Lloyd V. Briggs

History and Records of the First Congregational church, Hanover, Mass.

And Inscriptions From the Headstones and Tombs in the Cemetery at Centre Hanover, Mass., 1727-1894

Lloyd V. Briggs

History and Records of the First Congregational church, Hanover, Mass.
And Inscriptions From the Headstones and Tombs in the Cemetery at Centre Hanover, Mass., 1727-1894

ISBN/EAN: 9783337161897

Printed in Europe, USA, Canada, Australia, Japan

Cover: Foto ©Lupo / pixelio.de

More available books at **www.hansebooks.com**

HISTORY AND RECORDS

OF THE

FIRST
CONGREGATIONAL CHURCH,
HANOVER, MASS.,
1727—1865,

AND INSCRIPTIONS FROM THE HEADSTONES AND TOMBS IN THE CEMETERY AT

CENTRE HANOVER, MASS.,
1727—1894.

BEING VOLUME I. OF THE CHURCH AND CEMETERY RECORDS OF
HANOVER, MASS.

BY

L. VERNON BRIGGS,

AUTHOR OF "HISTORY OF SHIPBUILDING ON NORTH RIVER, MASSACHUSETTS," MEMBER
OF THE OLD COLONY COMMISSION (HISTORICAL) BY APPOINTMENT FROM GOV.
GREENHALGE IN 1895, MEMBER OF THE NEW ENGLAND HISTORIC-
GENEALOGICAL SOCIETY, AND OF THE BOSTONIAN SOCIETY.

BOSTON, MASS.:
WALLACE SPOONER, PRINTER, 17 PROVINCE STREET.
1895.

COPYRIGHT BY
L. VERNON BRIGGS,
1895.

DEDICATED

IN

AFFECTIONATE RESPECT

TO

Clifford Ramsdell,

WHO FROM YOUTH

HAS BEEN

EVER A PATIENT, FAITHFUL AND

TRUE FRIEND.

the oldest date is that erected to "Mr. Thos. Ramsdell, A. D. 1727," the same year that the town was incorporated and the church established here. There were undoubtedly many burials in this cemetery prior to that date, and on the older graves may yet be seen heaps of stones, placed there to keep the wolves and dogs from digging up the bodies. Little is left in these graves. In 1886, when making some improvements in the cemetery with money raised by concerts, I had occasion to have one or more of the old graves opened. A streak of black earth, a tuft of hair, and in one instance a few kernels of parched corn where the stomach ought to be, was all that was found by Mr. Andrew T. Damon, who opened the graves. I am indebted to Mr. Damon for many favors and much kindness during my acquaintance with him, extending over many years. No one now living knows more about the old cemetery than he.

In closing this preface I wish to especially commend this volume to all who have time to make a careful study of it. Many will find much to give them light on the characters who lived in this country town a century ago, and who had such difficulty in getting the wayward members back to the fold, in keeping the small boy quiet, and in raising enough money to support the minister. They were responsible for the present generations; do we all realize that we are equally responsible for the coming generations.

L. VERNON BRIGGS.

AUGUST, 1895.

CONTENTS.

For Index of Names See End of Volume.

CHAPTER I.
PAGE.
Formation of Church and Biographies of Its Ministers . . 1–51

CHAPTER II.
"Of the gathering of the church ordination and church meetings" . . 52–69

CHAPTER III.
Admitted to the church — 1728–1864 70–86

CHAPTER IV.
Marriages Performed by the Pastors of the First Congregational Church — 1728–1827 87–106

CHAPTER V.
Births — 1730–1819 107–116

CHAPTER VI.
Baptisms — 1728–1866 108–166

CHAPTER VII.
Dismissions, Suspensions and Excommunications from the church as recorded — 1757–1865 167–178

CHAPTER VIII.
Deaths Entered on the Records of the First Congregational Church — 1728–1867 179–213

CHAPTER IX.
Inscriptions from the Stones and Tombs in the Cemetery at Centre Hanover — 1727–1895 214–309

LIST OF ILLUSTRATIONS.

	PAGE.
PRESENT MEETING-HOUSE of the First Congregational Church. From a photograph by L. Vernon Briggs	Frontispiece
SAMUEL STETSON HOUSE, where meetings were first held. From a photograph by L. Vernon Briggs	2
PLAN of the parts of Scituate and Abington that were incorporated as Hanover, June 14, 1727. From an original drawing	7
HOUSE occupied by Rev. Samuel Baldwin during his pastorate. From a photograph by L. Vernon Briggs	8
HOUSE occupied by Revs. Mellen, Chaddock, Chapin, Smith, Duncan, during their pastorates. From a photograph by L. Vernon Briggs	14
MAP of Hanover, A. D. 1794. From an original drawing	24
REV. ABEL G. DUNCAN. From a photograph owned by his son	34
PRESENT PARSONAGE, built A. D. 1855, on land purchased of Sam'l Stetson	48
SHIP "Cronstadt." From " History of Shipbuilding on North River "	51
FIRST MEETING-HOUSE. From Barry's " History of Hanover "	86
SECOND MEETING-HOUSE. From Barry's " History of Hanover"	116
THIRD MEETING-HOUSE. From Barry's "History of Hanover"	166
PORTRAIT of Keoni Kalua	260
STONE ERECTED to Mr. Thos. and Mrs. Sarah Ramsdell, 1727–1773. From a photograph by L. Vernon Briggs	273
STONE ERECTED to Dea. Joseph Stockbridge and Mrs. Margaret, his wife, 1732–1773. From a photograph by L. Vernon Briggs	280
STONE ERECTED to Mr. John Stockbridge, 1768. From a photograph by L. Vernon Briggs	284
STONE ERECTED to Dea. Joseph and Mrs. Auna Stockbridge, 1783–1783. From a photograph by L. Vernon Briggs	286
STONE ERECTED to David Stockbridge, Esq., 1788. From a photograph by L. Vernon Briggs	294
STONE ERECTED to Mr. Lewis White, 1813. From a photograph by L. Vernon Briggs	298

HISTORY OF THE FIRST CONGREGATIONAL CHURCH, HANOVER, MASS.

CHAPTER I.

FORMATION OF CHURCH AND BIOGRAPHIES OF ITS MINISTERS.

THE early history of Hanover is identified with that of Scituate, to which town its territory belonged until 1727, excepting only a small portion which was taken from Abington. Therefore the church history, prior to 1727, of the people living in the territory, now known as Hanover, is to be found mainly in the church records of Scituate. This territory was settled in 1649; the part of Scituate lying about the harbor was settled in 1628, thus making Scituate the second settlement in Plymouth Colony, though not the second incorporated town.

When the inhabitants of Hanover, then numbering about three hundred souls, decided to petition to be set off a town by themselves, they were met with considerable opposition from the inhabitants of Abington, though the inhabitants of Scituate gave them no trouble. The General Court, receiving the remonstrance, appointed a committee, consisting of Lieut. Gov. Tailor and Elisha Cook, of the Council, and Ezra Bourne, Maj. Tileston, and Edward Arnold, of the House, to view the territory, and they reported in favor of its corporation, although they allowed it would

"Put the inhabitants of Abington under some difficulties respecting the supporting the public worship of God, for that several large tracts of land within the town did not pay towards the maintenance of the ministry."

It was decided to call the new town Hanover, probably after the Duke of Hanover, who had lately been called to the English throne, under the title of George I, and as yet the Colonies had seen little to give them cause to be otherwise than loyal to their Island government.

In the act incorporating the town of Hanover, June 14, 1727, it was stipulated as one of the conditions of the grant

"That the inhabitants of the said town of Hanover do within the space of two years from the publication of this act erect and finish a suitable house for the Public Worship of God, and as soon as may be procure and settle a learned Orthodox Minister of good conversation and make provision for his comfortable and honorable support, and that thereupon they be discharged from any further payment for the maintenance of the ministry &c., in the towns of Scituate or Abington for any estate lying within the said town of Hanover."

In pursuance of this proviso one of the first steps taken by the town was to provide for the support of Public Worship, and July 17, 1727, Mr. DANIEL DWIGHT, who had already preached in the town, was chosen to dispense the Word of God for three months.

Rev. Daniel Dwight was a descendant of Michael Dwight, of Dedham, Mass.. He was born October 28, 1707; graduated from Harvard College in 1726, and was never married. He preached occasionally, though for years he engaged in business. He died July 4, 1747, aged 39.

Messrs. Amos Sylvester and Thomas Josselynn were chosen to arrange with Mr. Dwight, and £7 s. 19 were subsequently voted as a remuneration for his services. Meetings were held at this time in private dwellings, and the house of Mr. Samuel Stetson, being nearest the centre of the town, and most convenient for the public accommodation, was principally used.

August 29th, of the same year, £60 was voted for the support of a minister, and Isaac Buck, Elijah Cushing and Joseph House were chosen to provide one. Nov. 13th, it was agreed to erect a meeting-house at the most convenient place, by the road called the Drinkwater Road, and Elijah Bisbee, Joshua Turner, and

SAMUEL STETSON HOUSE, WHERE CHURCH MEETINGS WERE HELD IN 1727, AND ON DIFFERENT OCCASIONS SINCE THEN.

Aaron Soule were chosen to select the site, and Job Otis was appointed to inform them of the town's desire. Dec. 13th, voted:

"That the size of the house be as follows: Length 48 ft.; Width 38 ft.; and height between joints 19 ft. to be completed by October 1st 1728."

Elijah Cushing, Joseph House and Abner Dwelly were chosen a building committee, and to see that the house was done in a workmanlike manner, but as cheap as possible. The house was erected at a cost of £300. Barry says:

"January 22, 1728, Isaac Bush was chosen agent to apply to the town of Scituate for aid in erecting the new meeting-house; a subscription paper was circulated by him, on which the sum of £90 was subscribed, but of which only £66 1s. 6d., were realized; and it was agreed that the money thus obtained should be proportioned on the polls and estates, towards defraying the charges. Mr. Buck was also agent to apply to citizens of Hanover for aid. Gifts of land were made by John Cushing, Job Otis, Nicholas Litchfield, Stephen Clapp, Sen., and others of Scituate; Rev. Thomas Barstow, of Taunton: and Joseph Barstow, and Samuel Barstow, of Hanover; the lots being laid out for the town by Caleb Torrey, and Stephen Clapp, of Scituate. The land on which the house was built, is said to have been given by Thomas Buck. Isaac Buck was the agent of the town to receive the deeds of the above lots.

"March 23, 1728, the town voted to take their part of the Government loan of £60,000, 'now in the Treasury at Boston,' and Joseph Barstow, Benjamin Curtis, and Samuel Barstow, were chosen to receive the same, and to let it out towards paying the carpenters. Gifts of lumber were made by several persons, and what was left, after the house was finished, was sold for the use of the ministry. The whole cost of the house appears to have been about £300.

"This first meeting-house stood on the same spot as the present house, and continued in use until 1765, under the ministry of Mr. Baldwin, when the second house was built. No records exist from which a correct idea of its appearance can be gained. An old lady, Mrs. Perry, living in Pembroke in 1853, and then 98 years old, born in 1755, and who was ten years of age when the second house was erected, has a distinct recollection of that event, but not of the looks of the original edifice. From the best information I can gain, I learn that it was a plain structure, in accordance with the simplicity of the times, facing the South; without steeple or chimney; the windows glazed with diamond-shaped glass; the walls unplastered; and unwarmed by stove or furnace; and here, for about forty years, the fathers of the town, with their wives and little ones, gathered together, from Sabbath to Sabbath, in summer's heat and winter's cold, listening devoutly to the ministrations of the Word of God, and chanting, to the quaint, old-fashioned tunes of the day, Sternhold and Hopkins' hymns, deaconed off to them line by line."

August 27th, 1728, Benjamin Curtis, Elijah Cushing, William Witherell, Thomas Josselynn, and Benjamin Curtis, jr., were chosen

"To advise with the neighboring ordained ministers as the law directs, in order for the settlement of the REV. BENJ: BASS in the work of the ministry;"

and subsequently it was voted that the sum of £130 per annum be paid as his salary. Nov. 23rd, 1728, it was voted to ordain Mr. Bass to the work of the ministry; and Amos Sylvester was chosen to make provision for the council. Rev. Benj: Bass was the son of Joseph and Mary Bass, of Braintree, and a descendant of Samuel Bass, who, with his wife Anne and one or two young children, came to New England in 1630, and settled first in Roxbury, and afterwards in that part of Braintree which is now Quincy. Benjamin was born in 1694, and graduated at Harvard College in 1715.

The ordination of Mr. Bass took place Dec. 11, 1728. Previous to this, Dec. 5th, was observed as a day of

"Fasting and Prayer to implore the Divine Presence and Blessing to attend the ministry of the Pastor elect, Benj: Bass, M. A., who had before this accepted the Town's call to the Pastoral office amongst them."

The church, consisting of ten members besides the pastor elect, was formed on this day, and they then subscribed the Church Covenant. The following names appear in the Church Records of those who constituted the church at this time, and signed the covenant:

Joseph Stockbridge, Elijah Cushing, James Hatch, John Tailor, Samuel Staples, Isaac Buck, Joseph Stockbridge, jr., Thomas Josselynn, Amasa Turner, and Samuel Skiff. The covenant signed by them is found further on in this book.

At the ordination of Mr. Bass the Rev. Mr. Eells, of Scituate, and Rev. Mr. Lewis, of Pembroke, were present and assisted in the services.

At a church meeting, held Jan. 10th, 1729, Joseph Stockbridge and Elijah Cushing were chosen deacons, and it was agreed to raise money by contribution to provide utensils for the Lord's Table. A contribution was accordingly made January 19th, it being the Sabbath, and with the proceeds there were bought

"Three pewter tankards, marked C. T., of 10 s. price each; five pewter beakers, costing 3s. 6d. each, and marked C. B.; two pewter platters, marked C. P.; a pewter basin for baptism; and a cloth for the Communion Table."

The communion was celebrated for the first time March 2nd, 1729, and the first service plate continued in use until 1768.

Feb. 15th, 1736, occurred the *death* of John Taylor, one of the *original members* of the Church.

March 7, 1742, the Church took a vote to see if the Society would sing in the new way, and it passed in the affirmative. Then, being desired to bring in their votes for a tuner, Mr. Ezekiel Turner was chosen by a considerable majority. Previous to this, singing, in most, if not all the New England churches, had been strictly congregational, the lines of the hymns being read off by the Deacon, who usually pitched the tune, and all who could sing joined in. By this vote, Sternhold and Hopkins' version of the Psalms was rejected, and Tate and Brady's was adopted. From the first the church steadily increased in numbers. On Nov. 4th, 1744, Susannah Rose, an Indian, was received by letter from the Indian Church of Mashpee in Sandwich.

The Church chose May 14th Joseph Stockbridge, Elijah Cushing, Benjamin Mann, Thomas Rose, Samuel Barstow, Joseph Ramsdale, and James Torrey, jr., to inspect the manner of the children of the church, as well as such as are in full communion, and endeavor when they walk disorderly to bring them to repentance and reformation.

April 8th, 1748, £14. 15s. was collected to buy good books to lend to such of the Society as stand in need of them, and would be glad to read them.

"With the above money," says Mr. Bass, "I bought in less than a week a parcel of books, whose Titles, Authors, and Price in Old Tenor may be met with in a book which is an exposition of the Epistle to the Colossians by Nicholas Byfield."

Those who borrowed the books were to return them in two months, and Mr. Bass wrote on the title-page of each book the letters C. B. C. S. H., which stand for Charity Book of the Congregational Society in Hanover.

The ministry of Mr. Bass, which was quiet and undisturbed, passed peacefully on until May 23, 1756, when he died, in the 63rd year of his age, after a settlement of 27 years, 5 months, and 15 days. During this period 83 persons joined the church, and 588 were baptized.

From his writings Mr. Bass appears to have been a man marked more by common sense, than by brilliancy of diction, withal a little inclined to facetiousness, yet open-hearted, and frank, and laboring diligently for the welfare of his people. He was often consulted by neighboring churches, and acted as Moderator in Ecclesiastical Councils. In the midst of the excitement which prevailed during the latter years of his ministry, occasioned by the preaching of Whitefield, and the rise of the "new lights," he preserved his own hold on the good-will of

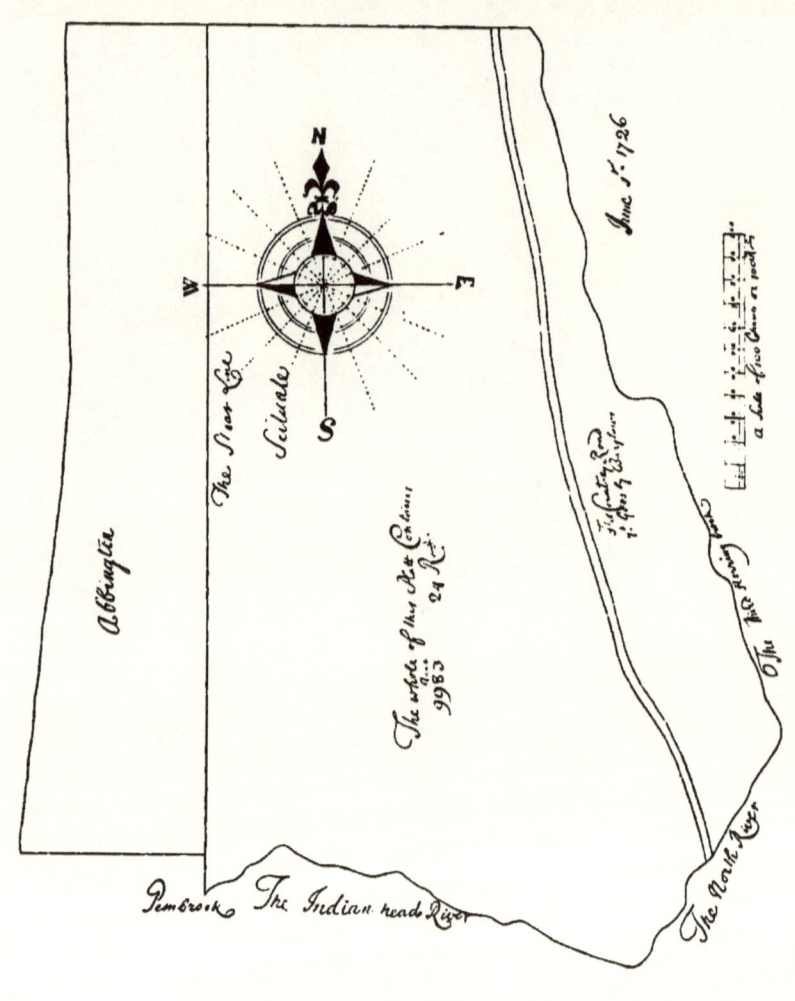

MAP OF PARTS OF THE TOWNS OF ABINGTON AND SCITUATE, INCORPORATED AS THE TOWN OF HANOVER, JUNE 14, 1727.

his society, and left his people in a state of as great prosperity as was enjoyed in any of the adjoining towns. His habits were simple and his manner of living frugal and unostentatious; yet his was ever a hospitable board, to which his parishioners and friends were cordially welcomed. He took great interest in the children of his parish, and never passed a child in the road without noticing it. The children so loved him, that whenever they saw him approaching, they would arrange themselves in a row, and as he drew near, greet him with bows and courtesies, while smiles of joy illumined their faces. As an illustration of his facetiousness, it is related, that having received an invitation to settle at Eel River, Plymouth, and being asked if he should accept it, he replied: "No, Eel River may do for small fish, but it is not large enough for Bass."

After the death of the Rev. Mr. Bass, Ezekiel Turner, Esq., Joseph House, and Michael Sylvester were chosen a committee by the town June 14th, 1756, to join a committee chosen by the Church, to supply the pulpit with preaching, and Aug. 30th, the church having laid before the town their choice of MR. SAMUEL BALDWIN for their pastor, the town concurred in the choice. It was voted, that he should receive as his salary £73. 6s. 8d. per annum. (He was son of David Baldwin, of Sudbury, gr. son of Henry, and gt. gr. son of Henry, of Devonshire, England, who settled at Woburn in 1650. He graduated from Harvard College 1752, and married Hannah, dau. of Judge John Cushing, Jan. 4, 1759, by whom he had nine children.) Mr. Baldwin declined to become pastor for this sum. Oct. 11th, it was voted

"to give him £80. and to build for him within 18 months a dwelling-house 40 ft. long, 30 ft. wide, and 17 ft. between joints, with two stacks of chimneys, a plain roof, with a suitable number of windows with crown glass, and to be painted inside and outside, such a color or colors as shall be agreeable to his mind, and to build and finish under the house a cellar 30 ft. long, and 14 ft. wide, pointed &c., and everything, both inside and outside, both wood work, iron work, and joiner's work, with two cupboards and as many closets in said house as may be convenient, all to be done to the turning of a Key, and to be underpinned in a suitable manner, to the acceptance of Mr. Baldwin, and this to be a free gift as a settlement."

Mr. Baldwin accepted this proposal. Feb. 7th, the dimensions of the house were altered to 38 by 32 ft. It was voted to pay for the building in money, and to give Joseph Curtis £160 for building and completing it.

Mr. Baldwin acknowledged the receipt of the house March 5th, 1759, as his settlement gift.

Oct. 8th, 1756, it was voted that Mr. Baldwin be ordained Dec. 1st, if the Thanksgiving be not on that week, but if it is, the ordination to be on the second Wednesday of December. It was also voted to give Capt. Josselynn £16 to provide handsome and suitable entertainment for the ordination, and he agreed to do it for that sum. The ordination took place Dec. 1st.

Under the ministration of Mr. Baldwin, the meeting-house was soon filled; and accordingly, June 25th, 1764, it was voted to open the same in two parts, and put in a new piece in the middle, 13 ft. or 14 ft. in length. This vote was re-considered Oct. 22nd, and it was voted to build a new house of the following dimensions—

"62 ft. in length, 43 in width, and 22 ft. between joints according to the plan in the office of the town clerk."

At the same time it was voted that each person should enjoy their pews as heretofore, only giving way for the new additional pews to be built. The committee was empowered to dispose of the old meeting-house, and the new additional pew room to the undertaker or undertakers of the meeting-house aforesaid, or to any other person or persons in part pay for the work aforesaid. Mr. Joseph Tolman was the contractor for the erection of the new house; and May 20th, 1765, it was voted to have a steeple to the meeting house, provided the money for the same can or shall be raised by subscription. This steeple was built,

RESIDENCE OF REV. SAMUEL BALDWIN, 1756-1784.
(THE HOUSE IS NOW OCCUPIED BY MR. SOPER.)

and the new house was erected on the site of the old one. It stood facing the south. At the east end was the women's porch extending from the ground to the eaves, and projecting from the building a few feet. In the entry was the stairway leading to the gallery, and overhead was the powder-room, in which the *town's stock of powder was kept during the Revolution.* The men's porch was at the west end, also projecting from the building and rising above the eaves, with a long tapering spire surmounted with a vane. This spire was removed about 1784, when a bell was presented to the Society by Mr. Josselynn, and a new steeple with a suitable belfry was erected. Within, the walls were plastered, the pews square, the galleries spacious, and the accommodations for the worshippers comfortable and decent.

While this house was building, meetings were held in a pine grove near by, and here Mr. Baldwin's daughter Hannah was baptized.

On Oct. 30th, 1768, Lord's Day, the Church was presented with four silver cups on the communion table, by orders, and at the expense of Deacon Stockbridge. The cost of each cup being £25, and each bearing this inscription: "The Gift of Deacon Joseph Stockbridge to the Church of Christ in Hanover, 1768."

The affairs of the Society, from this time until the War of the Revolution, continued in a state of great prosperity, and the salary of Mr. Baldwin was regularly paid and promptly; but the derangement of the finances of the country, on account of the war, led to difficulties in many religious societies, and finally to a dissolution of the connection, which had so long and so happily subsisted between Mr. Baldwin and the Society in Hanover. Nov. 28th, 1779, Mr. Baldwin was led to preach a farewell sermon to the people of Hanover for the want of support, and on the 8th of March he asked a dismission, which was granted and confirmed by a vote of the town.

Mr. Baldwin remained with the Society 23 years, 3 months and 3 days. During this period, 107 persons united with the Church, and 632 were baptized. As a pastor, his services gave general satisfaction, and as a preacher, his talents were not only highly respectable, but his manuscripts show that he was a ready and eloquent writer, and his discourses display good judgment, keen perceptions, and strong common sense.

Mr. Baldwin was led to espouse the cause of America in the struggle with Great Britain, and throughout the war took a deep interest in his country's success. He was a chaplain in the army, and gave eloquent exhortations to his own flock at home, and to the minute-men of the town. His mind became affected, and for a period of four years previous to his death he was partially deranged, but was faithfully cared for by his devoted wife. It is said that on one occasion during this time, one of his neighbors, a Miss Studley, called to converse with Mrs. Baldwin upon events of the war. Mr. Baldwin was lying on his bed, apparently unmindful of what they were saying, in his usual state of apathy. Suddenly he arose and went to his study. He returned with the manuscript of a discourse which he had delivered to the minute-men. Standing in the doorway he read it from beginning to end. Mrs. Baldwin, thinking that his mind was restored, was led to rejoice; but when he had finished reading, he carried the manuscript back, and returning laid himself on the bed and became silent as before.

He died Dec. 1st, 1784, about one year after peace was declared. Grave-stones were erected to his memory and to that of his devoted wife by vote of the town March 9th, 1796.

After the withdrawal of Mr. Baldwin, several candidates presented themselves, and were heard by the Society. REV. JOSEPH LITCHFIELD received a call, with a salary of £90 per annum, in silver money, at 6s per dollar, or gold equivalent, or in paper bills at the rate or value the General Court or Assembly shall settle the same, and 12 cords of firewood at his door, within a mile from the meeting-house. Dec. 27th, 1780, was fixed upon as the day of his ordination. Captain Joseph Soper was to provide entertainment for the council. The council met, and were in session two or three days; but he was not ordained, many of the Society being opposed to his settlement. A second attempt was made, which resulted in his rejection and withdrawal.

Rev. Joseph Litchfield was born in Scituate, and graduated

from Brown University in 1773. He came to Hanover from York, Me. He descended from Lawrence Litchfield, who bore arms in Barnstable, Mass., in 1643. He died in Kittery, Me., Jan. 28th, 1828, aged 78 years.

After several other candidates were heard, to some of whom a call was extended, a more unanimous call was extended to REV. JOHN MELLEN, of Sterling. He was settled Feb. 11th, 1784, Capt. Joseph Soper making the entertainment for the council. Invitation was sent to six churches, but one of them, that of Cambridge, was not represented, owing to the death of the aged Rev. Dr. Appleton.

In 1785, a donation of $100 was given to the Society by Col. Joseph Josselynn, and it was agreed that a bell should be purchased with it, provided that enough could be raised by subscription to make up the difference between that and the cost of the bell. In Nov., 1785, a bell was purchased of Col. Aaron Hobart, of Abington, and a committee of twenty,

"with all the rest of the town that see cause to assist,"

was chosen to hang it. Not long after, this bell was broken, owing to the want of skill on the part of the person appointed to ring it. It was re-cast, and when it was hung, Dec. 18th, 1788, Dea. Bass and Dea. Robbins, with Benjamin Stetson were chosen to give the sexton directions in regard to ringing the bell.

In 1789, it was voted to paint the meeting-house. The walls were to be of a stone yellow, the roof of Spanish brown, and the corner-boards and window-frames and sashes were to be white. May 30th, 1791, it was voted to give Capt. Timothy Rose £3 to take care of, sweep and sand the meeting-house, and ring the bell for that year.

A committee was chosen Oct. 14th, 1793, to get the meeting-house underpinned, and to procure a stock-lock for the door. June 9th, 1797, there was a committee chosen to seat the singers, and alterations were made in the house to provide for their accommodation. The same year, $300 was voted as the salary of

Mr. Mellen, and from that time, his salary was paid in Federal currency. In 1802, the bell was again re-hung. The year following Capt. Albert Smith presented to the town a number of Lombardy poplar trees, which were set out near the meetinghouse. Not one of these is now standing. The last one was cut down by Mr. Samuel Stetson.

In 1805, owing to the infirmities of age, Rev. Mr. Mellen terminated his ministry, and moved to Reading, where he closed his long and useful life July 4th, 1807, at the age of 85.

His life was an eventful one. He was born in Hopkinton, March 14th, 1722, and was graduated at Harvard College in 1741, teaching school the same year for £85, in Sudbury. He was ordained the first pastor of the church in Sterling, Dec. 19th, 1744, where he continued probably at the head of the clergy of Worcester County until Nov. 14th, 1774.

Barry says: "His connection with this society, which had continued for thirty years, was dissolved in consequence of disputes, occasioned by his endeavors to maintain what he considered the true discipline of the churches, and by his adoption of doctrinal sentiments, not wholly in accordance with those generally prevailing at the time. 'He, with others, as tradition says, had sensibly departed from the standard of faith that had been generally received in the New England Churches, and had extended his speculations in such a manner as to give great offence to some who had not pursued the same course of reasoning. In 1756, he delivered an eloquent series of discourses addressed to parents, children and youth, which contained sentiments highly obnoxious to many of his brethren in the ministry. These were published, and were extremely well received by his people. In the unguarded hours of social conversation, too, he, as was well understood, rejected many of the articles of the popular faith. Nor were his people dissatisfied with him on this account, but rather for publicly co-operating in the censure of those doctrines which it was supposed he embraced in the truth of the gospel. It was now understood, by some of the most intelligent of the parish, that their minister was verging towards doctrines that he had publicly disclaimed. In 1765, he published a volume of sermons on the doctrines of Christianity. These contained a learned system of scholastic theology, maintaining a middle course between the two extremes of Calvinism and Arminianism. Upon some of the controverted points it is not easy to understand which side his speculations favor most. The volume is highly creditable to his memory as a scholar and a theologian, and when published was considered an acquisition to the literature of the country. When his people produced their allegations against him, in 1773, they urged but few instances of false doctrines, and of these he fully exculpated himself before a council. The principal charge of this character was, that he had said that God was the author of sin. The sermon was produced where it was said to be contained. He stated that he had never held this doctrine in its gross sense, but only that sin was by permission, &c. The council cleared him as his church had previously.' He is described, in the work from which we have just quoted, as a man 'liberally endowed by nature with a strong and energetic mind, which was highly improved by diligent and successful cultivation, and he obtained a high rank as a preacher and scholar.'

"Besides the volume of doctrinal sermons, to which we have referred, and his sermon to parents, &c., his other published works were a Sermon at the Ordination of Rev. J. Palmer, 1753; —a Discourse at a General Muster, 1756;—on the Mortal Sickness among his People, 1756;—on the Conquest of Canada, 1760; —on the Death of Sebastian Smith, 1763;—Religion productive of Music, at Marlboro', 1773;—a Sermon at the Ordination of Rev. Levi Whitman, 1785;—a Discourse before a Lodge of Freemasons, 1793;—and a Thanksgiving Sermon, 1796.

"A few of these, as will be seen by the dates, were delivered after his settlement in Hanover. He is spoken of here with much affection by his old parishioners; and was a man of sociable habits, lively in conversation, fond of a jest, and of ardent feelings. Many anecdotes are related of his ministry."

He died at Reading, Mass., July 4th, 1807, aged 85 years, leaving three sons, all of whom became prominent.

July 23, 1806, REV. CALVIN CHADDOCK, of Rochester, was installed pastor of the society; the entertainment being provided by Lemuel Dwelley, at an expense of $125. Seven churches were invited; but five only responded.

During the ministry of Mr. Chaddock the academy at the Corners was built, and Mr. Chaddock had the charge of it until his removal from the place, in 1818, after a settlement of 12 years.

He was the son of Capt. Joseph Chaddock, who died in Hanover, in June, 1812, aged 88, and Barry says, "was, perhaps, a descendant of the Chaddocks of Watertown. He graduated from Dartmouth, in 1786, married Melatiah Nye, of Oakham, and settled first in Rochester. He was Representative from the town of Hanover in 1811. As the result of his marriage there were twelve children."

He is described as a ready preacher, a man of great natural eloquence, fluent in speech, and one whose discourses were generally popular.

One of his pupils at his school says of him, that "with a mind richly gifted by the Father of Spirits, he possessed a native, simple, and truly genuine eloquence. His bosom, a fountain of the tenderest sympathies, spontaneously gushing forth, moved him often and copiously to weep with them that weep. To the afflicted, to the mourner in Zion, his words of consolation were the breathings of angelic sweetness, while the truth of God, heard from his lips, in tones of deepest solemnity, thrilled the hearts of assembled multitudes. Of like passions with others—by no means faultless—yea, even specially composed with infirmity—yet in conflict with his spiritual foes, he was more than conqueror."

It was voted June 4th, 1807, that any person might write out his experience upon being admitted to the church. It was also voted that the pastor notify Mr. Church of his appointment to the Deaconship.

An adjournment was then voted until Aug. 1st. At that time the church met and voted to excuse Mr. Church from serving as a deacon at his request. Then they voted to postpone the choice of a deacon until another year.

RESIDENCE OF REV. JOHN MELLEN, 1784–1805; REV. CALVIN CHADDOCK, 1806–1818; REV. SETH CHAPIN, 1819–1824; REV. ETHAN SMITH, 1827–1832; REV. ABEL G. DUNCAN, 1833–18—.

(NOW THE RESIDENCE OF ANDREW T. DAMON.)

During Rev. Calvin Chaddock's pastorate 19 were baptized, according to the record, and 26 were admitted to the church. The peaceful close of his useful life was passed on the sunny plains of western Virginia.

The Church met on Thursday, Feb. 4th, 1819, at the schoolhouse near the meeting-house, and voted unanimously to invite REV. SETH CHAPIN to take pastoral charge of the church.

Rev. Mr. Chapin, having accepted the call, and having given his answer, the church met at the house of Deacon Benjamin Bass, on Monday, 22nd of March, and the pastor elect by particular request acted as Moderator. Dea. Barstow and William Torrey were chosen a committee, with the pastor elect, to revise the old covenant, which was first formed at the gathering of the church in 1728, and lay it with amendments, and also some articles of faith prefixed to it, before the church for their approbation. It was then voted, that in case Rev. Mr. Chapin was installed, he should be considered as belonging to the church in Hanover, *ex officio*, and that the ceremony of removing his relation from the church in Barrington should be dispensed with. Letters missive for a council were sent to the following churches: 3rd Plymouth, Halifax; 2nd Abington; 2nd Medway; 1st Wrentham, Rehoboth, and Barrington. The council met April 21, 1819, all the churches invited being represented.

"Rev. Seth Chapin was the son of Seth and Eunice Chapin, of Mendon, Mass.; and was born June 25, 1783. His father was an officer in the Revolutionary Army, and was stationed, a portion of the time, in Rhode Island, being engaged in Sullivan's celebrated expedition. The son pursued his studies, preparatory for college, under the Rev. Dr. Crane, of Uxbridge, entered Brown University in 1804, graduated in 1808, studied theology at Andover, which place he left in 1811; and in November of that year was installed as pastor of the church in Hillsboro', N. H. Here he remained until 1816; and the following three years were spent in Rowley, Mass., Mansfield, Conn., and elsewhere. In 1819, he was settled in Hanover, and remained until 1824, after which he preached in East Haddam, Conn., Hunter, N. Y., Attleboro', Mass., and Granville, Mass. In

1845, he relinquished the duties of his profession, and engaged in agricultural pursuits, with such ardor and success, in the language of his son, as to 'have the pleasure of matching the wonderful Georgic transformation, and saw

> "Ingens
> Exiit ad coelum ramis felicibus arbos
> Miraturque novas fondes et non sua poma."

"He married Mary Bicknell, second daughter of the Hon. Joshua Bicknell, of Barrington, May 28, 1810—her father having been 'for more than fifty years prominent in the councils of the State; and a man of such unflinching political integrity as to have received the title of 'old Aristides.' By this marriage he had two sons, the elder of whom, Henry, graduated at Brown University in 1835, received the degree of L. L. B., at Harvard College, in 1838, and settled as a physician in Providence, R. I. The younger son read law with the Hon. A. C. Greene, of Rhode Island, and settled in Alabama, where he died September 11, 1836, at the early age of 21. Mr. Chapin, the father, died in Providence, R. I., April 19, 1850, æ 67. His widow survived and resided with her son in Providence. As a preacher, Mr. Chapin was earnest and faithful; his discourses being instructive and copiously illustrated. As a scholar, he was diligent and studious; and several of his occasional productions were published. He was successful in his calling; a man of usefulness, and indomitable perseverance; and he left behind him a good name as an inheritance for his surviving son."

At the beginning of Mr. Chapin's ministry the church numbered 75 members, 20 of whom were males. After the preparatory lecture, June 4th, the church adopted the articles of faith which were presented by the committee chosen for this purpose, and the adoption of the covenant, presented by the same committee was postponed until the next preparatory lecture. The next preparatory lecture was on Aug. 13th, at which the covenant was, after much deliberation, adopted almost unanimously. At that time the church voted to set apart a day of fasting and prayer, and for renewing the covenant. The day was to be designated by the pastor, and the parish were to be invited to unite with the church in observing the day. The church also passed four important resolutions, covering requirements of admissions.

Oct. 1st was set apart as a day of fasting and prayer, and the church solemnly renewed their covenant vows and received two new members according to their rules. At a church meeting, held in the meeting-house April 19, 1820, the importance of attending to church discipline was considered, and a committee of three was chosen to converse with those members who had for a long time neglected the communion and public worship, or who had otherwise publicly offended. The same committee of examinations was continued for another year.

Oct. 21st, Deacon Joseph Brooks was chosen a delegate, with the pastor, in compliance with a letter missive from the Prudential Committee of the American Board of Commissioners for Foreign Missions, to attend an ecclesiastical council in North Bridgewater, the 31st of the same month, for the purpose of setting apart Mr. Daniel Temple and Mr. Isaac Bird as ministers of the Gospel and missionaries, and on the 2nd of January, 1822, the church was represented by the pastor and Dea. Barstow in an ecclesiastical council in Abington, for the purpose of ordaining Mr. Samuel Spring as pastor over the Congregational Church in that place.

About this time the church experienced a great loss in the death of Dea. Joseph Brooks, who had, for a great many years, served the church faithfully, and had been appointed on a great many committees, chosen at different times for different purposes. So we find, that after meeting on the Sabbath, Jan. 6th, 1822, the members voted that it was proper to

"hold a day of fasting and prayer on account of the many deaths in the church during the preceding year, and especially that of the lamented Dea. Jos. Brooks; also to seek direction in the choice of a brother to fill his place, and to humble themselves before God, on account of the low state of religion, and the unfavorable aspect of surrounding circumstances."

Accordingly, the 15th day of Feb. was observed as a day of fasting and prayer, and religious services were held in the house of worship. Although the members made choice of a deacon, he absolutely declined to serve, so that they postponed any further action. In the following year, the church accepted an invitation to send the pastor and a delegate to attend an ecclesiastical council in Barrington, R. I., Feb. 25th, for the purpose of ordaining Mr. Francis Wood as pastor of the church in that place.

In October, of the same year, a very singular meeting was held. A certain person had presented himself for admission into the church, by virtue of a letter of dismission and recommendation from a neighboring church, and had stood propounded longer than the usual time. No objections were made to him, and the pastor made some remarks, expressing his satisfaction with the views and religious experience of the person presented. When a vote was called there was entire silence, and accordingly the pastor, who was moderator, declared there was no vote, and the subject of receiving the member was postponed until the brethren should have an opportunity to converse with the person. At this meeting, the pastor voted a new measure, which was objected to on the part of the members of the church. He wished them to nominate a neighboring minister to preside as moderator at a future church meeting, before which he wished to present some business. Though he repeatedly urged the importance of making such a nomination, the members refused to do so, and the meeting was postponed until the members had time to consider and to inform themselves relative to the practice of other churches in such cases.

In the following November, the subject of church discipline was again considered, and at two meetings, after a long discussion, in which it was contended by some members, that a public acknowledgment of their faults before the congregation, on the part of members who had publicly offended was inexpedient and unprofitable, and by some contrary to Scripture. It was finally unanimously voted that members of the church should be required to make acknowledgment and manifest their penitence only before the church. Nevertheless, if they chose, they could do so before the congregation.

Again the pastor and church felt a need for a day of fasting and prayer, and the 1st of January, 1824, was set apart, and the several neighboring churches, having agreed to set apart the same day, this church met in the house of the pastor to pray for its own pastor and church, and also for the pastor and churches also assembled for the same purpose in other places.

It seems that after a year and a quarter, the members had had time to converse with the person, in regard to whom they were so silent, for we find that they were ready to vote, and did vote to receive him, Jan. 27th, of this year. Feb. 19th the pastor resigned his office, and asked for an ecclesiastical council to meet on the 21st day of April, for the purpose of dissolving the pastoral relation. The church granted his request, and in their records expressed their "deep contrition and humiliation before Almighty God under his providential frown upon them," feeling it to be their "painful duty, all existing circumstances considered, to concur with their beloved pastor." Accordingly, in union with the parish, committees were chosen and a council was summoned by letters missive. The council met, and after examining into the case, regularly dismissed him, expressing the deep interest they felt in the "afflictive circumstances in which it has pleased a sovereign God to place this church and people by this decision." His dismissal was caused by a want of pecuniary support. The salary agreed upon, when he was settled, was $500, which seems to have been collected and paid without much difficulty, for the first three years of his ministry. Soon after the beginning of the fourth year, a committee was sent to him, to see if he would accept a less sum, which had been subscribed. To their communication he returned a respectful answer July 6th, 1822, stating, that with the prospects before him, he was not prepared to say that he dared venture to hope that anything less would defray his necessary expenses. During the fourth year his salary was raised by taxation, but the fifth year the parish returned to the subscription plan, and at the close make the following minutes:—

"Considering the diminished and impoverished state of this parish, they do not think it expedient to raise money to defray the Rev. Mr. Chapin's salary for the ensuing year."

Those were critical times, especially for the feeble Congregational Churches in Massachusetts. By a recent decision of Chief Justice Parsons, of the Supreme Court of this State, the autonomy of the churches had been destroyed. By this decision, in the Dedham case, no church could hold property, or in fact could have a legal existence aside from the parish or society with which it was connected. It took from the churches all their possessions, and put all their funds, and even their communion ware, at the entire control of the society, the majority of whom, in many cases, might be made to vote to employ ministers who would preach against the doctrines of the Congregational churches. Had it not been that this parish was a close corporation, the church might, in its feebleness, like many others, have passed over into another denomination.

In view of the straitened circumstances and embarrassments of Rev. Mr. Chapin, they affectionately recommended him to the sympathy of the people among whom he labored, in the hope that they would make such exertions for his relief as the case would require. The council, in their result, expressed their continued and undiminished confidence in him, in his Christian integrity, and their respect for his ministerial talents and attainments, and they commended him to others with whom his lot may be cast, and they commended this church to the unfailing protection of the great Head of the Church.

During his ministry 12 persons were admitted into the church and 27 were baptized. After the dismissal of Mr. Chapin, the church did not despair, but began to look around for a new pastor, for one who might make it more easy, or at least more practicable to sustain the ordinances of the gospel in this first church of the town. They were, however, without a settled pastor until 1827, when they gave to REV. ETHAN SMITH a call. During this time they were not without the ministrations of the gospel. In the same year after the departure of Mr. Chapin they were much cheered by the ladies. The parish received— from certain ladies living in this and adjoining towns, not subject to taxation (as they say), who had formed themselves into a society which they termed "The Female Helping Society,"— a communication to be laid before the parish. In this communication these ladies said: That, in view of the reduced numbers and resources of the society, they have obtained one hundred and thirty or forty dollars, which they would like to give the parish to aid in securing another minister, and they very respectfully added, that, if it met the concurrence of the parish, they would be particularly gratified if the parish would engage Mr. Noah Emerson. The parish, anxious to meet such generosity in a suitable manner, made an offer to Mr. Emerson to become their pastor, which, for some reason, was not accepted.

While the church was without a pastor, the members of the church held their meetings, and attended to church discipline, and the reception of members. Eighteen persons were by them received into the church, and the pulpit was more or less supplied by different preachers. The parish also became interested and engaged in building a NEW MEETING HOUSE—the THIRD ONE. Those were spirited times, on account of the different views entertained, and the earnest discussions resulting therefrom.

According to the records this meeting-house was built before the call of Rev. Mr. Smith to be the pastor; for March 19th, 1827, the church held a meeting in the new meeting-house, and voted to extend a call to REV. ETHAN SMITH to become their settled pastor. The parish concurred with the church, and the following churches were invited: The 2d and 3d churches in Abington; 2d in Weymouth; church in Braintree; Union Church in Braintree and Weymouth; church in Hanson; 1st church in Scituate, and 2d in Cohasset.

Barry says: "That the Rev. Ethan Smith, the 7th pastor, was born in Belchertown, Mass., Dec. 17, 1762. He married in 1791, Bathsheba Sandford, second daughter of Rev. David Sandford, of Medway, Mass. He was in Haverhill, N. H., nine years, and was dismissed for want of support. He was installed in the ministry at Hopkinton, N. H., March 12, 1800, and continued there about 18 years, during 16 of which he was Secretary of the New Hampshire Missionary Society. He was afterwards settled at Hebron, N. Y., about 4 years; at Poultney, Vt., about 5 years; at Hanover, Mass., 5 years; and then spent a season as a city missionary in Boston. His publications were, 1. A Dissertation on the Prophecies, two editions; 2. A View of the Trinity, two editions; 3. A View of the Hebrews, two editions; 4. Lectures on the Subjects and Mode of Baptism, two editions; 5. A Key to the Figurative Language of the Bible; 6. Memoirs of Mrs. Abigail Bailey; 7. A Key to the Revelation, two editions; 8. Prophetic Catechism; 9. Two Sermons on Episcopacy; 10. Farewell Sermon at Haverhill, N. H.; 11. First Sermon after Installation at Hopkinton; 12. Two Sermons on the Vain Excuses of Sinners, preached at Washington, N. H.; 13. Sermon on the Moral Perfection of God, preached at Newburyport, Mass.; 14. Sermon on the Daughters of Zion Excelling, preached before a Female Cent Society; 15. Sermon on the Happy Transition of Saints, preached at the Funeral of Mrs. Jemima, consort of Rev. Dr. Harris, of Dunbarton; 16. Sermon at the Ordination of Rev. Stephen Martindale, at Tinmouth, Vt.; and 17. Sermon at the Ordination of Rev. Harvey Smith, at Weybridge, Vt.

"His children were Myron, born in Haverhill, N. H., 1794, and died 1818, aged 24; Lyndon Arnold, born at Haverhill, 1795, graduated at Dartmouth College, married a daughter of Rev. Dr. Griffin, and settled as a physician in Newark, N. J.; Stephen Sandford, born at Haverhill, 1797, and settled as pastor of the Congregational Church, Westminster, Mass.; Laura, who died in infancy; Carlos, born in Hopkinton, 1801, graduated at Union College, and settled as pastor over the Presbyterian Church in Massillon, Ohio; Grace Fletcher, wife of Rev. Job H. Martin, died in Haverhill, Mass., 1840; Sarah Towne, second wife of Rev. J. H. Martin, of New York; Harriet, wife of William H. Sandford, of Boylston, Mass.; and Ellen, wife of C. B. Sedgwick, Esq., of Syracuse, died May 23, 1846, aged 33. The wife of Mr.

Smith died in Pompey, N. Y., April 5, 1835, aged 64. He was living in 1847, in Boylston, Mass., but has since deceased.

"During the ministry of Mr. Smith the second meeting-house was torn down, and the third, or present house erected; which stands in the centre of the town, facing the East, and is a modest structure, surmounted by a steeple, and in the belfry hangs the old bell given by Mr. Josselynn, in 1785, and recast in 1788."

Rev. Ethan Smith had offered to become a member of the church on the condition, that if his moral character or conduct should be called in question he should be tried only by a council mutually chosen for the purpose, and the church had received him on this condition as a member. His wife, Bethesda, presented a letter from the church in Poultney, Vt.

In March, 1830, the church was invited to sit in council, by pastor and delegate, to aid in forming the Third Congregational Church, Plymouth, into two churches. Deacons Barstow and Cook were chosen, that one of them might accompany the pastor, as they shall agree.

At the monthly church meeting, held June 3d, 1831, the church voted, that in the future, examinations of candidates be as usual by the committee, but also in the presence of the church, and that other members besides the committee have opportunity to ask questions.

Sabbath noon, June 12th, a letter missive was read to the church from Kingston, requesting the aid of the church in the installation of a pastor over the evangelical church in that place. Dea. Isaac Cook, with Dea. Barstow, as alternate, was chosen delegate with the pastor. Again on Sabbath, Nov. 6th, a letter was read from a committee of the church in Halifax, requesting the church to aid (with a number of other churches mentioned in the letter) in an *ex parte* council, to give advice relative to difficulties between their pastor and themselves, the pastor having utterly declined to unite in calling a mutual council. This church voted not to comply with the request; at which the pastor, Mr. Smith, was grieved, deeming the vote uncharitable and irregular.

About this time the pastor, being called to take a journey, hired a REV. MR. WOODBURY, of Boston, to supply his pulpit two Sabbaths. Mr. Woodbury, though a total stranger to Mr. Smith, was well recommended, and was a candidate in good standing. After preaching one Sabbath, the church was convened on the following Thursday, Dec. 1st, and with Dea. Isaac Cook as moderator, voted to send the following communication:

"*Congregational Church in Hanover to the Rev. Mr. Woodbury.*

"SIR: Having heard you preach last Lord's Day, and believing as we do that your preaching is subversive of the Gospel of Christ, and contrary to the confession of faith adopted by this church, and dangerous to the souls of men, we, therefore, request that you would not preach to us the next Lord's Day."

This, as well as a case of church discipline the year before, shows that the church had a regard for discipline and its well being. The last Sabbath in Dec. of the year 1831, Mr. Smith having received an invitation from the Board of Overseers of the City Missions, of Boston, to engage as a city missionary, requested of the church a dismissal, and accordingly a council was called, and he was regularly dismissed Jan. 12th, 1832. The council were unanimous in their conclusions, and expressed themselves as highly gratified to find, from the documents, that there was a state of very desirable harmony existing between the pastor and his church and society; and that nothing had been exhibited, or even suggested, as detrimental to the ministerial, the Christian, or moral character of the pastor. In his youth, Mr. Smith learned the trade of "tanner and currier and shoemaker." At the age of 18 he became a soldier in the Revolutionary War, and was stationed at West Point when Benedict Arnold attempted to betray the fort and the country into the hands of the enemy. It was not until he had reached the age of 21 that he began preparation for a liberal education. At the age of 30 he was a well-educated man, having been graduated with honor at Dartmouth College. He spent some time in studying theology, with the distinguished Dr. Burton, of Thetford, Vt. His first settlement was at Haverhill, N. H., where he remained

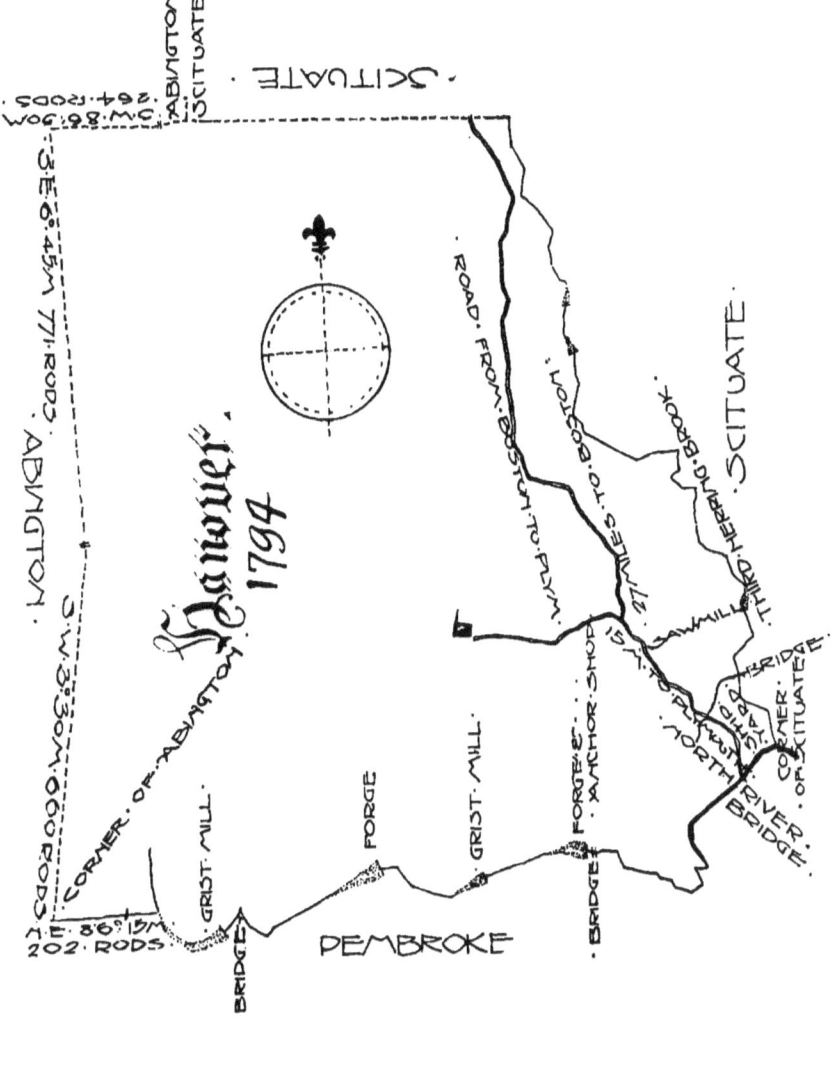

about 9 years. He was settled in Hopkinton, N. H., about 18 years, and when he was settled in Hanover, it was his fifth place of settlement. After he left Hanover, he labored about a year in Boston, as city missionary, and then was employed in the State of New York. His wife died in 1835, leaving him to travel alone the journey of life. He had ten children, eight of whom reached adult years. The whole period of Mr. Smith's ministry was 59 years. He was a great student of the Bible. His son, Rev. Carlos Smith, says of him: "He was an indefatigable Bible student, and beyond all the men I ever knew, familiar with the Bible. It was with him THE BOOK. He pored over it with ever fresh delight. I remember hearing him say, in his old age, 'new beauties were opened up to him continually.' He had a warm and deep sympathy for all classes of men, however ignorant and degraded, and for all of those Christian and benevolent societies and operations which are adapted to promote human elevation and human happiness." He spent the closing years of his life with his children, particularly with his daughter, the wife of William H. Sanford, of Boylston, where he died in the year 1849. It is remarkable that three of his sons were in the ministry, as pastors, and three of his daughters were wives of pastors.

At a regular church meeting, held April 4th, 1833, a committee of three was chosen, consisting of Dea. Isaac Cook, Dea. Elijah Barstow, and Elisha Bass, to visit those members whom they judged to walk disorderly, and to make a report to the church at some future day. The same committee was appointed to make inquiry respecting the articles of faith. On the 8th day of the following June, a regular meeting of the church was held in the vestry, and Dea. Elijah Barstow being chosen moderator, an invitation was extended to the REV. ABEL G. DUNCAN to become their pastor, and Elisha Bass was appointed a committee to communicate to Mr. Duncan the doings of the church. The following is the answer to their invitation:

To the Cong'l Chh. in Hanover and the Society connected therewith.

BRETHREN AND FRIENDS: Having prayerfully considered your invitation to settle among you in the Gospel ministry, and the leadings of Divine Providence, I now cheerfully consent to take the oversight of you, and to minister to you in holy things, on the conditions proposed. Praying that you may share with your children and the Israel of God in the blessings of his gracious covenant, I subscribe myself your servant for Christ's sake. A. G. DUNCAN.

Hanover, Aug. 2d, 1833.

Accordingly, a council was convened at the house of Rev. Abel G. Duncan, Aug. 22d, for the purpose of installing him pastor, if thought proper. The council was composed of representatives from the following churches : 2d church, Abington; 3d church, Abington; 2d church, Randolph; Union church, Braintree and Weymouth; church in North Wrentham. Also Rev. Stephen Thurston of West Prospect, Me., afterward of Searsport, Me., was invited and was present. The members of the council were unanimous in voting that they were satisfied, after due examination into Mr. Duncan's doctrinal opinions, his views of experimental piety, his aptness to teach, and his views relative to entering the ministry of the Gospel. Installation services were held in the church at 2 o'clock, when the following persons took part : Rev. Moses Thatcher, of North Wrentham, offered the introductory prayer ; Rev. Stephen Thurston preached the sermon; Rev. Jonas Perkins, of Braintree, made the prayer of installation; Rev. Daniel Thomas, of 2d church, Abington, the moderator, gave the charge to the pastor; Rev. D. Brigham, of 2d church, Randolph, gave the right hand of fellowship; and Rev. Lucius Alden, of 3d church, Abington, the scribe, offered the concluding prayer. In the month of October following, Mr. Duncan and his wife were received as members of the church. Rev. Abel G. Duncan was born in Chester, Vt., in 1802. He graduated at the Bangor Theological Seminary in 1828, was settled for four years in Jackson and Brooks, Maine, and was installed in Hanover Aug. 22d, 1833. He proved himself a faithful minister and an excellent citizen, having had the honor to represent the town for six years in the State Legislature, and having been for many years chairman of the school committee. Mr. Duncan remained in Hanover a little more than twenty years, and was active in school matters, and in the cause of temperance and that of anti-slavery. During his ministry the church experienced three special seasons of revival, and 60 persons by profession and letter were added to the church. Soon after Mr. Duncan became pastor, two persons were excommunicated; one for breach of covenant "in going to the Baptists without consulting with the church, and neglecting to give the church satisfaction," and the other for having "embraced the heresy of Universalism." In May, 1835, Joshua Perry was chosen delegate with the pastor to attend a council in Scituate, in order to install Rev. Luke Spofford pastor over the Trinitarian Church. In the following month the pastor, with Wm. Church, were sent to meet in council to advise the church in South Weymouth in relation to their affairs. In the month of July following, a day of fasting and prayer was observed by the church in view of certain "favorable indications of good to Zion." During the years that follow, we find that church meetings were regularly held, and from time to time persons were admitted into church membership, and in August, 1839, a committee of three, consisting of Deacons Barstow and Cook and Br. Elisha Bass, were appointed to converse with any members who might be guilty of breaking covenant or transgressing the divine precepts. In 1836, the church having considered the matter, caused to be printed a small pamphlet containing twenty-nine doctrinal articles of their creed and their covenant. Each article is followed by a list of passages from the Bible as proof texts. It seems that a certain promissory note called the Mellen note, had become a source of difficulty in parish meetings. By this note the parish was obligated to pay to the church six dollars annually for the expenses of the communion services. At a regular church meeting held Aug. 5, 1836, this note was relinquished and given up. In the summer of the year 1840, the meeting-house was painted white, and the stoves were removed into the entry. The aisles of the house were also carpeted. While there were some signs of outward prosperity, we find the pastor mourning over the very low state of religion, so that in those days there were tides of religious interest. During the last half of the year 1841, the church was engaged in a controversy with one of its members in regard to the doctrines, and at meeting after meeting the matter came up, and a committee was appointed also to wait upon him and report. This case of discipline was remarkable for the length of time consumed and the many meetings called in the controversy. Had the women been allowed to vote it might have been settled much sooner.

In regard to the favorable indications of a revival, a day of fasting, humiliation and prayer was observed March 9th, and March 25th we find the record that a series of meetings was held during the week, and Revs. Powers and Ward, of Abington, Lewis, of South Weymouth, Colman, of Scituate, and Perkins, of Weymouth and Braintree, preached. The weather was unfavorable, but the Holy Spirit was present and good results were manifest. April 7th it is recorded that REV. JAS. R. CUSHING, of E. Haverhill, held a series of meetings, preaching nine times. June 22d, Dea. Elisha Barstow died, after a few days' sickness, at the age of 73. It is recorded of him that he was a worthy man, "who for some months past has appeared very much devoted to the work of the Lord." We find the pastor in making this record giving expression to the feelings of his heart: "Ah! Lord God! Wilt thou make a full end of the remnant of Israel? Turn us again and cause thy face to shine, and we shall be saved." At the close of the year 1842, the pastor left an interesting record. We find recorded for the first time, in the year 1847, the amount of monthly benevolent contributions for the year. The amount was $85. Twenty of this was given to the A. B. C. F. M., twenty to American Missionary Association, and twenty-five to American Home Missionary Society. We find also at the close of the year 1849, the same amount and the same appropriations. In the year 1851, the pastor met with a severe loss. Sabbath evening, October 12th, Mrs. Lucia Harlow, wife of the pastor, died at the age of 56, after twelve weeks of severe suffering, borne with Christian meekness, patience, fortitude and submission. She was a descendant of Govs. Bradford and Carver, and possessed a spirit worthy of her Puritan stock. At one time during her illness she remarked, in an ecstacy, "Precious Savior! I shall soon be with him," and her last audible accents breathed forth his name, "Precious Jesus." The following year the pastor was cheered by receiving into the church among many others, his two children, William Paley and Lucia Ann. In the year 1853, a donation of twenty dollars was given to the pastor by the Misses Sarah and Rhoda Ford to purchase a Pulpit Bible and Hymn Book for the use of the pulpit. At a regular church meeting in 1834, it was voted that the pastor be requested to record the fact that the table and chairs used at the communion are the property of the church by regular purchase with money raised by the church. In the year 1854 occurred the division of the church, "though," according to Rev. Mr. Allen, in his history of the church, "it was a friendly division, and as those mostly concerned thought to be a necessary one." Thirty-two persons, members of the church, were dismissed and recommended, March 10th, for the purpose of being organized into a church at the Four Corners, for the better accommodation of themselves and their families, and others living in that vicinity. Among them was numbered a large proportion of the church's most reliable and active supporters.

Soon after this division, it seemed necessary to the pastor to bring his long and faithful ministry in this place to a close. Accordingly there was read in the meeting-house Sunday, April 2d, 1854, the following communication to the church:

To the Congregational Church in Hanover:

"Grace be unto you and peace from God our Father, and the Lord Jesus Christ." I came unto you as soon as I was sent for, and for these twenty years and over have been laboring to fulfil the 'intent ye sent unto me' to accomplish; and for the past two years God had given that measure of prosperity which appeared to be the promise of better days for this church and society. But a change has come over us, and the condition of things seems to indicate that another should come in my stead and reap that whereon he has bestowed no labor. PERMANENCY in the Pastoral Office seems to give way to the love of novelty and change, and the churches are in the course of experiment which, in the opinion of the General Association, will result most unfavorably to their interests. I have considered it my duty heretofore, to make sacrifices of feeling and of interest for the retarding of such a result. But wishing no longer to stand up for a principle so rapidly lost sight of in the excitements and changes of the day; feeling it to be no longer a duty in view of the circumstances of your present condition; realizing that my motives and sacrifices for the principle have not been, and still are not, appreciated by this people; and being willing, while I commit my way to the Lord, to bide my time, I most freely yield to the desire of a change, having in common with the most devoted friends of this beloved church an earnest desire for its perpetuity, peace and prosperity. I, therefore, do now resign into the hands of the great Shepherd and Bishop of Souls, from whom I received it by solemn installation, and into your hands, the pastorate of this church, the resignation to take effect on and after the first day of May next; and I respectfully request you to unite with me in calling a mutual council to advise relative to the matter. While I take this opportunity to express my gratitude for your multiplied favors, for which I pray that God may richly reward you, I ought in justice to say that my stipulated compensation has always been inadequate to meet my necessary expenses, more especially for the last few years, since the manifest lessened value of money, while my own means for making up your lack of remuneration have been sensibly diminished. The necessary result has been, notwithstanding all my struggles to avoid it, that I am unable fully to meet the claims on me, which are justly due. I prefer no claims, but do appeal to the generosity and magnanimity of those to whom I have ministered; not because I so much desire a gift, but I desire that fruit may abound to their account. Although you have suffered a great diminution of your members, strength and influence, yet I trust that you will be united and will speedily secure a sound and godly ministry, and that you will humbly and prayerfully in faith and active, zealous effort, wait on the Lord for his blessing. May the light of this ancient Zion never be quenched, but shine with the pure radiance of truth and holiness from generation to generation. And suffer me to ask your continued prayers for one who has rejoiced in your joys, and sorrowed in your sorrows, and who has above all things desired and labored for your salvation, and the salvation of your children. Yours in the bonds of the Gospel,

A. G. DUNCAN, *Pastor.*"

This resignation was accepted by the church, and it was voted that the council to be called be the same that shall meet at the "Four Corners," April 12th, 1854, to organize the Congregational Church there contemplated. Deacon Cook and Josiah Chamberlain were chosen to unite with the pastor in calling the said council and in representing the church before it; and Deacon Cook was chosen to attend with the pastor the council to be convened at the "Four Corners," to assist in the organization of the brethren who have been dismissed, and others who may unite with them into a Congregational Church, to worship in the new house recently erected in the village. Accordingly the council met at the house of Dr. Garratt, Hanover Four Corners, now the residence of James T. Tolman, and organized by the choice of Rev. James W. Ward as moderator, and Rev. Isaac C. White scribe. The churches invited were represented as follows:

Church in Abington Centre, Rev. J. W. Ward.
                                   Joshua Whitmarsh, Delegate.
Hingham,   Rev. E. P. Dyer, Pastor.
                     Isaac N. Damon, Delegate.
Hanson,   Rev. S. L. Rockwood, Pastor.
                     Deacon I. F. Stetson, Delegate.
East Abington,   Rev. H. D. Walker, Pastor.
                     Deacon ———, Delegate.
Scituate,   Rev. Daniel Wight, Pastor.
                     Deacon J. Cudworth, Delegate.
North Abington, Rev. J. C. White.

The council, after fully considering the papers and the facts, voted to dissolve the pastoral relation, and recommending that those who had enjoyed his ministrations should raise at least two hundred dollars as a mark of their continued affection and regard, and their desire to do justice to one who had labored long and faithfully in the Gospel ministry. They cordially recommended Mr. Duncan to the churches of Christ as a Brother beloved, a sound, faithful preacher of the Gospel, as one who had long sustained the relation of a discreet and affectionate pastor. They also expressed their deep sympathy for the enfeebled church, and somewhat disheartened by the diminution of members. We find that during his ministry in this place, Mr. Duncan baptized 117 persons, infants and adults, besides receiving a large number into the church. After closing his ministry in this place, he resided and was acting pastor in the Congregational Church in Assonet for eleven years, and after living in Scotland, a part of Bridgewater, for about five and one-half years, acting pastor there, he came back to Hanover in 1873, to spend the few remaining days of his pilgrimage, having reached the age of more than three score years and ten. Here, with health enfeebled in his house on King Street, he resided for about ten months with constantly failing prospects of recovery, much of the time upon a bed of sickness, until April 23d, 1874, when he quietly passed away. As he had lived a Christian life, so he died a Christian death, exclaiming shortly before he breathed his last, in the full triumph of a Christian hope: "Oh, precious, precious Saviour! Wonderful, wonderful Saviour! His name shall be called wonderful, counsellor, the mighty God, the everlasting Father, the Prince of Peace." The Rev. Mr. Allen, a successor, in his historical account, says: "Mr. Duncan held the pen of a ready writer. Not only did he prepare his written sermons with great care and facility, but he wrote not a little for the press in fugitive and occasional pieces. I know, however, of only four works which were issued in his own name. The first is an address which he delivered in Boston, in 1838, before the Physiological Society, of the city, and was published there. The second is a sermon which he preached in 1853, at the funeral of Mrs. Mary Anna (Perkins) Wight, the wife of Rev. Daniel Wight, of Cohasset. The third is a religious tract which was published by the Boston American Tract Society, on the subject of Baptism, for the manuscript of which they offered a premium (I think) of fifty dollars, and which they appraised to him. The fourth is a little book, called the "Pastor's Manual," a very good and useful work, and often of great convenience in the performance of pastoral duties. Besides these he prepared several volumes of his own sermons in manuscript for the press, which were not published on account of the risk in expense which he would have to assume, and in the same way a volume of religious meditation in prose and poetry by himself, was prepared for publication, but for the same reason failed to come before the public." Mr. Duncan was a man of much more than ordinary talent and perseverance. After he was fifty years of age he began the study of the Hebrew language. The children of Mr. Duncan were Laura J., who married Nahum D. King, of North Adams, and died October 22d, 1859, aged 30 years. Lucia A., who married Henry S. Dean, of Taunton, and died April 3, 1881, aged 48 years; and William Paley, of Cambridge, a lawyer by profession, in practice in Boston, who studied at Williston Seminary, Easthampton, and at Amherst College, and married Abbie F. Crane, daughter of Capt. John Crane, of Freetown, and has two sons, John F. and Payson Williston, a daughter, Laura Mabel, born October 30, 1865, died March 31, 1867.

Reference has been made to the literary ability of Rev. Mr. Duncan. He was, indeed, a man of rare scholarship as a linguist, having an intimate knowledge of ancient and several modern languages, reading each tongue with facility, and in *belles-lettres* was equally gifted. He was a skilled logician and a wise counsellor in denominational church polity, and his advice was frequently sought by the several churches and ministerial associations in Plymouth, Norfolk and Bristol Counties. His modest and friendly demeanor at all times commended him even to those who opposed him in opinion. One incident is remembered concerning him in this connection. A man called at his house one evening during his pastorate at Hanover, and assailed him with violent language about a certain matter of opinion only. Mr. Duncan heard him silently to the end, and then with singular dignity and kindness, replied only in these words: "*Rebuke not an elder.*" Suffice it to say, the excited caller was so much impressed by the manner and simple words of the pastor, that (in the language of Scripture) "there was a *great calm*." He could be severe if occasion required, yet his severity was tempered by a gentle dignity through it all, which conciliated as well as reproved.

The separation of the First Congregational Church and society was, in fact, a source of much grief to him, and while he had feelings of utmost kindness for the promoters of the measure, many of whom were his warm personal friends, yet it had great influence in saddening his declining years, and to the very last he could not speak of the event without emotion and regret. He rejoiced in the Godly succession of ministers over the old church, particularly in the ministry of the Rev. Mr. Allen. While he displayed much interest in the new Second Parish, yet his thoughts and affections seemed to centre in and revert to the ancient First Church, the home of his early love and care; and his remains now rest beside those of the wife of his youth in the old churchyard, near the beautiful new church edifice erected on the site of the venerable structure consumed by fire, in which old sanctuary they unitedly labored, mid joy and trial, smiles and tears for so many years, in the Master's work, until they "*fell on sleep*."

The ladies of the congregation erected a plain but beautiful tablet to the memory of his wife greatly beloved by them, at her grave, and his children placed a similar one at their father's grave, with this inscription on the same (as he directed shortly before his decease) "*Simply to Thy Cross I Cling*"; and there in "God's Acre," with a great company of his parishioners and fellow-townsmen, whose funeral obsequies he performed, his body rests, near the beautiful burial lot of his beloved brother in another communion, Rev. Samuel Cutler, awaiting with him and them the resurrection dawn.

The church though considerably enfeebled, yet rallied, and at a regular meeting held Jan. 13th, 1855, in the meeting-house, presided over by Deacon Cook, invited REV. JOSEPH FREEMAN, to become their pastor and teacher. Accordingly, Mr. Freeman came in answer to the call on the 21st of February,

REV. ABEL G. DUNCAN.

and preached on the 25th the first sermon as pastor elect. On Sunday, March 11th, the Lord's Supper was administered, fourteen members of the church being present, and three from sister churches. "It was a good season." April 5th was observed as a day of public fasting, humiliation and prayer. A sermon was preached in the forenoon, and a social meeting was held in the afternoon. At the close of the service a meeting of the church and parish was called, and Elisha Bass, Josiah Chamberlain and Deacon Cook were chosen a committee to call an ecclesiastical council for the purpose of installing Rev. Mr. Freeman as pastor of the church and society. Pursuant to letters missive from the First Congregational Church in Hanover, an ecclesiastical council convened in the meeting-house on Wednesday, April 18th, 1855, for the purpose of examining, and if judged expedient, of installing Rev. Joseph Freeman as pastor. The council was organized by the choice of Rev. Samuel L. Rockwood as moderator, and Rev. F. A. Fiske as scribe. The pastors and delegates present from the churches invited were as follows:

Hanson,   Rev. Samuel L. Rockwood.
Hingham,   Rev. E. Porter Dyer,
        Brother S. G. Bayley, Delegate.
Abington, Third Church, Rev. H. D. Walker.
        Deacon P. Winslow, Delegate.
Hanover, Second Church, Rev. William Chapman.
        Brother George Eells, Delegate.
Frankfort, Me., First Congregational Church,
        Rev. S. H. Hayes.
Marshfield, Trinitarian Congregational Church,
        Rev. F. A. Fiske.
        Brother C. W. Macomber, Delegate.

A ministerial brother being present was invited to take part in the deliberations. The council were satisfied with the papers and examination, and Rev. Mr. Freeman was installed at 2 P. M. in the meeting-house, with the following public services :

1. Reading of Minutes by the Scribe.
2. Reading the Scriptures and Prayer by Rev. Charles Morgridge.
3. Sermon by Rev. S. H. Hayes.
4. Installing Prayer by the Scribe.
5. Charge to the Pastor by Rev. E. Porter Dyer.
6. Right Hand of Fellowship and Address to the People by Rev. H. D. Walker.
7. Concluding Prayer by Rev. E. P. Dyer.
8. Benediction by the Pastor.

Inasmuch as this was the last installation of a pastor over this church, it may be interesting to read the letter of invitation to be pastor, and the reply from Mr. Freeman.

HANOVER, Jan. 15, 1855.

Rev. Joseph Freeman,

Dear Sir: I am directed to communicate to you the following votes of the First Congregational Church and Society in this place. At a regular meeting of the church holden at their meeting-house on Saturday, the 13th inst., Voted, that we invite the Rev. Joseph Freeman to become the pastor and teacher of this church. At a regular meeting of the Society on the same day and place, Voted, that we unite with the church in extending an invitation to the Rev. Joseph Freeman to settle with us in the Gospel ministry. Voted, that we pay him six hundred dollars annually. The above votes were unanimous. I hope that you will accept our call, and come among us as soon as practicable. For the present we have engaged half of a large house near the meeting-house for you, until you can be better accommodated. Please answer as soon as possible.

ISAAC COOK.

PROSPECT, ME., Feb. 6th, 1855.

Deacon Joseph Cook, in behalf of the First Congregational Church and Society in Hanover, Mass.:

Dear Sir,—Your favor of the 15th ult., was duly received. A decided affirmative answer has been delayed until the present time, because it could not be properly given before I should know the results of an ecclesiastical council. The council convened to-day, and my pastoral relation with this people is now dissolved. I am happy to say that the short acquaintance I had with your brethren and friends gave me much pleasure, and I left feeling a cordial interest in them and their spiritual welfare. Your request has been made a subject of much thought and prayer to God for his blessing and guidance, for I desire to do what will be pleasing in his sight, and go only where He would have me. Without Him I can do nothing. Under a deep sense of my own weakness and want of conformity to Christ, I feel myself to be unfit for the responsible and holy office of one of His embassadors. But relying upon His grace and merciful presence, and trusting that I shall ever have the cordial co-operation and prayers of all who love His name, I have concluded to accept your call to the pastoral office. With respect to the compensation I accept your proposal, asking that you will grant me four or five Sabbaths annually for a vacation. I am pleased that you have provided accommodations for my family, and trust that we shall be happy in the enjoyment of them; but you will permit me to express the wish that a parish house may be built as early in the summer as practicable. If nothing in the Providence of God prevents me, I shall leave with my family, for Massachusetts next week; but may not supply your pulpit before the first Sabbath in March, subject, however, to your wishes. I shall then be ready for my installation at an early day as may seem desirable. Wishing you grace, mercy and peace in the Lord Jesus Christ, I remain, in Christian affection,
Yours,
JOSEPH FREEMAN.

REV. JOSEPH FREEMAN.

Mr. Freeman was born in Orrington, Me., the last day of December, 1814. His ancestors came from England and settled at Eastham, in this state. His parents were professed Christians. At the age of 19 he made a public profession of religion, and united with the Congregational Church in Orrington. His mind was then directed to the Gospel ministry, and he came to consecrate himself and his life to that work. He was licensed to preach the Gospel, and was graduated at Bangor Theological Seminary in 1842. He went immediately on a previous engagement to the Congregational Church in Strong, Maine, where he was ordained pastor in 1844; here he labored three years. He was then installed over the Congregational Church in Sandy Point (Stockton), Me., and remained nine years. From that place he came to Hanover, where he lived and labored until July 26th, 1869, when he was dismissed by a mutual council. When he was installed pastor there were 14 male members and 43 female, making a total of 57. With his ministry he began to record the times when the sacrament of the Lord's Supper was administered and the number of members present. June 15th, Rev. Mr. Duncan was present at the regular church meeting. It was voted to grant Mrs. Laura J. D. King, his daughter, a letter of dismission and recommendation to the Congregational Church in North Adams. October 14th, at the close of public worship, a meeting of the church was called by the pastor to decide whether they would join the Pilgrim Conference. The church voted to present their request at the next meeting of that body for admission, and Brother Ebenezer Thayer was chosen delegate to attend that week the conference held at South Marshfield. The request was presented by the pastor, and the church was received into the conference. An event occurred September 18th, when the pastor and his family moved in and occupied a new parsonage or parish house, which had been built for his occupancy. This house was not built by the parish society, but by individual members. At the beginning of the year following, we find the new pastor somewhat depressed on account of the low state of religion. Thus we find the record January 4th, 1856:

"Church met in conference at the house of Widow Stetson. Only 4 individuals were present. Prospects appeared rather gloomy."

In February the church did not meet in conference owing to the inclemency of the weather, and in March there was a good meeting and the Spirit of the Lord was present, and their hearts were encouraged. Yet it is added: "Religion is low, and wickedness abounds; but it affords no reason why God will not hear the prayer of faith and reveal His gracious power unto salvation." In connection with the Lord's Supper which was administered at noon, March 9th, he says: "It was a good season to our souls, but it does not seem to be the most appropriate time to observe this ordinance at noon. There is too much noise." In May there was present at the Communion the largest number of communicants during the year past, and the pastor's heart was encouraged. After public service on the Sabbath, October 19th, the church appointed Deacon Cook, Brother E. Bass and Brother S. S. Church delegates to the Pilgrim Conference which was to meet October 23d, with this church. The Pilgrim Conference met with this church Tuesday and Wednesday, October 23d and 24th. The meetings were very interesting, and it was hoped that permanent good would result. Rev. Mr. Bullard, of Boston, addressed the conference upon the subject of Sabbath Schools. Rev. Dr. J. Clark, of Boston, spoke on the subject of Home Missions. Rev. Mr. Babcock, of South Plymouth, preached the opening sermon. Rev. Mr. Brainerd, of Halifax, preached in the evening. Rev. Mr. Fiske, of North Marshfield, preached the closing sermon. Rev. Messrs. Rockwood and Babcock officiated at the Lord's table. For several months the church failed to meet in conference owing to storms, bad travelling and sickness. At the church meeting held March 4th, 1857, twenty-three were present. It was a very interesting meeting. Every one felt deeply, and there was much melting of heart and weeping before God.

The Holy Spirit was with them. The pastor closes with this desire of his heart: "Oh, may He work gloriously." March 11th twenty were present.

" There was much deep interest in the revival of the church and the salvation of souls manifested, much subdued feeling. The Holy Spirit seems to be moving the hearts of his people to call upon the Lord for his salvation to be revealed among this people. April 23d, meeting of the church and others interested in the subject of religion; twenty-two were present. Very good meeting. The Spirit of the Lord is with us. There have been a few conversions." May 1st, preparatory lecture. Good meeting, twenty-two present. The church generally seem much engaged in the cause of Christ. May 2d, administered the Lord's Supper. Large number of communicants present. Very solemn and interesting occasion. The Lord is reviving His work."

After public service Sabbath, May 17th, Deacon Cook and Brother Samuel Church were chosen delegates to attend the Pilgrim Conference at Carver, the 19th inst. The heart of the pastor was encouraged so that he breaks forth into praise to God, for His mercy and goodness. August 30th, Sabbath, after third service, Deacon Isaac Cook was chosen delegate in the absence of the pastor, who was away for six weeks on his vacation, to attend a council in Abington Centre for the purpose of ordaining Mr. Abbe as pastor over the Centre Congregational Church. On September 13th, 1857, the meeting-house was reopened after undergoing extensive repairs. A new sofa was put in the pulpit. A rich marble top communion table was presented to the church and society, and chairs also by James Stetson, Esq. A dedicatory service was held by the pastor. The pastor says:

" In His kind Providence God has smiled upon us during the time of making these repairs and improvements, and prospered the work of our hands. In this may we discern evidence of His pleasure in it. It was a work prompted neither by pride, nor by emulation. It was a work that was needed to be done. Reverence for the sanctuary, honor to God, comfort of worshippers asked for it. Cheerfully and kindly has it been done, and well done. May the richest blessings of the Father of lights, to whom it is all devoted, rest upon the people and upon their children and they receive double in mercies for all their labor."

October 11th, after public service in the afternoon, Deacon Cook, Brothers S. S. Church and Ebenezer Thayer were chosen delegates to attend the Pilgrim Conference to be held at Hanson, the 20th inst. Nov. 1st was a very interesting day. Thirty persons partook of the Sacrament, three were admitted to the church, one being baptized, and also five small children were presented for the ordinance of baptism. The heart of the pastor in common with the hearts of ministers throughout the country and Great Britain was greatly encouraged and cheered by the presence of the Holy Spirit, and the general interest prevalent in the meetings. Revivals abounded and this parish was in a somewhat revived state. February 14th, after public services, Brother Samuel S. Church was chosen delegate with the pastor to attend a council in Hanson, in reference to dismissing their pastor, Rev. Mr. Rockwood. April 4th, after public service, Brother S. S. Church was chosen to attend as delegate with the pastor a council in South Weymouth, for the purpose of installing Rev. S. H. Hayes pastor over the Union Congregational Church. May 19th, the Pilgrim Conference met at Plympton, and Deacon Cook and Brother Samuel S. Church were the delegates chosen to attend. About this time there was a case of church discipline. A great many years had passed since the church had found it necessary to exclude any of its members, but now, after investigating the case by a committee, it was thought best to suspend one of their members for a year, and at the end of that time he was excommunicated. August 15th, the people were pleased to hear again their former pastor, Rev. Abel G. Duncan, who was with them and preached twice, besides attending the funeral of Miss Sybil Hatch. September 26th, after public service, Brother S. S. Church and Deacon Cook were chosen delegates to attend the Pilgrim Conference. October 21st, Thursday, was observed as a day of fasting and prayer. There was a meeting in the meeting-house attended by twenty-five persons. It is described as a very good meeting. This was recommended to the churches by the Pilgrim Conference, in the hope that it might be the "beginning of better days." In March, 1859, we find again the complaint of the pastor as to the low state of religion. At the close of public services Sabbath, June 12th, a letter missive was read from the Second Congregational Church, in this town, and Deacon Cook was chosen delegate with the pastor to attend a council for the purpose of installing Rev. Mr. Aiken as pastor. In the spring of 1860, the pastor was afflicted with a short illness, and on March 4th, the Lord's Supper was administered by REV. MR. HOWLAND, of Abington. The Pilgrim Conference was held in South Plymouth, and Deacon Cook and Brother S. S. Church were chosen delegates. In recording the communion season of July 3d, the pastor speaks of it as a good season, and also states the fact that three young persons had recently been converted. July 16th, the pastor records the death of Widow Celia Judd. He says:

"She was received to this church August 5th, 1827, by Rev. Ethan Smith, pastor. She walked with the church till within a few years. She has been allured away and become interested in Spiritualism. Because of her feeble old age and broken state of mind, the church bore with her with long suffering and charity. She ever said to her pastor and others that she did not give up her faith in the Bible, nor her hope in Christ, nor her love to the church. Her accounts are with God and sealed. It is our hope that her error and inconsistency may have been forgiven, and that it may be well with her."

At the preparatory lecture September 13th, 1860, there was a good attendance of the sisters of the church, but none of the brothers were present. In the spring of 1861, Deacon Cook, and Brothers S. S. Church and Francis Chamberlain were chosen delegates to attend the Pilgrim Conference, and also in the fall, Brother M. Stoddard being chosen instead of Brother Chamberlain. The regular church meetings were held and attended as in previous years. The church and society having contributed five dollars for books and tracts for the soldiers in the army, received the following note of acknowledgement:

CAMP BARNES, HALL'S HILL,
VA., Oct. 4th, 1861.

To the First Congregational Church, Hanover, Mass.:

In behalf of Company G, 18th Regiment, I wish to tender to you our sincere thanks for the books and tracts received through Colonel Barnes for this company, and which I intend to distribute next Sabbath. Hoping they may do the good which you intended,

I am, your obedient servant,

WM. B. WHITE,

Captain Company G, 18th Regiment, Massachusetts Volunteers.

In the following spring, April 15 and 16, 1862, the Pilgrim Conference met with this church, and Deacon Cook, Brother S. S. Church and Brother Francis Chamberlain were chosen delegates as usual. We have no record of the proceedings. In the fall, the conference met at Halifax, and Deacon Cook, with Brothers S. S. Church and E. Thayer were chosen delegates. In November a letter missive was received from individuals in Chiltonville, and Brother S. S. Church was chosen to attend as delegate with the pastor a council for the purpose of organizing into a Congregational Church. Deacon Cook went instead of Brother Church. November 25th, Brother Church was chosen delegate to attend a council in Plympton, with the pastor, for the purpose of ordaining Mr. Stevens. At the beginning of the year 1863, January 18th, the meeting-house was burned. The fire was discovered less than an hour after the congregation had gone. It is supposed that the fire in some way or other was communicated from one of the stoves. The most valuable part of the furniture was saved. The next Sabbath, meeting was held in the parsonage, and REV. MR. WALKER, of East Abington (now Rockland), preached on exchange. The following Sabbaths, meetings were held in the house of Widow Samuel Stetson, where the people met for public worship in 1726. July 5th was a memorable day. Four young persons were received, one of them being the son of the pastor. The pastor and his wife also united with the church by letter from the Congregational Church, Stockton, Maine. At the communion September 6, there was a full attendance. The pastor says:

"Good season. Foretaste of the sweet communion of the church in Glory."

October 11th, after public services, Deacon Cook and Brother S. S. Church were chosen delegates to the conference to meet in Plymouth. The following Sabbath a letter missive was read from the Fifth Church in Chiltonville, and Deacon Cook was chosen delegate with the pastor to attend a council for the purpose of ordaining Mr. Alexander Fuller, Jr., over the church. After the fire, the society began to plan for rebuilding, and November 22d the congregation worshipped for the first time in the vestry of the new church, — the present building, — being the fourth building of the kind on the same site. November 26th was observed by the church as Thanksgiving Day. A good number assembled to bring offerings of praise before the Lord and present them for His great goodness and mercy. It was a good meeting. Sermon was on the text, I. Chron. 16, 36:

"Blessed be the Lord God of Israel forever and ever. And all the people said Amen, and praised the Lord."

The day was clear, mild and pleasant. APRIL 27TH, 1864, THE NEW CHURCH WAS DEDICATED to the worship of Almighty God. The order of exercises was as follows: 1. Anthem by the choir. 2. Invocation by Rev. B. Southworth, of Hanson. 3. Reading of Hymn by Rev. S. H. Hayes, of South Weymouth, 132d Psalm, beginning with 4th verse. 4. Reading of Scriptures, Psalms 95, 96 and 100, by Rev. Samuel Cutler, Rector of St. Andrew's Church, Hanover. 5. Prayer by Rev. James Aiken, Hanover. 6. Reading 141, Select Hymn, by Rev. Mr. Edwards, of South Abington. Singing. 7. Sermon by pastor. Text, Psalm 96, 8th and 9th verses. 8. Consecrating Prayer by Rev. Mr. Walker. 9. Anthem. 10. Benediction by pastor. The pastor records:

"The weather on the whole was favorable and the house was filled. We record our gratitude to God for His great goodness, and for a new sanctuary in which we may worship Him, and enjoy as a people the communion and fellowship of the Lord Jesus Christ."

In the following June, however, we find the record:

"Preparatory lecture. Few present. Religion low. People are busy in worldly affairs."

After public services, July 17th, a letter missive was read from the church in Carver, and Deacon Cook was chosen delegate with the pastor to attend a council for the purpose of ordaining a pastor. In the fall, the Pilgrim Conference met with the Fifth Church, Chiltonville, and Brother S. S. Church was chosen to attend as delegate. In the year 1865 Fast Day was observed by this church. April 13th, Deacon Cook and Brother Church were appointed delegates to the conference to meet at Kingston, the 19th inst., and to represent the church in respect to a national council to be held in Boston on the 14th of June, and to vote for the sending of messengers from the conference to that council. In the fall, Brothers Church and Chamberlain were chosen delegates to the Pilgrim Conference at South Plymouth. October 12th, 1865, the parish met with a severe loss in the death of Melzar Hatch. He was a constant attendant on public worship in all kinds of weather. Though he was not a professor of religion, he had great reverence for religion and religious ordinances. It grieved him to see them neglected habitually by men, or to witness the desecration of the Holy Sabbath. He was a man of public spirit, and his influence and work may be seen in many things. He was a strong friend and patriot during the great national conflict, ready and willing to aid, to provide liberal things for the soldiers, for the suffering, without distinction of color or nationality. He did much in aiding improvements in the cemetery.

His funeral was attended by a large gathering of people. After the communion November 5th, 1865, the church granted letters of dismission to Rev. Mr. Duncan and Almira Estes, who wished to unite with the Congregational Church in Freetown (Assonet). At the beginning of the year 1866, the church was called upon to sustain a great loss in the death of Deacon Isaac Cook, who died February 2d, peaceful and happy. The pastor enters the following record concerning him:

"He had been declining a long time. He had been a member of the church 39 years; deacon, 37 years; superintendent, 30 years. He was a good man and faithful. He loved the cause of Christ. He could say, 'I love Thy kingdom, Lord.' He loved the church. Her interests were dear to him. He remembered them as he drew near to death. He was a man of more than ordinary ability, well-informed and discriminating mind, clear and sound in his theological views, able to speak unto the edification of the brethren and sisters in the church, and of men of the world. He was ever ready and willing to do all he could for the support of the Gospel ordinances, and the comfort and support of the church and its prosperity. He rests from his labors, and his works do follow him."

March 28th, the church met in conference and made choice of Brother Samuel S. Church and Brother Francis Chamberlain as deacons. They accepted the office and were consecrated by the laying on of hands. It was an interesting meeting, and the pastor expresses the wish that the "blessing of God may follow it." Deacon Francis Chamberlain was chosen superintendent of the Sabbath School. During his pastorate, Mr. Freeman faithfully records the deaths of the members as they occur, with some remarks concerning them. So we find the record of one who for many years was a great sufferer. "July 15th, Widow Elizabeth T. House died in peace, and entered the promised rest. She had been in failing health for several months. Rev. Mr. Southworth, of Hanson, officiated at her funeral during the absence of the pastor."

"January 2d, 1867, Mr. Samuel Barstow died. He was a social, cheerful and obliging man, and had many friends, who mourn his death. He was not a professor, but was an habitual attendant on public worship, an active member of the parish, and one of the most liberal supporters of the Gospel. He gave $200 to the Parish Fund for the support of public worship."

January 14th, we find the record of the death of a prominent member, Mr. Elisha Bass.

"He died an easy and peaceful death in the blessed hope of Heaven. He was a grandson of Rev. Benjamin Bass, the first settled pastor. He was a well-read, sound, faithful, influential Christian. He was fluent, clear, logical and conclusive in thought, remarks and appeals. He was a pillar in Zion. He came to the grave in full age, like a shock of corn cometh in its season."

April 14th, after public service, Deacon Church was chosen delegate to the Pilgrim Conference. After the preparatory lecture, November 1st, ten persons being present, Deacon Church was again chosen to attend the conference, and it was voted to make contributions to the A. B. C. F. M. This church had not contributed to that Board for many years, but had sent to the A. M. Association instead. They also voted to accept the resignation of Deacon Chamberlain as superintendent of the Sabbath School. In the spring of 1868, Deacon Church and Brother E. Thayer were chosen delegates to the conference. But little is recorded during this year. In the year 1869, July 26th, we find a record of the death of Widow Lydia Stockbridge. She was found dead in her bed, as she had fallen asleep. "She had been a member for nearly half a century. She was a good woman, and prepared for her change when it came.

'So He giveth His beloved sleep.'"

So we come to the end of the great many records recorded by this faithful pastor during the fourteen years and more of his ministry. Now the time has come when he feels it his duty to resign his pastoral charge. Accordingly, he tendered his resignation of the pastoral office July 11th, 1869, and called for a mutual council. This was granted him by the church and society, and a council was called July 26th, at 10.30 o'clock. July 18th, letters of dismission and recommendation were granted to Rev. Joseph Freeman, Sarah H. Freeman and Willis H. Freeman at their own request, to unite with the Congregational Church, in York, Me., from which church he had received a call to become their pastor. The following churches were invited to be represented in council: North Scituate, South Marshfield, Kingston, Hanover, Second Church and Hanson. The council was convened at the time appointed, and Rev. Alexander J. Sessions, of Scituate, was chosen moderator, and Rev. E. Alden, of South Marshfield, scribe. The following persons constituting ecclesiastical council held this connection: First Church, Scituate, Rev. A. J. Sessions, Deacon Israel Cudworth; Second Church, Hanover, Brother J. M. Wilder, delegate; Church in Hanson, Rev. B. Southworth, acting pastor; First Church, Marshfield, Rev. E. Alden, Jr., pastor. By this council, Rev. Mr. Freeman was regularly dismissed and well recommended to the churches. During his ministry 24 persons were received into the church, and 18 adults and children were baptized. The church lost by death 20, and a few were dismissed to other churches. In the pulpit Mr. Freeman was dignified, commanding and solemn. He was a sound, doctrinal and practical preacher, not given to flowery flights in his style, nor to too large liberality in his sentiments. He was serious and earnest in his important professional work, and did much also for the improvement of the schools as a superintending committee. He was held in high estimation in the community generally, and among his ministerial brethren with whom he associated. After an interval of about two years, in which the pulpit was supplied for the Sabbath merely, or for a few consecutive Sabbaths by the same minister, REV. CYRUS WILLIAM ALLEN was engaged as a permanent supply. We find this record of the event: April 9th, 1871. The committee of the church and parish agreed with Rev. C. W. Allen to

PRESENT PARSONAGE, BUILT A. D. 1855. THE RESIDENCE OF REV. JOSEPH FREEMAN, REV. CYRUS W. ALLEN, REV. SAM'L E. EVANS AND REV. W. H. DOWDEN.

supply the pulpit of the First Congregational Church for one year for $550 and use of parsonage from May 1st, 1871, to May 1st, 1872. Samuel S. Church, committee of church, Lemuel Dwelley and Daniel Barstow, committee of parish.

Mr. Allen began to preach to this church March 26th, 1871, and became permanently engaged May 1st, and continued until July 12th, 1879, when he was released from further service at his own request. Mr. Allen was the ninth minister of this church and society. He was the son of Joseph and Betsy (Woodward) Allen and was born in Taunton on the 28th day of October, 1806. He was graduated at Brown University, (R. I.) in 1826, and at Andover Theological Seminary in 1829. In the same year he was licensed to preach by the Andover Association on the 22nd day of April. After leaving the seminary he spent the first five years of his ministerial life in Missouri and Illinois, as an agent of the American Tract Society, New York, as a missionary of American Home Missionary Society, and as a minister at different places, in which latter service he received $160 a year. He was ordained by the Missouri Presbytery in St. Louis, October 6th, 1833, St. Louis then being only a village. He was settled in Norton, Mass., July 8th, 1835, and dismissed by council March 1st, 1842. He was installed at Pelham, N. H., February 1st, 1843; at Coleraine, Mass., February 28th, 1849; at Hubbardston, December 29th, 1852, and was settled without installation in East Jaffrey, N. H., April, 1863. When he began labor in Hanover he was nearly 65 years of age. In his historical record delivered to this church April 27th, 1879, he speaks of his pastoral relation to the church and society. He says that he sustains

"the relation of what is called a stated supply, or an acting pastor. It is a relation which implies and requires all the duties and all the privileges of the real pastor, excepting merely the formalities of an ecclesiastical council, called for the purposes of installation and dismission. Such a minister can come and become a minister of a particular church and society, and can leave the same without such a council."

His wife, Mary (Folger) Allen of Nantucket, was a daughter of Gideon and Eunice (Macy) Folger, to whom he was married June 6, 1835. While at Norton he taught Latin for a while in the recently established Wheaton Female Seminary. His work brought on ill health, and after closing his pastorate at Norton he spent a year at Nantucket, regaining his health.

At Hanover was his last pastorate. When in 1879, increasing years and failing strength compelled him to relinquish his active connection with parish work, he retired to his son's house at West Roxbury, where he died from apoplexy, April 11th, 1875. He was a staunch defender of the faith of the fathers. His preaching was marked by little embellishment, but set forth his ideas always logically, always forcibly, yet simply and to the point. The best sermon he ever preached was his own everyday life. No one knew him but to love him. The Spirit of the Master spoke every day from the absolute self-forgetfulness of Mr. Allen's life.

He was a member of the school committee in each of the towns of Coleraine, Pelham, Hubbardston and Hanover. His wife survived him after a long, helpful and happy married life. She bore him the following children:

Dr. George Otis Allen, born in Norton, October 25, 1838, now deceased.

Rev. Rowland Hussey Allen, born in Norton, August 13, 1840, now deceased.

Henry Folger Allen, born in Norton, September 2, 1841, now a successful merchant residing in Boston.

Rev. Laban Wheaton Allen, born at Pelham, December 11, 1843, who died August 23, 1875.

Mary Abby, wife of George F. Sylvester of Hanover, born at Pelham, June 19, 1845.

Eliza Katherine Allen, born at Coleraine, 1850, and died at three years of age.

Williams Cyrus Allen, born in Gardner, Mass., who died at the age of 21 months.

Fanny Florence, wife of John F. Simmons of Boston, born at Hubbardston, April 25, 1855.

The foregoing is mainly in the words of the writer spoken of in the preface. Further than this I have not gone, because, at this point I approached Mr. John Tower, the editor of the *North River Pioneer*, and the faithful recorder of our local history, hoping he, as an authority on the history of the country around, would help me out on many perplexing details. He informed me that he was about publishing a History of Hanover, bringing Barry's History down to the present day and adding much new matter to the old, and correcting some of the latter. It was too late to stop my work; some of it was already in the press, so I present only what I had already secured, and leave the balance to be recorded by THE searcher among searchers of our local history, in his forthcoming valuable book, which every man, woman and child will anxiously wait for and certainly secure.

SHIP "CRONSTADT" ASHORE ON FALSTERBO REEF.—*See Hist. No. River.*

CHAPTER II.

"OF THE GATHERING OF THE CHURCH, ORDINATION AND CHURCH MEETINGS."

FROM THE ORIGINAL BOOK OF RECORDS.

THERE are several years of records missing which no one is responsible for excepting the different ministers whose duty it was to keep the records. I have endeavored to follow the original style of spelling, etc., changing only the arrangement.

The different methods of reckoning time, as is seen in some of the records which have two dates, is best explained in Don Gleason Hill's Book of Dedham Records, and which I give below:

The length of a year is the space of time required for the earth to revolve around the sun, namely: 365 days, 5 hours, 48 minutes, 49 seconds and seven-tenths of a second; but for convenience it has been found necessary to lump the fractions together so as to make up a day therefrom. As early as 45 B. C., Julius Cæsar, by the help of an Alexandrian philosopher, introduced the present arrangement of making the year consist of 365 days, with the addition of one day every fourth year, to absorb the odd hours. At the time of the Council of Nice, A. D. 325, the Vernal Equinox (the time when the days and nights are of equal length in all parts of the world) fell correctly on the 21st of March. But the addition of a whole day every fourth year was found to be too much by 11 minutes, $10\frac{3}{4}$ seconds, so that the beginning of the year was constantly being moved ahead of the point at which it was in the days of Julius Cæsar. In 1582, Pope Gregory XIII undertook to reform the Calendar. He found that since the Council of Nice there had been an over-reckoning of ten days, so that the Vernal Equinox fell on the 11th of March. To correct the past error he decreed that the 5th day of October,

1582, should be reckoned as the 15th; and to keep the year right in future, the overplus being 18 hours, 37 minutes, 10 seconds in a century, he ordered that every centurial year that could not be divided by 400 (1700, 1800, 1900, 2100, etc.,) should not be bissextile or leap year, as it otherwise would be; in other words, that the extra day should be dropped three times every four hundred years. The following rule has been made to determine in all cases the number of days in each year under the Gregorian method.

Every year whose number is divisible by 4, except those divisible by 100, and not by 400, consists of 366 days, and all others of 365 days.

The Catholic nations in general adopted the Gregorian style, but the Protestants were too much inflamed against Catholicism to receive from the Pope even a pure, scientific improvement. A bill to reform the Calendar was brought before the British Parliament in 1585, but was not passed, and for nearly 200 years the British people endured the inconvenience of the old style rather than adopt the Gregorian calendar. It was at length adopted in Great Britain and her colonies in 1752, when it became necessary to drop eleven days. But the Protestant populace of Great Britain were even then violently inflamed against the statesman who carried the bill through Parliament. They believed they had been defrauded of eleven days of their destined lives. It is said that for some time afterwards a favorite opprobrious cry to unpopular statesmen in the streets was, "Who stole the eleven days?" "Give us back the eleven days!"

The act of Parliament provided that after the second of September, 1752, the next ensuing day should be held as the fourteenth, and that three of the four centurial years should, as in Pope Gregory's arrangement, not be leap years. From 1582 both styles continued to overrun the true time in the same proportion until the year 1700, which was leap year under the Julian method, and gained an extra day, but under the Gregorian method came within the exception and dropped the extra day. In changing the dates in this volume, prior to September 2, 1752, so as to correspond with the new style, it will be necessary to add ten days to the date given in the record for all dates on or before February 29, 1700, and eleven days for all dates on and after March 1st of that year, where double dates are given.

Previous to the adoption of the Gregorian calendar, the year had different days of beginning at various periods in the same and different countries. In England, in the 7th and as late as the 13th century, the year began on Christmas day, but in the 12th century the Anglican Church commenced the year on Annunciation or Lady Day, March 25th, as did also the Civilians in the 14th century, and this continued until the adoption of the new style; but for a long period prior thereto, the historic year, so called, had commenced on the first day of January, so that at the time our records begin, and for a considerable period prior thereto, the two modes of reckoning the commencement of the year existed in Great Britain and her colonies — the civil, ecclesiastical or legal year with March 25th, and the historical year with January 1st. Boston almanacs made the change from March to January, in 1687, and the Boston News Letter in 1717.

The same act of Parliament which struck off the eleven days in September, 1752, enacted that the year should thereafter begin with January 1st. The two lines of introduction to the first book indicate that here "the year is accounted to begin the first day of the first Mo. called March." At first the months were more commonly called by their numbers than by their names. 1 Mo. for March, 2 Mo. for April, 3 Mo. for May, and so on; the months named from the Latin numerals, September, October, November and December, are frequently written 7ber, 8ber, 9ber and 10ber. To prevent confusion, the same practice was very early adopted here as elsewhere in the colony of double dating, i. e., giving both years to all dates between January 1st and March 25th; as, for instance, February 10, 1721-2, meaning February 10th of the year 1722, which began January 1st, and of 1721, which began in the preceding March, and this practice of double dating continued until the adoption of the new style by Parliament, September, 1752.

In the pages which follow there is a great field for study and research, and while I have found material that could be made much of in writings, I have not found the time in which to write it up, but shall leave each student of genealogy and history to pick out the choice bits here and there. To give the reader some idea of the difficulties under which I have labored while compiling this book, I give below some of the offices I have held during the year 1894, each of which claimed good portions of my time:

President of the Bath Electric Light & Illuminating Co., of New York.

Vice President and Honorary Counsel of the Associated Charities, Ward XVI, Boston.

Member of the Exchange Club, Boston.

Senior Warden of Phœnix Masonic Lodge, Hanover.

Member of the Sons of the American Revolution.

Treasurer of the Live Oak Phosphate Co., of Elmwood, Fla.

Director in the New England Hospital for Women and Children, Boston.
Member of Tufts College Medical School, Boston.
Director in Dr. Bowditch's Sanitarium, Sharon, Mass.
Fine Member First Corps Cadets, M. V. M., Boston.
Bank Notary.
Member Massachusetts Consistory 32°.
Treasurer Georgia Pyrites Company, of Temple, Ga.
Commissioner of North Carolina, by appointment received from the Governor of North Carolina.
Member Bostonian Society.
Member of the Hawaiian Club.
Member New England Historical and Genealogical Society.

There are other positions or duties which I have been destined to fill for times varying from a few days to a few months, which have taken much time that I would otherwise have been able to devote to this work. The records are, however, as complete as the originals from which they are taken, I having left out only a few words or dates where I have thought it wisest and best so to do. If any mistakes are discovered I hope they will be immediately reported.

December 5, 1728 was observed as a day of Fasting and Prayer, to implore the Divine presence and blessing to attend the ministry of the Pastor-elect vizt., BENJ. BASS, M. A., who had before this accepted the Town's call to the Pastoral office amongst them: On the said day the Church was gathered, consisting of ten besides the Pastor-elect, who then subscribed the Chh. Covenant vizt :

Joseph Stockbridge,   Isaac Buck,
Elijah Cushing,   Joseph Stockbridge, Jr.
James Hatch,   Thomas Josselyn,
John Tailor,   Amasa Turner
Samuel Staples,   Samuel Skiff.

THE COVENANT THEY SIGNED RUNS IN THESE WORDS:

We do give up ourselves and our offspring to that God whose name alone is Jehovah, Father, Son and Holy Spirit, as the one only true and living God, and unto our blessed Lord, Jesus Christ, as our only Saviour, Prophet, Priest and King over our Souls and only mediator of the Covenant of Grace promising (by the help and assistance of His spirit and grace) to cleave unto God and our Lord Jesus Christ by faith in a way of Gospel obedience as becometh the Covenant People forever, and we do also give up ourselves one unto another in the Lord, according to the will of God, freely covenanting and promising (the Lord helping of us) to walk together in holy union and communion as members of the same mystical body and as an instituted church of Christ rightly constituted and established in the true faith and order of the Gospel; and further we do oblige ourselves (by the help of Christ) in brotherly love to watch over one another and over all the children of the covenant growing up with us, and faithfully, according to our ability, to transmit the holy word and worship of God to our posterity; to cleave unto and uphold the true Gospel ministry as it is established by Christ in his Church, to have it in due honor and esteem, to subject ourselves fully and sincerely unto the government of Christ in his church, and duly to attend to the seals, censures and whatsoever ordinances Christ hath commanded to be observed by his People according to the order of the Gospel and withal we do further engage ourselves to walk orderly in a way of fellowship and communion with all our neighbor Churches according to the rules of the Gospel, that the name of our Lord Jesus Christ may be one throughout all the Churches to the glory of God the Father. AMEN.

The Rev. Mr. Eels of Scituate and the Rev. Mr. Lewis of Pembrook, came at the desire of the Christian Inhabitants in Hanover and assisted in the work of ye said day of Fasting and Prayer.

December 11, 1728 Benj. Bass, A. M. was by prayer & fasting with imposition of the hands of the Presbytery ordained a Pastor of the Church. The Rev. Mr. Eels of Scituate, Mr. Lewis of Pembrook, Mr. Hobart and Gay of Hingham and Mr. Checkley of Boston laid on hands. Mr. Gay began with prayer, Mr. Checkley preached, Mr. Eels gave the charge & Mr. Lewis the right hand of fellowship.

January 10, 1728-9 there was a Church meeting at which Deacon Joseph Stockbridge & Mr. Elijah Cushing were chosen Deacons and 'twas agreed to raise money by contribution to provide utensils for the Lord's Table &c.

The contribution was made on January 19th being ye Lord's Day and between that time and January 30th. were bought (with the money that was contributed) and brought to town three Pewter Tankards marked " C. T. " of ten shillings price each; Six Pewter Bakers costing three shillings & six pence each; marked " C. B. ; " Two Pewter Platters marked " C. P. ; " a pewter Bason for baptisms, marked ***, price ***. Price of each ***. A cloth for the Communion Table marked " C. H. " and this Book of Records.

July 31, 1733. The Brethren of the Church met and chose Mr. James Hatch and Mr. Isaac Buck, Deacons, who manifested their acceptance of the office.

April 1, 1739. The church voted a dismission of Joseph Stockbridge, Jr., to the Church of Christ in Pembroke.

November 25. The church brou't in their votes for a Deacon and Mr. Thomas Josselyn was chosen. The voters were 16 & given for him.

January 6, 1739-40. A letter was read from the First Chh. in Hingham ; in it they upon his desire, dismissed Thomas Wilks from his particular relation, to ye Chh. in Hanover, and it being put to vote, this Chh. of Hanover voted his reception to full and stated communion with them.

November 29, 1741. Thomas Toby was by a vote of the Chh. dismissed and recommended, according to his request, to the Chh. in Sandwich under the pastoral care of the Revd Mr. Fessenden.

March 7, 1742. The vote was called if the Society would sing what is commonly call'd the new way, and it pass'd in the affirmative *nemine contradicente;* then being desired to bring in their votes for a Tuner, Ezekiel Turner was chosen by a considerable majority.

November 4, 1744. Susannah Rose, an Indian, being recommended by the Indian Chh. at Mashpy in Sandwich to ye holy care & communion of ye chh. in Hanover ye sd. chh. of Hanover upon hearing ye Letter, voted to receive her to full & stated communion with them.

April 18, 1745. Mr. Thomas Rose was chosen by the Chh. into the office of a Deacon and in voting for another Deacon, the votes were so scattered that after several tryals without any ones having a majority of ye votes the affair was adjourned to Thursday ye 25th of April, 1745.

April 25. The Church met by adjournment to bring in their votes for a Deacon, and having brought them in, upon sorting them Samuel Barstow was found to be chosen by a majority of the votes that were brought in.

May 14. The Chh. chose the following brethren to inspect the manners of the children of the Chh. as well as such as are in full communion and endeavor when they walk disorderly to bring them to repentance & reformation: Joseph Stockbridge, Elijah Cushing, Benjamin Mann, Thomas Rose, Samuel Barstow, Joseph Ramsdale & James Torrey, Junior.

July 7. The Chh. at the desire of Jemima Bates, wife of Amos Bates, voted her a dismission and recommendation unto the Chh. in Rochester, under the pastoral care of the Revd Mr. Timothy Ruggles.

December 7, 1746. The Chh. voted to receive as a member in full communion, Mary Torrey, the wife of James Torrey, Junior, she having at her desire been dismissed and recommended to them by the Second Chh. in Scituate.

January 18. 1746 ($^{?}_{08}$) The Chh. voted a dismission and recommendation of their brother, Elisha Tobey to the Chh. of Christ in Falmouth, of which the Revd Mr. Palmer is Pastor.

November 22, 1747. The Chh. voted a dismission of their brother, James Torrey, Junior, and his wife, with a recommendation to the Chh. of Christ in Tolland, under the pastoral care of the Revd Mr. Steel.

1748. At a Church meeting on April 8 the Church reckoned with the Deacons Rose and Barstow and found due from Deacon Rose to the Chh. in old Tenor 00-06-03 and from Deacon Barstow in ye same tenor 1-1-5.

At the same meeting Mr. John Bailey, Junior, a brother of the Chh. gave the Chh. satisfaction which they to a man voted the acceptance of for an offence he had given for sinning with his tongue, which brother had had the character of a man that was in no way given to evil speaking, and it was well known that he was extreamly provoked when he in his passion uttered the words which gave the offense he made satisfaction for.

April 18. I, Benja. Bass, received at Deacon Rose's as he and Deacon Barstow reckoned it, good and bad together, Fourteen pounds fifteen shillings and nine pence, old tenor, it being a collection made by ye flock under my care to buy good books with to lend to such of the society as stand in need of em & would be glad to read them. With the above mentioned money I bought in less than a week after the collection, a parcel of books, whose titles, authors and price in old tenor may be met with in a book which is an exposition of ye Epistle to the Colossians by Mr. Nicolaus Byfield, vizt: on a leaf I found vacant immediately before the title page of said book : any one that borrows these books must use em well and return em in two months. That these books may be known I intend to put in the title page these letters : C. B. C. S. H. which stand for "Charity Book of the Congregational Society in Hanover."

August 28. The Chh. voted a dismission of Elijah Cushing,

esq., & his wife (they desiring it) from their special relation to them in order to their becoming members of a Chh. designed speedily to be gathered in the neighborhood.

July 23, 1749. The Chh. voted Brother Amasa Turner, at his request, a dismission & recommendation to the First Church in Lancaster.

September 30, 1753. The Chh. at his desire voted Brother Timothy Bailey a dismission to qualify him to be in a regular manner a member of a new Chh. going to be formed at the 2nd Precinct in North Yarmouth.

April 9, 1756. The Church met upon notice given the Lord's day next preceding and unanimously agreed in the following vote: Inasmuch as our brother, David Jenkins, was publickly charged by a certain person with being guilty of committing the sin of * * * * and the Church being this day met to consider what is proper to be done in such a case, and having notified said Jenkins of the time & place of meeting but he did not appear to give the Church any Christian satisfaction, therefore voted that it is the mind of this Church that our brother Jenkins refusing to meet the Church and endeavour to give them Christian satisfaction is wrong and unjustifiable & that he be suspended at present from the Communion at the Lord's Table until he shall desire the church to meet again in order further to consider his case, and that some two of the brethren be desired to deliver a copy of this vote to our brother Jenkins as soon as may be. Benjamin Man & William Curtis undertook to carry a copy of this vote to our brother Jenkins.

At the Tuesday meeting mentioned in the last page the following satisfaction for an offence given was offered to the Church and met with their unanimous acceptance . . .

I, the subscriber, having in an hour of temptation when I should have earnestly cried unto God for help and vigorously resisted the devil, grossly violated the * * * commandment in committing the sin commonly called * * * * * * , do hereby, and I hope for the glory of God, declare that I may remove the offence which I have given the Church of which I am a member that the Divine command which I have broken is holy, just & good, and I hope I shall walk very humbly with God for breaking it; fly to the blood of Christ which cleaneth from all sin for the pardon of that & all my sins, and as Christ' has commanded, watch & pray that I enter not into temptation & that I desire the Church's forgiveness & that their prayers may be joined with mine to the Father of Mercies with whom is forgiveness and that he may be feared, for all interest in his pardoning mercy and for grace that as I name the name of Christ I may depart from iniquity and live so as to adorn the Doctrine of God our Saviour in all things & at length receive eternal life from God in the way of a free gift though Jesus Christ our Lord.

JOSEPH RAMSDEL.

1756 Anno Domini, 1756. A continuation of the Church Records in the Town of Hanover:

Book 2d, containing admissions to full Communion. Dismissions from the Church: Those that have owned the Covenant and not admitted to full Communion: Baptisms, Deaths, Marriages and the Administration and votes of the Church on special occasions.

Beginning with December 1st, 1756.

1756 December 1. *Samuel Baldwin, A. M.*, was by Prayer with the imposition of the hands of the Presbytery ordained Pastor of the Church of Christ in Hanover. The Rev'd Messieurs Gay of Hingham, Cook of Sudbury, Storer of Watertown, Smith of Pembroke, Swift of Acton, laid on hands. Mr. Smith began with prayer, Mr. Cook preached, Mr. Gay gave the charge, Mr. Storer gave the right hand of fellowship, Mr. Swift made the last prayer.

The several pastors of the particular churches sent to assist in the ordination were the Revd Messieurs Gay of Hingham, Cook of Sudbury, Storer of Watertown, Smith of Pembroke, Swift of Acton, Wales of Marshfield, Hitchcock of Pembroke, Woodward of Weston, Dodge of Abington, Barns of Scituate.

ADMINISTRATION & VOTES OF THE CHURCH ON SPECIAL OCCASIONS.

October 30, 1768. Lord's Day. The Church in Hanover was presented with Four Silver Cups on the Communion Table by order and at the expence of Deacon Stockbridge. The cost of each Cup 25£ O. S. and each bearing this inscription, "THE GIFT OF DEACON JOSEPH STOCKBRIDGE TO THE CHURCH OF CHRIST IN HANOVER, 1768."

1st. It was moved to the Church by the Pastor whether they would vote their thanks to the Donor: the vote being called it passed unanimously in the affirmative.

2ly. On a motion made by the Pastor a vote was called whether an account of the above donation should be entered among the Church Records to be transmitted in gratefull memory of the donor and it passed in the affirmative.

3ly. Voted that the Pastor wait upon Deacon Jos'h Stockbridge, the donor, and give him the thanks of the Church, signifying these several votes, which was done accordingly.

pr. Samuel Baldwin, Pastor.

November 28, 1779. On the 28th Novr, 1779, I preached a farewell sermon to the people of Hanover for want of support, and on the eighth of March following I ask'd a dismission for want of support, which they granted, and it was confirmed by a vote of the Town.

February 11, 1784. On the 11th day of February, 1784, was instal'd to the Pastoral office in Hanover the REVD JOHN MELLEN, late of Lancaster, 2d Parish, now Sterling. Six Chhs. were sent to but Cambridge failed by reason of the Revd. & aged Dr. Appleton's death on the same week. Revd. Mr. Hitchcock of Pembroke gave the charge. Revd. Mr. Barns of Scituate gave right hand. His son, the Rev. Mr. Mellen of Barnstable, preached the sermon. Revd. Mr. Prentice of Reading, began with prayer & the Revd. Mr. Niles of Abington, concluded. Anthems sung by the Choir at the entering & leaving the meeting-house.

NAMES OF PROFESSORS AT LARGE.

June 27, 1784. David STOCKBRIDGE, Junr. & wife.
Sepr. 5, 1784. Joshua MAN & wife

Novr 28,		Job TILDEN & wife, also Snow CURTIS & wife.
Augt 7, 1785.		Benjam'n WHITE & wife.
May 28, 1786.		Morgan BREWSTER & wife.
Octr 22, 1786.		Ezra BRIGGS, Junr. & wife, after making their peace.
July 22, 1787.		James WOODWORTH & wife, after &c.
Novr 4,		Caleb WHITING & wife.
18,		Josiah CHAMBERLAIN & wife after making their peace.
Augt 3, 1788.		Wife of Josh. JOSLYN.
Aug. 10, 1788.		Ezekiel Turner HATCH & wife.
Sepr 14.		Nathl. BARSTOW & wife, also Homer WHITING & wife.
Octr 12.		Robert SALMON & wife.
1789.		Jóel SYLVESTER & wife, Oct. 11th.
1790.		John BARSTOW, July 25.
1792.		Ezra BEALES & wife, May 20th & child baptized.
	July 29th.	Bela MAN & wife.
	Aug. 5th.	Job YOUNG.
	Novr 18th.	Oliver WINSLOW & wife, she baptized.
1793.	July 14.	Charles MAN & wife, & wife of Joseph NEAL.
1794.	May 18.	John PERRY & wife.
	Novr 9.	Huldah WING, wife of William Wing.
	Octr 30.	William WHITING & wife.
1804.	April 29.	Cloe JOSLYN, wife of Almoner Joslyn.
1804.	Sepr 2d.	Benj. Healy CLARKE & wife. Also Jabez STUDLEY, Junr. & wife. Also Joseph EELLES & wife.
	30th.	Stephen BAILY, Junr. & wife. Also Amos BATES & wife.

RECORD OF CHH. VOTES PR. JOHN MELLEN.

August 13, 1784. The Chh. met and chose Brother Joseph Brooks, Deacon.

January 8, 1786. Received two Silver Cups for the Communion table, a legacy of the late Dea. Thomas Josslyn: Cost £7.4.0. The church voted they had received them & that they would have it recorded in the Chh. Book, as a token of their gratitude & to perpetuate the memory of the benefaction. Attest: John Mellen, Pastor.

1790 Lord's Day, July 18th. The Pastor introduced the following vote by observing that when persons are admitted into the Chh. & Kingdom of God out of a wicked world, it is to be supposed that may have been vicious and ungodly, but that they now truly repent & reform & are forgiven of God & therefore ought to be forgiven of men tho' accountable afterwards for their conduct to the Chh. & Society to w'ch they belong. But that upon their first repentance & embracing Christianity it does not appear scriptural or prudent to insist upon particular acknowledgments in some certain cases when it is not done in others—that many persons by this means are kept out of our Chhs & often join other persuasions because it is natural and very common for them to say that if a particular acknowledgment is required for one offence it ought to be for another and for all, but this not being the case they look upon themselves as injured & treated with partiality. If it be your minds therefore, brethren, that when persons are admittted to a public profession of religion & to Chh. Communion, a general penitent confession of past sin agreable to the Covenant, shall be deemed sufficient, please to manifest. Past in the affirmative: full vote.

1806. On the twenty third day of July, was instaled into the Pastoral Office in Hanover the REVD CALVIN CHADDOCK late of Rochester. Seven Chhs. were sent to, five only attended: the Revd. Mr. Strong of Randolf made the introductory prayer—the Revd. Mr. Niles of Abington, preached the sermon and made the consecrating prayer—the Revd. Mr. Barker of Middleborough gave the charge—the Revd. Mr. Norton of Waymouth gave the right hand and the Revd. Mr. Richmond of Halifax made the concluding prayer.

The following is a list of the present members of the Chh. in Hanover, both male and female:

MALES:

Saml. Barstow,	Josiah Smith,	Samuel Stetson,
Gideon Studley,	Stockbridge Josslyn,	Ezekiel Turner,
Lem'l Curtis,	Joseph Bates,	Snow Curtis,
Jonathan Pratt,	Benj. Bates,	Melzar Hatch,
Joseph Brooks,	Timothy Church,	John Stetson,
Seth Bates,	Benj'n Bass, Junr.	Calvin Curtis,
Timothy Robbins,	Turner Stetson,	Wm. Whiting,
John Hatch,	Oliver Winslow,	Constant Clap,
Benj. Bass,	Joel Sylvester,	Benj. Tolman,
Caleb Rogers,	Joshua Dwelley,	Nathl Jacobs,
Josiah Chamberlain,	Seth Rose,	Wm. Torrey,
Elijah Sylvester,	Elijah Barstow,	Elisha Bass.

} In Pencil on Original Records.

1807. June th. 4, 1807. There was a regular Church Meeting, the object of which was to choose a Decon, agree upon a Church Covenant, mode of admitting members, Rules of discipline, &c. There being a thin meeting, voted to adjourn to this day three weeks or to the 25th instant, at 3 o'clock, afternoon.

Hanover, June 25, 1807. The Chh. met according to adjournment.

1. Chose Mr. Turner Stetson a deacon in the room of Timothy Robbins, deceased. Mr. Stetson declined and Mr. Timothy Church was then appointed by a unanimous vote.

2. Voted that any person may write their relation upon being admitted into the Chh.

3. Voted that the Pastor notify Mr. Church of his appointment to the Deaconship. Adjourned to August 1st.

Hanover, Aug. 1st. The Church met according to adjournment.

1. Voted to excuse Mr. Church from serving as a Deacon upon his request.

2. Voted to postpone the choosing a Deacon until another year.

3. Voted that the original Chh. Covenant be the Covenant of this Chh. still.

1808. At a regular Church meeting, Jan'y, 31, 1808:

Voted, Deacon Joseph Brooks, agent, to hold a note of hand of one hundred dollars, given to the Church by the Rev. John Mellen.

1809. At a regular Church meeting, Sept. 30, 1809:

1. Voted, the Pastor, Deacon Joseph Brooks & Turner Stetson a Committee to converse with Mrs. Chapman and report next meeting.

2. Voted, Dea. Benj'n Bass, Elijah Barstow, Turner Stetson, Wm. Whiting and Timothy Church, a Committee to go and converse with certain members on account of neglect of ordinances and report next meeting.

3. Voted, to adjourn till the last Saturday in October, 1 o'clock, p. m.

Sunday, Oct. 15, 1809. The Church tarried after divine service.

Voted, to excuse Dea'n Bass from serving as one of the above Committee and appointed Dea'n Joseph Brooks in his room.

October 28, 1809.. The Church met according to adjournment and after opening the meeting by prayer the Committee chosen to inquire into the character of Mrs. Chapman reported that from the evidence they could obtain, in their opinion she was not a suitable character at present to be admitted into this church. Voted unanimously to accept the above report.

The Committee appointed to converse with certain members for neglect of duty report as follows, viz.: Dea. Brooks reports that he saw Calvin Curtis, who declined giving any reasons for neglecting Church ordinances but gave encouragement that he would attend the next Church meeting : he did not attend. Snow, Bashua, his wife, and Lydia Curtis, pled conscience and sent a writen request to be dismissed from the Church, but as their request contained no desire to be recommended to any other Church, therefore voted unanimously that their request cannot be granted. Elijah Barstow reported that Caleb Rogers requested time for further consideration. Josiah Chamberlain said he did not consider himself a member of the Church. Jonathan Pratt said he wished a dismission from the Church, but made no mention of a recommendation to any other Church. Wm. Whiting reported that Joel Sylvester and wife said they did not consider themselves members of the Church because they had joined themselves to a different denomination. Elijah Sylvester's wife said the want of health was the reason she did not attend divine ordinances: her husband said fear of unworthyness kept him away but wished to remain a member of the Church. Mr. Stetson reported that Josiah Smith and wife said they did not consider themselves members of the Church. Albert Smith's wife said in some respects she was a member of the Church and in some she was not, but on the whole she did not consider herself a member at present.

Voted, to choose a committee of two to converse further with Snow, Bashua and Lydia Curtis. Voted that Dea'n Brooks & Dea'n Bass be this committee. Voted that the reasons offered by Elijah Sylvester & wife for neglecting divine ordinances are satisfactory. Voted that the Pastor lay the subject respecting delinquent members before the association at their next meeting and request their advice. Voted to adjourn till the second Saturday in Novr next at 1 o'clock P.M.

Second Saturday in Nov'r 11, 1809. The Church met according to adjournment. There being but a few present voted to adjourn without day.

November 12. After divine service the church were desired by the Pastor to tarry. The Pastor then laid before the church the opinion of the Association respecting delinquent members which was that the same committee which was first appointed to go and converse with these persons be reappointed to go and converse with them a second time and make their report the next meeting. Voted Dea'n Joseph Brooks, Capt. Elijah Barstow, William Whitting & Turner Stetson be said committee. Adjourned.

August 13, 1810. Agreeably to notification the church met and after the opening of the meeting by prayer the church attended to the following things.

1st. They attended to the report of a committee chosen to converse with delinquent members, who reported that said members denied that the church had any jurisdiction over them and sent in a written communication, stating some reasons why they neglected their duty which not being satisfactory to the church the church proceded as follows:

Voted unanimously that Capt. Calvin Curtis, Lydia Curtis, Jonathan Pratt, Anne Lenth'l Smith, Nabby Smith, Caleb Rogers, Joel Sylvester, Snow Curtis, Bashua Curtis, Josiah Chamberlain, Josiah Smith and Sarah Sylvester be suspended from all fellowship and communion with this church for the space of two months. Voted that an answer to their communication be drawn and sent to the delinquent members and a notification of their suspension. Voted that the Pastor and Dea'n Joseph Brooks be a committee for the above purposes. Voted to choose a committee to converse with Olive Whitting who is about joining the Baptist. Voted that the Pastor, William Whitting and Constant Clapp be this committee. Voted to disolve this meeting.

1811. Hanover, May 24. At a regular Chh. meeting.

1st. Voted that Calvin Curtis, Jonathan Pratt, Caleb Rogers, Josiah Chamberlain, Anna L. Smith, Lydia Curtis, Josiah Smith and Nabby his wife, Joel Sylvester and Sarah his wife, Snow Curtis and Bashua his wife be excommunicated for persevering neglect of divine ordinances.

2d. Voted that the Pastor and Dea'n Joseph Brooks be a committee to notify the above named persons of their excommunication.

After hearing the report of the committee relative to Olive Whitting

3rd. Voted the subject be suspended for the present.
4th. Voted that Elijah Barstow be a deacon of this Chh.
5th. Voted to give said Barstow time to consider of the subject till the next meeting.
6th. Voted to disolve the meeting.

1817. Hanover, Augt 19, 1817. In consequence of previous notice the chh. in this place met at the meeting house for the purpose of seeing whether the said Church would agree with the Revd Calvin Chaddock in calling a council to dissolve the connection between him and them.

Voted to defer the consideration of the calling a council to the first Monday in Nov'r next. Voted that Turner Stetson be a committee to inform the Society of the doings of the Chh. Voted that Capt. Elijah Barstow be allowed to defer giving an answer to a previous request of the Chh. to the next meeting. Voted that this meeting be adjourned to the first Monday in Novr next at 1 o'clock P.M.

SAMUEL W. COLBURN, Mod'r.

Novr 3, 1817. The Church met according to adjournment.
Dea'n Brooks was chosen Moderator, Capt. Elijah Barstow was called upon to give an answer whether he would accept of the Dea'nship, he answered in the affirmative.

Voted to pospone the consideration of the Revd Calvin Chaddock's request for a dismission till the twenty-third day of July next at 2 o'clock P.M.

JOSEPH BROOKS, Mod'r.

1818. Hanover, July 23. The Congregational Church in Hanover met according to adjournment.

Voted the Revd Calvin Chadock their Pastor a regular dismission at his own request.

JOSEPH BROOKS, Moderator.

The other records of meetings, etc., will be found under the respective heads of the subjects they refer to.

CHAPTER III.

ADMITTED TO THE CHURCH, 1728–1864.

ADMISSIONS TO FULL COMMUNION.

Nos 1, 2   March 2, 1728–9   The sacrament of the Lord's Supper was administered the first time in the Chh. of Hanover on the same day Job OTIS was taken into the Chh. Joseph SMITH was also taken in the same day after a publick confession of the Sin of * * * * and profession of repentance for it.

No	Date	Name
3	April 6, 1729	Benj. MANN
4	May 4	Saml BARSTOW and
5		Joseph RAMSDEL
6	June 1	Mary BUCK
7	July 6	Robert MACKERDEY
8, 9		Thanful OTIS and Jane HANMER
10	August 3	Mary HATCH, Jeremiah Hatch's widow
11	September 7	Isaac HATCH
12	October 5	Mary JUSTICE, the wife of John Justice
13	March 15, 1729–30	Sarah RAMSDALE, widow
14	May 3	John BAILY
15 & 16	August 2	Elizabeth WILKS and Mary BASS, wife of B. Bass, Pastor
17	May 2, 1731	Sarah LAMBERT wife of John Lambert, Jr. after a publick confession of the sin of * * * *
18	September 5	Sarah TORY, the daughter of James Tory
19	January 2, 1731–2	Anna LAMBERT wife of John Lambert

20	May 14, 1732	Joseph SYLVESTER, a student of ye college
21, 22	October 14, 1733	William CURTISS Jr. & Elizabeth BAILEY wife of John Bailey
23	January 19, 1734-5	Joseph SHELDON
24	Feb. 9, 1734-5	Nathan BOURN
25	June 8, 1735	Sarah TOREY wife of James Torey
26	August 24, 1735	Abigail HATCH wife of Deacon James Hatch
27	Feby. 1, 1735-6	James TOREY, Junior
28, 29	Feby. 8, 1735-6	Seth STETSON and likewise Elizabeth STETSON his wife
30	November 11, 1736	Deborah HOUSE, wife of Samuel House
31	May 22, 1737	Thomas BOURN
32	September 9, 1737	Thomas TOBY
33	October 23, 1737	Jemima Bates
34, 35	August 7, 1738	Benjamin STETSON and his wife Lillis Stetson
36, 37	October 1, 1738	Timothy BAILY and his wife Sarah Baily
38, 39	August 5, 1739	Clement BATES and Agatha Bates, his wife ^{Her confession of her violation of the * * * commandment preceeding.}
40	September 2, 1739	Ann JOSSELYN
41, 42	October 7, 1739	Samuel BARSTOW and his wife Margaret Barstow
43	November 4, 1739	Martha CURTIS wife of William Curtis
44	December 2, 1739	Francis JOSSELYN, widow
45, 46	January 6, 1739-40	Thomas ROSE and Faith Rose, his wife
47	July 6, 1740	Mary RAMSDALE, wife of Joseph Ramsdale
48, 49	August 3, 1740	Joseph CURTIS and Mary his wife also
50		Abigail SYLVESTER wife of Benjamin Sylvester, Junr

51	July 12, 1741	Hannah CURTISS, wife of Sam'el Curtiss
52, 53	May 9, 1742	Elisha TOBY and his sister Martha PROUTY, she making a public confession of her violation of the * * * commandment
54, 55	June 20, 1742	Lydia SPEER and Ann TOBY
56, 57	September 5, 1742	John LAMBERT, an aged man & Elizabeth RANDALL, a maiden
58	October 3, 1742	Sarah CURTISS wife of Jesse Curtiss
59, 60	August 7, 1743	David STOCKBRIDGE and Deborah his wife
61	September 4, 1743	Lillis STETSON, daughter of Benjamin & Lillis Stetson
62	November 6, 1743	Naomi CURTISS the wife of Benja Curtiss, Junior
63, 64	June 3, 1744	Rebecca CURTISS also Rachel ROGERS
65	Sept. 2, 1744	John TILDEN
66	April 14, 1745	Sarah RAMSDALE wife of Gideon Ramsdale
67	May 5, 1745	Mary STODDARD, singlewoman
68	October 6, 1745	Thankful COLLIMORE
69	June 1, 1746	Martha DAMAN, a singlewoman
70	September 7, 1746	Elizabeth TORREY, wife of Thomas Torrey
71	September 6, 1747	Elizabeth STUDLEY the wife of John Studley
72	October 2, 1748	Elizabeth JENKINS the wife of David Jenkins
73	November 6, 1748	Sarah CURTISS, wife of Thomas Curtiss
74	July 2, 1749	Thomas CURTISS
75	September 3, 1749	Deborah LAMBERT, wife of Isaac Lambert
76	May 6, 1750	Keziah THOMAS wife of Isaiah Thomas
77	May 6, 1753	David JENKINS

78, 79	June 3, 1753	William CURTISS and his wife Martha
80	April 11, 1756	Nathanael JOSSELYN at the same time
81	-	Hannah STETSON, the wife of Robert Stetson
82 not 83		also "my daughter" Elizabeth SYLVESTER the wife of Edmund Sylvester.

ADMISSIONS TO FULL COMMUNION.

1757. March 27 The widow Hannah RAMSDALE upon confession of the Sin of * * * * * & professing her faith in Christ was admitted to full communion.
May 1 Elizabeth STAPLES
June 12 Samuel STETSON aged 85
July 3 Ann & Caroline WILKS
August 7 Joseph HOUSE & Abigail his wife
Octo. 9 Simeon CURTIS
Novr 6 The widow Hannah FORD owned the covenant, was baptized and admitted to full communion.
1758. Jany 15 Sarah FORD owned the covenant, was baptized and admitted to full communion.
Jany 15 Sarah BATES
April 2 Rhoda the wife of David HOUSE, Junr
April 9 The widow Margaret FITZ-GERALD and Anna the wife of Jno BRAY
April 23 Benjamin BATES, baptized &c:
May 7 Joseph BATES, baptized & admitted &c:
Mary BATES the wife of Joseph Bates
Jeremiah STETSON & Lucy his wife
The widow Hannah CURTIS
Ruth the wife of Thomas CURTIS
June 4 Sarah STAPLES after confessing the sin of * * * * *
Mary STAPLES
July 9 Sage the wife of Joseph HOUSE, Jur

July 30   Samuel Barstow, Jur & Huldah his wife after confession of the sin of * * * * *
Sepr 3   Betty BAKER baptized & admitted to full communion
Octr 1   Alice the wife of Daniel GARDNER
Novr 5   Ruth the wife of Caleb TURNER
Mercy BATES
1759.   April 1   Mrs. Hannah BALDWIN, the wife of the Revd Samuel Baldwin, Pastor of the Church.
August 5   Sarah PETERS & Hannah LADD were baptized & admitted to full communion.
August 19   Margaret FITZ-GERALD, Jur
Octo. 14   Ruth the wife of Uriah LAMBERT
Mary WING the daughter of Ebenezer Wing
Nov. 4   Elizabeth the wife of David JENKINS after confessing the sin of * * * * *
Sarah MAN
1760.   May 4   William WHITTEN & Mary his wife
   August 17   Caleb HOUSE & his wife Elizabeth after confession of the sin of * * * * * were admitted to full communion. She was baptized at the same time.
1761.   Octor 4   Mary BASS, Jr after confession of the sin of * * * * *
1762.   Sepr 5th   Samuel CURTIS
   Benj. MAN, Jr.
Abigail the wife of Benj. MAN, Jr.
Deborah STETSON the wife of Abijah Stetson
Mary MAN
1763.   April 10   Stevens HATCH & Ruth his wife
   April 10   Samuel WITHERELL Jr. & Ruth his wife
May 1   Gideon & Rosamond STUDLEY—before admission she was baptized.
July 3   Hannah wife of Joseph HOUSE
Octor 2   Hannah wife of Benj. WHITE
Octr 24   Joshua & Avis DWELLY
1765.   March 10   John & Thankfull STETSON
1766.   Jany 19   Shubæl MUNROE
   August 8   Solomon BATES Jr. and his wife Aquilla. At the same time he was baptized.
Octor 26   Othniel & Deborah PRATT

1767. April 4   Benjamin & Mercy BASS
June 7   Mary the wife of Shubæl MUNROE
July 5   Rachel TORREY the wife of Stephen Torrey
Solomon & Elizabeth BRYANT
Sibyl HATCH wife of Sam'l
August 2   Lemuel & Ruth CURTIS
Deborah PETERSON
1768. January 10   Theophilus & Freelove WITHERELL
June 5   CUBA, a *negro woman*, belonging to Sam'l Curtis upon recommendation from the 2d Church in Scituate from whence her relation was transferred.
July 31   Jane STOCKBRIDGE the wife of David Stockbridge, esqr
Sepr 4   Jonathan and Lucy PRATT
1769. April 2d   Mercy RAMSDELL the wife of Joseph Ramsdell, her relation being transferred from the church in Duxbury.
Sept. 10   Rebecca WITHERELL
1770. May 6   Joshua STAPLES
July 22   Stockbridge and Olive JOSSELYN.   She was baptized before admission.
1771. April 7   Joseph BROOKS
1772. April 5   Timothy and Mary ROBBINS
May 3   Sarah EELLS wife of William Eells
Octr 4   Rebecca JOYCE
1773. Aug. 1   Ruth JOSSELYN
Novr 7   Sarah GROSS baptized and then admitted to full communion.
1774. July 24   Seth and Anna BATES
Aug. 7   The widow Hannah TORREY
Octr 2   Sarah JOSSELYN
1775. June 4   John and Bathshua HATCH
July 2   Peleg EWELL
Sepr 10   Chloe CLAP wife of Capn. Jno. Clap
Oct. 1   John STUDLEY
Dec. 10   Timo & Elizabeth CHURCH
Aug. 4   Mary TURNER wife of Marlbry Turner
Oct. 6   Huldah CURTIS
1778. Nov. 1   The widow Betty STETSON

THOSE THAT HAVE OWNED THE COVENANT AND NOT ADMITTED TO FULL COMMUNION.

No. 1, 2 April 10, 1757   Nathl PALMER & Rachel his wife
3, 4   July 30, 1757   Marlbry TURNER & Mary his wife
5   Sept. 4, 1757   Stephen TORREY, Jur
6   April 2, 1758   David HOUSE, Jur
7, 8   July 30, 1758   Amos SYLVESTER, Jur & Desire his wife
9, 10   Novr 26, 1758   Amos WRIGHT & his wife Mary & were baptized
11   April 15, 1759   Robert EELLES & Ruth his wife
12   Septr 19, 1760   Thomas SYLVESTER
13, 14   August 16, 1761   John HATCH & Bathshua his wife
15, 16   June 6, 1762   Ezekiel MERRITT & Rachel his wife
17, 18   June 13, 1762   Gideon RANDALL & Rebecca his wife
19, 20   Sepr 19, 1762   Thomas ROSE, Jr. & Rhoda his wife
21   Jany 9, 1763   Seth BAYLEY & Lydia his wife
22, 23   July 10, 1763   Zachariah CURTIS & Lydia his wife
24, 25   July 31, 1763   David & Hannah JACOBS
26, 27   Sept 11th   Wm. Witherell EELLES & Sarah his wife after &c:
28, 29   Octr 16th   Job & Betty YOUNG   "   "
30   "   23rd   Samuel EELLES,   "   "
31   Nov. 17   Priscilla EELLES after &c :
32, 33   Jany 15, 1764   John & Sage JOSSELYN
34   Sepr 2, 1764   Luke STETSON
35, 36   June 23, 1765   Gershom & Deborah HOUSE
37   Octbr 13, 1765   Job and Hannah STETSON
38   Jany 20, 1766   Aquilla BATES
39   March 30   Solomon BATES, Jr.
40   May 18, 1766   Ruth CHAPMAN
41, 42   May 25   Benjamin & Mercy BASS
43, 44   June 8   Seth & Bathshua HOUSE
45, 46   June 15   Timothy & Elizabeth CHURCH
47, 48   29   Seth STETSON, Jr. & Lucy
49, 50   July 20   Benjamin & Bradbury STETSON
51, 52   Decem. 14   John CURTIS Jr. & Anna his wife
53, 54   April 12th   Timo & Lydia ROSE
55, 56   July 12   Solomon & Elizabeth BRYANT

No. 57 August 2 Jenny Gardner RIPLEY and was at the same time baptized.
58, 59 Octo. 23d, 1768 John WITHERELL & Content his wife
60 April 2, 1769 The widow Rebecca STUDLEY
61 July 23 Sarah CURTIS after confessing &c:
62 May 6, 1770 Joanna STUDLEY, after confessing &c:
63 May 20 Rachel DELANO, after &c:
64, 65 May 27 Ebenezer & Deborah EDDY
66 June 3 Widow Hannah BATES
67, 68 July 8 Prince and Eunice STETSON
69 Aug. 5 Leonard HILL
70, 71 Reuben CLARK & Dorothy CLARK
72, 73 26 Thomas and Susanna HATCH
74, 75 Thomas & Anna WILLETT
76, 77 April 28, 1771 Israel & Abigail PERRY, after &c:
78, 79 July 21 Atherton and Ruth WALES, after &c:
80, 81 Levi & Deborah CORTHELL
82, 83 Aug. 18 Isaac LAMBERT, Jr. & his wife Hannah
84 Sept. 22 Samuel WOODWARD
85, 86 Octor 13th James & Susannah ORR
87, 88 27 Joseph RAMSDALE 3d & Elizabeth
89 Novr 10, 1771 Gideon STETSON
90, 91 March 8, 1772 Asa & Abigail TURNER
92, 93 June 7 John HOUSE, Jr. and Jane his wife
94, 95 July 19 Amos and Betty TURNER
96, 97 Oct. 4 James and Zilpah CURTIS
98, 99 Octr 4 Thomas WHITTEN Jr. and Rachel his wife, after &c:
100 25 Samuel STAPLES
101 Novr 15 Sarah WHITTEN
102, 103 May 2 Daniel and Betty BARSTOW
104, 105 June 6 Elijah and Susannah STETSON, after &c:
106, 107 27 Thomas and Olive STETSON
108, 109 July 18 David and Susanna TORREY
110 Aug. 8th Robert WHITE
111, 112 January 2, 1774 Jabez & Keturah STUDLEY
113, 114 30 Melzer and Kezia CURTIS, after &c:
115 Augt 14th 1774 Sage STAPLES, after &c:
116 Sept. 4 John Tilden TORREY

No. 117, 118   Novr 13   Joshua & Margaret BARSTOW
   119, 120   Jany 1, 1775   Zebulon & Deborah BOWKER
   121   April 30, 1775   Widow Hannah RANDALL
   122, 123   June 25   William and Rebecca CURTIS
   124, 125   Hersey and Abigail GILBERT
   126   Aug. 13   Leah GARDNER wife of Elijah Gardner
   127   Decr 16, 1775   Bradbury PALMER
   128, 129   Jany 7th 1776   William and Ruth STOCKBRIDGE
   130   March 3   Lucy WHITTEN
   131, 132   June 23   Gershom CURTIS and his wife
   133, 134   Benjamin MAN, Jr. and wife
   135, 136   Octo. 13   Abner CURTIS, Jr. & wife
   137, 138   Novr 3   James and Lydia TORREY
   139, 140   June 29, 1777   Abel and Ruth CURTIS
   141   Aug. 10   Abigail SYLVESTER wife of Elisha Sylvester
   142, 143   Aug. 16, 1778   Ebenezer and Mary CURTIS
   144   Oct. 4   Thomas TORREY in private by reason of sickness
   145, 146   Jany 17, 1779   Joseph & Mary TORREY
   147, 148   April 11, 1779   Elias & Deborah WHITTEN after &c:

VOTES OF THE CHURCH ON SPECIAL OCCASIONS.

1776. May 5. Shubæl ROSE having made application to the Pastor on behalf of himself and Susanna his wife (who were members of the Church of England, but voluntarily dissented therefrom) for occasional communion. A representation was made by the Pastor of the state of their case, and of their request: A vote was called, and it past in the affirmative without any opposition, that they should be admitted to this privilege, agreeable to their Petition.

pr. SAMUEL BALDWIN, Pastor.

ADMISSIONS TO CHH. COMMUNION
pr. me John Mellen.

1784. May 16   Rebecca MELLEN, consort of the Pastor from the Chh. of Christ in Lancaster.

ORIGINAL RECORDS. 79

August 1   Admitted William* CURTIS & wife
No. 2 this year
1785.   Novr 6th   Admitted Ruth RAMSDALE
        No. 1
1786.   May 7th   Admitted Thankful DUNBAR, Abington
        Novr 12   Admitted Caleb ROGERS, Junr & wife
No. 3 this year.
1787.   None
1788.   July 13th   admitted Mercy BASS* daughter of Dea. Bass
        Octr 12   admitted Cloe JOSSELYN, daughter of Nath. Josslyn
No. 2
1789.   March 22   admitted Josiah CHAMBERLAIN & wife* She sick
        at home.
May 3d   admitted Widow Ruth TURNER & Calvin CURTIS & wife.*
She sick at home
Novr 1st   Admitted Keturah wife of Jabez STUDLEY*
No. 6
1790.   Augt 8   admitted wife of Seth BAILY & their daughter Allice*
        also the wife of Capn Albert SMITH
also our youngest daughter Charlotte MELLEN
22   wife of Cornelius WHITE*   She sick at home—at her earnest
desire read & took her consent, to ye Covt yesterday & a vote of ye
chh. this night.
Octbr 3   Admitted Seth BAILY*
also Lucy CURTIS daughter of Capt. Sim. Curtis*
Novr 7   Admitted Content WITHERELL, widow
No. 8
1791.   May the 1st   admitted Abigail BALDWIN
        Octr 30th   admitted Sarah WHITING, daughter of Thos
Whiting
No. 2
1792.   Augt 5   Admitted Mary wife of Job YOUNG
        Sepr 2d   admitted Cindrilla BASS & Huldah Bass
Octr 14   admitted Mary EELLES
No. 4
1793.   None admitted.
1794.   Feby 9   Admitted Mary widow of late Dr. HOBART
        Admitted Lydia CURTIS, daughter of Capn Lem'l Curtis

June 1st   Admitted Rebecca STUDLEY daughter of Gideon Studly
Augt 3d   Sarah CLARK wife of Belcher Clark made her acknowledgement and was forgiven & received by the Chh.
Octr. 5th   Admitted Edmund EASTMAN also Sarah BROOKS, Daughter of Deacon Joseph Brooks.
No. 6

1795.   May 31st   Elijah SYLVESTER & wife
   Octr 25th   Josiah SMITH & wife
Novr 29th   the wife of Elisha CURTIS, Junr
No. 5

1796.   July 3d   Admitted Benja BASS, Junr & wife
   10th   Phœbe MANSON & Lydia BATES
August 7th   Capn Joseph Soper & wife
Septr 18   John CURTIS* Senr by a vote of ye Chh. he old & confined ye Pastor to give him ye Covenant.
No. 7

1797.   July 2d   Wife of Josiah CHAMBERLAIN

1798.   June 10   admitted Timothy CHURCH & Rebecca his wife
   25th   admitted Olive CURTIS* in private, sick, according to a vote of the Chh.
Sepr 2   admitted the six following persons: Oliver WINSLOW & Sally his wife, Turner STETSON & Lydia his wife, Mary wife of Jacob SYLVESTER, Joseph BATES.
No. 9

1799.   Feby 10th   Admitted Joel SYLVESTER & wife
   Novr 17th   Joshua DWELLY & wife
No. 4

1800.   July 6th   Admitted Seth ROSE & wife also admitted Elijah BARSTOW & wife
Augt. 3   Admitted Mary wife of Stephen RANDAL
24th   Admitted Samuel STETSON & wife also Ezekiel TURNER & wife
Octor 5th   Abigail wife of Shubæl MUNROE also widow Christiana JOSLYN
11

1801.   Sepr 6   wife of Edward STETSON, Hannah
   Oct. 11th   Widow Sarah BARSTOW & Widow Ruth EELLES
Nov. 29   Elizabeth SYLVESTER

Decr 13 Snow CURTIS & wife
No. 5
1802. Sept. 5 Wife of Capn Tim'y ROSE, Lydia, also Bathseba widow of Michael SYLVESTER
2
1803. Oct. 2d· Melzar HATCH & wife
No. 2
1804. June 3d Admitted Ruth GROCE

ADMISSIONS
by me Calvin Chaddock
TO COMMUNION

1806. July 23 Militiah CHADDOCK, consort of the Pastor
Nov. 9 Jane DWELLY wife of Lem'l Dwelly
1807. May 10 *Joseph CHADDOCK
August 2 *William WHITTING & Betty his wife
1809. Jany 29 *Constant CLAPP
Molly MANN wife of Capn. Joshua Mann
Augt 6 *Lydia BARSTOW
Rachel WHITTING, Olive WHITTING
*Lydia CHAMBERLAIN, Lydia JOSSELYN
Oct. 1 Thankful WHITTING the wife of James Whit'g
Sarah EELLS the wife of Joseph Eells
Mary BASS
James WHITTING
Benjamin TOLMAN of Marshfield
1814. Apl 3 *Israel PERRY
Apl 10 Elisha BASS
Mary THOMAS, Pembroke. Recommended to the church in Brook, Maine, 1826.
1816. June 2 Frances DWELLY
Betsy MONROE
Capt. William TORREY & wife*
Julitte SYLVESTER
1817. June 1 Mrs. Ruth the wife of Isaac WILDER was received from the 1st Chh. in Weymouth.
1818. June 1 Nathl JACOB received from the 2d Chh. in Scituate.

1819. October 3 Michael TOLLMAN, by profession
Rusha wife of Sam'l EELLS by letter from the church in Scituate
Rebecca TOLLMAN, by profession
1820. September 3 Priscilla wife of Joshua STETSON, by profession
November 5 Mrs. Nabby BARKER, by virtue of a letter from the 2d Chh. in Scituate October 5
Oct. or Nov. 5 Ruth & Lydia, daughters of Turner STETSON, by profession
1821. August 5 Nancy wife of George CUSHING of Scituate, by a recommendation from the church in Park st. Boston
1822. April 6 Lydia, wife of Nathl PRATT, by profession
Miss Molly BARSTOW, by profession
1824. January 27 Levi NASH agreeably to a letter of dismissmal and recommendation from the Second Church in Weymouth
April 18 Lucinda EELLS
1825. May 20 William CHURCH, by profession
May 20 Elizabeth wife of Nathan DWELLY
Mary LITTLE, by profession & was baptized } daughters of W. Torrey
Elizabeth TORREY, by profession & was baptized
Bathsua DAWS, by profession & was baptized
Betsey DWELLY, by profession
Sybil HITCHCOCK, by profession
Anne DWELLY, by profession
Lydia MUNROE, by profession
Michael BATES, by profession
Abigail ROGERS wife of Ruben Rogers, by profession & was baptized
Mary Robins BATES, by profession & was baptized
December 4 Grace FOSTER, by profession and was baptized
Hannah Briggs WILDER, by profession
Lydia Farrow PROUTY, by profession and was baptized
Thankfull WHITING, by profession
Rebbeca WHITING, by profession
Bradbury Eells STETSON, by profession
1826. June 4 Widow Mary BATES, by profession
Isaac COOK, by profession and baptized
Bethiah COOK, by profession and baptized

Rufus BATES, by profession and baptized
Huldah BATES, by profession
Anjelina JOSELYN, by profession
October 29   Abigail NEAL, by profession
Roxana NYE, by profession
December 7   Eliza WHITING, by letter
1827.   August 3   Bathsheba SMITH, by letter
August 5   Cela JUDD, by profession
Grace F. SMITH, by profession
Elizabeth EELLS, by profession
Mary E. STETSON, by profession
Caroline STETSON, by profession
1828.   April 6   Christiana CLARK, by profession
Mercy WRIGHT, by profession
October 3   wife of William COPELAND, by profession
wife of Samuel STETSON, by profession
wife of William CHURCH, by profession
Eliza STUDLEY, by profession
Matthy PERRY, by profession
December 14   Albert STETSON, by profession
1829.   August 9   Josiah CHAMBERLAIN & his wife, by profession
Michel BASS, by profession
1830.   August 1   Ebenr THAYER, by profession
October 17   wife of Michal SYLVESTER, by profession
Mrs. Jane MERIAM, by profession
1831.   August 7   John C. WILDER, by profession
December 18   Sarah B. TOLMAN, by profession
1833.   October 00   At a regular meeting of the Church voted that the Pastor (Revd Abel G. DUNCAN) and his wife be received into the Church
Joshua PERRY and Mary T. his wife, by letter
1834.   August 00   Melvin STODDARD, by profession and was baptized
1836.   June 5   Isaac M. WILDER, by profession
Sarah B. EELLS, by profession
Ruth BATES, by profession
Almira ESTES, by profession
Abby W. DWELLY, by profession

Ann S. DWELLY, by profession
Abigail Jane ROGERS, by profession
Ruth B. STOCKBRIDGE, by profession
August 7   Mary, daughter of Samuel STETSON, by profession
October 2   Lucinda COPELAND, by profession and baptized
Almira BATES, by profession and was baptized

1837   October 1   Joseph EELLS, by profession
Betsey BARSTOW, by profession and was baptized

1840.   July 5   Mrs. Lydia S. BARSTOW wife of Dan'l Barstow, Jr., by profession

1843.   January 1   Samuel S. CHURCH and Sarah E. his wife, by profession

Lucy D. ROSE, by profession
Ebenr Barker HOWLAND, by profession
March 7   John SYLVESTER and Lucy J. his wife, by profession

1849.   January 7   Mrs. Saba D. BARSTOW, by profession and was baptized

Mrs. Lucy J. REED, by profession and was baptized
Widow Sarah W. TOLMAN, by profession and was baptized

1850.   January 3   Mrs. Sophia A. HOLMES, by letter from the church in Woburn

1852.   March 5   Benjamin S. WATERMAN, by letter from First Trinitarian Cong'l Church in Scituate

Elizabeth T. HOUSE, by letter from First Cong'l Church in Marshfield
November 7   Lucy, widow of Elijah SYLVESTER, by profession
Abby Eells, wife of Capt. Thomas BARSTOW, by profession
Sarah Jane SYLVESTER, by profession
Lydia Lane STOCKBRIDGE, by profession
Wm. Paley DUNCAN, by profession
Lucia Ann DUNCAN, by profession

1853.   January 2   Robert SYLVESTER, 2nd & Martha Almira his wife, by profession

Mary wife of Thomas O. BATES, Jr., by profession
William T. LAPHAM, by profession
Huldah Frances SAMPSON, by profession
Julia Ann PERRY, by profession
March 13   Samuel TOLMAN, Jr., by profession; a dissenter from the Episcopal Church in Hanover

Dea. George W. EELLS, by letter from the Chh. in Westerly, R.I.
March 25 Dr. A. C. GARRATT & Elizabeth his wife, by letter from the First Cong'l Chh. in Abington
April 29 Mary Thomas, wife of James T. TOLMAN, by letter from the First Trin. Cong'l Chh. in Scituate
James TURNER, by profession; a dissenter from the Episcopal Chh.
Priscilla Clark, wife of George W. EELLS, by profession; dissenter from the Episcopal Chh.
May 1 James Turner TOLMAN, by profession
Laura Jane DUNCAN, by profession
Charles Francis BOWMAN, by profession
Edwin TAYLOR, by profession
1854. January 8 Daniel E. DAMON, by profession
    Lemuel FREEMAN & Diana his wife, by profession
1856. September 7 Mrs. Meletiah C., wife of Philip CHAMBERLIN, by profession
Fanny, wife of J. CARY, by profession
1857. November 1 Mrs. Ruth J., wife of Reuben STETSON, by profession
Miss Priscilla JOSSELYN, by profession
Henry M. STETSON, by profession
1858. March 31 Mrs. Jane CHURCH, from the Baptist Church
    May 1 Mrs Juletta S. STETSON, by profession
Miss Alice STETSON, by profession
1860. September 16 Lucy, wife of Robert HERSEY, by profession
    Maria, wife of Charles DYER, by profession
Miss Eliza ROSE, by profession
George CHAMBERLIN, by profession
Francis CHAMBERLIN, by profession
Edward P. STETSON, by profession
November 18 Widow Ruth JOSSELYN, by profession
Mahala, wife of Frank CORBIN, by profession
1863. June 20 The Pastor, Rev. Joseph FREEMAN & Sarah H. his wife, by letter from the Church in Stockton, Maine
July 5 Willis H. FREEMAN (son of Pastor) by profession
Mary T. STETSON, by profession
Alice Jane HATCH, by profession and was baptized
Hannah P. STETSON, by profession

1864. January 3, Lucy W., wife of Joseph B. Sylvester, by profession

January 13 Widow Elizabeth T. W. House, by letter from the church in Marshfield.

FIRST MEETING-HOUSE OF THE FIRST CONGREGATIONALIST CHURCH AT HANOVER.
ERECTED 1728, ON THE PRESENT SITE.

CHAPTER IV.

MARRIAGES PERFORMED BY THE PASTORS OF THE FIRST CONGREGATIONAL CHURCH 1728–1827.

MARRIAGES

BY

BENJAMIN BASS, PASTOR OF THE CHURCH

IN HANOVER.

1728-29. January 16 David BRYANT, Junr of Scituate and Hannah TURNER of Hanover
February 20 Richard HILL and Jemimah RAMSDELL both of Hanover
May 15 Benjamin BARSTOW and Sarah BORDEN both of Hanover
July 7 Jonathan PETER and Margaret FRANK both of Hanover
October 9 Ezekiel PALMER and Martha PRATT both of Hanover
1730. April 23 Joseph RAMSDALE and Mary HOMER both of Hanover
June 15 Clement BATES and Agatha MERITT both of Hanover
*September 24 Matthew STETSON of Hanover and Hannah LINCOLN of Scituate
1730-31. February 18 Meletiah DILINGHAM and Phœbe HATCH both of Hanover
April 22 John LOVE of Pembroke & Susanna GUILFORD of Hanover
May 12 Eliab TURNER & Martha BARSTOW both of Hanover
June 4 Isaac BURDEN and Deborah TOBEY both of Hanover

August 4   Richard BUKER & Sarah PALMER both of Hanover Gone to the Clerk.
September 21   Isaac LAMBERT & Deborah PALMER both of Hanover
November 26   Samuel BARSTOW & Margaret STOCKBRIDGE both of Hanover
1731-32. February 7   Amos SYLVESTER, Junr of Hanover & Patience PALMER of Scituate
August 8   Jacob WILKE of Tiverton & Isabel BUKER of Hanover
November 9   Thomas HATCH of Scituate & the widow Mary HATCH of Hanover
December 14   Joseph HOUSE and Abigail STUDLEY both of Hanover
December 25   Samuel HOUSE & Deborah BARSTOW both of Hanover
1732-33. August 9   James MACCARTY & Elizabeth SMITH both of Hanover
October 30   Ezekiel LEED (or Lad) and Sarah BARSTOW both of Hanover
October 31   Isaac COLLEMORE of Scituate & Thankful CURTIS of Hanover
November 16   Isaac KEEN of Pembroke and Lydia JONES of Hanover
November 20   Daniel ROGERS and Ruth PARKER both of Hanover
November 29   Elisha CURTIS & Martha DAMON both of Scituate
1733-34. February 6   Samuel WHITEN of Hingham & Mary WING of Hanover
April 8   Uriah LAMBERT and Ruth BRYANT both of Hanover
June 10   Joseph RICCARDS of Pembroke & Lydia DILLINGHAM of Hanover
July 12   Joseph SHELDON of Westfield & Sarah TOREY of Hanover
August 15   Stephen TOREY and Rachel BATES both of Hanover
December 19   Joseph HARRIS of Bridgewater & Hannah TORREY of Hanover
1734-35. January 31   Meletiah DILINGHAM and Meriah GILFORD both of Hanover
March 6   Joshua STUDLEY of Hanover & Lydia PRATT of Pembroke
April 3   Hannibal and Bilhah ; Mr. Job OTIS's *negroes*
May 14   Thomas BRYANT, esqr. of Scituate & Mrs. Mary BARSTOW of Hanover
May 22   Theophilus WITHERELL of Hanover & Sarah RICCARDS of Pembroke
June 10   Tony SAMPSON & Esther PETER of Hanover

October 31   Amos BATES and Jemimah CASWELL both of Hanover
1736. April 19   Samuel WITHERELL & Rebecca FERRIS both of Hanover
April 22   Stephen WEBSTER of Pembrook & Bathsheba BRYANT of Hanover
1736-37. February 24   Paul WHITE of Marshfield & Elizabeth CURTIS of Hanover
July 27   Benjamin SYLVESTER & Abigail BUCK both of Hanover
1737-38. February 13   Nathanael STETSON and Rebecca BRISCO both of Hanover
March 9   Peleg STETSON and Mercy RAMSDALE
April 20   John BRAY and Anna KEEN both of Hanover
June 19   James TOREY, Junior & Mary TOBEY both of Hanover
August 23   Jeremiah ROGERS and Deborah BAILY both of Hanover
September 7   James HOUSE & Margaret CURTIS both of Hanover
October 5   William GUILFORD, Junr & Jane KEEN both of Hanover
November 6   John CURTIS, Junr & Mary BRYANT both of Hanover
November 22   Benjamin BARSTOW, Junior of Hanover & Ruth WINSLOW of Scituate
November 22   Daniel CONNER and Elizabeth TAYLOR both of Hanover
November 23   William CURTIS and Martha CURTIS both of Hanover
1738-39. January 25   Timothy MACOMBER of Dartmouth & Elizabeth ROGERS of Hanover
February 22   Dennis CARRIE and Rachel TORREY both of Hanover
April 2   Othniel PRATT of Hanover & Mary PRIOR of Duxborough
May 24   James CLARK and Margaret BUCK both of Hanover
September 20   Jesse CURTISS and Sarah MAN both of Hanover
1739-40. January 9   John HOUSE and Rebecca BUKER both of Hanover
January 9   John WOODWORTH, Junior & Margaret FORD both of Hanover
February 25   Edward CONOWAY of Pembroke and Elizabeth CANE of Hanover
May 15   Nathanael ROBBINS and Hannah WITHEREL both of Hanover
June 3   William WOOD of Dartmouth & Deborah ROGERS of Hanover
October 13   Abner TURNER and Mary MUNROE both of Hanover
October 27   Isaac GROSS and Ruth SYLVESTER both of Hanover

November 12   Michael SYLVESTER & Mary BARDEN both of Hanover
December 18   Samuel HESSORD & Mary WITHEREL both of Hanover
1740-41.   March 9   Benjamin CURTISS the 3rd and Naomi BAILY both of Hanover
May 7   James ROGERS and Rachel BAILY both of Hanover
August 20   Thomas CURTISS and Sarah UTTER both of Hanover
August 27   Ebenezer EAMES of Marshfield & Margaret BARSTOW of Hanover
December 14   Boston and Margaret *negroes* of Elijah CUSHING, esqr both of Hanover
December 25   Dick, Jonas BAILY's *negro* and Dassin (or Desire) Caleb BARKER's *negro* both of Hanover
1741-42.   February 4   Joshua PRATT and Honour TORY both of Hanover
May 10   Thomas TORY and Elizabeth TORY both of Hanover
June 7   Timothy BAILY and Hannah CURTISS both of Hanover
July 20   Jabez JOSSELYN and Mary LINDSEY both of Hanover
1742-43.   January 26   Nathanael SYLVESTER and Sage BARDEN both of Hanover
February 10   Edmund SPEAR & Molly STETSON both of Hanover
1743-44.   January 19   Adam PROUTY and Grace RAMSDALE both of Hanover
March 29   Joshua RIPLEY and Alice STETSON both of Hanover
April 28   Eleazer DONHAM of Plymouth & Elizabeth CONNER of Hanover
December 6   Jesse TORREY and Mary BUKER both of Hanover
1746.   May 13   Daniel COTHERELL of Bridgewater & Hannah ROSE of Hanover
December 24   John BARNES, Junior of Hingham and Margaret CURTISS of Hanover
1747.   July 8   Joshua STETSON of Scituate and Lillis STETSON of Hanover
November 13   William CURTISS, Junior and Martha MANN both of Hanover
1747-48.   February 24   Henchman SYLVESTER and Sarah STOCKBRIDGE both of Hanover
December 22   Jeremiah HALL and Elizabeth BAILY, Junr both of Hanover

1748-49. February 2 Ebenezer CURTISS and Elizabeth RANDALL both of Hanover

March 9 Windsor JONAS, *negro* and Mercy NEIL, *Indian* both of Hanover

October 26 John GOULD of Bridgewater & Rachel CURTISS of Hanover

November 23 Benjamin MAN, Junior & Abigail GILL both of Hanover

December 5 Oliver WINSLOW of Scituate & Bethiah PRIOR of Hanover

December 7 Joshua WHITEN of Hingham & Silence FORREST of Hanover

1749-50. February 19 Joshua BRYANT of Scituate & Elizabeth PERRY of Hanover

May 19 Joseph SOPER of Scituate & Ruth CURTISS of Hanover

July 5 Thomas HUBBARD of Abington & Jane BAILY of Hanover

November 1 Caleb SYLVESTER and Desire STETSON both of Hanover

1750-51. February 8 Jack & Bilhah, two *negroes* both of Hanover : being Mr. Job TILDEN's servants

December 25 William GOLD, Junior of Bridgewater & Mary CURTISS, Junior of Hanover

1752. January 16 Lemuel CURTISS & Ruth MAN both of Hanover

January 30 Edmund SYLVESTER & Elizabeth BASS both of Hanover

At this interval the records of thirteen marriages seem to be missing.

1754. February 12 John ROBINSON of Plymouth & Elizabeth STUDLEY of Hanover

December 26 Seth HARDIN of Pembroke & Susanna TAYLOR of Hanover

1755. February 13 Joseph HOUSE and Sage RANDALL both of Hanover

February 26 Daniel TOUR(?) of Hingham & Persis CURTISS of Hanover

February 27   Thomas PINCHIN, Junior of Scituate & Anna TAYLOR of Hanover
March 11   John RUGGLES, Junior Scituate & Susanna BARSTOW of Hanover
March 31   Elijah WATERS of Hingham & Mehetabel CURTISS of Hanover
November 25   Joseph RAMSDALE & Mercy PRIOR both of Hanover
December 25   Isaac PROUTY of Scituate & Priscilla RAMSDALE of Hanover
1756.   February 14   Nathanael HARDING, Junior of Pembroke & Rebecca TAYLOR of Hanover
February 26   Thomas CURTISS and Ruth ROSE both of Hanover
May 6   Jacob WHITTEN of Scituate and Ann GIBS of Hanover

MARRIAGES
BY
THE REVD SAMUEL BALDWIN.

1757.   Jany 19   Amos SYLVESTER & Desire ROSE both of Hanover
Jany 27   Samuel BARSTOW and Huldah HOUSE both of Hanover
Decem. 21   Seth BATES and Ann NEAL both of Hanover
1758.   Feby 23   James BARSTOW of Pembroke and Rhoda HOUSE of Hanover
Sept. 14   Lawrence EKINGS and Sylvester HOWLAND both of Hanover
1759.   Feby 15   Michael JACKSON of Abbington and Thankful STUDLEY of Hanover
April 5   George BENNIT of Abbington and Hannah North EELLES of Hanover
Novr. 22   William NORTON of Abbington and Sarah SYLVESTER of Hanover
Nov. 29   Thomas HILL of Pembroke & Mary WARDELL of Hanover
1760.   Jany 15   Elisha CURTIS of Scituate and Betty STUDLEY of Hanover

Jany 17 Michael SYLVESTER and Ruth TURNER both of Hanover
Jany 23 Lieut. Elisha HOUSE and Orphan PETERSON both of Hanover
May 25 Newport and Kate two *negro* slaves belonging to Nathl SYLVESTER, both of Hanover
June 5 Robert GARDNER, Jur of Hingham & Sarah MAN of Hanover
August 3 Joshua BAKER of Rochester & Lydia CLARK of Hanover
Nov. 27 David CUDWORTH of Scituate & Rebecca STETSON of Hanover

1761. Jany 3 Joseph BATES and Widow Elizabeth CURTIS both of Hanover
May 25 Joseph HOUSE and Widow Hannah RANDALL both of Hanover
Sepr 7 Nathl TURNER of Pembroke & Lucinda TURNER of Hanover
Nov. 12 Thos. ROSE, Jr. and Rhoda ROGERS both of Hanover
Decem. 3 Abner SYLVESTER & Susanna STETSON both of Hanover
John STETSON & Thankful CURTIS both of Hanover
Stevens HATCH and Ruth PRIOR both of Hanover
Decem. 17 John WITHERELL and Content CONNEWAY both of Hanover
Joshua CURTIS and Abigail HOUSE both of Hanover
Decem. 24 Joshua DWELLY & Avis RAMSDALE both of Hanover
Decem. 31 Theophilus WITHERELL and Freelove STETSON both of Hanover

1762. Jany 14 Gideon STUDLEY and Rosamond CHURCH both of Hanover
Jany 21 Zechariah CURTIS of Scituate & Lydia PALMER of Hanover
Feby 11 Seth BAYLEY and Lydia BARSTOW both of Hanover
March 30 Daniel ALDEN of Stafford, in the Colony of Connecticut, esqr and Rebecca CURTIS of Hanover
April 8 Amos BERRY and Sarah PETERS both of Hanover
June 6 Job YOUNG and Betty STOCKBRIDGE both of Hanover
Decem. 30 Jonathan PRATT and Lucy CHURCH both of Hanover

1763. August 11 Mark ROGERS and Mary BRAY both of Hanover
Novem. 24 Seth LATHAM of Bridgewater and Rachel HOUSE of Hanover

1764. Jany 19 Leonard HILL of Pembroke & Jerusha BATES of Hanover

Feby 16   Daniel CROOKER of Pembroke & Abigail STUDLEY of Hanover

N.B. August 2, 1764. A list of the above marriages have been exhibited to the Town Clerk.

Nov. 29   Seth WITHERELL and Hannah CLARK, Jr. both of Hanover
Decem. 20   James STILL, *Indian man*, & Sarah TOTO, *Indian woman* both residents in Hanover
1765. January 3   David RIPLEY and Priscilla DUNBAR both of Hanover
January 10   Joseph STUDLEY & Rebecca STETSON, Jr. both of Hanover
March 28   John CURTIS, Jr and Anna CURTIS both of Hanover
April 7   Hezekiah BUNKER of Sherborn in Nantucket and Margaret FITZ-GERALD of Hanover
April 11   Seth STETSON, Jr. & Lucy STUDLEY both of Hanover
April 30   Benj STETSON and Bradbury EELLES
July 18   Job SYLVESTER and Margaret STETSON both of Hanover
Sept. 5   Timothy CHURCH and Elizabeth ROSE both of Hanover
Novr 11   Othniel PRATT and Deborah HATCH both of Hanover
1766.   Jany 19   Joseph NICKERSON and Lurana NEEL both resident in Hanover
Jany 23   Timo. ROSE and Lydia SOPER both of Hanover
Thos. COLLEMORE of Scituate & Elizabeth TURNER of Hanover
March 13   John CHAPMAN, Jr. of Pembroke and Ruth TORREY of Hanover
May 1   Solomon BRYANT of Plympton & Elizabeth CURTIS of Hanover
July 3   Abner CURTIS of Hanover and Sarah FORD of Scituate
July 27   Jesse CURTIS of Hanover and Hannah PETERSON of Scituate
Octo. 16   Lemuel BATES and Mercy WITHERELL both of Hanover
Decr 14   Samuel STETSON and Alice ROGERS both of Hanover
1767.   January 1   Joseph RAMSDELL the second and Mercy BATES both of Hanover
January 29   Daniel PARKMAN of Abbington & Hannah HOUSE of Hanover
January 29   Thomas BATES and Hannah TORREY both of Hanover
April 2   Samuel HARDEN of Pembroke and Mary ROGERS of Hanover

1768. Jany 18 Elijah CUSHING of Pembroke and Mary TURNER of Hanover

Mar. 17 Ebenezer EDY of Pembroke and Deborah PALMER of Hanover

April 3 Atherton WALES and Ruth TURNER, Jr. both of Hanover

April 21 Benjamin CLARK and Tabitha CHUBBUCK both of Hanover

N.B. July 4, 1768 A list of the above marriages were exhibited to the Town Clerk.

July 28 Seth BAYLEY and Alice NEAL both of Hanover
Novr 27 Samuel HAYFORD and Diadama BISHOP both of Hanover
Decemr 8 Cornelius TURNER and Michal SYLVESTER both of Hanover

1769. Jany 12 Thomas HATCH and Susanna CURTIS both of Hanover

Jany 26 Joseph NICHOLSON and Desire PETER, *Indians*, resident in Hanover

March 2 Josiah MAN, Jr. of Scituate and Sage CLARK of Hanover
May 4 Samuel BRIMHALL of Abbington and Hannah RAMSDELL
May 11 Thomas WILLIT of Boston and Anna LAMBERT of Hanover
Octo. 12 Levi CORTHELL of Abbington and Deborah CURTIS of Hanover
Octo. 19 Elisha FOSTER, Jr. of Scituate and Grace BARSTOW of Hanover

1770. Feby. 8 James ORR and Susanna TILDEN both of Hanover
Mar. 22 Nicholas BOWKER and Tamzin WOODS both of Hanover
June 6 Thomas CURTIS, Jr. and Abigail STUDLEY both of Hanover

1771. Jany 31 Bosworth COLLIER of Hull and Anna HOUSE of Hanover

Feby 11 Jonathan BATES of Rochester and Ruth STETSON of Hanover
June 30 Asa TURNER and Abigail MAN both of Hanover
July 4 Daniel BARSTOW and Betty TILDEN both of Hanover
Sepr 5 David TORREY and Susanna ROGERS both of Hanover
Sepr 5 Gamabiel BATES of Hanover and Mary CARVER, Jr. of Pembroke
Octo. 17 James CURTIS and Zilpah STETSON both of Hanover

Nov. 21 Lot RAMSDALE and Rachel TORREY both of Hanover
1772. Feby 16 John BARNS, Jr. of Hingham and Martha CURTIS the third of Hanover

N.B. March 23, 1772 A list of the above marriages were exhibited to the Town Clerk.

April 9 Elijah STETSON and Susannah CURTIS of Hanover
April 12 Benja THOMAS of Marshfield and Betty ROBBINS of Hanover
June 18 Thomas STETSON and Olive MAN both of Hanover
Decem. 30 Elisha WITHERELL of Chesterfield and the Widow Rebecca STUDLEY of Hanover
1773. Feby 25 Stephen MOTT of Scituate and Nabby STAPLES of Hanover
Sepr. 12 Isaac JOSSELYN of Pembroke and Lois RAMSDALE of Hanover
Decem. 23 Joseph BATES, Jr. and Tamzin BOWKER both of Hanover
1774. Jany 13 Oliver POOL and Sarah RAMSDALE both of Hanover
May 19 Charles TOLMAN of Scituate and Mary SYLVESTER of Hanover
Oct. 9 William STOCKBRIDGE and Ruth BAYLEY both of Hanover
Nov. 6 James COLE, Jr. of Scituate and Lucy HOUSE of Hanover
1775. Jany 5 William CURTIS, Jr. and Deborah CURTIS both of Hanover
March 16 James TORREY and Lydia CASWELL both of Hanover
July 6 Stephen DAMAN of Scituate and Rebecca CURTIS of Hanover
Novr 8 Joseph BICKNALL, Jr. of Abbington and Nabby TURNER of Hanover
Nov. 23 Elisha SYLVESTER, Jr. of Scituate and Abigail PALMER of Hanover
Nov. 23 James CLARK, Jr. of Hanover and Deborah CUDWORTH of Pembroke
1776. Feby 12 Abel CURTIS and Ruth TURNER, Jr. both of Hanover
April 4 Ebenezer WING, Jr. and Betty OLDHAM both of Hanover

April 28   John OLDHAM of Pembroke and Lydia SYLVESTER of Hanover
June 13   Elijah GILBERT and Widow Hannah RANDALL both of Hanover
Octr 20   Adam PERRY of Pembroke and Elizabeth HOUSE of Hanover
Decem. 2   Tilson GOULD Pembroke and Mary HATCH of Hanover
1777.   Jany 1   Marlbry TURNER and Abigail CURTIS both of Hanover
Jany 2   David TORREY of Hanover and Miriam MANSON of Scituate
March 20   Robert WHITE and Anna HOUSE both of Hanover
May 1   Eelles DAMON of Scituate and Huldah CURTIS of Hanover
July 20   Elisha CURTIS of Scituate and Elizabeth CHURCH of Hanover
Aug. 29   Nathanael HOUSE and Lillis PALMER both of Hanover
Sepr 7   Amos PERRY of Scituate and Sarah JOSSELYN of Hanover
Nov. 18   Joseph WATERMAN, Jr. of Hallifax and Lucy Josselyn MUNRO of Hanover
1778.   Jany 15   Joseph TORREY and Mary TORREY both of Hanover
March 12   Jacob WHITE of Abington and Hannah Witherell EELLES of Hanover
April 30   Abner HOUSE and Abigail SYLVESTER both of Hanover
July 9   Docr Gad HITCHCOCK or Pembroke and Miss Sage BAILEY of Hanover
Sepr 6   William GRAHAM of Spencer and Hannah HATCH of Hanover
"   Samuel WHITTEN and Elizabeth GARDNER both of Hanover
Novr 4   Richard EUSTICE and Mercy RAMSDALE both of Hanover
Decem. 10   Isaac TURNER, Jr. and Mary WHITTEN both of Hanover
Decem. 24   Joseph CURTIS and Lydia OLDHAM both of Hanover
1779.   Jany 14   Solomon SHAW, Jr. of Abington and Betty Delingham of Hanover
June 17   Mr. Adams BAILEY, Jr. of Bridgewater and Miss Mary LITTLE of Hanover
June 27   William MORRILL (or Morrice) of Scituate and Rhoda HOUSE of Hanover
July 15   Ephraim PALMER of Scituate and Desire OLDHAM of Hanover
Sepr 16   Luther ROBBINS and Anna BARKER both of Hanover

Decem. 23   David STOCKBRIDGE, Jr. and Ruth CUSHING both of Hanover

Decem. 26   Caleb ROGERS, Jr. and Widow Hannah BATES both of Hanover

1780.   Feby 17   Ephraim STETSON and Olive RAMSDALE both of Hanover

Feby 24   Samuel GROSS and Betty TORREY both of Hanover

A LIST OF PERSONS MARRIED

BY ME

JOHN MELLEN

Pastor of the Chh. in Hanover.

1784.   Feby 19   Abel WHITING and Priscilla PEAKS both of Hanover

May 13   Ezra BRIGGS, Junr and Margaret CURTIS both of Hanover

Octr 21   Capn Luther BAILEY and Sylvester LITTLE both of Hanover

Novr 8   Benjamin STETSON and Widow Betty YOUNG both of Hanover

Novr 25   Josiah CHAMBERLAIN of * * * * & Lucy PRATT of Hanover

Decr 30   Levi BATES and Lydia SYLVESTER both of Hanover

1785.   Jany 20   Caleb HOWLAND of Plymouth & Mary SYLVESTER of Hanover

March 13   George STERLING and Ruth BAILEY both of Hanover

March 31   Morgan BREWSTER and Martha STETSON both of Hanover

May 8   Homer WHITING and Anna STUDLY both of Hanover

Oct 4   Nath'l HILL of Pembroke and Mary RAMSDALE of Hanover

Nov. 1   John Reed JOSELYN and Nabby STUDLY both of Hanover

Decr 25   Clement BATES, Junr & Rebecca STETSON both of Hanover

1786.   Feby 2   Saml Baker PERRY of Pembroke & Anna BATES of Hanover

April 11   Jabez BATES and Elizabeth BARKER both of Hanover

April 13 Asa WHITING and Debbe DWELLY both of Hanover
April 23 Caleb WHITING and Suse Gill MAN both of Hanover
Aug. 31 Nath'l BARSTOW of Scituate and Elizabeth CUSHING of Hanover

1787. Jany 25 Paul WEBB of Scituate and Deborah SYLVESTER of Hanover
March 12 Dr Nath'l PARKER of Salem and Mary MELLEN of Hanover
May 17 Joseph RAMSDALE and Elizabeth ELLIS both of Hanover
Aug. 23 Capn. Albert SMITH of Pembroke & Anna Lenthel EELLES of Hanover
Novr 1 Robert SALMON and Mary BALDWIN both of Hanover
Novr 29 Joseph Dawes RAMSDALE of Hanover and Eunice NASH, Scituate
Novr 29 Oliver BONNY and Cynthia Sylvester JOSSELYN both of Hanover
Novr 29 Elisha CURTIS, Junr of Scituate and Hannah CURTIS of Hanover

☞   Sent to the Town Clerk.

1788. Jany 27 Shubæl MUNRO, Jr. and Abigail STETSON both of Hanover
Feby 7 John Burden BARSTOW of Scituate and Betsy EELLES of Hanover
May 8 Ezekiel Turner HATCH and Hannah BAILY both of Hanover
Decr 7 Benjamin DWELLY of Pembroke and Bradbury STETSON of Hanover

1789. March 1 Ezra BRIGGS, Jr. of Hanover & Lydia SOUTHWARD of Duxbury
April 2 Morris Hobbs CLARK of Hingham and Mary GROSS of Hanover
April 12 Asa WHITING and Bette WHITING both of Hanover
June 25 Revd Ebenezer DAWES, Scituate and Betty BAILY, Hanover
July 20 Nath'l ELLIS and Mary RAMSDEL both of Hanover
Nov. 26 William WING and Huldah Copeland EELLES both of Hanover

1790. Jany 7 Capn Marlbry TURNER & Deborah STOCKBRIDE both of Hanover
Mar. 28 Saml HILL, Junr of Pembroke and Hannah WITHERELL of Hanover
Apl. 15 Jonathan PRATT and Lydia CHAMBERLAIN both of Hanover
April 15 Ezra BEALS of Pembroke and Lucy HATCH of Hanover
July 12 Zattu CUSHING of Abington & Rosamond STUDLEY, Hanover
Nov. 25 Job SYLVESTER, Jr. and Lydia PHILLIPS both of Hanover
Decr 13 Simeon CURTIS, Junr and Bathsheba SYLVESTER, both of Hanover
1791. Feby 1 Job YOUNG of Turner and Polly CURTIS of Hanover
Feby 3 Prince WATERMAN and Lucinda BATES both of Hanover
March 3 Saml GROCE and Submit GARDNER both of Hanover
March 27 Saml BATES and Hannah STETSON both of Hanover
Oct. 12 Luke LONDON of Marshfield and Jane COZENO of Hanover, *negroes*
Nov. 6 Samuel WHITCOMB and Lydia RAMSDELL both of Hanover
Dec. 6 Joseph NEAL, Cohasset and Sarah MAN of Hanover
1792. Jany 5 Thomas YOUNG, Bridgewater and Bethiah Cushing BALDWIN of Hanover
Jany 15 Lieut. Saml BARSTOW of Pembroke and Sibil HATCH of Hanover
Feby 9 John JONES of Lunenbourg and Polly TURNER of Hanover
March 4 Richard HILL and Sarah SYLVESTER both of Hanover
April 29 Heman HOLMES, Kingston and Mercy BASS of Hanover
May 3 William Austin KENT of Concord, New Hampshire and Charlotte MELLEN of Hanover
July 22 Joshua JENKINS of Scituate and Kezia MERRIT of Hanover
Nov. 1 Thomas BATES and Lucy BATES both of Hanover
1793. Feby 10 Curtis BROOKS and Anna SOUTHWARD both of Hanover
March 3 Dea. Benjamin BASS and Mary EELLES both of Hanover
June 13 Benjamin BAILEY of Greenland and Lydia SYMMONS of Hanover
Sepr 26 Arad WOODWORTH of Western & Debby STUDLY of Hanover

Nov 7. Nath'l STETSON (the third) of Hanover and Temperance CURTIS of Scituate

Decr 19 Elijah SYLVESTER and Mary ROBBINS both of Hanover

1794. Feby 6 Rufus ADAMS of Kingston and Ruth WALES of Hanover

March 13 Josiah SMITH, Jr. of Pembroke & Nabbe EELLES of Hanover

April 3 Thomas MACUMBER, Jr. of Marshfield and Betsy CURTIS, Jr. of Hanover

June 1 Cyrus LEAVIT of Turner and Sarah PRAT of Hanover

June 29 James LINCOLN of Taunton & Lucinda BAILEY of Hanover

Oct. 21 Walter ROGERS of Marshfield and Betty BARSTOW of Hanover

Nov. 16 Joseph CUSHING and Kezia CURTIS, Junr both of Hanover

Dec. 4 Benjamin BASS, Junr and Lucinda SYLVESTER both of Hanover

1795. Jany 8 Joseph KEEN, Jr., Pembroke and Cloe WING, of Hanover

Feby 1 Turner STETSON and Lydia ROSE, Jr. both of Hanover

May 3 Thomas WILLET, Abbington and Eunice Turner STETSON, Hanover

Sept. 29 John THATCHER, Barnstable and Mary SYMMONDS of Hanover

Nov. 3 Simeon WASHBURN, Kingston and Hannah MORTON of Hanover

1796. April 14 Cooms HOUSE and Deborah BROOKS both of Hanover

April 28 Paul BATES & Frelove WITHEREL both of Hanover

June 9 Timothy ROSE, Jr. of Hanover & Mercy JOSLYN of Pembroke

July 17 Levi CASWELL and Allice CLARK, Jr. of Hanover

August 28 Isaac TURNER and Rebecca CURTIS, Senr both of Hanover

Nov. 27 Timothy CHURCH and Becca STETSON both of Hanover

1797. Feby 2 John YOUNG and Ruth EELLES, Jr. both of Hanover

Feby 15 Elisha BARKER, Pembroke and Rebecca CURTIS, Hanover

March 2   Ozias WHITING and Rebecca CURTIS both Hanover
March 16   Joshua DWELLE and Rachel HATCH both of Hanover
June 8   Thomas WHITING, Jr. & Hannah MAN, Jr. both of Hanover
August 13   Josiah TUBBS, Junr of Pembroke and Lucy STETSON, Jr of Hanover
Oct. 5   Isaac JOSLYN, Junr and Christiana JOSLYN both of Hanover
Oct. 29   John HATHAWAY of Camden and Deborah CUSHING, Hanover
Nov. 30   Samuel JENKINS, Junr of Scituate to Hannah ROBBINS, Hanover

1798.   Jany 10   Jonathan PRAT and Desire PALMAR both of Hanover
Feby 4   Robert BARKER and Deborah BAILY both of Hanover
May 8   Seth GARDNER of Hingham and Susanna Hatch, Hanover
Nov. 1   Benjamin STETSON, Jr. and Betsey EASTIS, both of Hanover
also same day
John CURTIS ye 3rd and Sally MAN both of Hanover
Nov. 8   Elijah BARSTOW, Scituate and Lucy EELLES, Hanover
Decr 4   Seth ROSE and Lucy DWELLY both of Hanover

1799.   Jany 1   Edward STETSON and Hannah PERRY both Hanover
Jany 29   Samuel STETSON and Zilpah STETSON both of Hanover
Feby 28   Ezekiel TURNER and Lydia STETSON both of Hanover
March 3   Lemuel FREMAN of Scituate and Esther SAMPSON of Hanover
Decr 15   Isaac WITHINGTON of Dorchester and Mary TURNER of Hanover

1800.   Feby 3   Joseph RAMSDEL, Junr and Ruth STOCKBRIDGE, 3rd both of Hanover
Feby 11   Benjamin TOLLMAN, Jr. Marshfield and Rebecca STUDLY, Hanover
Feby 20   Thomas WINSLOW and Ruth GROCE of Hanover
Feby 23   Jabez STUDLY, Jr. and Chloe Man CLARK both of Hanover
July 2   Zahary DAMMON and Sarah BROOKS, both Hanover
Augt 3   David TURNER and Mary GROSS of Hanover
Augt 31   Barker RAMSDEL and Lucy ELLIS both of Hanover
Nov. 27   Robert EELLES and Huldah BASS both of Hanover

1801. Mar. 24 Joseph Dawes RAMSDEL and Widow Sally SYLVESTER both of Hanover
April 23 John ELLIS and Nabby SYLVESTER both of Hanover
July 28 Almorin JOSLYN of Hanover & Chloe WHITTEN, Pembroke
Augt 12 Calvin BATES of Hanover and Elizabeth STETSON of Pembroke
Sept. 15 David POOL of Abbington and Abigail STUDLY of Hanover
Oct. 4 Joseph JACOB and Anna DAMMON, Jr. both of Hanover
Oct. 19 Thomas STETSON, Junr of Pembroke and Betsey STUDLY, Jr. of Hanover
Nov. 7 Dr. David BAYLY and Joanna CURTIS both of Hanover
Nov. 26 John WOODWORTH and Lois JOSLYN both of Hanover
Nov. 29 Reuben CURTIS and Abigail BAILY both of Hanover
Decem 30 Cornelius WHITE and Rebecca BATES both of Hanover

Sent to ye Clerk

1802. Jany 3 Melzar HATCH and Sally BARSTOW both of Hanover
Aug. 8 Isaac WILDER of Hingham and Ruth MANN of Hanover
Oct. 10 Benjamin Hely CLARK and Mary NEAL both of Hanover
Oct. 10 Barnabas STETSON of Abington and Lucy BARSTOW of Hanover
Nov. 25 Amos BATES and Sybil ROBBINS both of Hanover

also same day

Joseph EELLES and Sarah BASS both of Hanover

1803. Jany 16 Joseph BROOKS, Junr and Mary TOWER both of Hanover
Jany 30 James STUDLY and Mary Hobart, Jr. both of Hanover
Feby 8 Levi FISH and Hannah BATES both of Hanover
Apl 21 Jesse STODDARD, Abington and Rachel STUDLY, Jr. of Hanover
May 15 Richard EASTIS and Saba CURTIS both of Hanover
June 9 Stephen BAILY, Junr and Ruth HATCH both of Hanover
June 26 Elijah PACKARD and Priscilla PERRY both of Hanover
Sepr 15 Miller SMITH of Pembroke and Jane Reed STOCKBRIDGE of Hanover
Nov. 29 Nathaniel PRAT of Halifax and Elizabeth T. GROCE Hanover

Decr 14 Asa BATES of Weymouth & Hannah RAMSDALE, Hanover

Taken off for ye Clerk to this place.

1804. Feby 23 Joshua YOUNG of Scituate and Mary Lenthal EELLES of Hanover

April 1 George LONGLEY and Priscilla CROOKER both of Hanover

May 6, Joseph ELLMS, Junr, Scituate and Elizabeth ROBBINS of Hanover

June 3 William E. SMITH and Elizabeth DAMMON of Hanover

Octr 18 Roland SYLVESTER of Durham and Ruth BARSTOW of Hanover

Oct. 20 Joshua STETSON and Priscilla DWELLY both of Hanover

1805. Jany 7 Samuel BAKER, Junr of Marshfield and Eunice PERRY of Hanover

March 3 Nathl CURTIS of Hanover and Mrs. Nancy STODDER of Scituate

MARRIAGES

BY ME

C. CHADDOCK.

1806. July 27 John GARNER of Bridgewater to Betsey TILDEN of Hanover

Aug. 17 William SAMSON of Bridgewater to Sally CLARK of Hanover

Sep. 28 Thomas BARSTOW, Jr. of Scituate and Elie THOMAS of Hanover

1807. Jany ** Thomas FARRON of Townsend to Orpha CURTIS of Hanover

April 27 Dryden JUDD, resident in Hanover to Lide BATES of Hanover

May 17 Samuel STETSON and Nabby Stetson MUNROE both of Hanover

May 21 James BATES of Hanover and Hannah WALKER of Pembroke
July 12 Thomas Merit BATES and Sylvia WING both of Hanover
Nov. 26 George VIAUGHAN of Middleborough and Mercy ESTIS of Hanover
1808. Oct. 6 Revd Thomas COCHRAN of Camden and Mary BARSTOW of Hanover
1809. Jany 1 Eleazer JOSSELYN and Hannah STUDLEY both of Hanover
Feby 5 Jacob CAPRON of Attleborough and Deborah BATES of Hanover
July 23 Alpha TRIBOU of Bridgewater and Ruth CLARK of Hanover
Sept. 10 Simeon GILBERT of Barre and Nancy RAMSDELL of Hanover
Oct. 5 Enos BATES and Lydia TILDEN, Junr both of Hanover
Oct. 11 Thomas Oldham BATES and Rebekah BATES, Junr both of Hanover
Decem. 17 Israel PERRY and Relief SOPER both of Hanover
" Gideon STUDLEY, Jur and Sally BUTLER both of Hanover
Decem. 31 Jesse CURTIS, Junr and Sarah NASH both of Hanover
1810. Jany 1 Ells DAMMON and Elinor BROOKS both of Hanover
Jany 11 Thomas PERRY and Sarah RAMSDELL both of Hanover
Aug. ** John LONDON and Susanah PRINCE (*Blacks*) both of Hanover
Octo. 21 John TRIBOU of Bridgewater to Mary TILDEN of Hanover
Nov. 1 Ithamer WHITTING of Abington to Abigail MAN of Hanover
1811. March 7 Nath'l STETSON and Joanna PRATT both of Hanover
Aug. 25 David TOWER and Patience PALMER both of Hanover
Novr 12 John Dunbar GARDINER of Hingham to Susanna Gill WHITTING of Hanover
1812. March 4 William BATES and Betsey BATES both of Hanover
April 26 Reuben PETERSON, Junr of Duxbury and Mary WHITE of Hanover
Sept. 6 Joseph DAMON and Lucy TOWER both of Hanover

1813. Sept. 23   Paul PERRY and Chloe BAILEY both of Hanover
Novr 21   Elias BARREL of Bridgewater and Deborah TILDEN of Hanover
Decemr 16   Nathaniel BISHOP and Abigail BATES both of Hanover
Decem. 21   Ephraim STETSON of Abington and Nabby BARSTOW of Hanover
1814. Sept. 25   Ezra PHILIPS of Pembroke and Luie CHAMBERLAIN of Hanover
June 15   Piam DAMON and Olive WHITTING both of Hanover
1815. August 20   John DILLINGHAM and Hanñah Turner WING both of Hanover
Sept. 10   William ESTES of Hanover and Bethiah JOSELYN of Pembroke
Novr 26   John ESTES and Eliza Barker ELLIS both of Hanover
1816. Feby 14   Orin JOSELYN of Pembroke and Mary C. MANN of Hanover
Mar. 18   Joshua CURTIS of Abington to Nancy STUDLEY of Hanover
May 19   Samuel G. BOWMAN of Bath and Maria STOCKBRIDGE of Hanover
May 22   Zadock BEAL of Abington to Tryphena WHITTING of Hanover
June 16   Stephen CURTIS of Scituate and Lucinda BAILEY of Hanover
Sept. 15   Isaac COOK and Bethiah Baker PERRY both of Hanover
Sept. 29   Harris M. TOTMAN of Scituate and Sarah S. GROSE of Hanover
Oct. 2   David WHITMAN, Junr of Weymouth and Betsy POOL of Hanover
Oct. 27   Seth VINAL of Marshfield and Hanner Bailey HATCH of Hanover
Decem. 1   Thomas SIMMONS of Scituate and Bethiah GRAY of Hanover
1817. Jany 18   Charles HOWARD of Bridgewater and Betsey WADE of Hanover
1818. March 10   Joshua PERRY and Mary THOMAS, 2d, both of Pembroke
March 30   Benjn Darling TORREY and Louisa PERRY both of Hanover
June 14   John DAVENPORT and Eliza REED both of Hanover
1827. August 23   Revd Job Henry MARTIN and Grace F. SMITH
December 3   Mr. Joseph RAMSDELL of Weston and Elizabeth EELLS

CHAPTER V.

BIRTHS.
1730–1819

1730. October ** Elizabeth, daughter of Thomas and Elizabeth WILKS
October 30 Mary, daughter of Benjamin and Mary BASS
October 31 John, son of John and Elizabeth BAILY
November 17 Clement, son of Clement & Agatha BATES
November ** Mary, daughter of Joseph & Patience CORNISH
December 17 Jonathan, son of Joseph & ...... PERRY
December 27 ......, daughter of Joseph & Mary BATES
1730-31. January 6 Mary, daughter of Joseph & Mary RAMSDALE
February 8 Sarah, daughter of Benjamin & Martha MAN
February 23 Benjamin, son of Benjamin & Lillis STETSON
March 1 Desire,.daughter of Ezekiel & Tabitha VINEL
March 22 Deborah, daughter of Solomon & Deborah BATES
April 5 ......, child of William & Honour TORY
May 5 Rachel, daughter of Joseph & Rachel SMITH
June 7 ......, daughter of Edward & ...... EASTICE
June 21 ......, child of David & ...... HOUSE
June 28 Deborah, daughter of Ezekiel & Bathshua TURNER
July 2 Sarah, daughter of John & Elizabeth STUDLEY
July 10 ......, daughter of Sylvanus & Hannah WING
August 5 ......, son of Henry and ...... MERRIT

August 23 ......, daughter of Isaac & Deborah Burden
August 24   Matthew, son of Matthew & Hannah Stetson
Sept. **   Joseph, son of Joseph & Mary Curtis
October 27 ......, child of Matthew & ...... Eastice
November 9   Lemuel, son of William & Margaret Curtis
November 28   Hannah, daughter of Isaac & Mary Buck
December 18   Rebeckah, daughter of Josiah Curtis
December 29 ......, son of Meletiah & Phœbe Dillingham
1731-32.   January 4 ......, daughter of Jacob & Ruth Baily
January 19   Jane, daughter of John & Elizabeth Baily
February 3 ......, son of James Hatch, Junior
February 14 ......, daughter of Caleb & ...... Barker
February 20 ......, daughter of William & Hannah Ford
February 27   Thomas, son of Benjamin & Sarah Barstow
February ** ......, son of John & Susanna Love
March 1   Joseph, son of Elijah & Elizabeth Cushing
March **   Mercy, daughter of Job & Thankful Otis
May ** ......, child of John & Juel Dilingham
July 14   Avis, daughter of Joseph & Mary Ramsdale
July 15   Mary, daughter of Benjamin & Hannah Curtis
July 26   Isaac, son of Isaac & Deborah Lambert
August 20   Hannah, daughter of Isaac & ...... Hatch
August 23   Joseph, son of Benjamin & Martha Man
August 28   Caleb, son of John & Sarah Lambert
September 1 ......, daughter of Jonathan & Margaret Peters
September 12   Ruth, daughter of Joseph & Lydia House
September 13   Ruth, daughter of Thomas & Faith Rose
October 2 ......, daughter of Seth & ...... Stetson
October 9 ......, son of Eliab & Martha Turner
eodem die   Susanna, daughter of Samuel & Margaret Barstow
October 14 ......, daughter of Joseph & Mary Bates
November 10   James, son of Clement & Agatha Bates
December 23 ......, daughter of Thomas & Elizabeth Elmer
1732-33.   January 5   Sarah, daughter of Richard & Sarah Buker
February 3 ......, daughter of Joseph & Patience Cornish
March 7   Joshua, son of Joseph and Rachel Smith

March 8   Ann and Susanna, daughters of Thomas & Elizabeth WILKS
March 21   ......, daughter of Benja. & Rachel TAYLOR
March 22   Job, son of Benja. & Lillis STETSON
May **   ......, son of Sylvanus & Hannah WING
May 23   Margaret, daughter of Richard & Margaret FITZGERALD
May 31   ......, child of Edward & ...... EASTICE
May 31   ......, child of John & Susanna LOVE
June 4   Sarah, daughter of Samuel & Hannah EELS
June 8   ......, daughter of Matthew & ...... EASTICE
July 27   Lincoln, son of Matthew & Hannah STETSON
August 5   David, son of Joseph & ...... PERRY
August 13 ......, daughter of Robert & Margaret YOUNG
September 7   ......, son of Amos & Patience SYLVESTER
September 17 ......, daughter of Henry & Margaret MERRIT
September 23 Joshua, son of Joseph & Mary CURTIS
September 26 Thomas, son of Thomas & Ann JOSSELYN
October 30   Betty, daughter of John & Elizabeth STUDLEY
November 14   Thankful, daughter of Benjamin & Martha MANN
November 16   Joseph, son of Joseph & Abigail HOUSE
December 15   Lemuel, son of Job and Thankful OTIS
1733-34 January **   ......, son of David and Bethiah CURTIS
          January 25   ......, son of William & Hannah FORD
February 22 James, son of Benjamin & Sarah BARSTOW
March 6   ......, son of Jacob & Ruth BAILY
March **   ......, child of John & Juel DILINGHAM
March 18   Elizabeth, daughter of Benjamin & Mary BASS
April 22   Mary, daughter of Elijah & Elizabeth CUSHING
May 8   Shedrach, son of James HATCH, Junior
June 3   ......, daughter of Thomas & Faith ROSE
June 30   ......, son of Thomas & Thankful JONES
July 7   ......, son of Joseph & Mary BATES
July 26   ......, daughter of Samuel & Mary WHITEN
July 28   Samuel, son of Samuel & Margaret BARSTOW
August 4   ......, daughter of Richard & Sarah BUKER
August 17   Seth, son of Josiah & Sarah CURTIS
August 30   ......, daughter of Isaac & Mary BUCK
August or Septr Jemima, daughter of Solomon & Deborah BATES
September 5 Priscilla, daughter of Joseph and Mary RAMSDALE

September ** Zerirah, daughter of Uriah & Ruth LAMBERT
September ** Hannah, daughter of Joseph & Lydia HOUSE
October 6 Stevens, son of Isaac & Sarah HATCH
October 24 ......, child of Jonathan & Margaret PETERS
November 13 ......, son of Joseph RAMSDALE
November 14 ......, daughter of Ezekiel & Martha PALMER
December 1 ......, daughter of William & Margaret CURTIS
1734-35. January 2 ......, son of William & Hannah FORD
January 14 Charity, daughter of Daniel & Ruth ROGERS
January ** ......, child of Stephen & Rachel TOREY
February 3 ......, son of Eliab & Martha TURNER
February or March ......, child of Joseph & Hannah HARRIS
March 22 ......, daughter of Meletiah & Meriah DILINGHAM
April 18 Betty, daughter of John & Sarah LAMBERT
April 30 Ezekiel, son of David & Bethiah CURTIS
May 4 John, son of Thomas & Ann JOSSLYN
May 7 Olive, daughter of Timothy & Sarah BAILY
May 25 Deborah, daughter of John and Ann HOUSE
June 4 Seth, son of Seth & Elizabeth STETSON
June 4 John, son of Thomas & Elizabeth WILKS
May or June Ruth, daughter of Benjamin & Martha MANN
July 7 ......, daughter of Sylvanus & Hannah WING
July 7 Hannah, daughter of Matthew & Hannah STETSON
July 14 ......, daughter of Job & Thankful OTIS
July 11 Deborah, daughter of Joseph & Patience CORNISH
July 28 Experience, daughter of Joseph & Mary CURTIS
August ** ......, son of Clement & Agatha BATES
September ** Rhoda, daughter of Joseph & Abigail HOUSE
October 13 Huldah, daughter of Samuel & Deborah HOUSE
November 17 ......, daughter of Joshua & Lydia STUDLEY
December 25 Sarah, daughter of Joseph & Sarah SHELDON
1735-36. January 26 Susanna, daughter of Benjamin & Lillis STETSON
February 15 Jacob, son of Benjamin & Sarah BARSTOW
February 16 Remember, daughter of Nathan & Lydia BOURN
February 23 James, son of Robert & Margaret YOUNG
February 26 ......, daughter of Benjamin & Susanna TAYLOR

March 11 ......, son of Joseph & Mary BATES
March 13 Gideon, son of John & Elizabeth STUDLEY
March 16 Katherine, daughter of Richard & Margaret FITZGERALD
March 25 William, son of Joseph & Mary PERRY
April ** ......, child of Richard & Sarah BUKER
April ** ......, child of Henry & Margaret MERRIT
May 4 Betty, daughter of Elijah & Elizabeth CUSHING
May ** ......, child of John & Juel DILINGHAM
May 16 ......, child of James & ...... HATCH
June ** Ruth Clay, daughter of Uriah & Ruth LAMBERT
June ** Hannah, daughter of Thomas & Faith ROSE
July 31 ......, son of Amos & Jemimah BATES
October 3 Ann, daughter of Thomas & Ann JOSSELYN
Thomas, son of Joseph & Mary RAMSDALE
......, child of Samuel & Rebecca WILKS
Seth, son of John & Ann HOUSE
......, child of Samuel & Hannah EELS
......, child of Meletiah DILINGHAM
1736-37. March ** Sarah, daughter of Gideon RAMSDALE
March ** Samuel, son of Lydia BARSTOW
April ** William, son of William & Mary SYLVESTER
May ** Sarah, daughter of Thomas & Elizabeth WILKS
May ** ......, child of David & Bethiah CURTIS
June ** ......, child of John & Sarah LAMBERT
June 12 Ruth, daughter of Ezekiel & Ruth TURNER
June 23 Timothy, son of Timothy & Sarah BAILY
July ** ...... & ......, Twins of William EASTICE
July 13 ......, child of Isaac & Deborah LAMBERT
August 13 Mary, daughter of Benjamin & Martha MANN
August 20 Joseph, son of David & Deborah STOCKBRIDGE
October ** ......, child of Ebenezer WING
October ** ......, child of Edward EASTICE
October 13 Joshua, son of Richard & Lydia PROUTY
October ** ......, son of Paul & Elizabeth WHITE
November 10 Deborah, daughter of Matthew & Hannah STETSON
November ** Thomas, son of Seth & Elizabeth STETSON
1737-38. January 12 ......, child of Eliab & Martha TURNER
January 16 ......, son of Clement & Agatha BATES

January 22 ......, daughter of Samuel & Hannah EELS
January ** ......, child of Benjamin & Sarah BARSTOW
February ** ......, daughter of John & Susanna LOVE
February ** ......, child of Isaac HATCH
February 18 Elisha, son of Samuel & Deborah HOUSE
February 27 Mary, daughter of Nathan & Lydia BOURN
April 3 ......, daughter of Benjamin & Abigail SYLVESTER
April 5 A son of Ruth SYLVESTER
April 23 ......, son of Amos & Patience SYLVESTER
April or May ......, child of Robert & ...... BARKER
May 15 or 16 Gideon, son of Joshua & Lydia STUDLEY
June 12 Rebecca, daughter of Joseph & Mary PERRY
June 19 Lette, daughter of Robert and Margaret YOUNG
July ** ......, child of Joseph & Mary BATES
July ** Thomas, son of Thomas & Faith ROSE
August ** ......, child of Samuel & ...... PERRY
August ** Jabez, son of John & Elizabeth STUDLEY
August 19 Nathanael, son of Benjamin & Lillis STETSON
August 23 Isaac, son of Peleg & Mercy STETSON
September 5 ......, child of ...... CHAPMAN
September 6 or 7 ......, son of William & Hannah FORD
September ** ......, child of Nathanael and Rebecca STETSON
September ** John, son of Gideon & ...... RAMSDALE
September ** Deborah, daughter of Elijah & Elizabeth CUSHING
October ** Relief, daughter of Benjamin and Hannah CURTIS
November ** ......, son of Jeremiah & Rachel ROGERS
......, child of John and Juel (Gail?) DILINGHAM
December 17 Mehetabel, daughter of Ebenezer & Mehetabel CROSBY
1738-39. January 19 Caleb, son of Joseph and Abigail HOUSE
February 20 Margaret, daughter of Samuel and Margaret BARSTOW
March 12 Sarah, daughter of Timothy & Sarah BAYLY
March 29 Ruth, daughter of Joseph and Patience CORNISH
April ** ......, child of John and Sarah LAMBERT
April 9 Bathshua, daughter of Ezekiel & Ruth TURNER
April 22 Betty, daughter of David & Deborah STOCKBRIDGE
Michael, son of David & Bethiah CURTIS
Samuel, son of Samuel and Jane PERRY

April 22   James, son of James & Mary TOREY
July **   Leonard, son of Richard & Jemimah HILL
July 4   Seth, son of John & Elizabeth BAILY
July **   Stephen, son of Joseph & Mary CURTIS
July 17   ......, child of Joshua and Mary STAPLES
August 2   ......, daughter of William & Martha CURTIS
August 20 ......, child of Jonathan and Margaret PETERS
August 21 ......, son of Benjamin & Abigail SYLVESTER
August 26 ......, child of John and Mary CURTIS
October ** Lydia, daughter of Thomas & Elizabeth WILKS
December 26 Mary, daughter of Samuel & Hannah EELS
1739-40. January 16   ......, daughter of Joshua & Lydia STUDLEY
January ** ......, child of James & Margaret CLARK
February ** ......, son of William & Elizabeth EASTICE
March 5   Grace, daughter of Benjamin & Lillis STETSON
March 9   ......, daughter of Eliab & Martha TURNER
March 11   ......, son of William and Jane GUILFORD
March **   ......, son of Benj. & Sarah BARSTOW
March 31   ......, child of Isaac & Deborah LAMBERT
April 7   Benjamin, son of Matthew & Hannah STETSON
April **   ......, daughter of Stephen & Rachel TORREY
April 10   ......, son of Clement & Agatha BATES
April 16   Elijah, son of Jesse and Sarah CURTIS
April **   Deborah, daughter of Samuel & Deborah HOUSE
May 3   Charles, son of Samuel and Margaret BARSTOW
June 5   ......, child of Samuel and ...... PERRY
June 9   ......, child of Joseph and Mary BATES
June **   ......, child of Isaac & Sarah HATCH
June 14   ......, child of John and Rebecca HOUSE
June 16   ......, son of Samuel & Rebecca WITHEREL
July **   ......, child of Peleg and Mercy STETSON
July 22   Ezekiel, son of Ezekiel & Ruth TURNER
July **   Mercy, daughter of Ebenezer CROSBY
July 26   ......, child of William and Martha CURTIS
August 3   Isaac, son of Micah and Mary STOCKBRIDGE
August 8   Jere'h, son of Seth and Elizabeth STETSON
September 12 ......, child of Jeremiah and Deborah ROGERS

ORIGINAL RECORDS.

September **   Elizabeth, daughter of Thomas and Faith ROSE
September 27   Lucinda, daughter of Caleb and Ruth TURNER
October 15   ......, son of Othniel and Mary PRATT
1740-41. February **   ......, daughter of James and ...... (Alvira or Alice) CORNISH
February or March   ......, child of Amos and Jemima BATES
March   ......, child of Nathanael and Hannah ROBBINS
March   ......, daughter of Joseph and Mary RAMSDALE
March 17   ......, son of Melatiah and ...... DILINGHAM
March 21   ......, daughter of Isaac and Ruth GROSS
March 29   Stockbridge, son of Thomas & Ann JOSSELYN
March 29   Chandler, son of Joseph and ...... PERRY
March 30   Timothy, son of James and Mary TORY, Junior
April 7   Bradbury, daughter of Samuel & Hannah EELS
April 14   Samuel, son of Samuel & Deborah HOUSE
May 4   ......, daughter of Ezekiel & Martha PALMER
May 5   ......, daughter of Benjamin and Sarah BARSTOW
May 12   ......, daughter of John and Elizabeth STUDLEY
May 19   ......, daughter of Joshua & Lydia STUDLEY
May 24   ......, child of John & Rebecca HOUSE
May or June   ......, child of William TORY
June 6   Benjamin, son of Benjamin and Mary BASS
June 6   ......, child of ...... CHAPMAN
June 16   ......, child of Elijah & Hannah CUSHING
June   ......, child of James and Margaret CLARK
June 30   Mary, daughter of John and Sarah LAMBERT
June 29   ......, daughter of Solomon & Deborah BATES
July   Amos, son of Ezekiel & Ruth TURNER
July 23   Thomas, son of Seth & Elizabeth STETSON
August 3   Naomi, daughter of Abner & Mary TURNER
August   ......, child of Jacob & Ruth BAILY
August 23   ......, child of David and ...... CURTIS
September 10   ......, son of William & Martha CURTIS
eodem die   ......, child of Benjamin & Naomi CURTIS
September 14   ......, daughter of Michael & Mary SYLVESTER
October   ......, child of Joseph & Sarah SHELDON
October   ......, child of Joseph & Abigail HOUSE
November 13   ......, son of Joshua & Elizabeth BARSTOW

November 13 ......, child of David and ...... HOUSE
November ......, child of Daniel and Ruth ROGERS
November ......, child of John and ...... BRAY
November 24 ......, child of James & Rachel ROGERS
December 7 John, son of David & Deborah STOCKBRIDGE
December 14 Caroline, daughter of Thomas & Elizabeth WILKS
December Content, daughter of Gideon & ...... RAMSDALE
1742. April Thankful, daughter of Joseph and Mary CURTIS
April ...... TAMPLIN
May Cornelius, son of Caleb and Ruth TURNER
May Hannah, daughter of Thomas & Sarah CURTIS
May Job, son of Amos & Patience SYLVESTER
June 16 Seth, son of Samuel & Margaret BARSTOW
June 20 ......, son of Thomas & Ann JOSSELYN

January 18, 1753: was born Edmund Sylvester the son of Edmund SYLVESTER and his wife Elizabeth

November 11, 1754: was born Elizabeth Sylvester, daughter of Edmund and Elizabeth SYLVESTER

Births of the Children of Benjamin BASS & Mercy his wife.

Mercy BASS, born September 14, 1766
Benjamin Bass, born June 26, 1768
Cindrilla Bass, born December 30, 1770
Huldah Bass, born May 16, 1773

Aldin Bass, born January 31, 1776
Sarah Bass, born December 14, 1778
Elisha Bass, born July 23, 1781
Mary G. Bass, born August 18, 1784

1805. July 22 Fanny, daughter of Samuel & Abigail STETSON
1809. January 1 Zilpha, daughter of Samuel & Abigail STETSON
1810. October 31 Reuben, son of Samuel & Abigail STETSON
1811. January 27 Horace Tower, son of Samuel & Rusha EELLS
1813. February 6 Henry Blanchard, son of Samuel & Rusha EELLS
July 26 Abigail, daughter of Samuel & Abigail STETSON

1815. January 15 John, son of Samuel & Abigail STETSON
June 7 William Witherell, son of Samuel & Rusha EELLS

1816. September 17 Mary, daughter of Samuel & Abigail STETSON

1818. January 4 Nancy, daughter of Samuel & Rusha EELLS
June 1 Samuel, son of Samuel & Abigail STETSON
November 8 Elizabeth Jane, daughter of Samuel & Rusha EELLS

1819. January   Ruth Bailey, daughter of Lebbeus & Lydia STOCKBRIDGE

SECOND MEETING-HOUSE OF THE FIRST CONGREGATIONAL CHURCH AT HANOVER,
ERECTED A. D. 1765, ON THE PRESENT SITE.

CHAPTER VI.

BAPTISMS.

1728–1866

[*For other Baptisms see Chapter III.*]

1728-9. March 23 Reuben, the son of William & Margaret CURTIS
Sarah, daughter of Joshua & Rebecca STAPLES
1729. April 13 Persis, daughter of Joseph & Lydia HOUSE
April 27 Benjamin HANMER (adult) and
John STUDLEY, adult
June 8 Mary, daughter of Ezekiel and Baths'a TURNER
and
Elizabeth, daughter of Amasa & ......TURNER
August 10 MR. EELS, baptized Lillis and Desire, daughters of Benja. and Lillis STETSON
August 31 Mary, daughter of Joseph & Mary CURTIS
September 7 Mary, daughter of John and Mary JUSTICE
Rebecca Mann, daughter of Benjamin & Martha MANN
September 21 Elizabeth, daughter of John & Elizabeth BAILEY
October 5 Priscilla, daughter of Samuel & Lydia BARSTOW
1729-30. January 4 Eunice Buck, daughter of Isaac & Mary BUCK
Feby 15 Ruth, daughter of John and Sarah LAMBERT

Feby 22 Sarah JONAS, an adult *molatto* after a public confession of the sin of fornication
March 8 Nathanael, son of Elijah and Elizabeth CUSHING
        Samuel, son of Samuel and ...... STAPLES
        Ezekiel SPRAGUE, his master, James Tory, publickly promising to take care he should have a religious education.
March 15 Thomas, son of Amos and Elizabeth SYLVESTER
April 26 Windsor, son of Sarah JONAS a *black*, his master, John BAILY promising to give him a religious education.
May 10 Richard, son of Richard and Jemimah HILL, they making a publick confession of their violation of ye * * * commandment.
June 14 Job, son of Job and Thankful OTIS
August 2 Sarah, daughter of Joseph & Lydia HOUSE
August 9 Thomas, son of Ezekiel & Martha PALMER
August 16 Mehetabel, daughter of Isaac & ...... HATCH
October 4 Rachel, daughter of Benjamin & Hannah CURTIS
November 8 Mary BASS, the Pastor's daughter, baptized by the REVD MR. LEWIS of Pembroke
December 13 Elizabeth, daughter of Thomas & Elizabeth WILKS, baptized by the REVD MR. ALLEN late of Bridgewater
1730-31. January 3 Jonathan, son of Joseph & Mary PERRY, by MR. EELES
January 10 Sarah, wife of Benjamin BARSTOW and George their son
January 24 John, son of John and Elizabeth BAILEY
February 28 Benjamin, son of Benjamin & Lillis STETSON
eodem die Mary, daughter of Joseph & Patience CORNISH
April 4 Sarah, daughter of Benjamin and Martha MANN
        and
        Desire, daughter of Ezekiel and Tabitha VINAL
April 25 Abner, son of Josiah and Sarah CURTIS
May 16 Anna LAMBERT, an aged woman
June 6 Mary, wife of Joseph RAMSDALE, and Mary their daughter
July 4 Deborah, daughter of Ezekiel & Bathshua TURNER
August 29 Matthew, son of Matthew & Hannah STETSON
September 12 Sarah, daughter of John & Elizabeth STUDLEY
September 26 Joseph, son of Joseph and Mary CURTIS, by MR. EELS
October 10 Deborah, daughter of Solomon & Deborah BATES

October 31   Nehemiah, son of John & Naomi WARREN
December 19   Lemuel, son of William & Margaret CURTIS
eodem die   Rebeckah, daughter of Josiah CURTIS
1731-32. February 20   Hannah, daughter of Isaac and Mary BUCK
eodem die   Elizabeth, daughter of Mary BUNTING, a single woman who made a publick confession of her sin of * * * *
March 12   Joseph, son of Elijah and Elizabeth CUSHING
March 26   Jane, daughter of John & Elizabeth BAILY
March 26   Mercy, daughter of Job and Thankful OTIS
July 16   Avis, daughter of Joseph & Mary RAMSDALE
August 6   Mary, daughter of Benjamin & Hannah CURTIS
August 27   Joseph, son of Benjamin & Martha MANN
eodem die   Hannah, daughter of Isaac & ...... HATCH
September 17   Ruth, daughter of Joseph & Lydia HOUSE
October 1   Caleb, son of John and Sarah LAMBERT
October 15   Susanna, daughter of Samuel & Margaret BARSTOW
November 5   Ruth, daughter of Thomas & Faith ROSE
1732-33. March 18   Ann and Susanna, twin daughters of Thomas & Elizabeth WILKS
March 25   Job, son of Benjamin & Lillis STETSON
April 1   Thomas, son of Benjamin & Sarah BARSTOW
June 29   Isaac, son of Isaac & Deborah LAMBERT
August 5   Lincoln, son of Matthew & Hannah STETSON
September 23   Joshua, son of Joseph and Mary CURTIS
September 30   Thomas, son of Thomas & Ann JOSSELYN
eodem die   David, son of Joseph and Mary PERRY
December 23   Lemuel, son of Job and Thankful OTIS
1733-34. January 6   Thankful, son of Benjamin & Martha MANN
February 24   Joseph, son of Joseph & Abigail HOUSE
March 24   Stephen, son of Thomas & Hannah STOCKBRIDGE of Scituate

and

Elizabeth, daughter of Benjamin and Mary BASS   } By Mr. Eels of Scituate.

April **   James, son of Benjamin and Sarah BARSTOW
May 12   Mary, daughter of Elijah & Elizabeth CUSHING
May 19   Betty, daughter of John & Elizabeth STUDLEY

June 2   Amos, son of Amos & Patience SYLVESTER
June 9   Sarah, daughter of Richard & Sarah BAKER, her mother owning the covenant &c.
July 28   Desire, daughter of Thomas and Faith ROSE
August 4   Samuel, son of Samuel and Margaret BARSTOW
August 25   Seth, son of Josiah and Sarah CURTIS
September 8   Priscilla, daughter of Joseph & Mary RAMSDALE
October 13   Stevens, son of Isaac and Sarah HATCH
October 20   Jerusha, daughter of Solomon & Deborah BATES
October 27   Sarah, daughter of Deacon Isaac BUCK & Mary his wife
November 24   Mary, wife of Samuel WHITTEN of Hingham (and daughter of Batchelor WING of Hanover) and Joanna, a daughter after a publick confession by said Whitten and his wife of ye violation of ye * * * commandment.

1734-35.   January 12   Were baptized four persons, viz.:
Mary, the wife of Joshua STAPLES,
Joshua, the son of Joshua STAPLES,
Mehetabel, daughter of William and Margaret CURTIS,
Betty, daughter of Ezekiel & Martha PALMER.

March 30   Zerviah, daughter of Uriah & Ruth Lambert, the mother having made a public confession of her violation of the * * * commandment.
April 6   Seth STETSON and his children Jeremiah & Elizabeth
April 20   Bethiah, the wife of and Nehemiah, the son of David CURTIS
May 11   John, son of Thomas & Ann JOSSELYN
June 1   Betty, daughter of John & Sarah LAMBERT
June 8   Ruth, daughter of Benjamin & Martha MANN
eodem die   John, son of Thomas & Elizabeth WILKS
June 15   Lydia, daughter of Robert & Margaret YOUNG; her mother having made a public confession of her violation of the * * * commandment.
July 13   Seth, son of Seth and Elizabeth STETSON
Ezekiel, son of David and Bethiah CURTIS
Olive, daughter of Timothy and Sarah BAILEY
July 27   Hannah, daughter of Matthew & Hannah STETSON
August 24   Abigail, wife of Deacon James HATCH
August 31   Experience, daughter of Joseph & Mary CURTIS

Septbr 14 Betty, wife of Isaac STETSON
October 5 Samuel, son of Nathan and Lydia BOURN
October 12 Deborah, daughter of Joseph & Patience CORNISH
October 26 Huldah, daughter of Samuel & Deborah HOUSE
November 9 Rhoda, daughter of Joseph & Abigail HOUSE
1735-36. January 18 Deborah, daughter of Isaac & Deborah LAMBERT
February 1 Susanna, daughter of Benjamin & Lillis STETSON
February 8 Sarah, daughter of Joseph and Sarah SHELDON
February 15 Deborah, daughter of John and Ann HOUSE
February 22 Remember, daughter of Nathan & Lydia BOURN
April 4 Jacob, son of Benjamin and Sarah BARSTOW
May 23 William, son of Joseph & Mary PERRY
May 30 Gideon, son of John & Elizabeth STUDLEY, and James, son of Robert and Margaret YOUNG
June 6 Betty, daughter of Elijah & Elizabeth CUSHING
July 25 Hannah, daughter of Thomas and Faith ROSE
August 17 Job, son of Josiah and Sarah CURTIS, in private
August 22 Mary, daughter of Samuel and Mary WHITTEN
October 3 Ann, daughter of Thomas & Ann JOSSELYN
November 7 Joshua, son of Joshua and ...... TURNER, likewise Thomas, son of Joseph & Mary RAMSDALE
1736-37. March 13 Sarah, daughter of Gideon & ...... RAMSDALE
March 20 Lydia, daughter of Samuel & Margaret BARSTOW
                                     by MR. EELS of Scituate
April 24 Seth, son of John and Ann HOUSE, likewise William, son of William & Mary SYLVESTER
May 22 Sarah, daughter of Thomas & Elizabeth WILKS
June 19 Ruth Clay, daughter of Uriah & Ruth LAMBERT, and Ruth, daughter of Ezekiel and Ruth TURNER
June 26 Timothy, son of Timothy and Sarah BAILEY
July 3 Hannah, daughter of John and Sarah LAMBERT
July 24 Paul, son of David & Bethiah CURTIS
August 14 Mary, daughter of Benjamin & Martha MANN
August 28 Joseph, son of David & Deborah STOCKBRIDGE
September 18 Anna, daughter of Isaac & Deborah LAMBERT
October 16 Joshua, son of Richard & Lydia PROUTY

October 23   Amos, son of Amos and Jemimah BATES
November 8   Abia, daughter of John and Abia EELS
November 13   Deborah, daughter of Matthew & Hannah STETSON
December 4   Thomas, son of Seth and Elizabeth STETSON
1737-38.   January 17   Thomas, son of Clement & Agatha BATES
   March 5   Mary, daughter of Nathan & Lydia BOURN
April 2   Elisha, son of Samuel and Deborah HOUSE
April 9   Gideon, son of Benjamin and Sarah BARSTOW
June 25   Jerusha, daughter of Benjamin & Abigail SYLVESTER
July 2   Clement, James & Seth, sons of Clement & Agatha BATES
   Samuel, son of Richard and Sarah BAKER
July 23   Rebecca, daughter of Joseph & Mary PERRY and
Lette, daughter of Robert & Margaret YOUNG
July 30   Joshua & Gideon, sons of Joshua & Lydia STUDLEY and
Thomas, son of Thomas & Faith ROSE
August 13   Abner, son of Amos & Patience SYLVESTER
August 20   Nathanael, son of Benjamin & Lillis STETSON
October 8   Jabez, son of John and Elizabeth STUDLEY, likewise
   Sarah, daughter of Ezekiel & Martha PALMER &
   John, son of Gideon & ...... RAMSDALE
October 15   Deborah, daughter of Elijah & Elizabeth CUSHING
November 5   Relief, daughter of Benjamin & Hannah CURTIS
December 31   Mehetabel, daughter of Ebenezer & Mehetabel CROSBY
1738-39.   March 4   Margaret, daughter of Samuel & Margaret
   BARSTOW
April 8   Caleb, son of Joseph & Abigail HOUSE and
Sarah, daughter of Timothy and Sarah BAILEY
April 22   Bathshua, daughter of Ezekiel & Ruth TURNER
April 29   Betty, daughter of David & Deborah STOCKBRIDGE   } By Mr. Brown of Abbington
   Joseph, son of Joseph & Mary RAMSDALE
June 17   Samuel, son of Samuel & ...... PERRY and
Ruth, daughter of Joseph & Patience CORNISH and
Clement BATES, an adult, after a confession of his violation of the * * * commandment.
June 24   Michael, son of David & Bethiah CURTIS
July 1   James, son of James & Mary TOREY
July 8   Seth, son of John & Elizabeth BAILEY and

Leonard, son of Richard & Jemimah HILL
July 15 Stephen, son of Joseph & Mary CURTIS
July 22 Ruth, daughter of Oliver & Agatha WINSLOW
September 2 Betty, daughter of John & Mary CURTIS
September 30 Benjamin, son of Benjamin & Abigail SYLVESTER
October 7 Lydia, daughter of Thomas & Elizabeth WILKS

1739-40. January 13 Mary, daughter of Samuel & Hannah EELS
 March 18 Grace, daughter of Benjamin & Lillis STETSON
April 13 Charity, daughter of Daniel & Ruth ROGERS, likewise Benjamin, son of Matthew & Hannah STETSON, and Lydia, daughter of Joshua & Lydia STUDLEY
April 20 Jenny, wife of William GUILFORD, Junior & Paul their son
 Thomas, son of Clement & Agatha BATES
April 28 Deborah, daughter of Samuel & Deborah HOUSE
May 4 Charles, son of Samuel & Margaret BARSTOW
July 6 Thomas, son of Isaac & Deborah LAMBERT
July 27 Ezekiel, son of Ezekiel & Ruth TURNER
August 3 Mercy, daughter of Ebenezer & Mehetabel CROSBY
August 24 Ezra, son of Amasa & ...... TURNER
Sept. 14 George, son of Samuel and ...... PERRY, also Isaac, son of Micah and Mary STOCKBRIDGE
Sept. 28 Elizabeth, daughter of Thomas & Faith ROSE
October 19 Lucinda, daughter of Caleb & Ruth TURNER
November 23 Anna, wife of John BRAY & Elizabeth their daughter

1740-41. January 18 Jonathan, son of Othniel & Mary PRATT
 March 29 Avis, daughter of Joseph & Mary RAMSDALE
April 5 Stockbridge, son of Deacon Thomas & Ann JOSSELYN
 Timothy, son of James TORY, Junior & Mary his wife
April 19 Bradbury, daughter of Samuel & Hannah EELS
May 10 Hannah, wife and Nathanael, son of Nathanael ROBBINS likewise Benoni STUDLEY, Junior
June 7 Elijah, son of Jesse and Sarah CURTIS and Benjamin, son of Benjamin and Mary BASS
June 14 Samuel, son of Samuel & Deborah HOUSE
June 21 Chandler, son of Joseph and ...... PERRY
June 28 Abigail, daughter of Joshua & Lydia STUDLEY; by MR. D. LEWIS

July 5   Sarah, daughter of Benjamin & Sarah BARSTOW and Hannah, daughter of Ezekiel & Martha PALMER
July 12   Rebecca. daughter of John & Elizabeth STUDLEY
July 19   Amos, son of Ezekiel & Ruth TURNER
July 26   Thomas, son of Seth & Elizabeth STETSON
August 2   Mary, daughter of John & Sarah LAMBERT
August 21   Naomi, daughter of Abner and Mary TURNER
August 30   Prince, son of Abigail & ...... STETSON
September 21   Mary, daughter of Joseph & Sarah SHELDON
October 11   Nathanael, son of Oliver & Agatha WINSLOW
November 29   Abigail, daughter of Joseph and Abigail HOUSE
December 13   John, son of David & Deborah STOCKBRIDGE
December 20   Caroline, daughter of Thomas & Elizabeth WILKS
December 27   Content, daughter of Gideon & ...... RAMSDALE
1741-42.   January 3   John, son of John CURTISS, Junior and Mary his wife
April 4   Hannah, daughter of Henry and Hannah MUNROE
April 10   Abel, son of Jesse and Sarah CURTISS
April 18   Sarah, daughter of Ebenezer & Mehetabel CROSBY also Abigail, daughter of Benjamin & Abigail SYLVESTER
May 16   Thankful, daughter of Joseph and Mary CURTIS also David, son of David & Bethiah CURTISS and
Cornelius, son of Caleb & Ruth TURNER
May 30   Thomas, Rhoda & Mark, children of Jeremiah & Deborah ROGERS who previously made a publick confession of their violation of the * * * commandment.
June 13   Molly, daughter of Isaac & ...... STETSON
June 20   Job, son of Amos & Patience SYLVESTER also Seth, son of Samuel & Margaret BARSTOW
June 27   Hannah, daughter of Thomas & Sarah CURTISS
August 15   At Pembr. Waltheia, daughter of Moses BASSET of Kingston
September 26   Joshua, son of Joshua & Lydia STUDLEY also TITUS "*my negro boy.*"
October 3   Joseph, son of Joshua & Elizabeth BARSTOW, they making a public confession of their violation of the * * * commandment
October 10   Joseph, son of Joseph & Patience CORNISH also Rachel, wife of Stephen TOREY with Stephen & Ruth their children:

the parents making confession of their violation of the * * * commandment.

October 17   Hannah FAIRFIELD, a young woman brought up by Mr. James HOUSE also
Abner, son of Abner & Mary TURNER and
Susanna, daughter of Isaac & Deborah LAMBERT
October 24   Rhoda, daughter of Samuel & ...... PERRY and
Timothy, son of Nathanael & Hannah ROBBINS
October 31   Ruth, daughter of Daniel & Ruth ROGERS
November 7   Joshua, son of Clement & Agatha BATES
1743.   March 27   Samuel, son of John & Sarah LAMBERT
       March 28   Ephraim, son of Peleg & Mercy STETSON : the mother entering into covenant with God and confessing her breach of the * * * commandment.
April 3   Elizabeth, daughter of Ezekiel & Ruth TURNER
April 17   Samuel, son of Benjamin and Lillis STETSON
April 24   Ezra, son of Benjamin & Martha MAN also
Othniel, son of Othniel & Mary PRATT
May 15   Caleb Rogers and Mary the daughter of Caleb & Mary ROGERS
May 22   Deborah, daughter of Saml & Deborah HOUSE
June 26   Mary, daughter of Joshua & Elizabeth BARSTOW
July 3   Joseph, son of Amasa & ...... TURNER
July 10   Joseph, son of Joseph & Mary RAMSDALE,
July 17   Peleg STETSON after a confession of the sin of * * * * ; also Isaac, son and Mercy, daughter of Peleg & Mercy STETSON, also Ezra, son of Benjamin and Naomi CURTISS, who made confession of the sin of * * * *
July 31   Deborah, daughter of Caleb & Hannah RANDALL
August 7   Ruth, daughter of David & Bethiah CURTISS
September 11   John, son of John & Rebecca HOUSE; they making a public confession of their violation of the * * * commandment.
September 25   Thomas, son of John & Sibll TILDEN
October 16   Michael, son of William & Jane GILLFORD
November 20   Timothy, son of Thomas & Faith ROSE
December 18   Sarah, daughter of Benja. & Abigail SYLVESTER
1743-44.   January 8   Hannah, daughter of Jeremiah & Deborah ROGERS

February 5   John, son of Oliver & Agatha WINSLOW
April 1   Elisha, son of James TOREY, Junior and Mary his wife
April 15   Abigail, daughter of Ezekiel & Ruth TURNER, and
Ruth, daughter of Thomas & Ann JOSSELYN
May 13   Gideon, son of Gideon & ...... RAMSDALE
Stephen, son of Benjamin CURTISS & Naomi his wife
Deborah, daughter of Thomas & Sarah CURTISS
May 20   Jesse, son of Jesse & Sarah CURTIS
May 27   Lydia, daughter of Edmund & Molly SPEAR
Henry & Mary, children of John & Ann BRAY
June 10   Samuel, son of Seth and Elizabeth STETSON
June 17   Ephraim, son of Peleg & Mercy STETSON
July 1   Daniel, son of Samuel and Margaret BARSTOW
July 8   Isaac, son of Elijah & Elizabeth CUSHING &
Zaccheus, son of John & Sarah LAMBERT
August 12   Gershom, son of Joseph & Abigail HOUSE
October 2   Abel, son of David & Silence HOUSE, his master Samuel CURTISS promising to give him a religious education ; also Susanna, daughter of David & Silence HOUSE, her master Nathanael STETSON promising to give her a religious education.
October 27   Baily, son of James & Rachel ROGERS, who died within a few hours after he was born.
1744-45.   January 13   Joanna, daughter of Joshua & Lydia STUD-
LEY at ye same time
Hannah, daughter of Nathanael & Hannah ROBBINS
March 31   Jerusha, daughter of Benjamin & Abigail SYLVESTER
April 7   Margaret, daughter of Abijah STETSON also
Gamaliel, son of Clement & Agatha BATES
Alice, daughter of Caleb & Mary ROGERS
April 14   Abner, son of John and Rebecca HOUSE, and ye same time Ruth, daughter of Nathanael and ...... GILL
April 21   James, son of Joshua & Elizabeth BARSTOW, and David, son of Stephen & Rachel TORREY and
Mary, daughter of Abner & Mary TURNER
June 2   Lettice, ... of Richard and Jemimah HILL
June 16   Susanna, daughter of Bezaleel & ...... CURTISS
July 28   James, son of Samuel & Deborah HOUSE
August 4   Delight, daughter of Timothy and Hannah BAILEY

August 27   Japheth, son of Joseph & Mary RAMSDALE
September 8   Peleg, son of Isaac and Thankful COLLIMORE
November 24   Ebenezer, son of Bezaleel and ...... CURTISS
December 1   Thomas, son of Thomas & Elizabeth TOREY
December 8   Sarah, daughter of Benjamin and Ruth STORER
December 29   Sarah, daughter of Thomas & Elizabeth WILKS
1745-46.   February 23   Elijah, son of James & Mary TOREY
March 2   Bathshua, daughter of Joshua and Elizabeth BARSTOW also
Elizabeth, wife of Joshua SIMMONS and Joshua their son
March 7   Sarah, daughter of Caleb & ...... RANDALL
March 12   Mary, daughter of Michael & Mary SYLVESTER
March 23   Elijah, son of Abijah & ...... STETSON
March 30   Joshua, son of Joshua & Alice RIPLEY
April 20   Benjamin, son of Othniel & Mary PRATT also
Deborah, daughter of Jesse and Sarah CURTISS and
James, the * * * * * son of Martha DAMMON who made confession of the sin of * * * *
May 11   Ann, daughter of Joshua and Lydia STUDLEY
May 18   David, son of Gideon & Sarah RAMSDALE
June 8   Elizabeth, daughter of Joshua and Elizabeth SIMMONS
June 22   Margaret, daughter of Deacon Samuel & Margaret BARSTOW also Edmund, son of Edmund & Mary SPEAR
September 21   Ann, daughter of John and Rebecca HOUSE
October 5   Caleb, son of Caleb & Ruth TURNER
November 3   Deborah, daughter of Ebenezer & Joanna WRIGHT
November 9   Hannah, wife of Robert STETSON
November 23   James Clark, also Ruth, Mary, Reuben & Hannah, children of said James CLARK & Margaret his wife
November 30   Sarah, daughter of Job and ...... TILDEN
1746-47.   March 1   Benjamin, son of Benjamin & Naomi CURTISS the same day
Sarah, daughter of Thomas & Sarah CURTISS
March 8   Margaret & Katharine FITZGERALD, daughters of Richard & Margaret Fitzgerald, their mother (a widow) making her publick confession of her violation of the * * * commandment.
March 15   Reuben, son of Robert & Hannah STETSON
March 29   Isaac, son of Benjamin & Abigail SYLVESTER

April 26   Anna, daughter of Taylor & ...... BROOKS
May 24   Nathanael, son of Thomas & Elizabeth TORREY
June 7   Joseph, son of Joseph & Patience CORNISH; also
Isaac, son of Isaac & Deborah LAMBERT and
Levi, son of Peleg & Mercy STETSON
July 12   Grace & Sarah, daughters of Adam & Grace PROUTY
August 23   David, son of David & Elizabeth JENKINS
August 30   James, son of Simeon and ...... CURTISS
September 6   Susanna, the daughter & Amasa, the son of Amasa and ...... TURNER and ye same day
James, son of James and Margaret CLARK
September 27   Abigail, daughter of Joshua & Elizabeth BARSTOW
October 4   Paul, son of Clement & Agatha BATES
October 18   Sarah, daughter of Samuel and Deborah HOUSE
November 1   Sarah, daughter of John & Sarah LAMBERT
November 8   Abigail, daughter of Joseph & Alice NEAL
1747-48.   January 10   Luther, son of Job and Mary STETSON
April 3   Hezekiah HOLMES, apprentice to Mr. Melatiah DILLINGHAM
April 10   Gershom, son of Jesse & Sarah CURTISS
April 17   Lillis, daughter of Joshua & Lillis STETSON
April 24   John, son of Nathanael & ...... GILL
May 1   *At the new meeting-house in Pembroke*, Content, daughter of Nicolas & Content WEBSTER
May 8   Lydia, daughter of Joshua & Lydia STUDLEY, also
Deborah, daughter of Othniel & Mary PRATT and
Caleb, son of Caleb & Mary ROGERS
May 15   Olive, daughter of Timothy and Hannah BAILEY
May 18   Caleb, son of Caleb and ...... CHURCH
May 22   Anna, daughter of William & Martha CURTISS; likewise
John, son of Jeremiah and Deborah ROGERS
May 29   Grace, daughter of Samuel and Margaret BARSTOW
June 26   Samuel, son of Richard & Jemimah HILL
July 17   Briton, a *negro* infant born in the house of Mr. Edward JENKINS of Scituate, and given to Mr. John STUDLEY, of Hanover, soon after its birth.
August 7   Betty, daughter of Job and ...... TILDEN also
Mary, daughter of Benjamin SYLVESTER, Jr. & Abigail his wife

September 18 Margaret, relict and Margaret, daughter of John WOODWORTH, Junior, who died at Cape Breton : and the same day Hannah, daughter of Robert STETSON & his wife
October 2 Mary, daughter of Bezaleel CURTISS & his wife
November 6 Elizabeth, daughter of Thomas & Elizabeth WILKS
November 20 Joshua, son of Joshua & ...... PALMER
November 27 Betty, daughter of Nathanael & Hannah ROBBINS
December 11 Ruth, daughter of Caleb TURNER, Jr. & his wife Ruth
1748-49. January 22 Seth, son of James and Margaret CLARK
February 5 William, son of William CURTISS, Junr & Martha his wife
April 9 John & Lucy Bray, children of John & Anna BRAY
April 16 Betty, daughter of Peleg and Mercy STETSON and Nathanael, son of Benjamin CURTISS, Jr. & Naomi, his wife
April 23 were baptized the following persons
Mary and Samuel, children of Joshua STAPLES and Mary his wife; also
Betty and Sage, children of Joshua STAPLES & his wife Elizabeth
May 7 Lydia, daughter of Alice Neal, relict of Joseph NEAL, *who was killed ye fall preceeding by a loaden cart going over him.*
May 14 were baptized the following persons :
Isaiah, son of David & Elizabeth JENKINS
Lydia, daughter of Joshua and Elizabeth SIMMONS
Warren, son (I suppose) of Thomas and Elizabeth TORREY
July 2 Joshua, son of Joshua & Elizabeth BARSTOW
September 3 Keziah, daughter of Dr. Jeremiah HALL & his wife Elizabeth
1749-50. March 4 Caleb, son of Nathanael & Abigail GILL & ye same day
Asenath, daughter of Simeon & Asenath CURTISS
April 1 Prince, son of Bezaleel and ...... CURTISS
Rachel, daughter of Stephen & Rachel TORREY and
Mary, daughter of Othniel & Mary PRATT
April 22 William, son of William & Mary WHITTEN
Sarah, daughter of Jesse & Sarah CURTISS
April 24 Ezra, son of Joseph & Jane PALMER of Scituate ; in private the child being near death and Mr. Eels ill.
April 29 Nabbe, daughter of Clement & Agatha BATES

May 6   Mary, daughter of Samuel & Deborah HOUSE
June 10   Thomas, son of Thomas & Sarah CURTISS
June 24   Desire, daughter of Adam and Grace PROUTY
July 1   Elizabeth, daughter of Ebenezer & Elizabeth CURTISS; also Sarah, daughter of Shubael and Mary MUNRO
July 22   John son of Joshua and Lydia STUDLEY
August 26   Lydia, daughter of Benjamin SYLVESTER, Junior & Abigail his wife, the day after Mr. Eels's sudden death.
September 9   Alexander, son of Caleb TURNER, Junior & his wife Ruth
September 16   Mica & Kezia, son and daughter of Isaiah & Kezia THOMAS
October 14   Jesse TORREY & ......, the children of the said Jesse Torrey & his wife ......, James, Ruth & Hannah Torrey
November 16   Calvin, son of Joshua & Elizabeth BARSTOW; and the same day
Mercy TOTO, an *Indian* woman and George Toto, her son, as also Rhoda Toto, her daughter; the mother making confession of her repeated violation of the 7th commandment.
1750-51.   January 20   Nathanael, son of Job and ...... TILDEN.
February 24   in Scituate, Nathanael, son of Zechariah DAMON, Junr and his wife Hannah Lenthal (EELLS before marriage) the daughter of the Reverend Mr. Nathanael EELLS late Pastor of ye South Chh. in Scituate, who died very suddenly about half a year before; vizt: August 25.
March 3   Elizabeth, daughter of Jeremiah HALL and Elizabeth his wife
March 17   Zilpah, daughter of Abijah & ...... STETSON
March 24   Thomas, son of Nathanael & Hannah ROBBINS
March 31   John, son of Jeremiah ROGERS and Deborah his wife
April 14   Thankful, daughter of John & Anna BRAY
April 21   Peleg, son of Peleg & Mercy STETSON, and
Miriam, daughter of Taylor & Miriam BROOKS
May 5   Deborah, daughter of Abner & Deborah CURTISS
May 12   Betty, daughter of Clement & Agatha BATES
May 19   Martha, daughter of David & Elizabeth JENKINS and Martha, daughter of William & Martha CURTISS
May 21   Deborah, daughter of William & Mary SYLVESTER of Scituate (in private, she being very sick)

June 2 Ebenezer, son of Joshua & Elizabeth SIMMONS
July 7 Mary, daughter of Robert & Hannah STETSON
August 1 Lettice, daughter of Joseph and (I think) Mary TOLMAN in private, she being sick, and so sick, that she died the next day.
August 4 Susie, the daughter of Isaac & Thankful COLLIMORE and the same day
Jenny, daughter of Joshua & Elizabeth STAPLES and
Deborah, daughter of Joshua & Lydia PALMER
August 11 Mehetabel, daughter of Elisha and Sarah CURTISS likewise Joshua, son of Joshua & E izabeth BRYANT
August 18 Elizabeth, daughter of Thomas & Elizabeth TORREY
September 22 Deborah, daughter of Joshua & Silence WHITTEN
September 29 Bethiah, daughter of Oliver & Bethiah WINSLOW, and Lillis, daughter of Isaac & Deborah LAMBERT
October 13 Timothy, son of Timothy and Hannah BAILY
November 10 Abigail, daughter of Benjamin MAN, Junior & his wife Abigail
December 1 William, son of Ebenezer and Elizabeth CURTISS and John, son of John BAILY, the third and Ruth his wife, who made confession of their violation of the * * * commandment.
1752. February 3 Desire, daughter of Caleb and Desire SYLVESTER
March 8 Rebecca, daughter of Joshua & Lydia STUDLEY
March 15 Ambrose Low, son of Nathanael JOSSELYN & his wife
April 12 Joseph, son of Richard and Jemimah HILL
April 26 Abigail, daughter of John and Sarah LAMBERT
May 10 Joseph, son Abiel COBB & wife
May 17 Adam, son of Adam & Grace PROUTY
June 7 Anna, daughter of Stephen and Rachel TORREY, also Ezekiel, son of Joshua & Elizabeth BARSTOW and
Susanna, daughter of Caleb and Mary ROGERS
June 14 Joshua, son of Joshua & Lillis STETSON
July 12 Deborah, daughter of Thomas and Ann JOSSELYN
July 26 Charles, son of Jesse & Sarah CURTISS
August 16 Abel, son of William & Martha CURTISS
October 15 Abel, son of William and Mary WHITTEN
October 29 Jeremiah, son of Jeremiah and Deborah ROGERS, also Luther, son of John BAILY, Junr and his wife Ruth

November 12   Abner, son of Abner & Deborah CURTISS
December 31   Deborah, daughter of Benjamin SYLVESTER, Junr and his wife Abigail
1753.   January 20   Nathanael, son of James & Margaret CLARK: in private, he being very sick.
March 25   Amos, son of Taylor & Miriam BROOKS
Jacob, son of Benjamin & Naomi CURTISS and
Edmund, son of Edmund & Elizabeth SYLVESTER
(?) Edmund, son Edmund & Elizabeth SYLVESTER
April 8   Job, son of Samuel & Deborah HOUSE
April 22   Lemuel, son of Lemuel & Ruth CURTISS
April 29   Betty, daughter of Clement and Agatha BATES
Ruth, daughter of Othniel & Mary PRATT
May 6   Simeon, son of James & Margaret CLARK
May 20   Barker, son of Caleb TURNER, Junior & Ruth his wife
Nathanael, son of Jesse and Mary TORREY
May 27   Abigail, daughter of Shubael & Mary MUNRO
June 3   Sarah, daughter of Job TILDEN & ...... his wife
July 22   Benjamin, son of Benjamin MANN, Junior, and his wife Abigail
August 12   Sarah, daughter of Thomas & Elizabeth TORREY
August 19   Laban, son of Peleg & Mercy STETSON
September 2   William, son of David & Jane STOCKBRIDGE also
Sarah, daughter of Nathanael JOSSELYN & his wife
September 9   Ebenezer, son of Joshua and Elizabeth SIMMONS
October 21   Noah, son of John & Anna BRAY
November 4   Abia, son of Abia and Sarah COBB
1754.   January 6   Experience, daughter of Bezaleel & Mary CURTISS; in private, she being very sick.
January 13   Lydia, daughter of Thomas & Sarah CURTISS
January 27   Philip, son of Thomas & Ann JOSSELYN
March 24   Josiah & Snow Randall sons of Caleb & Hannah RANDALL, also
Seth, son of Jeremiah & Deborah ROGERS
April 7   Bachelor, son of Robert & Hannah STETSON also
Nathanael, son of James and Margaret CLARK
April 14   Susanna, daughter of Simeon & Asenath CURTISS
April 21   Olive, daughter of Benjamin MANN, Jr. & his wife Abigail

April 28 Nabby, daughter of Joshua and Elizabeth STAPLES
May 5 Mary, wife of Jacob SYLVESTER,
Lucy, wife of Jeremiah STETSON,
Sarah, the daughter of Joseph & Mary BATES
Caleb, the son of Caleb & Desire SYLVESTER and
Lucy, daughter of Jeremiah & Lucy STETSON
June 30 Priscilla, daughter of Joshua & Lydia PALMER
July 7 Lillis, daughter of Nathanael & Abigail GILL also
Jael, daughter of William & Martha CURTISS
September 7 Were baptized four children of Benjamin WHITE and his wife ...... (the wife owning the covenant as we speak) vizt. Niah (meant perhaps Peninnah? Robert? Hannah and Benjamin, the father's name, who was not considered in the baptism of the children
October 13 Isaac, son of Adam and Grace PROUTY
Hannah, the wife of Benjamin STUDLEY & Eliab their son
Hannah, wife of Richard HILL, Junior & Nathanael their son
and Joseph, the son of Joseph & Abigail CURTISS
October 27 Richard BUKER, Junior, and Phœbe, daughter of said Richard Buker & Phœbe his wife
Hannah, daughter of Isaac HATCH, Junior & his wife Hannah
November 10 Mary, daughter of Joshua & Elizabeth SIMONS
1755. January 19 Obadiah, son of Benjamin and Abigail SYLVESTER
and the same day
Elizabeth (my) grandchild the daughter of Edmund and Elizabeth SYLVESTER
March 10 Betty, daughter of Samuel and Deborah HOUSE; in private being very sick within a few days after her birth.
March 16 Sarah, daughter of Thomas and Sarah BARSTOW
April 13 Experience, daughter of Bezaleel and Mary CURTIS
April 20 Jesse, son of Jesse and Mary TORREY
June 1 David, son of David and Jane STOCKBRIDGE
at the same time the two following children
Deborah, daughter of Jeremiah and Deborah ROGERS
Mary, daughter of Lemuel and ...... WHITTEN
June 23 Lucy, daughter of John and Anna BRAY
July 27 Jabez, son of Othniel and Mary PRATT

August 10   Abigail, daughter of Caleb & Hannah RANDAL
and the same day
Snow, son of Reuben and Mary CURTISS
August 31   Nathanael, son of Nathanael JOSSELYN and his wife Sarah
September 21   Clement, son of Clement & Agatha BATES
October 5   Lucy, daughter of Thomas and Elizabeth TORREY
October 19   Betty, daughter of Peleg STETSON and Mercy his wife
and
Cornelius, son of Benjamin WHITE and wife
October 26   Joseph, son of Nathanael and Hannah ROBBINS
November 9   Michal, daughter of Michael SYLVESTER and his wife Mary, who died near a fortnight before (she was the daughter of Capt. Thomas BARDEN) also Barden, a son of ye same parents and Michael, another son of the same parents, likewise Mary, a daughter and the youngest child of said parents.
and at the same time
Abigail, daughter & Hatherly, son of John and Elizabeth BARSTOW
November 30   Desire, daughter of Caleb and Desire SYLVESTER
December 14   Ezra, son of Benjamin and Abigail MANN
December 21   Ruth, daughter of Lemuel and Ruth CURTISS
December 28   Lucy Josselyn, daughter of Shubael & Mary MUNRO
1756.   January 11   Mercy BATES
and
Mary, daughter of Ebenezer WING and Mary his wife
March 21   Mary, daughter of William and Mary WHITTEN
May 2   Elizabeth, daughter of Joseph and Sage HOUSE
May 13   Joanna, daughter of Ebenezer and Mary WING; in private, she being very sick
Decemr 5   Caleb, the son of Robert STETSON & Hannah his wife
Decemr 12   Simeon, the son of Simeon CURTIS & Asenath his wife
Samuel, the son of Joshua SYMMONDS & Elizabeth his wife
Samuel, the son of Wm. CURTIS & Martha his wife
1757.   Jany 9   Rachel, the daughter of Jeremiah STETSON & Lucy his wife
Jany 16   Olive, the daughter of Edmund SYLVESTER & Elizabeth his wife
Faith, the daughter of Thomas CURTIS & Ruth his wife

Jany 23   John, the son of Abishai SOLE & Abigail his wife
March 13   Noah, the son of Joshua STAPLES & Elizabeth his wife
Seth, the son of Joseph CURTIS & Abigail his wife
March 27   Hannah, the daughter of Thos. RAMSDALE, deceased and Hannah his wife
April 10   Bezaleel, the son of Nath'l PALMER & Rachel his wife
April 17   Foster, the son of Joshua BARSTOW & his wife Elizabeth
May 22   Thomas, the son of Thos. BARSTOW & his wife Sarah
May 29   Francis, the son of Nath'l JOSSELYN & his wife Sarah
Mary, the daughter of Jesse TORREY & Sarah his wife
Joseph, the son of Stephen TORREY, Jur & Sarah his wife
June 5   Mercy, the daughter of Joseph RAMSDALE & Mercy his wife
Benj. & Abner, 'the sons of Benj. STUDLEY & Hannah his wife
June 12   Robert, the son of Caleb TURNER & Ruth his wife
Elisha, the son of Othniel PRATT and Mary his wife
Samuel, the son of Lemuel WHITTEN & his wife
June 19   Thankfull, the daughter of Jno. BRAY & Anna his wife
July 3   Job, the son of Job TILDEN & his wife
Mary & Sarah, the daughters of Isaac HATCH, Jr. & Hannah his wife
July 30   Marlbry & Nabby, the children of Marlbry TURNER & Mary his wife
August 14   Joel, the son of Benj. SYLVESTER, Jur & Abigail his wife
August 28   Luther, the son of Nath'l ROBBINS & Hannah his wife
Sepr 4   Thomas, a boy that lives with Mr. Thos. WILKS
Luther, son of Stephen TORREY, Jr. & Sarah his wife
Sepr 18   Levi, the son of Benj. MAN, Jur & Abigail his wife
Oct.   Betty, the daughter of Bezaleel CURTIS & his wife
Novr 13   Amos, the son of Jesse CURTIS & his wife
1758.   April 2   Nath'el, the son of David HOUSE, Jr. & Rhoda his wife
April 30   Hannah, the daughter of Isaac BUCK & Mary his wife
May 7th   Mary, the daughter of Shubael MUNRO & Mary his wife
Joseph, the son of Joseph HOUSE, Jr. & Sage his wife
May 14   Avis, the daughter of Wm. WHITTEN & Mary his wife
June 4   Sarah & Ruth, the daughters of Sarah STAPLES
June 18   Henchman, the son of Caleb SYLVESTER & Desire his wife
July 9   Hannah, the daughter of Othniel PRATT & Mary his wife
July 30   Margaret, the daughter of Wm. CURTIS & Martha his wife

July 30   Samuel, the son of Samuel BARSTOW. Jr, & Huldah his wife
Amos, the son of Amos SYLVESTER, Jr. and Desire his wife
Octor 1   Waterman, the son of Joseph JOSSELYN, Junr & Mercy his wife
Daniel, Lydia, Calvin & Car, the chiidren of Daniel GARDNER and Alice his wife
Octor 22   Job, the son of Samuel BARSTOW, Jr. and Huldah his wife
Novr 26   Amos WRIGHT
Amos, Debbe, Benjamin, Charles, Samuel & Joseph, the children of Amos WRIGHT and Mary his wife
Decemr 3   Molly Gardner, the daughter of Edmund SYLVESTER and Elizabeth his wife
Decemr 3d   Mary, the daughter of Joseph RAMSDALE, Jr. and Mary his wife
1759.   March 4th   Eunice, the daughter of James CLARK & Margarett his wife
April 8th   Olive, the daughter of Lemuel CURTIS & his wife
April 15   Ruth, the daughter of Robert EELLS and Ruth his wife
May 20   Wm: the son of Jno. NICHOLSON & Lydia his wife
Joshua, the son of David HOUSE, Jr. and Rhoda his wife
June 4   Thankfull, the daughter of Lemuel WHITTEN & his wife
July 8   Huldah, the daughter of Isaac HATCH, Jr. and Hannah his wife
Ruth, the daughter of Thomas CURTIS and Ruth his wife
July 15   Joshua, the son of Benjn MAN, Jr. and Abigail his wife
August 26   Elizabeth, the daughr of Joshua STAPLES and Elizabeth his wife
Lydia, the daughter of Joseph RAMSDALE & Mercy his wife
Elisha, the son of Joshua SYMMONDS & Elizabeth his wife
Cloe, the daughter of Nath'el JOSSELYN & Sarah his wife
Sepr 23   Mercy, the daughter of Daniel GARDNER & Alice his wife
Nov. 4   Leah, the daughter of David JENKINS & Elizabeth his wife
Nov. 18   Abigail, the daughter of the Revd Saml BALDWIN & Hannah his wife
Barker, the son of Simeon CURTIS & Lucy his wife
1760.   Jany 27   Ruth, the daughter of Stephen TORREY, Jr. & Sarah his wife
Feby 24   Samuel, the son of Thomas TORREY & Elizabeth his wife

April 13 Gideon, the son of Joseph HOUSE, Jr. & Sage his wife
May 4 Betty, the daughter of Wm. WHITTEN & Mary his wife
June 1 Hannah, the daughter of Benj. STUDLEY & Hannah his wife
July 13 Alice, the daughter of David JENKINS & Elizabeth his wife
Eli, the son of Jeremiah STETSON & Lucy his wife
Joseph, the son of Samuel BARSTOW, Jr. & Huldah his wife
Orphan, the daughter of Jesse CURTIS, deceased & Sarah his widow
August 17 Rhoda, the daughter of Caleb HOUSE & Elizabeth his wife
August 31 Japhet, the son of Eliab STUDLEY and Elizabeth his wife
Sepr 19 Matthew, the son of Thos. SYLVESTER & Sarah his wife
Octor 5 Betty, daughter of Jesse TORREY & Mary his wife
Novr 16 Isaac, son of Isaac HATCH, Jr. & Hannah his wife
Thomas, son of Amos SYLVESTER & Desire his wife
Jabez Rose, son of Benj. BATES & Betty his wife
Novr 30 Bethiah, daughter of Edmund SYLVESTER & Elizabeth his wife

1761. Jany 19 Miranda, daughter of Joshua BAYLEY & Abigail his wife
Feby 15 Bathshua, daughter of Michael SYLVESTER & Ruth his wife
Mar. 22 Lillis, daughter of Lemuel CURTIS & his wife
Mar. 29 Lucinda, daughter of Lemuel WHITTEN & his wife
Apl. 12 Samuel, son of the Revd Samuel BALDWIN & Hannah Baldwin
Apl. 19 Betty, daughter of Robert EELLES & Ruth his wife
John, son of Joseph JOSSELYN, Jr. & Mercy his wife
Apl. 26 Abigail, daughter of Caleb HOUSE & Elizabeth his wife
May 10 Lucy, daughter of Simeon CURTIS & Lucy his wife
June 14 Elizabeth, daughter of Joshua BARSTOW & Elizabeth his wife
Shubael, son of Shubael MUNROE & Mary his wife
August 16 Bathshua, daughter of John HATCH & Bathshua his wife
August 30 Deborah, daughter of David STOCKBRIDGE & Jane his wife
Joshua, son of Joshua PALMER & his wife
Sept. 6 Joshua, son of Nath'l & Sarah JOSSELYN
   13 Rebecca, daughter of Thomas BARSTOW & his wife
   20 Isaac, son of George BARSTOW & his wife

Caleb Randall, son of Isaac HATCH, Jr. & Hannah his wife
Novr 29   Rhoda, daughter of David HOUSE, Jr. & Rhoda his wife
1762.   Jany 24   Paul, son of Bezaleel CURTIS & his wife
      Mar. 14   Cloe, daughter of Joshua STAPLES & Elizabeth his wife
April 25   Joseph, son of Nath'l ROBBINS & Hannah his wife
May 23   William, son of William WHITTEN & Mary Whitten
    30   Elisha. son of Waitstill TURNER & Mary Turner
June 6   Hannah, daughter of Thomas CURTIS & Ruth Curtis
Rachel, daughter of Ezekiel MERRITT & Rachel his wife
June 13   Nathanael, son of Thos. BARSTOW & Sarah his wife
Gideon, son of Gideon RANDALL & Rebecca his wife
July 4   Alice, daughter of Daniel & Alice GARDNER
July 25   Betty, daughter of Ezekiel MERRITT & Rachel his wife
Stephen, son of Joseph HOUSE, Jr. & Sage his wife
August 1   John, son of Jno. HATCH and Bathshua his wife
August 22   Nabby, daughter of Joshua BAYLEY & Abigail his wife
Sept. 12   Job, son of Jesse TORREY & his wife
Sept. 19   Deborah, daughter of Thomas ROSE, Jr. & Rhoda his wife
Oct. 31   Jeremiah, son of Jeremiah STETSON & Lucy his wife
Nov. 9   Olive, daughter of Samuel WITHERELL, Jr. and Ruth his wife in private by reason of the child being sick
Nov. 14   Martha, daughter of Robert STETSON and Hannah his wife
Benjamin, son of Benjn & Betty BATES
Nov. 21   Jacob, son of Amos SYLVESTER, Jr. & his wife Desire
Decemr 12   Seth, son of Seth BAYLEY & Lydia his wife; in private by reason of sickness
1763.   Jany 11   Ruth, daughter of Stevens and Ruth HATCH; in private by reason of the child being sick
Feby 27   Samuel, 2d, son of the Revd Samuel & Hannah BALDWIN
April 10   Samuel WITHERELL, Jr. baptized
Mary, daughter of Caleb HOUSE & his wife Elizabeth
April 17   Melzer, son of Marlbry & Mary TURNER; in private by reason of sickness
April 24   Reuben, son of Lemuel CURTIS & his wife
May 1   Anna, daughter of Gideon and Rosamond STUDLEY
June 12   George, son of Gideon STETSON & Elizabeth his wife; in private by reason of sickness

June 19   Asenath, daughter of Simeon & Lucy CURTIS
Lillis Turner & Grace, daughters of Caleb & Desire SYLVESTER
July 10   Alice, daughter of Daniel TEAGUE & his wife
Gamaliel, son of Joshua & Abigail BAYLEY
Zechariah, son of Zechariah & Lydia CURTIS
July 17   Sarah, daughter of Benjamin MAN, Jr. & Abigail his wife
July 31   David, son of David & Hannah JACOB
Huldah, daughter of Samuel BARSTOW, Jr. and Huldah
Augt 28   Huldah Copelin, daughter of Robert & Ruth EELLES
Hannah, daughter of Job & Hannah STETSON
Sept. 11   Lydia, daughter of Joshua & Elizabeth SYMMONDS
Sarah, Hannah Witherell, Mary Lenthell, daughters of Wm. Witherell EELLES & Sarah his wife
Octo. 2   Sarah, daughter of Amos & Sarah BERRY
Octor 16   Betty, daughter of Job and Betty YOUNG
Octor 23   Edmund, son of Edmund & Betty SYLVESTER
Lois, daughter of Stephen TORREY, Jr. and his wife
Debby, daughter of Joshua & Avis DWELLY
Samuel, Bezaleel, Benjamin, sons of Samuel & Priscilla EELLES
Novr 13   Christiana, daughter of Nath'el JOSSELYN & wife
Nov. 17   Priscilla, wife of Samuel EELLES in private by reason of sickness
1764.   Jany 15   John Reed, son of John & Sage JOSSELYN
          Feby 12   Joshua, son of David HOUSE, Jr. and Rhoda
April 8   Margaret, daughter of Seth & Lydia BAYLEY
April 15   Betty, daughter of Elisha and Betty CURTIS
Rebecca, daughter of Gideon & Rebecca RANDALL
May 6   Jemima, daughter of Robert and Hannah STETSON
May 13   Hannah Pratt, an adult person, daughter of Joshua PRATT
     20   Margaret, daughter of Lemuel & ...... WHITTEN
June 10   Bethiah, daughter of Daniel & Alice GARDNER
June 17   John Burdin, son of Thomas & Sarah BARSTOW
Ezekiel Turner, son of John & Bathshua HATCH
July 1   Joseph, son of William & Mary TORREY
July 8   Joseph, son of Caleb & Desire SYLVESTER
Grace, daughter of Wm. & Mary WHITTEN
August 5   Asenath, daughter of George & ...... BARSTOW
...... & Lucinda, children of Isaac and Hannah HATCH

August 25 ......, son of Joseph HOUSE, Jr. and Sage his wife
Ruth Howland, daughter of Luke STETSON
Joseph Dowse, son of Joseph & Mary RAMSDALE
Sepr 2 Mercy, daughter of Shubael & Mary MUNROE
Mary & James, children of Benj. STUDLEY & wife
Sept. 9 Nabby, daughter of Bezaleel CURTIS & his wife
Octor 6 Mary, daughter of Waitstill and Mary TURNER in private
    7 Zenos, son of Benj. & Hannah STUDLEY
   28 Susy Gill, son of Benj. MAN, Jr. & Abigail his wife
Nov. 18 Lemmy, son of Joshua & Avis DWELLY
   25 Sagy, daughter of John & Sage JOSSELYN
Decr 9 Thomas, son of Thos. ROSE, Jr. & Rhoda
1765. Feby 6 John, son of John & Thankfull STETSON
    March 10 John, son of Amos SYLVESTER, Jr. and his wife Desire
Philip, son of Samuel BARSTOW, Jr. & his wife Huldah
March 31 Priscilla, daughter of Wm. Withll & Sarah EELLES
May 12 ......, child of Joshua & Abigail BAYLEY
......, child of Samel WITHEREL, Jr. & Ruth
May 19 Joseph, son of Benj. & Betty BATES
   26 Deborah, daughter of Elisha & Orphan HOUSE
June 2 Isaac, son of Daniel TEAGUE & wife
   9 Job, son of Job & Betty YOUNG
  23 Deborah, daughter of Gershom & Deborah HOUSE
July 21 Hannah, daughter of the Revd Samuel & Hannah BALDWIN
   28 Christiana, daughter of Nathel JOSSELYN & wife
Sept. 1 Eliab, son of Jesse & Mary TORREY
   Joseph & Lydia Stetson, children of Marlbry & Mary TURNER
Oct. 13 Susanna, daughter of Job & Hannah STETSON
Decr 1 Belcher, son of Edmund & Betty SYLVESTER
Perez, son of David & Hannah JACOB
Decr 8 Anna Lenthell, daughter of Robert & Ruth EELLES
Seth, son of Seth & Lydia BAYLEY
1766. Jany 20 Dowty, son of Solomon & Aquilla BATES
   March 9 Sagy Randall, daughter of Joseph HOUSE, Jr. & Sage
March 29 Beulah, daughter of Lemuel WHITTEN & wife

March 30 Levi & Solomon Wheaton, sons of Solomon BATES, Jr. and Aquilla
April 29 William, son of Joshua & Elizabeth SYMMONDS
May 11 Abigail, daughter of John & Thankfull STETSON
    18 Orpah, daughter of Ruth CHAPMAN
June 8 Rebecca, daughter of Seth & Bathshua HOUSE
    15 Timothy CHURCH
    29 Becca, daughter of Seth STETSON, Jr. & Lucy
July 13 Amos, son of Amos & Sarah BERRY
    20 Bradbury, daughter of Benj. & Bradbury STETSON
    26 John, son of Job & Betty YOUNG
July 26 Car, son of Daniel & Alice GARNETT
August 3 Nabby, daughter of Benj. STUDLEY & wife
August 10 Sarah, daughter of Gideon & Rebecca RANDALL
Sarah, daughter of Gideon & Rosamond STUDLEY
August 24 Homer, son of Wm. & Mary WHITTEN
    31 Jenny Dowty, daughter of Thos. & Sarah BARSTOW
Sept. 21 Mercy, daughter of Benj. & Mercy BASS
Sarah, daughter of Gershom & Deborah HOUSE
Octo. 19 Robert, son of Michael & Ruth SYLVESTER
Martha, daughter of Elisha & Betty CURTIS
Octo. 26 Deborah, daughter of Othniel & Deborah PRATT
Nov. 30 Charles, son of Benj. MAN, Jr. & Abigail
Dec. 14 Cynthia Sylvester, daughter of John & Sage JOSSELYN
Joshua, son of Joshua & Avis DWELLY
Decem. 14 Hannah, daughter of Waitstill and Mary TURNER
Anna, daughter of Jno. CURTIS, Jr. and Anna
1767. February 8 Thomas, son of Stevens & Ruth HATCH
    April 12 Timothy, son of Timothy & Lydia ROSE
April 26 Lydia, daughter of Wm. Witherell & Sarah EELLES
May 3 Desire Rose, daughter of Amos SYLVESTER, Jr & Desire
Bela, son of Joshua & Abigail BAYLEY
Rhoda Rogers, daughter of Thomas ROSE, Jr. and Rhoda
May 10 Deborah, daughter of Seth STETSON, Jr. and Lucy
    24 Ezekiel & Rhoda Vinall, children of Ezekiel & Rachel MERRITT
May 30 Benjamin, son of Benjn and Bradbury STETSON
July 12 Elizabeth, daughr of Solomon and Elizabeth BRYANT

August 2   Mary, daughter of Simeon & Lucy CURTIS
August 16   Molly, daughter of Benj. and Betty BATES
      24   House, son of Samuel and Huldah BARSTOW
Sept. 27   Richmond, son of David & Hannah JACOB
Lydia, daughter of Zechariah and Lydia CURTIS
Oct. 4   Lydia, daughter of Elisha & Orphan HOUSE
Decemr 6   Robert and Nabby (twins) children of Robert and Ruth EELLES
1768.   January 3   Charlotte, daughter of John CURTIS, Jr. and Anna
January 10   Theophilus & Freelove WITHERELL and their children Deborah and Freelove
January 31   Christopher, son of Edmund & Betty SYLVESTER
March 13   Bathshua, daughter of Seth and Bathshua HOUSE
April 10   Lucinda, daughter of Michael and Ruth SYLVISTER
May 29   Timothy, son of Timothy & Elizabeth CHURCH
June 5   Molly Waterman, daughter of Samuel WAYFORD and wife
June 5   Othniel, son of Othniel & Deborah PRATT
June 12   Rosamond, daughter of Gideon and Rosamond STUDLEY
July 3   Betty, daughter of Daniel TEAGUE & wife
Laban, son of Daniel and Alice GARNETT
Benjamin, son of Benjamin and Mercy BASS
August 14   Jane, daughter of Job and Betty YOUNG
      21   Thankfull, daughter of John and Thankful STETSON
Sept. 4   Lucy Pratt, the wife of Jonathan PRATT
Sept. 18   Lucy & Jonathan, children of Jonathan and Lucy PRATT
Oct. 2   Molley, daughter of Thomas and Sarah BARSTOW
Thomas, son of Thomas ROSE, Jr. & Rhoda
Gershom, son of Gershom and Deborah HOUSE
Octo. 23   Ruth, daughter of John and Bathsheba HATCH
John WITHERELL and his children John, Hannah & Edward
Oct. 30   Molley, daughter of Marlbry & Mary TURNER
Levi, son of Joseph HOUSE, Jr. and Sage
Nov. 13   Perez, son of Benj. MAN, Jr. and Abigail
Decem. 4   William Witherell, son of Wm. Witherell & Sarah EELLES
Jedediah, son of Joshua & Avis DWELLY
Joseph, son of Joseph & Tamar CARYL
Mary, daughter of the Revd Samuel & Hannah BALDWIN

1769. March 19 Hannah, daughter of Amos SYLVESTER, Jr.
Desire
Lydia, daughter of Timothy & Lydia ROSE
April 2 Hannah, daughter of Seth STETSON, Jr. & Lucy
Rebecca Studley, and Lucy Studley, daughters of Rebecca STUDLEY
April 16 William Pitt, son of Joshua and Abigail BAYLEY
    30 Sarah, daughter of Lemuel & Ruth CURTIS
Eunice, daughter of Jno. and Sage JOSSELYN
April 30 Edward, son of Benj. and Bradbury STETSON
May 14 Jabez, son of Jonathan & Lucy PRATT
July 2 Hannah, daughter of David & Hannah JACOB
Betty, daughter of Solomon & Elizabeth BRYANT
July 23 Lydia, daughter of Sarah CURTIS
August 4 Isaac Jones, son of Joseph WOODWORTH & wife: in private by reason of sickness
August 27 Lucinda, daughter of John & Content WITHERELL
Sept. 10 Rebecca, the wife of Samuel WITHERELL
Charles, son of Job & Betty YOUNG
October 15 Elias, son of Stevens & Ruth HATCH
    22 Samuel, son of Solomon BATES, Jr. and wife
Novr. 26 Barker, son of Simeon & Lucy CURTIS
1770. February 11 Bethany, daughter of Lemuel WHITTEN and wife
April 8 Juliette, daughter of Michael and Ruth SYLVESTER
Lucinda. daughter of Elisha & Betty CURTIS
May 6 Betty and Anna, children of Joseph and Sarah WOODWARD
James, son of Joanna STUDLEY
May 20 Mary, daughter of Lemuel & Rachel DELANO
    27 John, son of Robert & Ruth EELLES
Ebenezer & Waterman, sons of Ebenezer and Deborah EDDY
Alice, daughter of Seth and Alice BAYLEY, in private by reason of sickness
June 3 Thomas, son of Thomas & Hannah BATES
July 8 Mary, daughter of Elisha and Orphan HOUSE
Nathanael Sylvester, son of Prince and Eunice STETSON
July 22 Olive, daughter of Stockbridge & Olive JOSSELYN
Aug. 5 Betty, daughter of Benj. & Betty BATES
Jerusha & Richard, children of Leonard HILL

Aug. 5   Dorothy, daughter of Reuben & Dorothy CLARK
   12   Sadoc, son of Daniel TEAGUE & wife
   26   Olive, daughter of Joseph HOUSE, Jr. and Sage
Seth, son of Seth and Bathsheba HOUSE
Thomas, son of Thomas and Anna WILLET
Israel, son of Thomas & Susanna HATCH
Sepr 9   Zipporah, daughter of Jno and Bathsheba HATCH
Octor 21   Chloe, daughter of John CLAP, &c.
Novr 18   Alice, daughter of Seth and Alice BAYLEY
Lemuel Holmes, son of Lemuel & ...... DELANO
Novr. 25   Avis, daughter of Joshua & Avis DWELLY
Decemr 16   Curtis, son of Joseph and Lydia BROOKS
1771.   Jan. 6   Lydia, daughter of Lemuel & Ruth CURTIS
         13   Nathanael, son of Seth STETSON, Jr. & Lucy
Feby 3   Chloe, daughter of Benja MAN and wife
   24   Cindrilla, daughter of Benja & Mercy BASS
Mar. 24   Samuel, son of Samuel and ...... STAPLES
April 7   Lucy, daughter of Edmund and Betty SYLVESTER
April 28   Melzer, son of Gershom and Deborah HOUSE
Israel, son of Israel & ...... PERRY
May 5   Elisha, son of Jonathan and Lucy PRATT
   12   Grace, daughter of Daniel and Alice GARNETT
   26   Bethiah Cushing, daughter of the Revd Samuel and Hannah BALDWIN
June 9   Deborah Cushing, daughter of Job and Betty YOUNG
July 14   James, son of James HOUSE, deceased and his widow Grace House; the lad about 17 years old, baptized on his mother's aut.
July 21   John, son of John and Thankfull STETSON
Lucinda, daughter of Solomon & Aquilla BATES
July 21   Ruthy & Atherton, children of Atherton and Ruth WALES
Levi, son of Levi and Deborah CORTHELL
Aug. 4   Nathan, son of Ebenezer and Deborah EDDY
Aug. 18   Rebecca, daughter of Elisha & Betty CURTIS
Isaac, son of Isaac LAMBERT, Jr. and Hannah
Aug. 25   Seth, son of Timo & Lydia ROSE
Sept. 22   Samuel WOODWARD, aged 20 years
Octo. 6   Charles & Lydia, children of David HOUSE, Jr. and Rhoda his wife

Octo. 13 Susanna Orr, the wife of James ORR
James, son of James and Susanna ORR
Octo. 27 Joseph, son of Benja and Bradbury STETSON
Mary, daughter of Joseph RAMSDALE, 3rd & Elizabeth
Novr 10 Susanna, Elizabeth & Mary, children of Gideon and Elizabeth STETSON
Philip, son of John and Content WITHERELL
Nov. 24 Jenny, a *Negro-child*, servant to Jacob & Mary SYLVESTER

1772. March 8 Stockbridge, son of Stockbridge & Olive JOSSELYN
Abigail, daughter of Asa & Abigail TURNER
March 22 Eunice Turner, daughter of Prince and Eunice STETSON
April 5 Hannah, daughter of Timo and Mary ROBBINS
    12 Lydia and Esther, daughters of Isaac and Hannah HATCH
       Lydia, daughter of Seth & Alice BAYLEY
    19 John, son of John CURTIS, Jr. and Anna his wife
    26 Lucy, daughter of John and Bathsheba HATCH
May 17 Susanna, daughter of Thos. & Susanna HATCH
    24 Sarah Hill, daughter of Thomas & Anna WILLET
    31 Olive, daughter of Gideon & Rebecca RANDALL
June 7 Jane House, the wife of John HOUSE, Jr. and Deborah, their daughter
June 7 Jeremiah, son of Thos. ROSE, Jr. and Rhoda his wife
    28 Peter, son Atherton and Ruth WALES
July 5 Solomon, son of Solomon & Elizabeth BRYANT
    19 Betty, daughter of Amos & Betty TURNER
Aug. 9 Robert, son of Michael & Ruth SYLVESTER
    30 Thomas, son of Israel & ...... PERRY
Sept. 1 Roland, son of James & Zilpah CURTIS, in private by reason of sickness
Sept. 11 Rufus, son of Joseph HOUSE, Jr. and Sage his wife; by reason of sickness in private
Sept. 17 Lemuel, son of Lemuel WHITTEN and wife; by reason of sickness in private
Octor 11 Nathanael, son of Robert and Ruth EELLS
Thomas WHITTEN, Jr. and his son named William Peaks
Oct. 25 John Washburn, son of Samuel and Elizabeth STAPLES
Oct. 25 Lydia Holmes, daughter of James & Susanna ORR

ORIGINAL RECORDS.

November 8 Richmond, son of Isaac & Hannah HATCH
        15 Sarah Whitten, adult daughter of Thomas WHITTEN
        Hannah and Rachel Farrar, children of Joseph CARYL
        & wife
        22 Joseph, son of Joshua and Avis DWELLY
1773. March 14 Seth, son of Seth STETSON, Jr. and Lucy
        21 Prissy, daughter of Joseph RAMSDALE, 3d and Elizabeth
May 2 Bridget, daughter of Jno. HOUSE, Jr. and Jane his wife
Betty, daughter of Daniel & Betty BARSTOW
May 9 Lydia, daughter of Joseph & Lydia BROOKS
   16 Leonard, son of Ebenezer and Deborah EDDY
Thomas, son of Isaac LAMBERT, Jr. and his wife Hannah
May 29 Hannah Stockbridge, daughter of Timo. & Elizabeth CHURCH
Huldah, daughter of Benja and Mercy BASS
June 6 Lemuel, son of Lemuel & Ruth CURTIS
Asenath, daughter of Elijah and Susanna STETSON
June 27 Thomas, son of Thomas and Olive STETSON
July 18 David, son of David & Susanna TORREY
Aug. 8 Christiana, daughter of Widow Sage JOSSELYN
Peninnah, daughter of Robert WHITE
Aug. 22 Bethiah. daughter of Job and Betty YOUNG
Mary, daughter of Timo & Mary ROBBINS
Aug. 29 Lucy, daughter of Edmund & Betty SYLVESTER
Sept. 5 Joseph, son of Seth and Alice BAYLEY
Octo. 10 Mary, daughter of Jonathan & Lucy PRATT
   24 Lucy, daughter of Gideon & Rosamond STUDLEY
Novr 21 Lemuel, son of Lemuel WHITTEN and wife
Rachel, daughter of Thomas WHITTEN, Jr. & Rachel
1774. January 2 Charles, son of Benja & Bradbury STETSON
        Rebecca, daughter of Jabez and Keturah STUDLEY
January 30 Kezia, daughter of Melzar & Kezia CURTIS
March 13 Timothy, son of John and Content WITHERELL
   20 William, son of the Revd Samuel and Hannah BALDWIN
April 10 Ruth, daughter of Amos & Betty TURNER
    17 Rachel, daughter of John and Bathshua HATCH
    Mary Niles, daughter of Atherton & Ruth WALES

April 17 Melzer, son of Melzer and Kezia CURTIS
    24 William, son of John CURTIS, Jr. and Anna his wife
May 6 Christopher, son of Solomon and Elizabeth BRYANT; in private by reason of sickness
May 8 Daniel, son of Daniel and Betty BARSTOW
    15 Temperance, daughter of Prince & Eunice STETSON
    29 Zilpah, daughter of John and Thankfull STETSON
June 11 Michal, Daugr of Seth and Anna BATES; in private by reason of sickness
June 19 Joseph, son of Robert and Ruth EELLES
Betty, daughter of Orphan HOUSE
Joseph, son of Mary MAN
July 3 Lucy, daughter of Benjamin & Betty BATES
Abigail Stockbridge, daughter of Stockbridge & Olive JOSSELYN
July 31 Seth, Joseph Neal, Paul, Thomas, Joshua, Anna, Becca and Enos, children of Seth & Anna BATES
Aug. 14 Sarah, daughter of Sage STAPLES
Sepr 4 John Tilden TORREY, an adult, aged
Oct. 2 Joseph, son of Seth and Alice BAYLEY
David, son of Lemuel and Rachel DELANO
Oct. 8 Simeon, son of Seth WITHERELL and Hannah; in private by reason of sickness
Oct. 9 John, son of Solomon BATES, Jr. & Aquilla
Nov. 6 Snow, son of David HOUSE, Jr. and Rhoda
    13 Ezekiel, son of Joshua and Margaret BARSTOW
    27 Charles, son of Timo and Lydia ROSE
Pompey, *negro-lad* of Col. STOCKBRIDGE
Decemr 4 John, son of John HOUSE, Jr. and Jane
    11 Charles, son of Elijah and Susanna STETSON
1775 Jany 1 Abigail, daughter of Zebulon BOWKER & wife
    15 Bethiah, daughter of Timo. & Mary ROBBINS
February 21 Eunice, daughter of David and Hannah JACOBS; in private by reason of sickness
April 30 Olive, daughter of Widow Hannah RANDALL
June 4 Olive, daughter of Thos. & Olive STETSON
    18 Hannah, daughter of Israal PERRY & wife
June 25 Charles, son of Isaac LAMBERT, Jr. and Hannah
Abigail, daughter of Hersey & Abigail GILBERT

William Gilbert, son of William and Rebecca CURTIS
July 16   Samuel, son of Seth STETSON, Jr. & wife
Joshua, son of Samuel STAPLES & wife
Aug. 13   Betty, daughter of Lemuel & Rachel DELANO
Betty, Townsend Smith, Oliver, Levi, Isaac, Sarah & Chloe, children of Elijah and Leah GARDNER
Aug. 20   Martha, daughter of John and Martha BARNS
Sepr 10   Rebecca, daughter of William & Sarah EELLES
Joseph, son of Joseph RAMSDELL, 3rd & Elizabeth
Sepr 12   Joseph, son of Samuel WITHERELL, Jr. & wife; in private by reason of sickness
Octr 1   Lucy, daughter of Joshua and Avis DWELLY
    11   Asa, son of Daniel TEAGUE & wife
Oct. 15   Ward, son of Seth & Anna BATES
Caleb, son of Benja & Bradbury STETSON
Zebulon, son of Zebulon and Deborah BOWKER
Novr 5   Olive, daughter of Mary MAN
Decr 16   Bradbury Palmer, daughter of Elisha PALMER; in private by reason of sickness
Decr 17   Mable, daugr of Kelah MINGO, *negro woman*
1776.   January 7   Caleb, son of Benja & Abigail MAN
    Joseph, son of William & Ruth STOCKBRIDGE
January 21   Ruth, daughter of Hersey and Abigail GILBERT
Feb. 25   Jeremiah, son of Melzer and Kezia CURTIS
March 3   Lucy WHITTEN, adult
    10   Rebecca, daughter of Seth and Alice BAYLEY
    17   Alden, son of Benja & Mercy BASS
April 21   Rachel, daughter of Atherton and Ruth WALES
Sarah, daughter of Joseph & Lydia BROOKS
May 5   John, son of John & Bathshua HATCH
Thomas, son of Thomas & Susanna HATCH
May 19   Elizabeth, daughter of Timo and Mary ROBBINS
June 9   Hannah, daughter of Gideon and Rebecca RANDALL
    23   Sarah, daughter of Jonathan and Lucy PRATT
Briggs, son of Gershom CURTIS and wife
Hannah, daughter of Benja MAN, Jr. & wife
July 28   Gideon, son of Gideon & Rosamond STUDLEY
Zilpah, daughter of James and Zilpah CURTIS

Aug. 4   Susa, daughter of David and Susanna TORREY
   12   Philip, son of Elisha CURTIS; in private by reason of sickness
Aug. 18   Lucy, daughter of Capt. Robt & Ruth EELLES
Sepr 22   Jabez, son of Jabez and Keturah STUDLEY
Thomas, son of Thos. WHITTEN, Jr. and wife
Oct. 6   Huldah CURTIS.   Adult
Oct. 13   Davis, son of Abner CURTIS, Jr. and wife
Lucy, daughter of the Revd Samuel & Hannah BALDWIN
Oct. 27   Elitheer, daughter of John CURTIS, Jr. and Anna
Nov. 3   Elijah, son of James and Lydia TORREY
Decemr 1   Ezekiel, son of Amos & Betty TURNER
1777.   Feby 16   Charles, son of Elijah STETSON
   March 23   Betty, daughter of Joshua and Margaret BARSTOW
Sally, daughter of Benja. MAN, Jr. & wife
April 6   Lydia, daughter of Solomon and Elizabeth BRYANT
April 13   Lucy, daughter of Seth STETSON, Jr. and wife
June 1   Abigail, daughter of Seth & Alice BAYLEY
   Gershom, son of John and Jane HOUSE
    8   Sally, daughter of Peleg EWELL and wife
   Lucinda, daughter of Lemuel WHITTEN and wife
   Ruth, daughter of Thomas STETSON and wife
   15   Ruth, daughter of Timo & Lydia ROSE
   Isaac, son of Elijah and Leah GARDNER
   29   Eli, son of Seth and Anna BATES
   Lucy, daughter of Stockbridge JOSSLYN & wife
   Abel, son of Abel & Ruth CURTIS
July 6   Eunice, daughter of Israel PERRY & wife
   27   Prissy, daughter of Joseph RAMSDALE, 3rd & Elizabeth
Augt. 10   Abigail, wife of Elisha SYLVESTER and Ruggles their son
Aug. 10   Elisha, son of Benja and Bradbury STETSON
   Rufus, son of William & Rebecca CURTIS
   17   Sarah, daughter of Benja. BATES and wife
   24   Lucy, daughter of Daniel and Betty BARSTOW
   Jesse, son of James & Lydia TORREY
Sept. 14   Nathanael, son of Lemuel and Ruth CURTIS

Sept. 30   Barney, son of the Widow Rachel MERRITT; in private by reason of sickness
Octr 1   Kinsman, Deborah, Calvin, and Charles, children of Levi & Deborah CORTHELL
Octr 5   Joseph & Lydia, children of ...... BRIGGS
    19   David, son of David and Susanna TORREY
Novr 9   Ruth, daughter of William & Ruth STOCKBRIDGE
    16   Diana, daughter of Gershom CURTIS & wife

1778.   March 29   Robert, son of Atherton & Ruth WALES
    April 12   Gamaliel, son of John & Bathshua HATCH
April 19   Deborah, daughter of Zebulon & Deborah BOWKER
May 10   Desire, daughter of Abner CURTIS, Jr. & wife
    15   Drusilla, daughter of Job and Mercy CASWELL; in private by reason of sickness
May 24   Levi, John & Mercy, children of Job & Mercy CASWELL
June 21   Cornelius, son of Hersey & Abigail GILBERT
July 12   Melzer, son of Melzer and Kezia CURTIS
    19   Josiah, son of Elijah & Hannah GILBERT
Aug. 2   Joshua, son of John and Thankfull STETSON
    9   Eleanor, daughter of Joseph and Lydia BROOKS
    16   Clarissa, daughter of Ebenezer & Mary CURTIS
Sept. 13   Lydia, daughter of Major John & Chloe CLAP
Oct. 4   Thomas TORREY, adult; in private by reason of sickness
Oct. 18   Perez, son of Lemuel WHITTEN and wife
    Ruth, daughter of Benja. MAN, Jr. & wife
    22   Susy, daughter of Levi and Deborah CORTHELL; in private by reason of sickness
Oct. 24   Lydia Peterson, daughter of Daniel TEAGUE & wife; in private by reason of sickness
Oct. 25   Joshua Staples, son of Sage MORSE
Nov. 1   Melzer, Susanna, Abijah, Luther, Calvin and Adam, children of the widow Betty STETSON
Dec. 6   Abigail, daughter of Gideon & Rosamond STUDLEY
Decem. 20   Sarah, daughter of Benja and Mercy BASS
Elitheer, daughter of John CURTIS, Jr. and Anna his wife
1779.   Jany 17   Mary Bowker, daughter of Joseph and Mary TORREY
Feby 21   Caleb, son of Gideon & Rebecca RANDALL

Feby 28 Lydia, daughter of Ebenezer & Deborah EDDY
March 14 Edward, son of Capt. Robert EELLES & wife
April 11 Elias WHITTEN, an adult person and his daughter Ruth, child of Elias & Deborah Whitten
May 2 Luthun, son of Amos & Sarah PERRY
   16 Mary, daughter of John & Jane HOUSE
       Gideon, son of Abel & Ruth CURTIS
   23 Rebecca, daughter of William & Rebecca CURTIS
June 13 Barker, son of Joseph RAMSDALE, Jr. and Elizabeth
Paul, son of Ebenezer & Mary CURTIS
July 4 Joanna, daughter of Jonathan & Lucy PRATT
Septr 9 David, son of Robert WHITE, in private by reason of sickness
Octr 31 Thankfull, daughter of Seth STETSON, Jr & Lucy his wife
Novr 14 Sibyl, daughter of Timothy ROBBINS & wife
Novr 28 Molley, daughter of Benja & Bradbury STETSON
Nov. 28 Joseph, son of Joseph & Mary TORREY
1780. June 11 Fanny, daughter of the Revd Samuel & Mrs. Hannah BALDWIN

BAPTISMS,

PR. ME

JOHN MELLEN

1784. March 28 Sarah, child of Dea. Timothy ROBBINS
       May 30 Benjamin, child of Elias WHITING
June 27 Charles, child of Thomas WHITING, Jr.
also William Read, child of William STOCKBRIDGE
also David, child of David STOCKBRIDGE, Jr.
July 25 Rukecy, child of Lemuel WHITING
also Samuel, child of John CURTIS, Jr.
Augt 18 Sally, daughter of Solomon BATES; in private

Augt 22   Mary Gardner, daughter of Benjamin BASS
Sepr 5   Joanna, daughter of Melzar CURTIS
Sept. 5   Sarah, daughter of Elias WHITING
also Joshua, son of Joshua MAN
Sept. 12   Reuben. son of Seth STETSON
Octo. 3   Horatio, son of Israel PERRY
Calvin, son of William STOCKBRIDGE
Octo. 10   Calvin, son of Joshua BARSTOW
Ruth, daughter of Abel CURTIS
Betsey, daughter of Isaac TURNER
Octo. 24   Reuben, Mary & Hannah, children of Caleb ROGERS
Novr 7   Joshua, child of Gideon STUDLY
   14   Emily, grandchild of Benj. SYLVESTER
   28   Ruth, daughter of Col. Amos TURNER
Reuben, son of Snow CURTIS
Lydia and Joseph, children of Job TILDEN
December 5   Hannah, child of Elijah GILBERT
1785.   April 24   Turner, child of Gershom CURTIS
   May 1   John, child of Atherton WALES
May 29   Sophia Adams & Sylvia, children of Mrs. Orphan GURNEY
July 14   James, child of Capt. Seth BATES; in private; sick
Augt 7   Lewis & Cyrus, children of Benjamin WHITE
Nov. 6   Molley, child of Joshua MAN
Philip, child of Ruth RAMSDALE
1786.   April 16   John, son of Dea. Timothy ROBBINS
   April 30   Hannah, daughter of Dea. Joseph BROOKS
May 28   James, son of Stockbridge JOSSLYN
Martyn, son of David STOCKBRIDGE
William, son of Morgan BREWSTER
June 18   Michal, daughter of Ebenezer CURTIS
June 25   Paul, son of Israel PERRY
Ebenezer, son of Elisha SYMMONDS
July 16   Bela, son of Snow CURTIS
August 13   Amos, son of Elias WHITING
   20   Charles Chauncey, son of Joshua BARSTOW
Octo. 15   Pamela, daughter of Elisha RECORDS
   Mary, daughter of Benjamin WHITE
   22   Martha & Rachel, children of Ezra BRIGGS, Junr

Octo. 29 Seth, son of Coll. Amos TURNER
Lydia, daughter of Daniel BARSTOW
Calvin, son of Adam PERRY
Betty, daughter of Job TILDEN
Novr 5 Sylvia, daughter of Solomon BATES
Priscilla, daughter of Isaac TURNER
Novr. 12 Ruth Torrey, daughter of Caleb ROGERS, Jr.
19 Asa WHITING, an adult person
1787. March 29 Marshal Lincoln, son of Dr. Peter HOBART
June 10 Laurentia, daughter of Melzar CURTIS
July 22 Olive, daughter of Thos. WHITING, Jr.
Ruth & Anne, children of James WOODWORTH; in private; sick
July 30 William, son of Col. Amos TURNER; in private; sick
Augt. 12 Elijah & Sylvester, children of James WOODWORTH
Sept. 16 Saba, daughter of William CURTIS
23 Lucy, daughter of Benjamin FARRAR
Octo. 28 Nathaniel, son of John CURTIS
Nov. 4 Caleb WHITING, an adult person
Susee Gill, daughter of Caleb WHITING
Nov. 4 Charles, son of Gershom CURTIS
18 Lucy, daughter of Josiah CHAMBERLAIN
1788. June 15 Agnes, daughter of Peter SALMON
Benjamin, son of Joshua MAN
Martha, daughter of Elisha SYMMONDS
June 22 Levi, son of Snow CURTIS
July 13 Lebbeus, son of William STOCKBRIDGE
Horatio, son of David STOCKBRIDGE, Jr.
Augt. 3 Sarah, wife of Joshua JOSSLYN
10 Ezekiel Turner, son of Ezekiel Turner HATCH
13 Edmund, son of Elias WHITING in private, being sick
Sept. 14 Betsy Cushing, daughter of Nathl. BARSTOW
Homer & Anna, children of Homer WHITING
21 Ezra, son of Ezra BRIGGS, Jr.
28 Gideon, son of Adam PERRY
Octr 5 Lydia, daughter of Josiah CHAMBERLAIN
12 Christopher, son of Stockbridge JOSSLYN
Robert & Samuel, twin sons of Robert SALMON
18 Sophia, daughter of Joshua BARSTOW

Nov. 16   Reuben, son of Solomon BATES
1789.   May 10   Calvin, Edward, James, Labbeus & Mary, children of Calvin CURTIS
May 17   Caleb, son of Caleb WHITING
June 14   Martha, child of Capn Calvin CURTIS, sick at home
June 21   Jonathan, a *negro man* that lives with Major BAILEY
Augt 23   Benjamin, son of Joel SYLVESTER
Sept. 6   Church & Deborah, son & daughter of Jonan PRATT
    Nabby Baker, daughter of Israel PERRY
    20   Charles, son of James WOODWORTH
Sepr 20   Job, son of Job TILDEN, Jr.
Octo. 4   Judson, son of Joshua JOSSLYN
    11   Martyn, son of Seth STETSON
    Susanna, daughter of Melzar CURTIS
    Bathsheba, daughter of Snow CURTIS
1790.   May 2   Joseph, son of Capn Albert SMITH
    June 27   Amos, son of Ezekiel Turner HATCH
July 4   Samuel, son of William CURTIS
    11   Deborah, daughter of Nathl BARSTOW
July 25   Sarah & Betsy Eelles, children of John BARSTOW
Sept. 5   Elias, son of the widow of Elias WHITING
    12   John, son of Robert SALMON
    19   Anson, Walter & Thomas, sons of the widow Sylvina ROBBINS
    26   Sylvia, daughter of Benjamin WHITE
Sepr 26   Betty, daughter of Elisha RECORDS
Oct. 17   Betsey, daughter of William STOCKBRIDGE
    Asa, son of Asa WHITING
    24   James, Israel, Rebecca, Abigail & Lucy, children of Seth BAILEY
    31   Sylvia, daughter of Isaac TURNER
1791.   Jany 24   Tamsen, wife of Joseph BATES, in private, sick
    May 1   Luther, son of Melzar CURTIS
May 22   Deborah, daughter of David STOCKBRIDGE
    Polly, daughter of Nathaniel BARSTOW
    29   Lucius, son of John CURTIS, Jr.
June 12   Lucy, daughter of Caleb WHITING
July 3   Nabby, daughter of Capn Daniel BARSTOW

July 3   Polly, daughter of Job TILDEN, Jr.
Augt 14 Benjn Chamberlain, son of Jonathan PRAT
Oct. 9   John, son of John BARSTOW
    16   Robert, son of Snow CURTIS
Dec. 4   Elisha, son of Elisha SYMMONDS
         Ambrose Low & Ira Lewis, twin sons of Joshua JOSSLYN
,   25   William, son of Robert SALMON
1792. May 20 Ezra, son of Ezra BEALES
         June 3 Joseph, son of Joel SYLVESTER
June 24 Matilda, daughter of David JACOBS, Jr.
July 22 Martin, son of Thomas WHITING, Jr.
    29   Anna, Fanny & Bela, children of Bela MAN
Augt 5   John Cushing, son of Job YOUNG
    14   Avis, daughter of Isaac TURNER, in private
Octo. 21 Elijah, son of Asa WHITING
Oct. 21 Triphena, daughter of Homer WHITING
Novr 18 Sally, wife of Oliver WINSLOW
Oliver, son of the above Oliver WINSLOW
1793. April 7   Albert, son of Capn Albert SMITH
         June 9   Sage Man, daughter of Caleb WHITING
July 14 Benjamin, son of Joseph NEAL
Abigail, daughter of Charles MAN
Sepr 29 ......, child of Job TILDEN
Octo. 6 Mary Randal, daughter of Snow CURTIS
Job, son of Job YOUNG
Oct. 13 Sylvia Bailey, daughter of William STOCKBRIDGE
Ruth, daughter of David STOCKBRIDGE ; Abraham, son of Joshua JOSLYN
1794. May 18 Molly Cushing, daughter of Lieut. Joshua MAN
         Polly Barker, daughter of John PERRY
June 8   Elisha, son of Elisha SYMMONDS
    29   Hannah, daughter of John BARSTOW
Sept. 28 Hannah Bailey, daughter of Ezekiel HATCH
Oct. 12 ......, child of Isaac TURNER
    19   Sarah, daughter of Joel SYLVESTER
Nov. 9   Huldah Eelles, daughter of Wilm & Huldah WING
    23   Hannah Eddy, daughter of Benjamin WHITMAN
1795. May 17 Debbe Dwelly, daughter of Asa WHITING
         31   Elijah, son of Elijah SYLVESTER

June 21   Ruth, Sarah, Francis, David & Reuben, children of Belcher CLARK & Sarah his wife
July 21   Hannah FORD; adult; in private bec. of sickness
Aug. 2   Melzar Hatch, son of Ezra BEALS
Sept. 6   John, son of Joseph NEAL
          Caleb, son of Caleb WHITING
      13 Adoniram, son of Benjamin FARRAR
Oct. 25   Mary, daughter of Albert SMITH
Nabbe Eelles, daughter of Josiah SMITH
Novr 8   Hiram, son of David JACOB, Junr
Edward, son of John BARSTOW
Novr 17   Hannah, wife of Elisha CURTIS, Jr., in private, unwell
1796. May 1 Frederick JOHNSON, an adult
          July 3 Benjamin, son of Benja BASS, Jr.
July 10   Phebe MANSON, an adult
Lydia BATES, an adult
Sept. 25 Joshua, son of Joshua MAN
Nov. 13   Lucy Barker, daughter of Job YOUNG
      20 Agnes, daughter of Robert SALMON
          Lucy, daughter of Josiah SMITH
1797. April 2 Mercy Tolman, daughter of Benja BASS, Jr.
          30 Benjamin, son of Benjamin WHITMAN
July 2   Nabbe, daughter of Josiah CHAMBERLAIN
      9   Sallee, daughter of Job TILDEN
Sept. 17 Sarah, daughter of Joseph NEAL
Sage, daughter of Caleb WHITING
Sept. 24 Elizabeth Tory, Mary & Ruth, adults, daughters of Samuel GROCE
Elizabeth, adult daughter of Lot RAMSDEL
Decem. 3 Benjn Hearsey, son of Elisha SYMMONDS
      10 John, son of Albert SMITH, esqr.
Decr 25   Isaac, son of Joel SYLVESTER, in private, sick
1798. Jany 14 Ruth Copeland, daughter of Josiah SMITH
          March 4 Nancy Delano, daughter of Seth BATES, Jr.
April 29 Charles, son of Dr. Melzar DWELLY
May 20   Joshua Barker, son of Job YOUNG
Elizabeth Briggs, daughter of Elijah SYLVESTER
June 10   Rebecca, wife of Timothy CHURCH

June 10   Timothy, son of said Timothy CHURCH & wife
Asa, son of Asa WHITING
Maria, daughter of David JACOBS, Jr.
July 15   John, son of Joel SYLVESTER
Aug. 26   Turner STETSON, adult & father of a family
Sept. 2   Joseph BATES, aged 65, admitted into ye Chh. same time
Turner & Ruth, children of Turner STETSON
Oct. 28   Lemuel, son of Lemuel DWELLY
Nov. 11   William, son of Willm WING of Hartford, Connect; his wife's account.

1799.   March 3   David, son Capn Joshua MAN
    April 21   Lydia Rose, daughter of Turner STETSON, in private, sick
July 7   Michael, son of Benja BASS, Jr.
    Elizabeth Bowen, daughter of Josiah SMITH
  14   Bathsheba, daughter of Snow CURTIS
  21   Joseph Cushing, son of David STOCKBRIDGE
Aug. 18   Thomas Miller, son of Albert SMITH. esqr.
Octo. 6   Mary, daughter of John CURTIS, lately deceased
Nov. 10   Sally Smith, daughter of Dr. Melzar DWELLY
  17   Josiah, son of Josiah CHAMBERLAIN
    Joshua, son of Joshua DWELLY

1800.   April 20   Ezra, son of Caleb WHITING
    June 29   William, son of Timothy CHURCH
July 6   Simeon, son of Job YOUNG
Seth, son of Seth ROSE
Nathaniel, son of Elijah BARSTOW
Augt. 3   Lydia Rose, daughter of Turner STETSON
  24   Samuel STETSON, an adult.
    Lydia, wife of Ezekiel TURNER
    Rachel, daughter of Joshua DWELLY
Sepr 7   Zilpah, daughter of Samuel STETSON
Hariot, daughter of Ezekiel TURNER
Octo. 5   William, son of Snow CURTIS
Abigail Stetson, John, Mary Josslyn, & Charles, children of Shubael MUNRO on his wives' account
Oct. 5   Christiana & Isaac, children of Christiana JOSLYN
  12   Marcia & Stephen, children of William STOCKBRIDGE

Oct. 12 Benjamin, son of John BARSTOW
Nov. 9 George Washington, son of Elisha SYMMONDS
Mary, daughter of Charles JOSLYN, Pembroke
Dec. 21 Ruth Copeland, daughter of William WING, of Hartford, Connecticut

1801. May 17 John, son of Benjn BASS, Junr
    24 Marrie, daughter of Charles MAN
June 7 Elizabeth, daughter of Albert SMITH, esqr
Sepr 6 Edward, son of Edward STETSON, on wife's account
Sepr 20 Maria Angelina, daughter of Benjamin WHITMAN, esqr.; in private, sick
Oct. 11 Salome, daughter of John BARSTOW
  18 William, son of Ezekiel TURNER
Nov. 1 Mary Lenthal, daughter of Josiah SMITH
Lucy Dwelly, daughter of Seth ROSE
Decr 20 Henry Maurice Lisle, son of Benjamin WHITMAN, esqr

1802. April 4 Hariot, daughter of Dr. Melzar DWELLY
    25 Jerusha, daughter of Joel SYLVESTER
June 6 Hulda Bass, daughter of Robert EELLES
Lucy Eelles, daughter of Elijah BARSTOW
July 4 Thomas Foster, son of Josiah CHAMBERLAIN
Samuel Stetson, son of Timothy CHURCH
July 11 Eliza, daughter of Edmund STETSON
Aug. 1 Peter Russell, son of Robert SALMOND
Sepr 5 Philinda DAMON, an adult
Oct. 5 Ruth GROCE, adult & in years but very sick
Oct. 10 Elizabeth & Joanna, *twins* of Elisha SYMMONDS
Nov. 14 John, son of Joshua DWELLY
  28 Sarah Barker, daughter of Capn Albert SMITH
    Barker Curtis, son of Job YOUNG

1803. Feby 13 Josiah Miller, son of Josiah SMITH
  July 10 Christopher Sylvester, son of Benj. BASS, Junr
Albert, son of Samuel STETSON
Sept. 11 Mary Eelles & Bradbury Eelles, *twins* of Edward STETSON
Oct. 2 Aristides, son of Turner STETSON
   Melzar, son of Melzar HATCH
  23 Betty, daughter of Asa WHITING
  30 Avis, daughter of William WHITING

1804. March 15   John Milton, son of Dr. Melzar DWELLY
      May 13   Ezekiel, son of Ezekiel TURNER
June 24   Charles, son of Seth ROSE
Aug. 19   ......, son of Charles JOSLYN
Sepr 9   Thomas, son of Benjn Healy CLARK
         Keturah & Eliza, daughters of Jabez STUDLEY, Junr
         Sarah Bass, daughter of Joseph EELLES
     23 Jerod, son of Caleb WHITING
Oct. 7   Amos, son of Amos BATES
     28 Ruth, daughter of Stephen BAILY, Junr
     — Fany Smith, daughter of William WING

BAPTISMS

BY THE

REVD JOSEPH BARKER.

1805. August   Jane Rusel, daughter of Lemuel DWELLY
               Barden & Michal, *twin* children of Benja. BASS, Jr.
               Robbert, son of Robbert EELLS
               Benja Healy, son of Benja H. CLARK
               Lucinda, daughter of Joseph EELLS
               John, son of Jabez STUDLEY, Jr.
               Sarah, daughter of Melzar HATCH
               Martin, son of Timothy CHURCH

BAPTISMS

BY ME

CALVIN CHADDOCK.

1806. Aug. 12   Benj. Day, son of Benj. FILLIMORE
      Sept. 28 Elijah, son of Elijah BARSTOW
Martin, son of Seth ROSE
Almira, daughter of Joshua DWELLY

1807. April 30   Lydia Stetson, daughter of Ezekiel TURNER
Aug. 23   Mary Stone & Nancy, both daughters of Calvin & Militiah CHADDOCK
Sept. 13   Ruth Turner, daughter of Benj. BASS, Jr.
1808.   May 29   Bathshua Turner, daughter of Melzar HATCH
July 24   Sarah Barker, daughter of Capt. Albert SMITH
July 24   George, son of Jabez STUDLEY, Jr.
Sept. 18   Elizabeth Rose, daughter of Timothy CHURCH
Oct. 2   Lucy, daughter of Ezekiel TURNER
Decemr **   John Shaw Sumner, son of Calvin & Militiah CHADDOCK
1809.   July 9   George Russel, son of Lemuel & Jane DWELLY
1810.   July 29   Mary, daughter of Isaac & Mary TOTMAN
1814.   Sept. 11   Joseph, son of Joshua & ...... DWELLY
Robert, son of Joseph & Sally EELLS
1819.   June 6   Ruth Bailey, daughter of Lebbeus & Lydia STOCKBRIDGE
Horace Tower, Henry Blanchard, William Witherell, Nancy, Elizabeth Jane, children of Samuel & Rusha EELLS
Fanny, Zilpha, Reuben, Abigail, John, Mary, Samuel, children of Samuel & Abigail STETSON
1820.   September 3   Angelina, Cassandria, Avis Dwelley, John, James, children of Joshua & Priscilla STETSON
July 2   James Gardner, George Williams, children of Joseph & Sarah EELLS
September 3   Melitiah Chaddock, daughter of Samuel & Abigail STETSON
1821.   October 28   Betsey Homer, daughter of Lebbeus & Lydia STOCKBRIDGE
1822.   October 6   A child of George and Nancy CUSHING
October 13   Rebecca Mellen, daughter of Samuel & Abigail STETSON
1824.   April 17   Edwin Williams, Nabby Eells, Andrew, children of Elijah & Lucy BARSTOW
1825.   May 20   Helena Maria Thompson, daughter of Samuel & Rusha EELLS
May 20   Wm. Ebenezer, son of Bathshua DAWS
May 20   Libeus, son of Libeus and Lydia STOCKBRIDGE
May 20   Melatiah Chaddock, daughter of Samuel & Abigail STETSON

August 6   Lucy Williams, daughter of William & Lucy CHURCH
A child of Levi & ...... NASH
1826.   June 4   George Mitchell, son of Rufus & Huldah BATES
June 25   Bethiah Baker, Abagail Neal, Nancy Newell, children of Isaac & Bethiah COOK
August 6   Jeremiah, son of Samuel & Abigail STETSON
Ruben Tower, Loisa, Andrew Jackson, Sylvia, Joshua, Mary, children of Joseph & Grace FOSTER
August 20   Ruben A., Zenas, Edwin, Abagail Jane, Hariot Newel, Andrew, children of Ruben & Abagail ROGERS
1828.   April 6   Mercy Tolman, Lucinda Bass, Hannah, Thomas, children of Mercy, wife of Thomas WRIGHT
April 27   Almira, George, Samuel, Charles, Henry, Louisa, William Priscilla, children of Christiana, wife of Zebulon CLARK
April 27   Betsey Fog, child of Rusha wife of Samuel EELLS
April 27   Sophrona Meed, child of Abigail wife of Reuben ROGERS
September 9   Lydia Lane, child of Lydia wife of Lebbeus STOCKBRIDGE
October 3   William, son of William & Lucy CHURCH
October 3   Henry Martyn, child of Samuel & Abigail STETSON
October 3   Matthy FERRY (or Perry) (an adult)
1829.   June 7   Mary Augusta, daughter of Christiana wife of Zebulon CLARK
June 7   James, son of Mercy wife of Thomas WRIGHT
August 9   Turner, son of Samuel & Abigail STETSON
August 9   Sophia, wife of Josiah CHAMBERLAIN
Josiah Warren, Nathaniel, Philip, William Henry, children of Josiah & Sophia CHAMBERLAIN
1830.   April 11   Sarah Loring, child of William & Lucy CHURCH
June 20   Reuben, son of Rufus & Huldah BATES
October 17   George Russell, Jane Russell, children of Mrs. Jane MIRIAM (widow)
November 21   Michael Robert, Edmund Quincy, children of the wife of Michael SYLVESTER
1831.   November 6   Myron Smith, child of William & Harriet SANFORD
1833.   April 7   Henry Martin, child of Samuel & Abigail STETSON by REV. MR. BRIGHAM

April 7 George, son of Thomas & Mercy WRIGHT; by REV. MR. BRIGHAM

1834. ...... Elizabeth Adams, child of George W. LOVELL and wife on her account

1835. ...... Lucy Hale, child of Josiah CHAMBERLAIN and wife on their account

July 12 Isaac, child of Isaac M. & Lucinda Eells WILDER, on her account

August 23 Ruth Turner, child of Geo. W. LOVEWELL and wife on her account

August 23 Eliza Maria, child of William CHURCH and wife; on their account

September 6 Zylpha Ann, daughter of Albert STETSON & wife and Fanny Stetson PERRY; on their account

Benjamin MUNRO, who was also received into the church according to a previous vote

1836. April Elisha Bass, child of Thomas and Mercy WRIGHT on her account

May 22 Mary Curtis, Benja Williams, Lucinda Thompson, children of Benja MUNRO and wife on his account

June 5 Almira ESTES, an adult

June 5 Abbie W. DWELLY, an adult

June 5 Anna S. DWELLY, an adult

June 5 Sarah Bass, Ruth, Albert Smith, Thomas Dunning, Analenthe, children of Joseph EELLS, Jr. and Sarah B. his wife; on her account

October 2 Lucinda COPELAND, an adult; Almira BATES, an adult

1837. May 29 Lorenzo Thomas, grandson of Dea. Isaac COOK and Bethiah his wife on their account and at their house the child being dangerously ill

June 4 Ruth Jenkins, Sybbil Robbins, Fanny, Betsey Russell, Rebecca White, Celia Ann Micheal, children of Widow Ruth BATES; on her account

August 6 William Henry, child of Benjamin MUNRO & wife: on his account

October 1 Betsey BARSTOW, an adult, on a profession of faith

Priscilla Bowker, child of Joseph & Sarah B. EELLS; at their residence on their account the child being dangerously sick

Lucinda Bass, child of Joseph and Sarah B. EELLS

1838. June 24 William Carver, child of Rufus BATES and wife by REV. DANIEL THOMAS on their account

Ruth Williams, child of M. W. and Ruth B. S. STETSON, by REV. DANIEL THOMAS on her account

July 22 George Barden, child of George W. LOVEWELL and wife, on her account

A child of Stephen JOSSELYN and Eliza his wife; on her account

October 8 Sarah Ann HARLOW, foster child of Rev. A. G. DUNCAN & wife and child Chs. Harlow: at the point of death; on their account.

1839. July 7 Mary Bradbury Eells, child of Martin and Caroline S. CHURCH, on her account

September 1 Joseph Eells, son of Isaac M. & Lucinda WILDER, on their account

September 1 John Calvin, son of John C. and Sarah T. WILDER, on their account

September 1 Elizabeth Brooks, daughter of Joseph & Sarah B. EELLS, on their account

1840. May 3 Lucius Williams, son of Wm. P. RUSSELL & Almira B. his wife, on her account

July 5 Laura Ann, child of George W. LOVEWELL and Michael B. his wife

July 19 Mary Tolman, daughter of Martin W. & Ruth B. S. STETSON

1841. January 3 Charles Ellis HARLOW, Foster child of A. G. DUNCAN & wife, on their account

July 4 George & Francis. *twin* children of Josiah and Sophia CHAMBERLAIN on their account

Lyman, child of William P. & Almira RUSSELL, on her account

1842. June 3 Lucinda Eells, child of I. M. and Lucinda E. WILDER at their house it being very sick

September 4 Marcus Packard, child of Wm. P. and Almira RUSSEL, on her account

September 11 David Brainerd, child of Benja. MONRO and wife, on his account

September 18 George Stevens, child of Stephen S. JOSSELYN and wife, on her account

October 30 William COPELAND, an adult, on a profession of his faith

October 30 Abner WOOD, an adult, on a profession of his faith

1843. January 1   Betsey Homer, child of Martin W. and Ruth B. S. STETSON, on her account

January 29   Samuel Harvey, Timothy, Julitta Sylvester, Sarah Elizabeth, Mary Adeline, Robert Sylvester, children of Saml. S. and Elizabeth CHURCH

January 29   Margaret Besse, Mary Besse, Ezra, children of Abner WOOD and wife on his account

January 29   Loama Burgess, Susanna Frost, Elizabeth Belcher, children of Robert SYLVESTER & wife

September 11   Josephine, daughter of George W. & Michel LOVEWELL

September 19   Sarah Jane, Benja. Franklin, Laura Adelaide, Lucy Ann, John Edwards, Amelia Frances, children of John SYLVESTER & wife

1844.   May 19   Hannah Melissa, child of Martin & Caroline CHURCH; by REV. MR. WIGHT of Scituate

June 2   Elizabeth Stetson, child of Wm. P. & Almira RUSSEL, on her account

June **   Sarah Emery, child of Robert & Sarah SYLVESTER, by REV. MR. WALKER

Benjamin, child of S. S. CHURCH & wife, by REV. MR. WALKER

July 14   Edward Payson, child of M. W. STETSON & Ruth B. Stetson on her account

1845.   October 8   Julitte, child of Robert & Sarah SYLVESTER

1847.   October 3   George Russel, son of Benja MONRO & Mary his wife on his account

1848.   March 14   Martin S. TORREY, being sick and very low, having professed his faith in Christ and desiring to be baptized was baptized in private by me agreeably to *Acts 8: 36-38*

August 6   Luther Wright, Sophia Ann, Josiah Bartlett, children of Rev. Cyrus HOLMES and wife

September 3   Priscilla Clark, child of George & Priscilla Clark EELLS on their account in private, the child being very sick.

N.B. Bro. Eells is a member of Church in Westerly, R.I. and Sister E. is a member of the Episcopal Chh. in Hanover.

September 24   Robert, son of Robert & Sarah SYLVESTER

October 8   James, son of George & Michal LOVEWELL, on her account: brought by her alone

October 15   Hannah, daughter of Martin & Ruth S. STETSON, on her account: brought by her alone

1849. January 7   Mrs. Saba D. BARSTOW, an adult
January 7   Mrs. Lucy J. REED, an adult
January 7   Widow Sarah W. TOLMAN, an adult
January 7   Charles, son of Widow Sarah W. TOLMAN
April 22   George Edward, Ellen Eells, children of Levett & Abigail STOCKBRIDGE, on her account
July 1   Wm. Estes, Bethiah Cook, Mary Glass, Lucy Paulina, Cela Judd, Eliza Butler, Augustine, children of Samuel & Lucy J. RIED, on her account
Charles Robert, child of Abner WOOD & wife, on his account
1850.   November 1   George Arthur, child of Martin W. & Ruth B. STETSON, on her account
1852.   November 7   Lucy SYLVESTER, an adult
1853.   January 2   William T. LAPHAM, an adult
Martha A. SYLVESTER, an adult
Julia Ann PERRY, an adult
Martha Ann, child of Melvin STODDARD & wife on their account
Benja. Coats & ......, children of Robert SYLVESTER, 2d & wife, on their account
April 16   Alfred Halleck, son of Dr. A. C. GARRETT and wife at their house she being very low
May 1   James T. TOLMAN, an adult, on profession of faith
Edwin TAYLOR, an adult, on profession of faith
June 26   Samuel, son of Samuel TOLMAN, Jr. & wife on their account
1854.   January 8   Daniel E. DAMON, an adult
January 8   Lemuel FREEMAN, an adult
January 8   Diana FREEMAN, wife of Lemuel Freeman
1857.   November 1   Priscilla F. JOSSELYN
November 1   Henry Eldon, Philip Herbert, children of Philip CHAMBERLIN & wife, presented by her
November 1   Ruth Ella, Ruby May, children of Reuben STETSON & wife, presented by her
November 1   Adelia Frances, child of John CAREY & wife, presented by her
1858.   May 1   Elliott Williams, child of Turner STETSON & wife, presented by her
1860.   September 16   Mrs. Lucy HERSEY, an adult
September 16   Emma Augusta, child of Martha STETSON & wife, presented by her

September 16   Jane Barstow, child of Robert HERSEY and wife, presented by her
September 16   Charles Heman, child of Charles DYER, Jr. & wife, presented by her

1861.   November 18   Widow Ruth JOSSELYN
  November 18   Mrs. Mahala CORBIN

1862.   September 7   Sarah Ellis, child of Turner STETSON & wife, presented by her

1863.   July 5   Miss Alice Jane HATCH, an adult
  July 5   Francis Waldo, child of Charles DYER, Jr. and wife, presented by her

1864.   November 6   Julia Ann SYLVESTER, adopted daughter of Joseph B. & Lucy W. Sylvester, presented by her

1866.   June 24   Mary Henry, daughter of Turner STETSON & wife, presented by her

THIRD MEETING HOUSE OF THE FIRST CONGREGATIONAL CHURCH AT HANOVER.
ERECTED A.D. 1827, ON THE PRESENT SITE.

CHAPTER VII.

DISMISSIONS, SUSPENSIONS AND EXCOMMUNICATIONS FROM THE CHURCH AS RECORDED.

1757–1865

1757. Novr 17 Thomas BOURN, dismissed & recommended to the Church of Christ in Sandwich

1760. April 6 Anna the wife of Jno. BRAY dismissed and recommended to the Church of Christ in Harpswell

1762. August 15 Rebecca the wife of Daniel ALDEN, Esqr. Dismissed and recommended to the Church of Christ in Stafford in Connecticut

1773. Feby 1 Tho WILKS and Wife and their children John, Ann and Caroline Wilks dismissed and recommended to the chh. of Christ in Abbington

December 19 Jeremiah and Lucy STETSON. Dismissed and recommended to the 2d Chh. in Pembroke

1776. March 3 Stevens and Ruth HATCH, dismissed and recommended to the Church in Spencer

Sepr 15 Ruth LAMBERT, dismissed and recommended to the church of Christ in No. 5

Decr 29 Othniel and Deborah PRATT dismissed and recommended to the Chh. of Christ in Spencer

DISMISSIONS AFTER REVD MR. MELLEN'S INSTALMENT.

1785. April 24 The Chh. dismist & recommended the Widow Hannah STETSON to the Chh. in Sylvester
1791. Jany 16 Dismissed Ruth the wife of Saml WITHEREL of Chesterfield to the Chh. in that town
1795. Octr 18 Dismissed & recommended Edmund EASTMAN to the Chh. in Limerick, he being now their Pastor elect
1796. Augt 14 Dismissed and recommended the wife of Job YOUNG to the Chh. of Christ in Belfast (Province of Main)
October 30 Dismissed & recommended Peleg EWELL to the Chh. in Francistown, New Hampshire; also
the Widow Content WITHEREL to the Chh. in Pittsfield
1800. Sepr 7 Dismissed & recommended the Widow Alice BAILY to the church of Christ in Freport
1802. May 2d Dismist & recommended wife of Elisha CURTIS, Junr to ye chh. in New Salem in New Hampshire
1825. March 4 Voted that Ezekiel TURNER, Benjamin BASS and Sarah CLARK be *suspended* from the fellowship and communion of this church for the space of three months.
November 16 Voted that Brother Ezekiel TURNER and Sister Sarah CLARKE be *excommunicated* from the fellowship and communion of this Church.

A request was communicated to the Church from Sister Mary TOLMAN requesting to be dismissed from this Chh. and recommended to the Chh. in Boston under the pastoral care of the Rev. William Jenks.

Voted to grant the request.

1826. April 3 Mary PERRY wife of Joshua : removed to the Chh. in ......
1828. August 1 Nancy CUSHING of Situate dismissed and recommended to the Rev. Mr. Jewett's church Situate

1829. August 7 Mrs. Meletiah CHADWICK (relict of Revd) letter to the chh. of New Bedford care of Rev. Mr. Holmes.

December 26 Grace F. SMITH was commended in usual form to the church in Edgartown, M. Vineyard.

1830. March 14 Mrs. Elizabeth RAMSDEL of Weston dismissed to the church in that place

November 5 Voted that the Widow Polly MANN be *excommunicated* from this church

1834. January [last Friday of] Voted that Jane MERIAM be *cut off from the Church* in going to the Baptists without consulting with the Chh. and neglecting to give the church satisfaction until she manifest true repentance and return with sincere confession of her violations of covenant.

January [last Friday of] At a regular meeting on * * * *, 1833 the case of Joshua DWELLEY was considered whereupon it appeared that he had embraced the heresy of Universalism and refused to listen to the admonitions or regard the labor of the brethren with him.

Voted that he be *cut off from the watch & fellowship of the Chh.*

October ** Roxana NYE dismissed to a Presbyterian chh. in Cincinnati, O.

1836. August 7 By vote of the church Elizabeth TORREY and Bashua DAWS recommended to the watch and fellowship of the church of Christ in North Yarmouth, Me.

1838. June 15 Mrs. Lydia F. P. BAKER: by letter of recommendation to 3rd Cong. Church in Abington

1841. June 4 Voted to give Brother Joshua PERRY a hearing in relation to his case, he having had a controversy with the Church in relation to certain points of doctrine and practice growing mostly out (of) his doctrinal views and the church after a series of meetings without satisfying him, having voted to postpone indefinitely the whole affair whereupon he withdrew from the Parish and from meetings & fellowship of the church for some months. He having expressed a desire to appear before the church, the church voted as above.

June 11 Church held a meeting to hear bro. Joshua PERRY who again brought before them his old controversy with some additional views.

July 2   Church conference. Mr. PERRY continued his remarks.

July 30   Church meeting. Mr. PERRY again labored on his points of doctrine and practice.

September 3   Church meeting. Mr. PERRY appeared again on the same subject: adjourned to meet on the 17th inst.

September 17   Church met. Bro. PERRY again before the Church.

Voted that Deacons Barstow & Cook & bro. E. Bass be a committee to look after any persons who have neglected to support gospel institutions & to attend public worship and any other cases that require discipline.

December 31   Church met. The comee on cases of discipline reported in part that they had labored with Bro. Joshua PERRY who in their opinion had embraced heretical opinions in relation to the agency of God and the doctrine of Regeneration & Sanctification by the efficient agency of the Holy Ghost & the doctrine of the atonement and who had also neglected gospel ordinances & fellowship with this church.

Voted that Mr. Perry be cited to appear before the chh. to answer to the above charges on Jan. 29, 1842.

1842.   January 29   At a regular meeting of the Church bro. Joshua Perry appeared and after some discussion the report of the committee was recommitted with instruction to obtain in writing from Mr. Perry a precise statement of the difference between him and the church in relation to the doctrines on which he is charged with heresy.

March 4   At a regular meeting the church received the report of the com'ee on Mr. Perry's case. The report did not contain a precise statement of the difference of belief but only an asseveration in general terms that he had never to his knowledge denied the doctrines as held by the church. The church after considering the subject at some length

Voted that in view of the favorable indications of revival to suspend the farther consideration of Mr. Perry's case for three months.

June 3   At a regular meeting the chh. resumed the consideration of Mr. J. Perry's case. He was questioned in relation to his belief of the work of the Holy Spirit. He affirmed that conversion was affected only by moral power which he defined to be the *truth* and the character of God combined and because the spirit has revealed the truth he may therefore be said to renew sinners. He was requested to state also why he had forsaken the ministrations of the word in this place and neglected to support gospel institutions. He affirmed that the church had no right to require him to come to the Lord's Supper. He affirmed also that he had lost his confidence in the Pastor. After considerable discussion it was

Voted to adjourn to Tuesday the 7th inst.

June 7 The church met according to adjournment. The case of Mr. Joshua Perry came again under consideration after prayer by the Pastor. The church, after a protracted discussion and consideration of the whole subject,

Voted to appoint brethren Dea. Cook, John C. Wilder and Elisha Bass, a committee to consider and report what action the church should take in relation to it.

The Committee reported as follows: "Whereas brother Joshua Perry has embraced sentiments essentially different from the confession of faith adopted by this church ; and whereas he has absented himself from the communion of the church and refuses to submit to the regular discipline of the church in confessing his faults, and making Christian satisfaction for them as he has covenanted to do." Therefore: Resolved that brother Joshua Perry *be no longer considered a member of this church* unless he confess his errors and faults and return to its communion within three months.

The report upon motion was adopted as the final action of the chh. 5 to 2 and one member not voting.

After prayer by Dea. Cook the meeting was dissolved.

July 1 At a regular church meeting the Comm'ee on Discipline entered a complaint against bro. William CHURCH for having for nearly two years forsaken the public worship of God and refusing to support the gospel with this church. The committee stated that they had labored with bro. Church without getting satisfaction and that he persisted in maintaining his position contrary to his covenant obligations :

Voted that bro. Wm. Church be cited to appear and answer to the charge brought against him.

July 29 Church met according to adjournment. Bro. Wm. Church's case was taken up for consideration. He refused to appear to answer to the citation but sent a communication in which he shifted the issue between him and the church : whereupon bro. Isaac Cook was appointed a committee to wait upon him and explain to him the views of the church in relation to his communication and endeavor to induce him to appear. Bro. Cook reported that he had labored in vain. After considerable discussion the church adjourned, after requesting the pastor to seek an interview with him.

September 2 The church met. Bro. Church remained contumacious. The Pastor reported that he had in company with Dea. J. Cook sought an interview with him but found him unchanged in his purposes and unable to give any reasonable satisfaction. After much discussion it was

Moved and carried that at the end of three months bro. William Church be *considered no longer a member in fellowship with this church* unless he shall within that time manifest repentance for his faults and make suitable confessions.

December 30 Voted that Bro. Rufus Bates be cited to appear before the church and justify (if he can) his general course for two or three years past.

1843. February 3 At a regular meeting of the church the case of bro. Rufus BATES was considered in relation to the following charges :

1st. Withholding support from the gospel ministry in the church.

2nd. Neglecting to attend on the preaching of the gospel and "other meetings of the church."

Bro. Bates had been cited to appear and give satisfaction. He did not appear. After much discussion of his case the church

Voted that Rufus Bates be and hereby is *excluded from the communion and fellowship and privilege* of this church. Dea. Cook was requested to inform him of the doings of the church.

March 3   The church met for prep. lecture & conference. The Committee of Discipline, Reported that they had commenced labor with bro. Albert STETSON "for neglect of the gospel & its institutions in this church." They had taken the first and second step but they had not gained their brother therefore they "told it to the church."

Whereupon voted that Bro. Albert Stetson be cited to appear before the church to answer for himself. Bro. Monro was requested to notify him.

March 31   At a regular meeting of the church the case of bro. Albert Stetson was considered. He was not present but a communication from him was rec'd and after much discussion & consideration of its reasons it was unanimously

Voted That the church are not satisfied the reasons assigned are a sufficient justification for an entire disregard on his part of all covenant obligations, *i.e.* in the church and that his case be deferred to the next meeting.

May 5   At a regular meeting of the church the case of bro. Albert Stetson was again considered. As he did not appear he was viewed as contumacious but in regard to the desires of some of the brethren it was

Voted that his case be deferred to the next conference.

June 2   The church met in regular church meeting. The case of bro. Albert Stetson was again under consideration. The Pastor read a second communication from him and after considering it it was

Voted to send bro. Chamberlin to request his attendance & hear the church who reported that Bro. Stetson still refused to appear before the church.

Whereupon after still further discussion and deliberation it was

Voted *nem. con.* "Whereas, bro. Albert Stetson has neglected the gospel and its institutions in this church and refuses to confess his fault and make Christian satisfaction, therefore, resolved that his connection with this church be and hereby is dissolved."

N.B.   Bro. Bass was requested to communicate this vote to him.

1845. June 9   Sister Ann S. HATCH was dismissed to unite with Rev. Dr. D. Tappan's Church in North Marshfield, prior to this date.

1847. December 31   Voted that Bro. Benjamin MONRO at his own request be dismissed and recommended to the church in Scituate.

1854.   March 10

William Copeland	Sarah Sylvester
Ebenr B. Howland	Julia A. Turner
James Turner	Huldah F. Sampson
Alfred C. Garratt	Martha A. Sylvester
Isaac M. Wilder	Lucinda Copeland
Robt Sylvester, 2nd	Ruth Wilder
James T. Tolman	Geo. W. Eells
Lucy Copeland	Wm. T. Lapham
Marcy B. Eells	Leml Freeman
Priscilla Eells	Robert Sylvester
Charles F. Bowman	Diana Freeman
Daniel E. Damon	Lucinda Wilder
Mary Tolman	Mary Bates
Rhoda Ford	Jane Copeland
Abby W. Stockbridge	Abby E. Barstow &
Sophia A. Holmes	Christiana Clark : were

dismissed to be organized into a Trinitarian Cong. Church at The "Four Corners" and when so organized they will be considered no longer as members of this church.

1855. June 15   Voted to grant Mrs. Laura J. D. KING, daughter of Rev. Mr. Duncan a letter of dismission and recommendation to the Congregational Church in North Asms at her own request. The letter was forwarded by the care of her father.

December 16   The following is the copy of a letter of dismission and recommendation of Mr. Benj. WATERMAN to the first Cong'l chh. in Scituate:

HANOVER, Feby 19, 1855.

The First Congregational Church in Hanover
   To The First Cong'l Chh. in Scituate.

REV. AND BELOVED:

Bro. Benjamin Waterman a member of this church in regular standing, having requested a letter of dismission and recommendation to you, the church have voted the same. When received by you his particular relation with us will be considered at an end.   ISAAC COOK, *Dea.*

Attest J. FREEMAN, *Pastor.*

December 17 The following is a note from the Rev. Mr. Wight, Pastor of the Cong'l chh. in Scituate:

"Bro. Benjamin Waterman of your church bro't a letter of dismission from yr. ch. and recommendation to ours (last July). He handed the letter to me but has not been present at our church meetings & so it has not been acted upon. As he has removed back to H. to reside, I have supposed it proper to return the letter having found it agreeable to him.

A true copy: Attest J. FREEMAN, *Pastor.*

1858. April 11 Voted at the request of Bro. Benjamin S. Waterman to give him a letter of dismission and recommendation to the Congregational Church in Centre Abington.

July 2 The case of brother * * * came up. Agreeable to the wish expressed by the chh. Bro. * * * stated some things as he understood them. He said that he had done nothing wrong and read a paper signed by those who had accused him of trespass against them, in the presence of Perez Simmons, esqr. exculpating him of all blame, but as there are many conflicting reports the brethren thought it might be well to look into the matter further and consequently appointed a committee for this purpose consisting of Dea. Isaac Cook, bros. Elisha Bass and Samuel S. Church.

July 27 Chh. met in conference. The committee chosen at the previous meeting July 2, were called to report on Bro. * * * case and they did so. After a free discussion and expression of feeling the following votes were passed:

Voted That we accept the report of our committee.

Voted That there is not sufficient evidence, to our minds, to sustain the charges brought against brother * * *.

Dea. Cook expressed the wish that if the committee were retained, to be excused from serving on the committee as the chh. did not perceive the necessity of a committee any further.

Voted That the committee be excused from further service.

The responsibility now seems to devolve upon each member to do what he can in the case; if he can get any more light on the subject or any valid evidence of bro: * * * being guilty to communicate the same to the chh.

August 2   Chh met for business agreeable to notice given on the Sabbath Aug. 1st. Bro. * * * case was further attended to. Bro. Bass moved that we reconsider the vote passed at the last meeting to wit :

That there is not sufficient evidence to our minds to sustain the charges brought against bro. * * *. Seconded by bro. Thayer.

After some discussion bro. Bass withdrew his motion for the purpose of adding an amendment :

Moved that whereas in the vote passed at the last meeting viz: there is not sufficient evidence to our minds to sustain the charges brought against brother * * * it was not designed to acquit bro. * * * and mistaken impressions have been received from it in some instances, we do hereby reconsider that vote : seconded by bro. Thayer, unanimous vote.

Moved by bro. Chamberlin that a committee of three be chosen to attend to the further prosecution of the business before the church.

Voted that Bro. * * * be suspended from the communion of this chh. for one year, unless within that time he can give satisfaction to the chh.

At the end of one year, if not settled before, the case is to be called up for final action. This is the understanding of the chh. as expressed in their remarks though no formal vote was taken upon it specifically.

Voted. That the pastor communicate to bro: * * * the vote of his suspension from the communion of this chh. for one year &c.

[This communication was made to Bro : * * * the evening of the same day.

Attest. J. FREEMAN, *Pastor:*

1859.   August 2   * * * The doings of the Church on the case of brother * * * at the last meeting on it one year ago, were read. Very few members were present so that it was not deemed advisable to take any important and decisive action on the case at that time. The committee were desired to visit brother * * * and confer with him on the whole matter before another meeting should be called.

Voted to adjourn to meet one week from next Saturday, 13th inst. at 3 o'clock P. M.

August 13. Church met for business according to adjournment. Only three members of the church were present. A portion of scripture was read and prayer was offered by the pastor. The record of the meeting on the 2nd. inst. was read. Bro. Chamberlin stated that the committee (a part of them) had waited on brother * * * since the last meeting. No action was taken on bro: * * * case because so few were present. Adjourned to meet on Monday next, 15th inst. at 3 o'clock P.M.

August 15. Church met according to adjournment a portion of Scripture was read and prayer offered by the Pastor. The record of the previous meeting was read: communications were made by the committee on Bro. * * * case. There were four brethren present. After expressing their views of the case they signified their readiness to proceed to take decisive action upon it. It was moved by Dea. J. Cook:

That whereas the charges brought against * * * a member of this church, have, in the minds of the church, been sustained, and he has failed to give satisfaction to the church by confession and repentance, he is hereby *cut off from the communion and fellowship of the church.*

The motion was seconded by Bro: Bass. The vote was unanimous.

Voted that the Pastor communicate this vote to Mr. * * *.

Prayer was then offered by the Pastor: Adjourned without date.

1860. October 28   At the request of Mrs. Elizabeth T. HOUSE as she expects to remove her residence to Duxbury where she formerly lived

Voted that she have a letter of dismission and recommendation to the church in Marshfield of which Rev. Mr. Alden is pastor.

1861. January 6. A letter was read by the pastor from Mrs. Lucia A. DEAN formerly Miss Duncan, daughter of former pastor, asking dismission from this chh. to the chh. in East Taunton and recommendation to the same. Church voted to grant it.

August 6. Bro. Benj. WATERMAN was not received to the chh. in Abington: probably he did not attend to his letter as he ought and he has now applied for a letter to the Cong'l ch. in Scituate to which he formerly belonged. I now forward to Dea. Marshall Litchfield bro. Waterman's letter returned to this chh. Dec. 1855.

August 18. Bro. Benjamin WATERMAN returned to me through Dea. Cook his letter to the Chh. in Abington.

1865. April 13 A letter was read by the pastor from Bro. John SYLVESTER & wife of Waverly asking dismission & recommendation to the First Cong'l chh. in Waverly & the chh. voted the same

November 5 After communion of the Lord's Supper the chh. stopped by request and the following letter was presented

FREETOWN, Oct. 31, '65

To the First Cong'l chh. in Hanover,
    REV. & BELOVED,

Being desirous of uniting with the Cong. Chh. in Freetown (Assonet) we hereby request letters of dismission from you and of recommendation to said church.

Yours in the bonds of the Gospel.

A. G. DUNCAN
for
ALMIRA ESTES.
A. G. DUNCAN.

The Church voted to grant the above requests.

December 10. The request of George CHAMBERLIN for letter of dismission and recommendation to the Cong'l Church in Milford was presented and granted by unanimous vote.

CHAPTER VII.

DEATHS ENTERED ON THE RECORDS OF THE FIRST CONGREGATIONAL CHURCH 1728–1867.

DEATHS

After I (BENJA. BASS) came to town.

1727-28. July 24 Captain Joseph BARSTOW.
  Josiah PALMER, senr.
  Rebekah, the wife of Joseph PERRY.
  Bradbury, the daughter of Abner DWELLY.
December 17 Mercy, the wife of Benja. BARSTOW.
  Mary, the wife of Meletiah DILLINGHAM.
1728-29. January 20 A *child* of Jabez JOSSLYN.
February 12 Mercy, daughter to the widow HEFFORD of Pembrook.
March 11 The *child* of Mr. Elijah CUSHING.
May 1 Luke son of Richard BUKER.
May 2 Edmund BUKER: son-in-law to Samuel Witherly.
June 28 Jonathan PRATT.
July 9 An *infant child* of Matthew EASTICE.
September 3 Ezekiel VINALL a child of about 6 months of age.
September 21 Rebecca, wife of Joshua STAPLES.
December 3 .... BUKER: a child.

1729-30. January 31   Susanna BARSTOW: widow: mother to Samuel Barstow.
June 14   Cæsar: a child: one of Deacon STOCKBRIDGE's *slaves.*
June 20   Mary, wife of Mr. Benjamin CURTIS, Senior.
September   A child of Matthew EASTICE
October 11   Mary, the wife of Richard BUKER.
October 24   Samuel BARSTOW: the *first chh. member that died in ye town.*
October 30   Henery JOSSELYN: the *oldest man in town for years together.*
October 31   Samuel PARRIS.
1730-31. February 18   Samuel, son of Samuel & Rebecca STAPLES.
February 25   Hanna, daughter of Samuel & Rebecca STAPLES.
March 27   A *child of* William & Honour TORY.
April 7   Charles STOCKBRIDGE.
June 15   ...... child of John and Juel DILINGHAM.
July 14   Bathshua, wife of Ezekiel TURNER.
July 27   Desire, daughter of Ezekiel and Tabitha VINAL.
                 A *mulatto child* of Jabez UTTER's.
December 19   ...... daughter of James HATCH, Jr.
1731-32. January 31   Phœbe, the wife of Meletiah DILINGHAM.
February 10   David CAIN.
February 22   ...... *daughter* of Jonathan & Margaret PETER.
March 10   Rebecca, daughter of Josiah & ...... CURTIS.
April 8   Eunice Low.
April 22   A *child* of Matthew & ...... EASTICE.
May 11   Thomas KENNEDY.
June 9   Mephibosheth DILINGHAM, son of Melatiah Dilingham.
September 1   Abner DWELLY.
September 7   Joseph son of Benjamin & Martha MAN.
October 17   Margaret, wife of Deacon STOCKBRIDGE.
November 2   The widow Mary BRYANT: of a great age.
1732-33. January 16   James BARSTOW.
March 15   ...... daughter of Caleb & ...... BARKER.
March 27   Susanna, daughter of Thomas & Elizabeth WILKS.
April 19   ...... daughter of Joseph & Patience CORNISH.
April 25   A *negro child* of Joseph RAMSDALE.
May 7   David SYLVESTER.
June 6   Mehetable wife of Theophilus WITHEREL.

July 18 Elizabeth wife of Thomas ELMORE.
September 19 Ezekiel VINAL.
October 15 Mary, wife of John STODDARD.
1733-34. January 10 John STODDARD : husband of ye woman last recorded.
January 26 ...... son of William & Hannah FORD.
March 1 Thankful, daughter of Benjamin & Martha MANN.
July 14 Jabez JOSSELYN.
August 3 Gideon STUDLEY.
December 12 Eli STETSON.
1734-35. March 13 Isaac, son of Isaac & Deborah LAMBERT.
1735-36. January 18 Deacon STOCKBRIDGE'S *negro man* Cuffy.
February 1 ...... daughter of Joshua and Lydia STUDLEY.
March 4 A *negro child* belonging to Elijah CUSHING, esqr.
April ...... RICCARDS of Pembroke.
May 26 Olive, daughter of Timothy & Sarah BAILY.
June 20 Josiah PALMER.
August 12. Elizabeth, daughter of William & Elizabeth GUILFORD.
1736-37. January A child of Samuel and Rebecca WITHERELL.
February 15 John TAYLOR.
March 4 William CURTIS.
March 8 Japhet the son of Honour TOREY and servant of Mr. Recompense TIFFANY : *drowned.*
March 10 Nathaniel TOREY, Junior.
May 29 The Widow NORTHY.
July 19 Hannah, daughter of Thomas & Faith ROSE.
August 5 Gideon, son of John & Elizabeth STUDLEY.
September 2 Hannah North, daughter of Samuel & Hannah EELLS.
October 26 Sarah, daughter of Gideon & ...... RAMSDALE.
December 5 Deborah, daughter of Joseph & Patience CORNISH.
December 20 A child of John LOVE.
1737-38. January 21 Thomas, son of Clement and Agatha BATES
February A *negro* of Mr. DILLY.
February 10 Lawrence CANE.
April 7 A son of Ruth SYLVESTER.
April 14 John FORD.
May 13 Sarah BARSTOW.
September 22 ...... a child of William & Hannah FORD.
October 6 Nathaniel, son of Benjamin & Lillis STETSON.

October 7 Mary, daughter of Nathan & Lydia BOURN.
1738-39. January 30 Hannah HOUSE.
February 13 Hannah STODDARD.
February A *negro* of Matthew EASTICE'S.
March 10 James, son of Robert and Margaret YOUNG : by *scalding*.
March 28 Mercy WADSWORTH.
June 1 Margaret, daughter of Samuel & Margaret BARSTOW.
June 7 Lydia, relict of Nathan BOURN, who died at Sandwich about a fortnight before.
June 25 Experience, daughter of Joseph & Mary CURTIS.
July 13 Naomi TURNER, widow.
August 4 Thankful OTIS.
August 12 ...... daughter of William & Martha CURTISS.
September 22 ...... son of Joshua and Mary STAPLES.
October 30 Sarah, an *Indian woman*.
November 19 Thomas, son of Seth and Elizabeth STETSON.
1739-40. March 21 Grace, daughter of Benjamin & Lillis STETSON.
April 6. Joseph, son of Joseph & Mary RAMSDALE.
April 16 ...... son of Benjamin & Sarah BARSTOW.
April 22 Bachelor WING.
May 6. Lydia, daughter of Joshua & Lydia STUDLEY.
May 7 Deborah, daughter of Samuel & Deborah HOUSE.
May 8. Stephen, son of Joseph and Mary CURTIS.
July 1 ...... child of John & Rebecca HOUSE.
July 9 Joseph BATES.
July 30 ...... child of William & Martha CURTIS.
July 31 Deborah PRATT.
August 10 ...... son of Seth and Elizabeth STETSON.
October 9 Sarah, wife of Timothy BAILY.
October 18 Ezekiel, son of Ezekiel & Ruth TURNER.

☞ At this interval the records of 29 deaths appear to be missing.

1743. November 5 Mary, wife of Joshua STAPLES.
December 7 Robert STETSON, a very old man: *near 100*.
1743-44. February 28 ...... CROOKER, a child exceeding suddenly.
May ...... child of Robert BARKER.
June ...... son of Robert BARKER.

June 17 ...... DOGGETT, a child.
June 24 ...... child of Edward EASTICE.
July 30 Capt. CUSHING's *negro child.*
August 10 Mehetabel CURTISS, daughter of Elisha.
August 11 Ezra, son of Benjamin & Martha MANN.
August 23 Sarah, daughter of Thomas & Elizabeth WILKS.
October 20 ...... daughter of Benja. SYLVESTER, Junr.
October 23 Rachel, wife of James ROGERS.
November 2 The widow TURNER: Caleb's mother: aged 86.
December 17 ...... child of Jeremiah & Deborah ROGERS.
December 22 Baily, only son of James ROGERS.
1744-45. March 19 Mary, relict of Deacon James HATCH.
May 16 An infant of James CORNISH & wife.
June 11 Prince HOWLAND: a young man of Marshfield *drowned in the Furnace Pond.*
September 3 ...... son of Ezekiel & Martha PALMER.
November Two children of ...... CROOKER: buried I think in *one* grave.
1745-46. January 4 Isaac, son of Elijah and Elizabeth CUSHING. and ye next day
January 5 Sarah, wife of James TORREY.
January 11 Martha PALMER.
February 18 Barden, son of Michael & Mary SYLVESTER.
March 7 Sarah, daughter of Caleb & ...... RANDALL.
March 18 Mary, daughter of Michael and Mary SYLVESTER.
May 30 A daughter of ye widow Elizabeth PERRY.
August or September A *negro infant* of Uriah LAMBERT.
October 20 Margaret, wife of Capt. James HOUSE.
October 22 Joseph, son of Joseph & Patience CORNISH.
November 6 Deborah, daughter of Ebenezer and Joanna WRIGHT.
November 14 Benoni STUDLEY: an aged man.
November 22 William TORREY of a *cancer* which began in his nose and which rendered him the most affecting spectacle of torture * * * I ever beheld.
November 25 The Widow Martha FORD.
December 29 or 30 Hope, wife of David TORREY.
1746-47. January or February A *negro* child of Elijah CUSHING, esqr.

February 11 RICHARD FITZGERALD, who had been *schoolmaster* in the town near twenty years.
March 27 Deborah wife of David STOCKBRIDGE
June 15 An infant of Joseph & Abigail HOUSE.
June 28 A child of Joseph & Alice NEAL.
September 24 Matthew EASTICE, Junr. a young man of between 20 & 21 years of age who in *making a rash attempt to swim over North River* with all his cloaths on heavy with water & mudd *was drowned* about 8 or 9 of ye clock in the morning.
November 18 Elizabeth, daughter of Thomas & Elizabeth WILKS.
Novb. or December Jupiter, a *negro man* of Mr. John CURTISS.
1747-48. February 7 A child of James and ...... CORNISH.
February An infant of ...... SYLVESTER.
April 17 Samuel, son of Seth and Elizabeth STETSON.
July 9 John, son of Jeremiah & Deborah ROGERS.
September 22 Joseph NEAL: who on the evening of the 16th day of the month *fell* (according to his own account) *before the wheel of his loaden cart* which went over him & yet left no mark.
September 24 Deborah, daughter of Othniel & Mary PRATT: aged 6 months and a few days: her distemper was a violent cough common among children & *strangled* her.
October 6 Nathaniel CURTISS: a young man almost 21.
December 19 or 29 Elnathan PALMER: aged about 86.
1748-49. January 10 Isaac STETSON.
January 12 Paul, son of Clement and Agatha BATES.
January 15 Joshua, son of Joshua and ...... PALMER.
January 23 Briton, a *negro child* of John & Elizabeth STUDLEY.
May 11 An infant of Sam'll WITHERELL.
June 14 Hannah, daughter of Thomas & Sarah CURTISS.
July 30 ...... child of Windsor & Mercy JONAS.
August 7 ...... RANSOM, who was killed in a moment by a *loaden cart running over his head.*
September 11 Shadrach HATCH.
October 23 Rebecca, daughter of John & Elizabeth STUDLEY.
October 24 Abigail, daughter of Joshua & Elizabeth BABSTOW.
October 28 A child of Robert BARKER.
November 19 An infant of Jeremiah & Deborah ROGERS.
1749-50. January 20 William, son of Benjamin CURTISS, deceased.
March 8 A child of Francis and ...... KANE.

March 23   William WITHEREL.
April 9   Mary wife of Joseph CURTISS.
April 14   ...... STAPLES, an infant.
May 31   ...... daughter of William & Elizabeth EASTICE.
June 18   ...... Ramsdale, son of Joseph and Mary RAMSDALE in the morning, and in the evening
　　　...... daughter of Jabez and Mary JOSSELYN by *drowning* in stream of water at the tail of a Tug wheel (or Forge?)
November 1   Jesse, son of Jesse and Mary TORREY.
November 9   An infant child of Elisha PALMER.
November 10   Sarah, the wife of Richard BUKER who had been for many years in great affliction.
November 29   John CURTIS.
1750-51.   January 17   John, son of Joshua & Lydia STUDLEY.
February 24 or 25   A child of Peg PETERS.
February 28   Hannah, daughter of Nathanael & Hannah ROBBINS: a child betwixt (I think, 6 & 7 years old) whose death *was occasioned & within a little more than two days accomplished by a wound at the inner corner of her eye* from a little stub root in ye ground on which she fell as she was getting over a scraggy fence.
March 17   An *Indian woman*: very suddenly on ye Lord's Day morning.
April 5   ...... son of Caleb & Mary ROGERS.
April 8   Sarah, daughter of Job and ...... TILDEN.
June 2   John, son of Jeremiah & Deborah ROGERS.
July 11   Mr. Hatherly FOSTER of Scituate: killed by *lightning*.
July 18   ...... son of David STOCKBRIDGE, esqr. and his wife Jane.
July 27   Seth, son of Josiah CURTISS: of the throat disorder.
August 7   A *negro child* of Ensign John BAILY.
September 4   The wife of Theophilus WITHERELL.
1752.   January 1   John LAMBERT an aged man after long confinement to his bed in uncommonly grievous circumstances.
January   An infant child of Othniel PRATT.
February 3   Abigail, daughter of Abijah STETSON.
May 2 or 3   ...... son of Eliab STUDLEY.
May 17   Joseph, son of Abiel COBB: baptised just a week before.
May 19   Abigail, daughter of Abiel COBB.
May 21   Deborah, another child of Abiel Cobb: She fell *a-bleeding at the nose* about 36 hours afore she died, which bleeding ceased not (if at all intermitted) till her death.

May 22 (perhaps)   A Child of John and Ann BRAY.
May 23   A child of Sylvanus and Hannah WING.
May 24   The wife of Abiel COBB.
May 28 or 29   Another Child of John and Ann BRAY.
May 31   Another Child of Sylvanus & Hannah WING.
June 2   Mr. John BAILY.
June 4   Jeroboam, the only son of Abiel COBB.
June 8   Katharine FITZGERALD.
July 16   Deborah ROGERS.
July 30   William, son of William and Mary WHITTEN.
September   Lillis, daughter of Isaac & Deborah LAMBERT.
November 17   An ...... child of Elizabeth SYLVESTER, maiden daughter of Amos Sylvester.
1753. January 3   Elizabeth, wife of David JENKINS.
January 15   Jeremiah, son of Jeremiah & Deborah ROGERS.
January 16 or 17 ...... son of Robert BARKER.
January 22   Betty, daughter of Clement and Agatha BATES.
January 27   Nathanael, son of James and Margaret CLARK.
February 11   Margaret FRANK, a Welsh woman: judged to have been about *96 years old.*
March 2   Mrs: ...... BAILY, relict of Mr. John Baily who died about 9 months before.
March 6   Mr. Ebenezer CURTISS.
March 11   Ruth ELLIS.
April 4   Nathanael TORREY.
June 4   James, son of Samuel & Deborah HOUSE.
June 11   Clement BATES, Junior, a promising young man about two and twenty years old.

    At this interval the records of 25 deaths appear to be missing.

1754. August 19   An infant of Joshua & Lillis STETSON.
August 21   Desire, daughter of Caleb & Desire SYLVESTER.
October 21   Jane HANMER.
December 26.   A *negro Infant.*
1755. March 11   The Widow VINAL, mother-in-law to Lieut. Job Tilden.
April 14   An infant son of Josiah and Alice CORNISH.
April 30   Edmund SYLVESTER, Junior, my lovely and only grand-son aged a little above two years and four months: may God make us heavenly minded and prepare us for eternal life in Heaven by this death.

July 22   Sarah, the wife of John LAMBERT.
August 26   The Widow Frances JOSSLYN
October 11   An *Indian woman* who died at Mr. Mordecai ELLIS'.
October 14   Patience, wife of Joseph CORNISH.
October 29.   Mary, the wife of Michael SYLVESTER.
October 31   The Widow Deborah HATCH.
November 2   An infant of Thomas PALMER.
November 30   Deborah, daughter of Jeremiah and Deborah ROGERS.
1756.   February 19   Dinah, a *negro*, Mr. Amos SYLVESTER'S servant.
March 29   John HOLMES an aged man after a few weeks abode in and support by ye town, the town of Pembroke in which he once owned a very good estate, having no more manhood than to fling him upon the Town of Hanover because they might do it by the law of the Province.
May 13   Caleb CHURCH.
May 13   The wife of Isaac TURNER.
May 14   Joanna WING.
May 16   Miriam, the wife of Tailor BROOKS.
May 23   The Revd. Benjamin BASS, Pastor of the Church in Hanover.
Ben Engin, an *Engin* of John BOSBY.
A *negro* of Joseph JOSLYN.
Joseph, son of Joseph CORNISH.
A child of Josiah CORNIS and Elie his wife.
John VINIOL *printis* of Charles BAILY.
Decem. 23 (8?)   The Widow Sarah JOSSELYN, the wife of Jabez Josselyn, deceased.
1757.   Jany. 24.   Margarett the daughter of Dea'n. Saml. BARSTOW and Margarett his wife.
Feb. 21.   Benj. CURTIS, aged 66.
Mar. 13.   Thomas RAMSDALE.
March 25.   Mary CURTIS, the wife of Reuben Curtis.
May 21.   Bilhah, Mr. Joshua BARSTOW's *negro-woman.*
June 29.   Joshua, the son of Amos WRIGHT and his wife.
July 21.   Mary WOODWARD the wife of Jno. Woodward.
July 25.   The Widow Sarah WITHEREL.
Sept. 2.   Capt. Benj. STETSON.
Sept. 14.   Asenath the wife of Simeon CURTIS.
Octo. 22.   Phillipi FOX.
1758.   Feby. 2.   David LAWSON.

Feby. 19   An infant, the daughter of Thos. TORREY and Elizabeth his wife.
April 23.   Henchman SYLVESTER.
May 15.   Reuben CURTIS.
Sepr. 7.   The Widow Sarah STOCKBRIDGE.
Nov. 15.   Elisha, the son of Othniel PRATT and Mary his wife.
Nov. 20.   Hannah, the daughter of Othniel PRATT and Mary his wife.
Dec. 6.   Jabez the son of Othniel PRATT and Mary his wife.
1759.   Jany. 11.   William CURTIS.
March 12.   Mary PRATT, the wife of Othniel Pratt.
April 15.   Jane BARON; an old woman for many years past maintained by the Town.
May 1.   Joseph Barstow, the son of Joshua BARSTOW and Elizabeth his wife.
May 17.   Abel, the son of Elijah GARNETT and his wife.
June 23.   Othniel PRATT.
June 27.   Lydia the wife of Joshua STUDLEY.
July 9.   Joshua STUDLEY.
July 22.   Jesse CURTIS.
July 30.   Mary Bates the wife of Joseph BATES.
August 1.   William the son of John NICOLSON and Lydia his wife.
August 4.   Joshua the son of David HOUSE Jr. and Rhoda his wife.
August 14.   Joseph CURTIS.
August 15.   David STUDLEY.
Decemr. 2.   Barker, the son of Simeon CURTIS and Lucy his wife.
Decemr. 26.   Irania DILLENO.
1760.   Jany. 7.   Abigail STUDLEY a widow-woman.
Feby. 12.   A *negro boy* of Mr. Job TILDEN'S.
March 14.   Benjamin SYLVESTER.
Sept. 28.   Joseph son of Nathll. ROBBINS & wife.
Octo. 1.   Thomas SYLVESTER.
Octo. 30.   Abigail the wife of Joseph HOUSE.
1761.   Jany. 28.   Miranda, daughter of Joshua BAYLEY and Abigail his wife.
May 20.   The Widow Joanna WING: *aged 100 years.*
June 23.   Samuel STETSON.
August 21.   Deborah the wife of Jeremiah ROGERS.
Septr. 17.   Samuel son of Joshua SYMMONDS and Elizabeth his wife.

1762. Jany. 1. John WOODWARD.
Feby. 3. Dinah, *servant* to the Revd. Samuel BALDWIN.
Feby. 8. Paul, son of Bezaleel CURTIS and his wife.
Feby. 11. Widow Elizabeth SYLVESTER.
March 20 Widow Ruth SYLVESTER.
March 31. Thomas WHITE.
May 7. Samuel, son of the Revd. Samuel BALDWIN and Hannah his wife. Died about 3 o'clock in the morning: aged 12 months and 28 days.
May 15. Anna STUDLEY, daughter of Joshua Studley and Lydia Studley, deceased.
July 23. Deborah, daughter of Samuel HOUSE and wife.
Novr. 10. Olive, daughter of Samuel WITHERELL Jr. and Ruth his wife.
Decem. 14. Deborah STETSON.
" 14. Seth, son of Seth and Lydia BAYLEY.
1763. Jany 12, Ruth, daughter of Stevens and Ruth HATCH.
Feby. 12. An Infant Son of Theops. WITHERELL and wife.
March 22. The Widow MARGARET FITZGERALD.
April 20. Melzer, the son of Marlby and Mary TURNER.
May 29. Martha, daughter of Sylvanus WING.
July 16. Gamaliel, son of Joshua and Abigail BAYLEY.
August 6. ......, wife of Isaac LAMBERT
      9 Peninnah, daughter of Benjamin WHITE and wife
     12 Lydia STETSON
Novr. 27 Priscilla EELLES wife of Samuel Eelles.
1764. Jany. 31 Christiana, daughter of Nathll. JOSSELYN and wife.
June 29 Ruth STETSON wife of Luke Stetson.
1765. Jany. 14. Abigail, daughter of Adam and Betty STETSON.
Feby. 6. John, son of John and Thankfull STETSON.
May 10. Thomas, son of Thomas ROSE Jr. and Rhoda.
July 1. Asenath, daughter of Simeon and Lucy CURTIS.
Aug. 28. Rebecca STETSON
Sept. 1. An Infant of Mercy PALMER'S
    24. Jacob, son of Amos SYLVESTER, Jr. and Desire his wife
Oct. 22. Susanna, daughter of Job and Hannah STETSON.
Decem. 30. Philip, son of Samuel BARSTOW, Jr. and Hulda.
1766. Jany. 5. ...... wife of Abner CURTIS.
Feby. 7. James, son of Benjamin STUDLEY and wife.
    24. Thomas ROGERS

Mar. 17. Joseph, son of Benjamin and Betty BATES.
Apl. 28 Richard CURTIS.
    29 Jeffry, *Negro* man of Coll. TURNER. *Drowned in the Furnace Pond.*
May 14 Lydia BRIGGS.
June 16. Joseph STUDLEY. *Killed by Lightning.*
July 20. Mary RAMSDELL, wife of Joseph Ramsdell, Jr.
Aug. 3. Sarah STAPLES.
Novr. 29. Elizabeth MAN.
Decem. 28. Lurana NICHOLSON. *Indian Woman.*
1767. Jany. 31 Sarah STAPLES
Feby. 5 Mercy, daughter of Shubael and Mary MUNROE.
Mar. 29 Elibabeth SYLVESTER
April 3. Gamaliel HATCH.
    12. Caleb TURNER.
    24 Widow Rebecca STETSON
May 22. Abner Turner, son of Simeon and Mary RAMSDELL.
June 27. Lemuel, son of Lemuel CURTIS, Sr: aged 14 years. *Drowned in his Father's Mill Pond.*
Sepr. 17. Lydia BAYLEY, wife of Seth Bayley.
1768. Feby. 27 Robert STETSON.
April 19. The Widow Dorcas RANDALL.
June 4. Robert, son of Michael and Ruth SYLVESTER. *Scalded to Death.*
    10 William TORREY.
    15 Mary TURNER, wife of Wait Turner.
Aug. 9. ...... HAYFORD, the wife of Samuel Hayford.
Oct. 10. An Infant Child, son of Lemuel and Mary WHITTEN.
Nov. 8. The Widow Ruth TURNER.
    13. Molley Waterman, daughter of Samuel HAYFORD
1769. Jany. 8 Phebe, a *Negro girl, Slave* to David and Hannah JACOB
    26 Martha MAN, wife of Benja. Man.
April 25 Simeon CLARK son of James Clark and wife.
June Jerusha SYLVESTER.
June 24. Reuben STETSON
    30 Jerusha HILL wife of Leonard Hill.
July 3. Deborah HOUSE
    7 Widow Bathsheba BRYANT.

Aug. 15. Widow Grace GILKY.
Sepr. Joseph BOZZARD: a stranger.
Sepr. 28. Charles, son of Job and Betty YOUNG
Octo. 22. Thomas BATES.
Decem. 30. A Son and Daughter, *Twins*, children of Isaac LAMBERT Jr: and wife.
1770. Jany. 2. David TORREY, aged 82.
    19 An Infant Son of Jabez STUDLEY & wife.
Feby. 19. Widow Rachel PIERCE.
March 2 Benjn. MAN.
March 8. Mary STODDARD
    24. Jno. LAMBERT.
April 12. Rose, *Negro woman* to David JACOB.
May Alice, daughter of Seth and Alice BAYLEY.
June 7 Joshua STAPLES
July 30 Ensign John JOSSELYN.
Nov. 2. Olive, daughter of Joseph HOUSE Jr. and Sage his wife.
Decemr. 29 Recompense TIFFANY.
1771. Jany. 19. An Infant, Daughter of Othniel and Deborah PRATT.
Feby. 13. An Infant, Son of Jabez STUDLY and wife.
March 9. Widow Mercy PALMER.
April 6. Lydia, daughter of Gideon STETSON.
    11 ...... Son of Benja. STUDLEY and wife.
July 3. An Infant, Daughter of Margaret PETERS.
July 19. Lucinda, daughter of Lemuel WHITTEN and wife.
Aug. 22. Joseph BRIANT: very suddenly.
1772. Feby. 24 Mrs. Mary BASS, Relict of the late Revd. Mr. Benja. Bass.
Mar. 16. An Infant, Daughter of Margaret PETERS.
May 26. Thomas, Son of Thomas ROSE, Jr. and Rhoda his wife.
Sepr. 22 Lemuel son of Lemuel WHITTEN and wife.
Octo. 2. Rufus, son of Joseph HOUSE Jr. and Sage his wife.
Decem. 2. Phebe BATES, wife of Joseph Bates, Jr.
1773. Jany. 10. Ruth ELLIS of Abington, wife of David Ellis: propounded to enter into the Church in Hanover the day before her death.
Jany. 17. Mary HARLOW, wife of Samuel Harlow.
Feby. 3. Lucy, daughter of Edmund and Betty SYLVESTER.

March 11. Deacon Joseph STOCKBRIDGE of Pembroke: a member of the Church in Hanover; *aged 100 years 8 months and 2 days.*
May 15. Bathshua HOUSE wife of Seth House.
June 21 Samuel HARLOW
July Mary WHITE, wife of Robert White.
Aug. 4. Widow Sarah RAMSDALE, aged *91 years.*
    10 Col. Ezekiel TURNER aged 72 years.
Oct. 9. Joseph, son Seth and Alice BAYLEY.
    17 Isaac GROSS
    19 Widow Deborah TORREY.
    22 An infant, Daughter of Jabez STUDLEY and wife.
1774. Feby. 13. Martha BRYANT, aged 84.
May 6. Sarah GROSS "Who dyed of the *Dropsy* after having been Tapp'd nine Times."
May 28 John WITHERELL
June 11. Michal, daughter of Seth and Anna BATES.
July 24 Ebenezer WRIGHT.
    Prissy, daughter of Joseph RAMSDALE, 3d. and Elizabeth.
Sept. 21 Caleb STETSON. He dyed at Hatia in the West Indies.
Oct. 11 ...... wife of John STUDLEY.
Nov. 9. Peninnah, daughter of Robert WHITE.
Decem. 17. Nathanael ROBBINS: "Killed in a well at Marshfield by reason of the *Earth's caving in upon and burying of him.*"
1775. January 10. Margarett WOODWARD
        28 Sarah CURTIS.
Feby. 4. Richmond, son of David and Hannah JACOBS.
    18 Stephen OTIS.
    28 Jane, Negro-Servant to David and Hannah JACOBS.
March 8 Ruth, Daughter of John and Bathshua HATCH.
April 27 John, son of John & Bathshua HATCH.
April 30 An infant, son of Isaac and Hannah HATCH.
July 14 Elijah STETSON, aged 89.
    23 Elizabeth GROSS.
Sepr. 8 Isaac, son of Elijah and Leah Gardner.
    13 Joseph, son of Samuel WITHERELL, Jr., and wife.
       John, son of Lot and Rachel RAMSDELL.
    24 Ruth, daughter of Amos and Betty TURNER.
    27. Olive, daughter of the Widow Hannah RANDALL.
       Betty, daughter of Lemuel DELANO and wife.
    30. Lemuel Holmes, son of Lemuel DELANO and wife.

Oct. 1. Mary, daughter of Lemuel DELANO and wife.
    5 Jesse BOOE, *servant* to Revd. Saml. Baldwin.
   10 An Infant son of Daniel TEAGUE and wife.
Oct. 12. Peleg KEEN, son of Ebenezer Keen: aged 19 "*Dyed in the service at Scituate:* entered among these records at the desire of his father."
Nov. 6. Widow Sage JOSSELYN
   26. Ezra MAN: *belonging to the American Army.*
Decr. 7 ...... wife of Elisha PALMER.
Decem. 26. An Infant, son of Lemuel and Mercy BATES
        An Infant, son of Eliab STUDLEY, Jr. and wife.
1776. Jany. 31. Samuel BARSTOW, son of Samuel & Huldah Barstow.
Mar. 2. Timothy CHURCH.
   17. Hannah JACOB, wife of David Jacob.
   30. The Widow Experience CURTIS: aged *96 years.*
April 6. The Widow Hanna.. TORREY, aged 81 years.
June 7. An Infant, Daughter of Joseph CARRELL and wife.
July 8 Sarah SYLVESTER, wife of Nathll. Sylvester.
July 10. Betty CURTIS, wife of Elisha Curtis.
Aug. 12. Philip son of Elisha CURTIS.
Sepr. 21. Zilpah CURTIS wife of James Curtis.
Oct. 3. Mary TURNER, wife of Marlbry Turner.
   27 Olive, daughter of Mary MAN.
Nov. 5. Lillis, daughter of Lemuel and Ruth CURTIS.
   6 Hannah, wife of Sylvanus WING.
Decem. 3. An Infant, son of Lemuel BATES and wife.
1777. Jany. 12 Roland, son of James CURTIS.
        25 Melzer, son of Melzer and Kezia CURTIS.
        29 Charles, son of Elijah and Susannah STETSON.
Feby. 9. Susannah STETSON wife of Elijah Stetson.
   21 Rachel, daughter of Ezra BRIGGS.
   26. Josiah CURTIS.
March 9. Ruth SOAPER, wife of Joseph Soaper.
   18 Jesse TORREY, Jr.
   19 Seth HOUSE
April 19. Mary TORREY, wife of Jesse Torrey.
May 14 John HOUSE
June 6. Lucy TORREY.

June 9. Elitheer, daughter of John CURTIS, Jr. and Anna his wife.
Sepr. 4. Thomas TORREY, Jr.
   29 Robert CORTHELL.
Oct. 17. Prissy, daughter of Joseph RAMSDALE, 3rd. and Elizabeth.
1778. Jany. 12 Eli, son of Seth and Anna BATES.
Feby. 19 ...... son of Widow Rachel MERITT.
April 12. Elizabeth BAYLEY, wife of Lieut. John Bayley.
   17. An Infant, still-born son of Timo. ROBBINS and wife.
   23 An Infant, son of Ebenezer WING Jr. and wife.
May 4. Orphan TORREY.
   18 Drusilla daughter of Job and Mary CASWELL.
July 11 Abigail, daughter of Seth and Alice BAILEY.
   15. Rebecca, daughter of Seth and Alice BAILEY.
Aug. 25 Rhoda HOUSE, wife of David House, Jr.
Sepr. 16. Charles, son of Timothy and Lydia ROSE.
   21 Reuben, son of Samuel and Alice STETSON.
   24 Deborah CUSHING, daughter of Job and Betty YOUNG.
      Deacon Thomas ROSE.
   28 Lieut. John BAYLEY.
   29 Ruth, daughter of Timo. and Lydia ROSE.
Octo. 2. Widow Sarah TORREY.
   6 Thomas TORREY.
   9. Betty, daughter of Job and Betty YOUNG.
   12. Joseph, son of Benja. and Bradbury STETSON.
   13 Caleb, son of Benja. and Bradbury STETSON.
   14 Rachel TORREY, wife of Stephen Torrey.
   16. Elisha, son of Benja. and Bradbury STETSON.
   18 Isaac TURNER.
   20 Charles, son of Benja. and Bradbury STETSON.
   21 Charles, son of Levi and Deborah CORTHELL.
      Lois, daughter of Isaac and Lois JOSSELYN.
   26. Lydia Peterson, daughter of Daniel TEAGUE and wife.
   27 Joseph RAMSDALE, Jr.
1779. March 10. DAPHNE, an old *negro-woman.*
         20. Mary Bowker, daughter of Joseph and Mary TORREY.
April 2. The Widow Elizabeth TORREY.
April 16. Joanna STUDLEY.
Sepr. 10 David, son of Robert and Anna WHITE.

1784. December 1. Revd. Samuel BALDWIN dyed after a long delirium.
1785. December 13th and 17th were intered Eliab STUDLY, 78 and Widow Martha CURTIS, aged 72.
1786. Jany 15. London, *negro-man* of Widow TURNER: about 19 years old.
    20   Dick, *negro-man* of Coll. BAILEY: supposed *about 90 years old.*
    25   The Widow Deborah STETSON: aged 81 or thereabout of old age.
    30   Lucy SYLVESTER aged 12½ years. of a *consumption.*
Feby. 10 Benjamin WHITE aged 65 complicated disorders.
March 29 Deborah BATES aged 52 *consumption & dropsy.*
    31   Lucy wife of Charles OTIS: aged 36 of a *consumption.*
June 19 Wife of Joseph RAMSDEL ætat 44 *consumption.*
Aug. 13 Becca, daughter of James WHITING: between 3 & 4 years old a *fever* and *canker.*
    26   Avis DWELLY, daughter of Joshua Dwelly: ætat 16 of a *nervous fever.*
Octr. 28. Child of Gamal: BATES: ætat 15 months: dyed with the *canker.*
Nov. 21. Jedediah DWELLY, son of Joshua Dwelly: aged 18. of a *nervous fever.*
Dec. 8. Betty WING: aged 40. dyed of a *consumption & dropsy.*
    25   Wife of Clement BATES aged 74. dyed of *old age.*
1787. Jany 8. Asa WHITING's wife; aged 24 dyed of a *fever:* ye 3rd of ye Dwelly family lately.
March 15 Joshua DWELLY: aged 51 years. of a *cancer.*
    28   Widow Sarah HATCH, aged 86. *Dropsy* with old age.
        Solomon BATES, aged 84 *old age* & suddenly.
April 30. Joseph JOSSELYN, esqr.: aged 88 *old age.*
June 24 Widow Persis TOWER: aged 80. of *old age.*
Aug. 3 Infant of Coll. Amos TURNER: aged 8 weeks. dyed *hooping cough*: set into fits.
Sep. 4. Widow Elizabeth STETSON: aged 83 dyed of *old age.*
Sept. 23 John STUDLEY, aged 83 dyed of *old age.*
Oct. 1. Nabby CURTIS, aged 24. dyed of a *Consumption.*
Nov. 13. Christopher SYLVESTER aged 20 dyed of a *consumption*: Atrophy.

Dec. 30   Anna CURTIS, aged 77   of old age : an invalid from her youth.

1788.   March 14   Clement BATES, aged 80.   dyed of *old age.*

24   Child of Gamaliel BATES, 7 months old   of worms.

April 13.   Wife or Dea. Samll. BARSTOW aged 80   of *old age.*

June 27.   Wife of Capn. Luther BAILY : ætat 35   paralitic disorder.

July 9.   Ezekiel PALMER, aged 87   of *old age.*

Aug. 15.   Daughter of Major Luther BAILY : an infant ætat 7 weeks never well.

16.   Wife of Ezra BRIGGS, Junr. aged 30   dyed of *consumption.*

22   Mr. Joseph RAMSDEL aged 80 : dyed of *old age.*

24   Infant son of Elias WHITING   of a strange inflamation & swelling.

Sepr. 19   Hannah STOCKBRIDGE *aged 95.*   dyed *old age.*

Decr. 3   Son of Bena. BATES, Junr. 19 months old   dyed of worms.

Decr. 12   Betty BATES, aged 36   dyed of a *consumption.*

23.   David STOCKBRIDGE, esqr. aged 75   long nervous languishment.

1789.   Mar. 14.   Wife of Levi MAN, aged 33   of a *bilious mortification.*

26.   Wife of Josiah CHAMBERLAIN, aged 24   of a *consumption.*

30   Infant daughter of Samll. NASH, 18 months old. tho't to be a *consumption.*

May 4.   Wife of Capn. Calvin CURTIS aged 31.   of a *consumption.*

July 7.   Daughter of Betty BATES : aged 10 months   of *fits.*

July 24   Wife of Homer WHITING aged 27.   of a delirium & *consumption.*

Aug. 12.   Infant son of Shubael MUNRO Junr. aged 2 days.   by nature imperfect.

21.   Widow Abigail CLARK aged 85   dyed of *old age.*

23.   Widow of Jona. PRAT aged 47   of a *bilious colic.*

Octr. 26.   Wife of Samuel CURTIS aged 72   of a *delirious languishment.*

Nov. 2.   Hannah BALDWIN aged 24   of a nervous delirious *consumption.*

28   Lucy, daughter of Thos. WHITING : aged 42.   *Lung fever.*

1790.   Jany. 2.   Widow Deborah PETERSON aged 80 : of *old age.*

Feby. 6.   Samuel CLAY aged 66.   *nervous consumption.*

Feby. 14 Son of Ezra BRIGGS Junr. 2 years old. *hereditary consumption.*
April 14 Thomas ROBBINS : aged 38. *drowned.*
    16 Infant daughter of Melzar CURTIS aged 9 months. dyed of a *fever.*
May 1. Capn. Joseph SOPER aged 87. *old age.*
    2 Nathll. JOSLYNN aged 68. of a *pleurisy.*
    4 Daughter of Melzar CURTIS aged 3 years 3 months. dyed of a *fever.*
    8 Widow Hannah BALDWIN aged 52 of a *lung fever*: relict of the Revd. S. Baldwin.
    17 Son of Shubael MUNRO Jr : Infant 9 hours old. Immature.
    20. Elias WHITING aged 37 *Lung fever* & highly nervous.
May 21 Oliver BONNEY aged 32 *Lung fever.*
June 21. Keturah wife of Jabez STUDLY aged 52. *Consumption.*
    28. Son of Nathll. SYLVESTER : aged 6 years of a *fever:* a weakly child.
July 1. Shubael ROSE, a *molatto:* 80 *old age* and long infirmities.
        also same day
    Ruth CURTIS, daughter of Capn. Lemuel Curtis : aged 35. *consumption.*
Sepr. 1 Wife of Cornelius WHITE aged 25 : dyed of a putrid *fever.*
    30 Son of Richard EASTIS ætat 7. of a *strangury.*
    23. Lydia, wife of Jonathan PRAT aged 35. dyed in child-bed. Infant son of Jonathan PRAT still-born.
1791. Feby. 5. Samll. STETSON aged 66 of a nervous *consumption.*
    7 Joseph BATES' wife aged 45 of a bilious disorder.
March 3. Bethiah SYLVESTER aged 30 of a family *consumption.*
June 3 Rufus, son of Wilm. CURTIS aged 14 suddenly, unknown disorder
        same day
    Son of Benjamin DWELLY aged 6 months. with *fits.*
August 5. Wife of Jess CURTIS aged 45 dyed of the *lock-jaw.*
Sepr. 25 Wife of William EELLES aged 62. dyed of a *consumption.*
Nov. 4 Daughter of Saml. GROCE aged 3 months.
    8 The widow of ...... HOUSE aged 78 of *old age.*
    23 Sage MAN aged 18 dyed of the *measles.*
Decemr. 19. Honble. Joseph CUSHING, *Judge of Probate* &c: aged 60. dyed of a nervous disorder ending in a delirium.

Decemr. 24. George STERLING aged 47   dyed of a num-*palsy* and long delirium.
1792. Jany. 24.   Elijah SYLVESTER, aged 25   nervous *fever.*
March 8   Wife of Bezaleel CURTIS aged 73.   dyed of a *consumption.*
April 4.   Wife of Dea. Benj. BASS aged 46   dyed of a slow putrid *fever.*
    7   Mingo, *Negro man* of Capn. Simn. CURTIS aged 70   dyed suddenly.
    27   Bezaleel CURTIS aged 81   dyed of *old age.*   Limbs and sense failed.
May 2.   Susannah, *negro-woman* of Dea. BASS aged 73.   *old age.*
May 17.   Sylvia, daughter of Major Luther BAILEY: aged 6 years. dyed of *canker.*
July 14.   Daughter of Isaac TURNER aged 7 years.   *Quinsy* and *canker.*
Aug. 6.   Daughter of Dea. BROOKS 6 or 7 years old.   *Canker* and *quinsy.*
    13.   Daughter of Ezra BRIGGS, Junr. ætat 8   *canker.*
    16.   Daughter of Isaac TURNER near a year old.   *canker.* a second child.
16 & 17.   *Two daughters* of Ezra BRIGGS, junr. one 6½ years old, the other 3 years old   both of the *canker.*
Aug. 17.   Wife of Dea. BROOKS: 47 : of the *canker.*
Sepr. 6.   Son of Levi CORTHEREL : 7 years old.   of ye *canker.*
Sepr.   A daughter of Levi COTHEREL: 4 years old.   also with the *canker.*
Sepr.   A son of William CURTIS : 3 years old.   *Canker* or throat distemper.
Sepr.   A son of Caleb WHITING : 3 years old.   Supposed to be imposhume in ye head.
Sepr.   Daughter of Joshua MAN : 7 years old   *canker.*
Oct. 3.   Son of Joshua MAN: 9 years old.   also *canker* or throat distemper.
    26.   Son of Neal BATES : 2 months old.   dyed of *fits.*
    29.   Wife of John BAILEY, aged * * * of a *consumption.*
Novr. 25.   Son of Atherton WALES aged 5 years.   dyed of the *Quinsy.*
Nov. 26.   Son of Elisha SYMMONDS : 2 years old.   also of ye *Quinsy.*
Decem. 12.   Daughter of Neal BATES : 6 years old: of the *canker.*

Decem. 17. Lucy CURTIS, daughter of Capn. Simn. 31 quick *consumption*: after *small pox*.
    27. Son of Neal BATES: 9 years old: dyed of ye *canker*.
Sepr. 1. Patience RANDAL, 27: at Freport *consumption*.
1793. Jany. 1. Son of Eliab STUDLY aged 6 years dyed of the *canker*.
    26. Daughter of Hannah GARDNER: fortnight old. * * *
Feby. 1 Daughter of James WHITING: 11 years old: of the *canker* or throat distemper.
March 10. Daughter of Japhet STUDLY: 2 years old throat distemper.
    24 Son of George STETSON not born alive.
April 19. Wife of Benjamin BATES 56 years of age. *consumption* and dropsy.
May 8 Son of Benjamin WHITE: 2 years old. said to be *Quinsy*.
    16. Son of Asa WHITING: 3 years old. dyed of the *canker* & quinsy.
June 26. William CURTIS aged 45 of a slow *consumption*.
July 15. Jesse TORY aged 68. dyed suddenly in a *fit*.
    28. Son of Seth STETSON 4 years old dyed with the *canker*.
Aug. 19. Son of Seth STETSON: 9 years old. dyed also with the *canker*.
Sepr. 5 Son of Widow Deborah WHITING, 4 years old. *Dysentery*.
    20 Our *Negro-woman* called BESS, 36 putrid *fever*.
    23. Thomas WHITING, aged 75 *dysentery* and putridity.
Oct. 4 Daughter of Homer WHITING: aged 6 years. *Dysentery*.
    11. Homer WHITING aged 28. dyed of *dysentery* and *canker*.
Daughter of Caleb WHITING: aged 9 months. *dysentery* & *canker*.
12 Avis WHITING aged 36 dyed of *dysentery* & *canker*.
17 Son of Thomas WHITING: under 2 years old. *dysentery*.
18 Daughter of *Negro*, named BRISTOL: 14 years old *Dysentery*.
25 Dr. PETER HOBART: aged 43 dyed of the *dysentery*.
Decr. 10 William EASTIS: aged 80. by *bleeding* at the nose.
1794. Jany. 13. Lydia BAILEY, daughter of Seth *Bailey*: aged 22 nervous *fever*.
Feby. 23 Samuel CURTIS, aged 86 of *old age*.
March 9. Theophilus WITHEREL: aged 57 nervous *fever*.
    20. Mary, negro-woman of Robert ESTIS, aged 76. *Dropsy*.

March 25   Widow Sarah CHURCH: *91*   dyed of *old age*.
April 14   Widow Alice NEAL: 82   dyed of *old age*.
June 20.   Son of Seth JOSLYN: 3 years old : a nervous *fever*.
           Widow Sarah SYLVESTER: 68 ætat   of a *consumption*.
Oct. 28.   Daughter of Snow CURTIS: 5 years old. of the *quinsy*.
Novr. 11.   Daughter of Thomas BATES ; *twin ;* 5 weeks old : of *fitts*.
1795.   March 25   Cuba : a *negro-woman* of Dea. BROOKS, 84 *old age*.
April 17   Hannah CHURCH, 22 years old : *consumption.*
     22   Infant son of Joseph CUSHING. aged 3 weeks. of *Fitts*.
May 2   Wife of Abner CURTIS aged 64   *consumption* & dropsy.
     7   Widow Mary STETSON about 90.   *old age* and palsy.
June 4   David STANDISH aged 70   dyed of the *gravel*.
     12   Melzar STETSON aged 30 years   of a long *consumption*.
     14   Shubael MUNRO aged 75.   *old age* & old ails.
     25   William Gilbert CURTIS : ætat 20   of a *consumption*.
June 28   Daughter of Wilm. STOCKBRIDGE : 2 years old.   dyed of the *quinsy*.
Aug. 7.   Hannah FORD : 54 years of age.   never well after ye *amputation of her leg*.
Oct. 8   Daughter of Thos. BATES a year old :   worms and *canker*.
Nov. 15   Wife of Elisha CURTIS : 55.   Bed-rid many years : emaciated and limbs contracted.
Dec. 4   Ruth, daughter of Stephen BAILY : ætat 20.   dyed of a *fever*.
     26.   Wife of Robert BARKER : aged 82   *a Friend*.
1796.   Jany 6.   Molly MACUMBER : 19 years old nearly.   *canker*-rash.
           21.   Daughter of David KINGMAN : 13 months old.   dyed of ye *canker*.
           24   Benja. SYLVESTER 87.   many years blind & dyed of a *cancer*.
           25   Son of Mordecai ELLIS : 13 years old.   dyed of *quinsy* and *canker*.
Feby. 9.   Robert BARKER aged 84   old age ; delirious : *a Friend*.
March 1.   Allice daughter of Seth BAILY : 25 years old   long decline or *consumption*.
April 15   Daughter of Sam. B. PERRY : 10 years old   of the *canker*.
     22.   Wife of Mordecai ELLIS, senr. aged 77.   of nervous disorders.
May 3.   Wife of Isaac TURNER, aged 40   dyed of child-bed illness.
     6.   Infant son of Lot RAMSDELL, Junr. fort-night old.

July 2.   Jonathan TURNER aged 82.   suddenly of an *apoplexy.*
    13.   Cloe, daughter of BRISTOL: *negro:* 19 years old.   of a consumption.
    29.   Widow Abigail SYLVESTER : aged 84   *old age* & palsey.
Augt. 5   David HOUSE aged 87   *old age* and long infirmity and confinement.
Sepr. 17. ...... of Booth ROGERS   of the *cholera-morbus.*
Oct. 12   Seth BAILY, 57   dyed of a *dropsy,* affecting ye *lungs.*
Nov. 4.   Daughter of David KINGMAN : aged 4 years.   *dysentery.*
1797. Jany. 20.   Ephraim PALMER : aged 43.   *consumption.*
    19   Infant son of Isaac TURNER: 9 months old   of the *quinsy.*
Feby. 1.   Ezekiel Turner HATCH: aged 33.   suddenly of an inflamatory *fever.*
    21.   Capn. Joseph STETSON aged 71   dyed of a *pleurisy fever:* only a weeks illness.
March 11.   Richard EASTIS : 51   *consumption* & pleurisy.
    20   Thomas BARSTOW : 66   dyed of *consumption* & dropsy.
June 2.   Wife old John CURTIS : 86   of fitts and *fever.*
    26.   Lucretia GILKIE.   *drowned* herself: insane.
July 18.   Wife of Josh. SYMMONDS, 76   of a long decline.
Sepr. 29   Richmond HATCH : 25   of a long decline.
Oct. 2.   Widow MAGOON : *90*   of *old age:* vomiting blood : sudden death.
Oct. 16.   Widow STUDLY : Eliab's widow : *90*   of *old age.*
Nov. 24   Daughter of Atherton WALES : aged 7 years   of a *fever.*
    27   Widow of Jesse TORY : 70 : fell down in a *fit* & dyed in a few days & sensible.
Decr. 7   Henry DILLINGHAM : 62 years old.   been long *deranged.*
    30.   Son of Joel SYLVESTER : 7 months old.   dyed of ye *hooping-cough.*
1798.   May 29.   Widow Hannah BAILY aged 66   dyed of ye bilious *colic.*
June 26.   Thomas GROCE : aged 51   dyed of a *dropsy* &c.
July 7   Olive CURTIS: daughter of Capn. Lemuel Curtis aged 40   *consumption.*
Aug. 8   Old Widow Hannah FORD: aged 88.   dyed of *old age.*
Aug. 12   Elisha PALMAR, 82   *old age.*
Sept. 20   Wife of Elisha BARKER aged * * * of a *consumption.*

Nov. 12 Michael SYLVESTER, aged 85. of *old age.*
Decr. 1 Jeremiah CURTIS son of Melzar Curtis: 23 years old. of a *fever* and nervous.
1799. Mar. 2 Wife of Job TILDEN, senr. aged 83. of ye *numb-Palsy.*
20 Sylvia CLARK, daughter of Belcher Clark, 25. *consumption.*
23 John CURTIS: aged *90 years.* Several years confined with age and *palsy.*
30 Isaac HATCH: aged 73 dyed of a billious disorder & *inverted* bowels.
April 22 Daughter of Turner STETSON: infant 12 days old. of *fitts.*
27 Gershom Curtis CORTHELL: aged 27. dyed of a *consumption.*
July 25 Anna BATES aged 54 dyed of ye bilious *colic.*
Aug. 24 David JACOB, Junr. aged 36 of a putrid *fever.*
25 a daughter of David JACOBS, Jun. aged 8 years. ye same *fever.*
28 wife of David JACOBS, Jun. aged 38 of ye same *fever.*
Sepr. 18 Abner CURTIS, aged 72 of a *consumption.*
Twin infant of Calvin BAILY.
27 John CURTIS, aged 57 of a *consumption.*
Oct. 24 Isaac JOSLYN, Junr. aged 26. of a strange malady in his *bowels.*
Nov. 3. The other *twin-child* of Calvin BAILY: 9 weeks old. both sons. ye same day Sage, daughter of Adam PERRY, aged 17. of a slow nervous *fever.*
Nov. 7. Infant daughter of Gamaliel BATES: 6 weeks old.
Dec. 24. Son of James WHITING: 2 years old. vomiting *blood.*
1800. Jany. 1. Widow of Joseph RAMSDEL: aged 84. of *old age.*
March 7 Capn. Simeon CURTIS: aged 80: old age and *fever.*
May 24 Sally BRIGGS aged 33: dyed of a *consumption.*
June 19. Capn. Robert Leuthal EELLES: aged 68. *Dropsy* and long decline.
July 28 Son of Thomas BATES: 2 years old. said to be *canker* in ye bowels.
29 *Twin Sons* of Shubal MUNRO: an hour old. dyed nearly together.
Aug. 23. Charlotte CURTIS daughter of Widow John Curtis: aged 34 of a *consumption.*

Sept. 29 Wife of Benjamin MAN, senr. : aged 66 of a *fever*.
Nov. 29. Daughter of Saml. STETSON : aged 11 months. of *fever* & astma.
1801. Jany. 29 Daughter of Isaac TURNER : 13 years old. supposed to be by worms.
April 16. Alethea CURTIS : aged 22 : daughter of Widow J. Curtis of a *fever*.
May 26 Daughter of Thomas BATES, 5 months old of *fitts* &c :
July 10. Daughter of David KINGMAN ; more than 2 years old. *hurt with mercury.*
Sept. 20 Daughter of Benjamin WHITMAN, esqr. 2 years old. of ye *dysentery*.
Oct. 15. David MAN : 84 years old. of a *fever* in *old age*.
    16. Bethiah, daughter of Dea. Timothy ROBBINS. aged 27 years. of a slow *fever*.
Novr. 7 Widow Lydia WHITING aged 82 *old age* and *fever*.
    8 Melzar CURTIS : esqr. 56 years old. Long decay and weakness.
    19 Dea. Saml. BARSTOW aged *94* had *dropsy* & astma a long time.
Dec. 24 Catharine, daughter of Atherton WALES : ætat 19 of a *fever*.

DEATHS
RECORDED BY ME
JOHN MELLEN;
Pastor.

1802. Jany. 10 : Sunday-morn, Mrs. Rebecca MELLEN my beloved Consort departed this life, after few days severe illness with old *astmatical* and other complaints : Enter'd on the 75 year of her age : was Intom'b on Thursday following.
Feby. 15 *Twin Son* of Josiah CHAMBERLAIN, 8 days old *sore mouth*.
March 21 Mary BASS in her 72d. year. long confinement and nervous *consumption*.
    26 Infant son of Wm. STOCKBRIDGE : aged 10 months : native weakness & *consumption*.
April 3. Michael SYLVESTER : aged 53 of a slow *consumption*.

May 10. Susanna ROSE: 75: *Indian Woman & a ✝tian.* a *fever.*
Oct. 15. Ruth ELLIS ætat 30 of nervous disorder and *fever.*
Nov. 3. Sally, daughter of Ben. BATES: 24 of weakness and decline.
Nov. 17 Widow Sarah CURTIS aged 80, of *old age* & slow decline.
same day Sally CURTIS, daughter of Leml. Curtis: 33 years old. *consumption.*
Nov. 28 Infant daughter of Capn. A. SMITH: aged about 3 days. suddenly.
Dec. 2. Child of Saml. DUNNEL, son. 20 months old. dyed with ye *quinsy.*
Dec. 28 Widow of David MAN: 88 *old age* &c:
1803. Jany 7 Son of Capn. A. SMITH: 3 years old violent *astma.*
  16. Wife of Thomas BATES: aged 29. *consumptive* complaint.
  26. Son of Almond JOSLYN, but two days old.
Mar. 13. Sally ELLIS, a maiden, 60 years old. Dyed rather suddenly.
April 17 Son of Snow CURTIS, aged 17 named Bela. nervous and *fits.*
Aug. 23 Widow Hannah STANDISH: 74 *dropsy.*
Sept. 10 Wife of Stockbridge JOSLYN, 54 of a *fever.*
Nov. 25 Robert EASTIS: aged 68 of a long decline.
Decem. 4 John TORRY, aged 88 long inclined to *insanity* & now blind.
1804. Jany. 6 Content RAMSDALE aged 51 of a *consumption.*
  Feby. 4 David HOUSE aged 73. a slow decay of nature.
March 29 Capn. Joseph SOPER, esqr. aged 67 consumption after a *wound.*
May 4. Sarah WHITING aged 20 insane: *drowned* herself.
June 13. Widow Ruth STERLING: 71 *insane.*
June 22 Abel CURTIS: 52 bilious *colic:* long deranged in a measure.
July 28 Isaac GROCE 48 dropsy and *astma:* in a degree non-compos.
Oct. 6. Benjamin RAMSDEL 83 age the *stranguary.*
Oct. 22 Ezra BRIGGS aged * * * *fever* &c:
1805. Jany. 6. Wife of Perez JACOBS (*land-lord*) aged 68 a *fever.*
  13 Infant son of Robert SYLVESTER: aged 2 or 3 months.
  16. Caleb ROGERS: 88 years old. of *old age:* at Turner Stetson's.
Feby. 4. Wife of John STETSON: 63. long decline or *consumption.*
Feby. 19 Widow of Thomas BARSTOW: aged 84 of *old age.*

ORIGINAL RECORDS. 205

AFTER THE INSTALATION
OF
REV. CALVIN CHADDOCK.

1806. July 26   Jacob SYLVESTER : aged 82.
July 29.   Moses BRIGGS: aged 33.
Oct. 31.   Widow Ruth SYLVESTER : aged 69.
1807. Jany. 5   Melzar HATCH : aged 40.
   same day   Zilpha STETSON wife of Saml. Stetson : aged 33.
Jany. 7   Widow Hannah ROBBINS : aged 86.
   Widow Lucy RAMSDALE : aged 89.
Jany. 21   Capt. Lemuel CURTIS : aged 75.
Feby. 24   Frederick JOHNSON : aged 27.
March 4   Joshua SIMMONS : aged 88.
March 10   Thomas HATCH : aged 62   *apoplexy.*
May 12.   Hannah ROGERS, the wife of Caleb Rogers : aged 59.
May 12.   LUCE the daughter of Asa POOL : aged 3 years.
May 13.   Joseph Dawes RAMSDALE : aged 45 years.
May 18.   Dean. Timothy ROBBINS : aged 64 years.
May 19.   Lydia STETSON, daughter of Ezekiel TURNER aged 17 months.
June 5   Samuel DONALD: aged 42 years.
same day   Widow Hannah CLAY : aged 76 years.
Aug. 11.   Hannah RAMSDALE : aged 51 years.   *dropsy.*
Aug. 12   Ebenr. CURTIS : aged 61 years   *consumption.*
Aug. 17.   Robert SYLVESTER: aged 36 years.   *dropsy.*
Oct. 25   Thomas BATES : son of Thomas Bates aged 3 years.
Nov. 3   Widow Miriam TORREY: aged 73.
Nov. 13.   Mary the daughter of Joseph JACOBS, Jr. aged 9 months.
Dec. 8   Almira, daughter of Joshua DWELLY.   aged 2 years.
Decemb. 11.   Abigail the wife of Israel PERRY : aged 61 years.
1808. Jany. 7   Mary, the wife of Dean. Benj. BASS : aged 68 years.
   Feby. 3   An Infant of Samuel ELLS : aged 24 hours.
   5   Sarah TILDEN : aged 54 years.
Feby. 12   Sophia, daughter of Seth CURTIS : aged 4 years.
Mar. 2   Rhoda ROSE : *black woman :* aged about *90 years.*
   8   Amos CURTIS : aged * * *.
   27   Zilpha GROSS : aged 56 years.

April 5   Bacheldor WING: aged * * *
June 11   Widow Jane Doten DONNEL: aged 42 years.
July 22   A *black* child of Stephen LONG: aged 5 months.
July 29. Widow CURTIS, relic of Capt. Lemuel Curtis: aged 72 years.
Aug. 29   Robert, the son of Robert ELLS: aged 3 years.
Oct 8   Eliza, daughter of Seth GANNIT: aged 17 mos.
Nov. 6   Temperance, the wife of Nathl. STETSON, aged 34 years.
Decem. 5. Mary HIFFORD: aged *92 years.*
Decem. 14 David JACOB: aged 79 years.
1809. January 22 Job TILDEN: aged 83 years.
          May 2.   Capt. John HATCH: aged 70 years.
Augt. 14 Hannah RANDAL: aged 18 years.
1810.   Hannah CLARK: aged 80.
          June Mordecai ELLIS: aged 93.
Sept. 5   Joseph son of Isaac BURRELL aged 2 months.
Oct. 23. Sarah, daughter of Benjn. EASTIS: aged 2 years & 8 mo.
Oct. 27   Col. John BAILEY; aged 80 years.
Nov. 15. Elijah RANDAL, Jr. who was *killed instantly by a stick of timber* in his twenty second year.
Decem. 9. Elizth. CURTIS: aged 52 years.
Decem. 12 Ann BATES: The wife of Col. Seth Bates: aged 72 years.
1811. Jany. 3 John CHAPMAN: *aged 105 years: 25 days.*
          John STETSON: aged 80 years.
Oct. 19. Elizabeth RAMSDALE: aged 58 years: wife of Joseph Ramsdale.
Decem. 13. Jesse CURTIS: aged 68 years.
Decem. 24 Molly SYLVESTER: aged 86 years: widow of Jacob Sylvester.
Decemb. 30 Abigail HANMAR: *aged 93.*
1812. Jany. 4 Lydia ROSE, wife of Capt. Timothy Rose: aged 79 years.
Jany. 28 Deborah, the daughter of Joseph BROOKS, Jr.: aged * * *
Feby. 26. Widow Mary Rogers: aged *96* years.
Mar. 21   Luce the wife of Nathl. JACOBS: aged 63 years.
March 25 Sarah Copland EELLS the daughter of Edward Eells 6 years.
May 3   James GREY: aged 57 years.
June 5   Abigail MUNROE, the wife of Shubael Munroe: aged 47 years.

June 4   Seth CURTIS: aged * * *
June 12 An Infant of Daniel BARSTOW, Jr.
June 24 Huldah EELLS, the wife of Mr. Robert Eells, aged 39 years.
June 25 Sally EELLS, the daughter of Joseph & Sally Eells. aged 9 years.
June 26. Capt. Joseph CHADDOCK aged 80 years.
July 4   Luce, the daughter of Mr. Timothy CHURCH, aged 2 years.
July 14. An Infant of Samuel STETSON of *fitts*.
Sept. 22 Elihab TORREY aged 47 years.
Sept. 22. Hanner Eells DAMON, aged 4 years.
Sept. 26. James WHITING, aged 61 years.
Decr. 4 Ruben FOSTER, son of Joseph Foster, aged 2 years.
1813. Jany. 13 Joseph GREEN, aged * * *
         Jeremiah BATES, aged * * *
Jany. 28 Lydia WRIGHT, aged *94 years*.
Apl. 3. Luis WHITE, aged 32 years.
    15   Bachelor WING's child: an infant.
May 3   Charles BAILEY's child aged 2 years.
May 16. The wife of Mathew EASTIS; aged * * *
     18 The child of said EASTIS. aged 10 mo.
June 1   Betsy STETSON, the wife of Benjamin Stetson aged * * *
July 15 The child of Ebr. CURTIS.
Aug. 15 The wife of Ebr. CURTIS.
Sept. 2 Widow STUDLEY.
         Ezra BRIGGS' child.
     5   John SMITH, aged * * *
    12   John MUNROE, aged * * *
    26   Capt. Clemt. BATES' wife, aged * * *
Nov. 12 ...... MAKEPIECE, aged 27 years.
    28   Jonathan PRATT, aged * * *
         Job DAMON's child; aged * * *
1814. Nathll. CLARK, aged * * *
         Feby. 9 Enos BATES, aged 40 years.
March 22 Widow Hannah WHITE, aged *93 years*.
May 23. A child of Calvin COTHREL: aged 2 years.
1815. Jany. 9 Ezekiel BARSTOW, aged 40.
         April 26 Widow Mary MUNROE, *aged 91*.
May 1   Peg PETER, a *black-woman*, aged 87.
May 2   Timothy CHURCH, Jr: aged 18 *drowned in North River*.

June 5   A child of Seth ROSE, aged 11 months.
Oct. 21 Elizabeth BARSTOW, aged 52 years.
Oct. 25 Wate TURNER, aged 92 years.
Oct. 31 Prince CURTIS, aged 65 years
Nov. 2   Ezra BRIGGS, aged 58 years.
Nov. 8   Mercy WING, aged 74 years.
Nov. 30 The wife of Col. Amos TURNER, aged 66 years.
Dec. 6. Melissa, the daughter of Edward STETSON, aged 9 months.
1816. Jany. 21   A child of Revd. ...... COOPER, aged 1 month.
          Mar. 8   Widow Keziah CURTIS, aged 67 years.
Mar. 27 Dean. Benjn. MANN, aged 89 years.
Mar. 28 Joseph NICK, a *black man* aged 76 years.
May 27   Sibyl, the wife of Amos BATES, aged 36 years.
June 22 A child of John WINSLOW, esqr. aged 6 months.
June 22 A child of Stephen JACOBS, aged 2 years.
Aug. 14 Gideon STUDLEY, aged 78 years.
Aug. 17 JACK, a *black man* aged 76.
Sept. 8 Zilphy EASTIS, aged 65 years.
Decem. 1   Jane, the wife of Lemuel DWELLY, aged 44 years. By hanging herself.
Decem. 7   Joseph BATES, aged 88 years.
1817. Jany. 19   Robert Clark STUDLY, son of Jabez Studly, Jr. aged 14 months.
Feby. 5   Nathaniel ELLIS, aged 60 years.
Feby. 18 ISRAEL PERRY, esqr. aged 73 years.
Feby. 20 Eliza Edwards DAMON, daughter of Piam Damon aged 4 weeks.
March 4   Widow Molly RANDAL, aged 83 years.
          Mary B. STOCKBRIDGE the daughter of Benjamin Stockbridge. aged 17 mo.
Mar. 13   Thomas BATES, aged 48 years.
Mar. 14   John CURTIS, Jr. aged 15 years.
Mar. 9   A child of Joseph MUNROE, aged 1 yr. & 6 mos.
Mar. 29   Priscilla, the daughter of Richard ESTES, aged 17 months.
April 4   John, the son of David TOWER, aged 10 months.
April 5   Patience, the daughter of David Tower, aged 5 years.
April 6   Lucy Williams, the daughter of Martin PALMER aged 5 years.
April   Eliza, the daughter of Almon JOSSELYN, aged 3 years.
May 10   Stockbridge JOSELYN, aged 77 years.

May. 11   Stephen CURTIS, aged 77 years.
June 9   Molly PETERSON, aged 79 years.
June 11   A child of Seth GARDINER, aged 1 month.
July 21   Thomas PERRY, aged 43.
Aug. 3   Catherine, the daughter of John BAILY, Jr. aged 6 years.
Aug. 6   Joseph RAMSDALE (Conversion) aged 74 years.
Sept. 1   Dean. Curtis BROOKS, aged 47 years.
Novr. 16 Samuel GROSS, aged 68 years by cutting his own throat.
Dec. 3   John the son of Capt. Elisha BARREL (?) Jr. aged 6 years. of the *quinsy*.
Decem. 30 Nathaniel BRIGGS, aged 53.
1818. Jany. 11 Widow Allice CLARK, relic of Nathl. Clark aged 75 years.
Jany. 12 Levi MANN, aged 60 years.
Jany. 19 An infant son of Richard ESTES.
Jany. 29 Nehemiah PALMER ; aged 79 years.
Feby. 20. Ruben CURTIS 2nd. : aged 34 suddenly.
Feby. 24 Widow Martha STETSON; aged 74.
Mar. 1 (?) Mary, the wife of Dean. Benjn. STOCKBRIDGE, aged 28 years.
Mar. 30. Isaac WILDER, aged 42 years.
May 14 Stephen, the son of Wm. STOCKBRIDGE aged 19 years.
May 22 A child of Isaac WILDER, aged 18 months.
May 26. Deborah WHITING, aged 61 years.
July 15 Mary, the daughter of Robert SALMON, aged 23 years.
1820. September 6 Ruth GROCE.
1824. September Freelove WITHERELL.
           November Bathshua HATCH, wd.
1825. February 8 Mary ROBBINS.
           ...... William WHITING.
1826. May Samuel BARSTOW.
           June 10 Sarah WHITING.
June 11 Mary WHITING, widow *aged 95*.
Jany. 28 Mary wife of William TORREY.
...... Levi NASH.
1831. August Seth ROSE.
           ...... Sally HATCH.
May 27 Ruth ELLS,

1832. August 2. Thankfull WHITING.
December 7 Rachel DWELLEY.
1834. Mary LITTLE.
1835. October 4. Bradbury E. STETSON: aged 32. "She was a valuable member and when descending the dark valley at first it was dark but soon said 'it was all light now.'"
1836. January 15 Abigail NEAL: aged 88 years and some months. "She rendered much services by pecuniary contributions to the Society, Chh. & Ministry. She left $200= to the Chh. & Soc. the interest of which is available."
June 21. Mary BATES, widow, aged 79: member of the church.
1837. ...... Lydia MONRO, aged 88: member of the church.
April Betsey MONRO, member of the church.
Rebecca TOLLMAN, member of the church.
September 17. Thankfull WHITING: aged 43: member of the church.
September 17 Sybil HITCHCOCK : member of the church.
1838. October 8 Sarah Ann HARLOW: an infant: foster child of Rev. A. G. DUNCAN and wife and child of Charles Harlow.
December 23 Oliver WINSLOW: aged 84 years.
1839. August 14 Mary E. STETSON, member of this church.
October Widow of Oliver WINSLOW : member of this church.
Dec. 10 Ruth wife of William STOCKBRIDGE: aged 85 years: member of this church.
1840. January 21 Lucy wife of Deacon E. BARSTOW: 63.
May 10 Widow Lucinda BASS member of the church : 73.
March 10. Elizabeth SYLVESTER, aged 85.
March 16. John Calvin, son of John C. and Sarah T. WILDER.
1842. June 23 Deacon Elisha BARSTOW: died after a few days sickness: "for many years a deacon of the chh. a worthy man who for some months past has appeared very much devoted to the work of the Lord: He died much demented. Ah! Lord God! Wilt thou make a full end of the remnant of Israel? Turn us again and cause thy face to shine and we shall be saved." The deacon was aged 73.
December 25 or 27 Miss Julitta SYLVESTER : 73. "For many years a faithful sister. Her end was peace and ardently desired by her. Lord! sanctify the loss to the chh. and remove thy judgments."
1844. February 25 Turner STETSON, aged 76. "Long a member of this church and a valued member of society."

August 29 Lydia S. COBB, daughter of Turner STETSON: many years resident in Abington.
November 24 Priscilla STETSON wife of Joshua Stetson: 64: suddenly.

1845. April 25. Lucy ROSE: 76: sister of the last named sister: united with the church under Rev. Mr. Mellen.

1847. October 3. Abigail CHAMBERLAIN: 84: who united with the church under Rev. Mr. Mellen.

1849. May 4 Miss Rachel WHITING: aged 74.
December 15 Mrs. Rusha EELLS, wife of Samuel Eells aged 67.

1850. June 1 Miss Molly BARSTOW: aged 81.
July 12. Widow Rebecca CHURCH, aged 77.
August 17 Widow Lydia PRATT: aged 81: In peace.
December 28 Mrs. Sarah E. CHURCH wife of Samuel S. Church: aged 42.

1851. March 26 Miss Cinderilla BASS: aged 80: *influenza*.
May 18 Mrs. Michal Bates STETSON wife of Thos. Stetson: Hanson: aged 70: *cancer*.
October 12 Mrs. Lucia Harlow DUNCAN. "Wife of Rev. A. G. Duncan pastor of this church; aged 56 (wanting 49 days) after 12 weeks of severe suffering borne with Christian meekness, patience, fortitude and submission. She was a descendant of BRADFORD & CARVER and possessed a spirit worthy of her Puritan stock. At one time during her illness she remarked in an ecstacy ' Precious Savior, I shall soon be with him' and her last audible accents breathed forth his name. 'Precious Jesus.' "

1853. May 16 Sister Elizabeth H. GARRATT : 39: peaceful and happy.

1854. February 24 Eliza S. wife of Stephen JUSSLYN: 50: after a protracted illness from *dropsey*.

1855. March 15 John C. WILDER, died at North Bridgewater in the faith of the Gospel. He was buried in Hanover on Saturday, March 17, in the burying ground near the centre chh. The funeral services were held in the meeting house of the 2nd Parish at the village:
December 10 Sylvia BATES: aged 84 years.

1858. February 15 Lucy CHURCH, wife of William Church, esqr.
Her death was sudden but she was willing to go if her Lord

would then take her. She was very calm and peaceful and expired without a struggle or a groan or moving a muscle. All was peace. Jesus was with her: She is now with him.

August * * * Miss Sybil HATCH.

1859. November 15 Lydia S. BARSTOW: died in the blessed peace of our Saviour. She was very happy in her sickness, near its close especially. May her death be sanctified to the church.

August 18 Samuel STETSON: died in the faith of Jesus Christ, suddenly in an *apoplectic fit:* aged 89 yrs. 3 mos. 8 dys.

1860. July 14 Widow Celia JUDD aged 77 years. She was received to this church, August 5, 1827 by the Rev. Ethan Smith, Pastor. She walked with the church till within a few years: she has been allured away and become interested in spiritualism. Because of her feeble old age and broken state of mind the church bore with her with long suffering and charity. She ever said to her pastor and others that she did not give up her faith in the Bible, nor her hope in Christ nor her love to the Church. Her accounts are with God and sealed: it is our hope that her error and inconsistency may have been forgiven and that it may be well with her.

1862. May 1. Mary G. BASS.

1863. March 7 Frances DWELLEY: aged 74.

March 9 Bethiah COOK, wife of Isaac Cook: aged 67.

August 28 Mrs. Nabby BARKER, member of this church 43 years: died aged *93 years & 8 months.*

October 26 Mrs. Michal LOVEWELL: wife of George W. Lovewell: aged 59 yrs. *Great grand-daughter of the first pastor* of this chh. Rev. Benj. Bass.

1864. August 17. Priscilla Josselyn STUDLEY, daughter of widow of Wm. Josselyn and wife of Edwin Studley.

1865. February 16. Hannah STETSON widow of Edward Stetson: aged 89 years 10 months. She died in holy faith in which she had lived many years. She attended chh. only a few weeks before her death.

October 12. Mr. Melzar HATCH died: In his death, his friends, the parish & town suffer deep affliction & a great loss. He was an early & earnest friend & laborer in the cause of temperance. Few men of the country have done more than he for the support of the institution of the Gospel. It was through his encouragement and liberal investment that the present parsonage was built and the lot secured:

he put in $300= or $400. When the late meeting house was burned and we stood by the smouldering ruins, he moved in the purpose to build a new one on that consecrated spot and in the first week he obtained the subscription of nearly $3000= promising $500= himself. He probably paid in about $600= besides personal labor for which he charged nothing, worth not less than $100= He gave the parish $600= toward the fund for the support of the Gospel ordinances. For a few years he has paid $100= towards the salary of the pastor besides liberal gifts to him. He had the oversight and care of the affairs and interests of the parish and was the treasurer and principal collector for many years. He was a constant attendant on public worship in all weather: though he was not a professor of religion he had great reverence for religion and religious ordinances. It grieved him to see them neglected habitually by men or to witness the desecration of the Holy Sabbath. He was a man of public spirit and his influence and work may be seen in many things. He has been a strong friend and patriot during the great national conflict and ready and willing to aid — to provide * * * things for the soldiers — for the suffering without distinction of color or nationality. He did much in aiding improvements in the cemetery. One of his last labors for the parish was to plant those trees now casting their shadows around the new church. His funeral was attended by a large gathering of people. It was a solemn occasion.

1866. February 2. Isaac COOK: after long decline: very peaceful and easy death: had been *deacon 37 years: Superintendent of Sabbath school 30 years* and member of the chh. 39 years: aged 73 years.

May 9. Widow Ruth BATES. Died in peace and comfort of the Holy Ghost. She had been a member of the chh. 30 yrs. She had been confined to her room 16 yrs. and unable to walk a step. She was an example of patience, meekness and faith. She suffered exceedingly in her last illness but she died easily. She sleeps in Jesus.

July 15. Widow Elizabeth T. HOUSE: "died in peace and entered the promised rest. She had been in failing health for several months. Rev. Mr. Southworth of Hanson officiated at her funeral as her pastor was absent."

1867. January 2. Mr. Samuel BARSTOW died.
June 11. Abigail ROGERS, wife of Reuben Rogers.

CHAPTER IX.

INSCRIPTIONS FROM THE STONES AND TOMBS IN THE CEMETERY AT CENTRE HANOVER.
1727–1895.

NATH'L CROCKER ADAMS
Born Nov. 14th 1846
Died April 7 1847

SIGOURNEY ADAMS
Born August 3d 1851
Died March 18th 1855
Amen

HARRIETT ELIZA
Wife of Daniel S. Adams
Born Nov. 24th 1821
Died May 6th 1888

"The Lord is my Shepard, I shall not want"

ELIZABETH A. STOCKBRIDGE
Wife of Dr. George O. Allen
Born Mch. 8 1847
Died Nov. 10 1878

OPHIR ALLEN
U. S. Navy

REV. LABAN WHEATON ALLEN
Born Dec. 11 1843
Died Aug. 23 1875

"Jesus said, I am the resurrection and the life"
"*Blessed are the pure in heart for they shall see God*"

REV. CYRUS W. ALLEN
Born Octo. 28 1806
Died April 11 1882
Aged 75 years 5 mos 14 days

"And I heard a voice from Heaven saying unto me, Write, Blessed are the dead which die in the Lord from henceforth, yea saith the spirit, that they may rest from their labours and their works do follow them"

GEORGE OTIS ALLEN M. D.
Born Octo. 25 1838
Died Octo. 3 1887

"Be ye also ready for in such an hour as ye think not the son of man cometh"

MARY (FOLGER)
Wife of Rev. Cyrus W. Allen
Born Nov. 15 1816
Died Aug. 13 1888
"The fragrance of her life below
Earth still shall know
The fullness of her life above
Unchanging love "

MRS. SARAH BAILY
Wife to Mr. Timothy Baily
who dyed October ye 8th *1740*
and aged 22 years

Sic Transit Gloria Mundi
Erected In Memory of
MRS. SILVESTER BAILEY
ye wife of Major Luther Bailey
She died June ye 27th 1788
Aged 30 years 4 months & 5 Days

From opening skies may streaming glories
 shine
And saints compare thee with days like
 mine

POLLEY BAILEY
Dau of Maj. Luther & Mrs. Silvester Bailey his wife
Died 1788

In Memory of SYLVIA B.
the Daughter of Majr. Luther Bailey
& Mrs. Silvester his wife
Born Feb. 25 1786
Died the 17th of May 1792
Aged 6 years 2 months 25 days

From Opening skies may streaming glories
 shine
And saints embrace thee with love like
 mine

In Memory of
MISS RUTH BAILEY
Daughter of Mr. Stephen Bailey
& Mrs. Abigail his wife
Who died December the 3rd 1795
In the 20 year of her age

LUTHER BAILY
Died Sept. 25 1799
Aged 27 days

MARTIN BAILY
Died Nov. 3 1799'
Aged 65 days
Twin children of Calvin & Sarah
Baily

In Memory of
MR. STEPHEN BAILEY
Who died Aug. 10 1806
Aged 68 years

Draw near my friend & take a thought
How soon the grave may be our lot
Make sure of Christ while life remain
And death shall be eternal gain

In Memory of
MR. CHARLES BAILEY
Who died June 11th 1820
in the 51st year of his age

Princes this clay must be your bed
 in spite of all your towers
The tall the wise the Reverend head
May lie as low as ours

Sacred to the Memory of
Mr. GEO. BAILEY
Who died March 29 1835
in the 33d year of his age
Also their infant child aged 6 months

Farewell my friends and kindred dear
Justice is done my body's here
To God my soul hath took its way
And shall return at the last day

OLIVE
Wife of Geo. Bailey
Died Feb. 23d 1880
Aged 76 yrs 6 mo
Also their Infant Child aged 6 mo's

In Memory of
RACHEL JANE
dau. of Mr. Benj. and Mrs. Rachel
Baily
Died May 15 1839 Aged 13 years

Farewell Father Farewell Mother I
must leave you
Death the chords of life has riven
Do not let my parting grieve you
Pray that we may meet in Heaven
Father and Mother Farewell
Farewell Brother Farewell Sister do not
grieve thus
God hath called me tis in vain
Pray that he may never leave us
Pray that we may meet again
My Loveing friends Farewell

HELLEN ELISABETH
Dau. of Gad J. & Lydia B. Bailey
Died Nov. 11 1849
Aged 5 years 11 dys

A bud plucked from Earth to bloom in Heaven.

In Memory of
MRS. CHLOE
Wife of Mr. Charles Bailey
Died Feb. 2d 1844 aged 73 years

Unveil thy bosom faithful tomb
Take this new treasure to thy breast
And give these sacred relics Room
To seek a slumber in the dust

In Memory of
MARTIN BAILEY
Who Died March 17th 1844
Aged 37 years.

Farewell dear friend a short farewell
Till we shall meet again above
Where endless joys and pleasures dwell
And trees of life bear fruits of love

RACHEL JANE
Dau. of Benjamin and Rachel
Bailey
Died Sept. 22d 1848
Aged 7 years 9 mos 2 days

Sleep on dear child and take thy rest
God called thee home he thought it best
There with the holy saints to dwell
Farewell thou dearest one farewell

In Memory of
SARAH C. BAILEY
Who died Feb. 7 1851
Aged 31 years

We mourn the sunshine of her smiles
The tendrils of her love
Ah was she loved too well the while
Ere she was called above

Mrs. Ruth
Wife of Mr. Stephen Bailey
Died May 16 1852
Aged 72 years

Lydia A.
Wife of John Q. Bailey
Died Oct. 5 1852
Æ 21

Weep not for me my husband dear
Dear children wipe the falling tears
Parents and friends loving and true
God takes but what he lent to you
Then with submission humbly bow
And kiss the rod that gave the blow

Reuben C. Bailey
Died May 8th 1853
Aged 22 years

George Bailey
Died Nov. 11 1855
Aged 78 years

Asenath
his wife died July 20 1855
Aged 74 yrs 2 mos

The Christian virtues having adorned their lives they died in hopes of a glorious immortality.

Horatio N. Bailey
Born—1834   Died—1860

His wife
Cordelia W.
Born—1836   Died—1860
I love thee still

Thankful
Wife of Gad Bailey,
Departed this life Mch. 28 1862
Aged 84 yrs 9 mos

"Blessed are the dead who die in the Lord"

Gad Bailey
Departed this life Dec. 13 1862
Aged 78 yrs 6 mos

Addie M. Bailey
Jan. 15th 1851
Nov. 13th 1866

W. Elwin Bailey
Died May 17 1869
Æ 18 yrs 7 mos 16 dys

Sarah M. Bailey
Died Sept. 4 1880
Aged 26 years 5 mos

Oh what must it Be to Be There.

Sylvia W.
Wife of Stephen Bailey
Died June 21st 1884
Aged 74 yrs 9 mos 17 days

Jacob G. Bailey
Died Jan. 24th 1888
Aged 70 years 9 mos 13 dys
At Rest.

STEPHEN BAILEY
Died Apr. 1 1890
Aged 80 yrs 23 days
"Gathering home one by one"

MELZAR WARREN
Bailey

STELLA W. (FOLSOM)
Dau. of S. W. & E. J. Bailey
Died July 29 1890
Aged 26 yrs 1 mo & 9 dys

ELLEN J. BAILEY
Wife of Elmer Whiting
Nov. 14 1853   Mch. 20 1891

SAMUEL
Son of the Rev. Sam'l Baldwin
Died *April 1763*   Aged 2 yrs

SAMUEL BALDWIN
2nd son of Rev. Sam'l Baldwin
Died at New York Apr. 4 1783
in the 22 year of his age

In Memory of the
REV. SAMUEL BALDWIN A. M.
who died Dec. 1 1784 in the
54 year of his age

In Memory of
MISS HANNAH BALDWIN
Dau. of Rev. Sam'l Baldwin
Died Nov. 2 1789
in the 25 year of her age

MRS. HANNAH BALDWIN
Consort of Rev. Sam'l Baldwin
Died May 8 1790 in the
52 year of her age

In Memory of
MISS ABIGAIL
Dau. of the Rev. Sam'l Baldwin
Died Dec. 22 1831   Aged 72

FRANCES BALDWIN
Dau. of Rev. Sam'l Baldwin
Born June 8 1780
Died Nov. 17 1865

In Memory of
MR. ELISHA BARKER
Who died October 18th 1781
In the 67 year of his age

In Memory of
MR. THOMAS BARSTOW
Who died March 20 1797
Aged 65 years

Reader stand still & drop a tear
Think on the dust that slumbers here
And when you read the fate of me
Think on the glass that runs for thee

In Memory of
MRS. SARAH BARSTOW
Widow of Mr. Thomas Barstow
Who died Feb. 20 1805
in the 74 year of his age

Wilt thou sad mourner at my stone appear
And think my mortal dust is mouldering here
Oh wilt thou come at evening hour to shed
The tears of memory o'er my narrow bed

Sacred to the Memory of
MR. ROBERT BARSTOW
Son of Col. John B. Barstow
Who died *at*
Falmouth in England
Octr. 13 1818   Aged 21 years.

In Memory of
MRS. SIBEL BARSTOW
Wife of Lieut. Samuel Barstow
Died March 25 1820
Aged 79 years

Death is a debt to nature due
I've paid the debt & so must you

Sacred to the Memory of
MISS LYDIA BARSTOW
Daugh. of Capt. Daniel Barstow
and
MRS. BETSEY BARSTOW
Died May 12 1822
In the 36th year of her age

Seven years in darksome night
But now I've gone to realms of light
To praise my God in endless rest
And be with Christ forever blest

In Memory of
LT. SAMUEL BARSTOW
Died May 4 1826
in **92D YEAR** of his age

How vain are all things here below
How false and yet how fair
Each pleasure hath its poison too
And every sweet a snare

In Memory of
MRS. BETSEY BARSTOW
Wife of Capt. Daniel Barstow
Died March 9 1826
In the 78 year of her age

Why do we mourn departing friends
Or shake at death's alarms
'Tis but the voice that Jesus sends
To call them to his arms

In Memory of
MISS GRACE BARSTOW
Daugh. of Capt. Daniel &
Mrs. Betsey Barstow
Died May 13 1829
Aged 19 years

To heaven my greatful soul descends
On God alone for help depends
His hand is my perpetual guard
His grace the source of my regard

Erected
To the Memory of
CAPT. EDWARD BARSTOW
Son of Col. John B. Barstow
Died Jan 27 1833
Aged 37 years & 7 Months

Grace B. (Foster)
Wife of Nathl. Barstow
Died Apr. 4 1834
Aged 26 years

Sacred
To the Memory of
Capt. Daniel Barstow
Died Feb. 24 1842
Aged 98 years

The patriarch died tho' spared
For near a hundred years
A long probation shared
And knew its hopes & fears
Mortals prepare to die
Prepare to meet your God
The four last things are nigh
Your doom awaits His nod

The grave of
Dea. Elijah Barstow
Born Feb. 13 1771
Died June 22 1842
In the 72 year of his age
also of
Lucy (Eells) his *Consort*
Dau. of Robert L. Eells Esq.
Born Aug. 12 1776
Died June 21 1840
In the 64 year of her age

*Blessed are the pure in heart
For they shall see God*

Mrs. Betsey (Eells) Barstow
Wife of Col. John B. Barstow
Died July 14 1851
Aged 91 YEARS

In Memory of
Miss Molly
Youngest daughter of
Thomas & Sarah Barstow
Born Augt. 1 1768
Died June 1 1850

Tell them to meet me in Heaven

Sarah R.
Died Jan. 14 1851
Aged 6 years
Etta H.
Died Oct. 6 1870
Aged 20 years
Children of Nathl. & Abby R.
Barstow

Col. John B. Barstow
Died Aug. 6 1854
Aged 91 YEARS

Frances Cutler
Dau. of Robert and Ann E.
Barstow
Died May 1st 1859
Aged 1 year 10 dy's

There came an angel to my home
The fairest out of Heaven
There went an angel from my home
An angel back to Heaven

Lydia
Wife of Dan'l Barstow
Died Nov. 16 1859
Aged 78 yrs

DANIEL BARSTOW
Died Feb. 20 1861
Aged 87 years

AMELIA F.
Wife of Augustus P. Barstow
Died Apr. 24 1862
Aged 21 yrs & 3 mos

ALBERT H.
Son of
H. B. & E. M. Barstow
Died Sept. 22 1863
Aged 2 yrs 16 dys

ALBERT
Son of
E. & C. O. Barstow
Died Apr. 7 1863
Aged 22 yrs 7 (?) mos

Thou art gone but not forgotten

HERBERT
Son of
Joseph & Elmira Barstow
Died Aug. 20th 1863
Aged 1 *month* 12 dys

Ot God to call us Homeward
h only son sent down
and now still more to tempt
our hearts has taken up our own

HANNAH BARSTOW
Died Oct. 9 1866
Aged 72 years

SAMUEL BARSTOW
1809—1867

SUSAN N.
Wife of
Henry B. Barstow
Died April 2 1867
Aged 28 years 5 months

We call her dead but ah we know
She dwells where living waters flow

THOMAS H. C. BARSTOW
Born
Oct. 23 1808
Died Nov. 8 1869

Now forgetful at thy feet
His tired head presses on its last long rest
And these sad garments of mortality
Put off we trust that to a happier land
He went a light and gladsome passenger

In Memoriam
HAVILAND BARSTOW
1st Asst
Engineer U. S. N.
Born June 11 1839
WENT DOWN IN THE
U S S ONEIDA
YOKOHAMA BAY JAPAN
Jan. 24 1870
standing at his post
of duty

BETSEY BARSTOW
1809—1872

Betsey Eells
Barstow
Died Mar. 8 1874
Aged 84 years

Benjamin Barstow
Born
16 December 1799
Died
3 September 1880

Saba D. Barstow
1807—1882

Major Daniel Barstow
1807—1882

Capt. Nath. Barstow
Born
Aug. 16 1799
Died
April 3 1885

Caroline O.
Wife of Elijah Barstow
Died Dec. 29 1888
Aged 75 yrs 4 mos

Grace F
Dau. of
Nathl. & Grace F. Barstow
Died May 6 1890
Aged 56 years

Abby Eells
Wife of
Thos. H. C. Barstow
Born Dec. 6 1812
Died Feb. 10 1889

The gift of God is
Eternal life
Through Jesus Christ our Lord

Abby R.
Wife of Nathl. Barstow
Born April 8 1809
Died April 23 1891

Rev. Benjamin Bass
First pastor of the
Congregational church in
Hanover
Died May 24 1756
Aged 61

Mrs. Mary
Wife of Rev. Benj. Bass & daut'
of the Rev. Ja. Gardner
former minister of Marshfeld
Died Feby 24 1772
Aged 61

In Memory of
Mrs. Mercy Bas
the wife of Deacon Ber. Bass
She died Apl. 4th 1792
in the 46th year of her age

In Memory of
MISS MARY BASS
Eldest Daughter of
Rev Benj. Bass
Died Mch. 21 1802
Aged 71 years

Sacred to the Memory of
MRS. MARY BASS
Wife of *Deac.* Benj. Bass
Died Jan. 7 1808
Aged 68 yrs

"Depart my friends dry up your tears
I must be here till Christ appears"

To the Memory of
DEAC. BENJAMIN BASS
Died Mch. 17 1821
Aged 79 yrs

"Whatsoever thy hand findeth to do do it with thy might for there is no work nor device nor knowledge nor wisdom in the grave whither thou goest"

In Memory of
BENJ. Bass
Died June 6th 1825
Aged 57 years
also
BENJ. BASS JR.
Died at New York 1824
Aged 30 years

Prepare to meet thy God

In Memory of
MRS LUCINDA BASS
Relict of Benj. Bass
Died May 9th 1840
in the 73 year of her age

*do not forget as you pass by
that one and all of you must die*

ROBERT
died Nov. 25th 1858
aged 6 ys 11 mo 13 ds

ISABELLA F.
died Oct. 2d 1844
aged 6 ys 8 mos 12 dys

JOHN D.
died Oct. 12th 1840
aged 9 mo 10 dys

JOHN D.
died Oct. 13th 1842
aged 1 year 6 mo 3 dys

LYDIA
died Sept. 28 1843
aged 3 mos 11 dys

GEORGE E.
died Nov. 12 1851
aged 10 mos 4 dys

Children of Robert and Lydia Bass

CINDRILLA
dau. of Dea. Benj & Mary Bass
died Feby. 25 1851
Æ 80

Mary C. Bass,
died May 1 1862
aged 77 yrs 10 mos

Elisha Bass
died Jan. 14 1867
aged 85 yrs 5 mos

Flora I.
dau. of Robert & Lydia Bass
died Nov. 10th, 1870
aged 17 years 1 mo 20 dys
It is sweet to be Remembered.

Col. Seth Bates
Tomb
No Inscription

In Memory of
Mrs. Rebeckah Bates
Wife of Capt. Clement Bates
& Daugh. of Mr. Seth Stetson
Born Dec. 17 1765
& died Sept. 27 1813
aged 47 years 9 Mos & 10 Days

Sybel R. Bates
Died May 26 1816
Aged 37

In Memory of
Mr. Gamaliel Bates
died Jan. 9th 1823
aged 78 years

Sophia
Dau. of Paul & Freelove Bates
Born Sept. 1 1801
Died Sept. 7 1825

In Memory of
Miss Betsey Bates
died Nov. 21 1825
aged 33 years

Frail man your vain pursuits forbear
To meet your God in Peace prepare

Paul Bates
Born Jan. 3 1762
Died Feb. 2 1826

Freelove
his wife
Born July 9 1766
Died Aug. 5 1837

In Memory of
Reuben Bates
son of Gamaliel & Mary Bates
died Jan. 31st 1829
aged 38 years

Laura Ann
dau. of Capt. Thomas M. &
Sylvia Bates
died Apl. 1st 1830
aged 6 yrs 3 mos

"Laura farewell we give thee up
Our father calls thee home
That Saviour folds you in his arms
Who said to children come"

Amos Bates
Died May 8 1833
Aged 64 yrs

Sacred to the Memory of
Mrs. Mary
wife of Mr. Gamaliel Bates
Who Died June 22d 1836
in the 81st year of her age

To the Memory of
Geo. W. Bates
son of Geo. & Lucy Bates
died Oct. 8th 1836
aged 2 years 7 mos

Sweet opening bud of innocence
Thy parents joy and pride
They fondly hoped thy frolic life
No evil would betide
Ere sin could blight or sorrow fade
Death came with friendly care
The opening bud to Heaven conveied
And bade it blossom there

In Memory of
Mrs. Bethiah B.
wife of Mr. Thomas M. Bates Jr.
who died March 11 1837
aged 20 years

See the fair cheeks of beauty fade
Frail glory of an hour
And blooming youth with sickning head
Droop like the dying flower

In Memory of
Capt. Clement Bates
Who died Nov. 30 1839
in the 85 year of his age

The grave of
Lydia P. Bates
Died Oct. 16 1837
Aged 1 year & 3 months
Also
George F. Bates
Died Aug. 28 1838
Aged 7 weeks
Children of Mr. Judson &
Mrs. Lydia Bates.

The infants wither like a flower
But live O death beyond thy power
Ye mourning parents kiss the rod
For He who gave and took was God

Henry Augustus
Son of Henry & Harriet N. Bates
died Dec. 9 1839
aged 1 year & 3 mos

The little spirit pure as light
Saved by redeeming love
Hath taken its eternal flight
To better worlds above

To
the memory of
Mrs. Rebecca Bates
Wife of Mr. Thomas O. Bates
died May 27 1841
aged 52 years

Pause friends for ready are your graves
To follow me yourselves prepare
Prepare in time while Jesus saves
O make religion all your care

Silas C. Bates
died Sept. 20 1848
aged 30 yrs 2 mos 11 ds

CEMETERY RECORDS.

ROBERT M.
son of Mr. Martin S. &
Mrs. Olive W. Bates
born Jan. 9 1845
died Sept. 4 1845

"Sleep on sweet babe and take thy rest
God called thee home he thought it best."

MARIA A.
dau. of Paul & Temperance C.
Bates
died May 20 1845
aged 15 yrs 9 mos 10 ds

MRS. MARTHA BATES
wife of Benjamin Bates
died feb. 23d 1849
aged 82 years

Her toils are past her work is done
and she is fully blest
She fought the fight the victory won
and entered into rest.

JAMES A.
son of James & Ann W. Bates
died Sept. 20 1851
aged 8 yrs 9 mos

Tis' hard to give thee up sweet one
tis' hard to give thee up;
but nature's sudden work is done
tis' the last bitter cup.

SARAH A.
dau. of Thomas & Mary Bates
died Sept. 9 1857
aged 3 yrs 6 mos

"Mother I am going home"

ELIZA P. dau. of
Paul & Temperance Bates
died Sept. 18 1853
aged 22 ys 9 mos & 2 ds

"Locked in the icy arms of death
Two Christian sisters slumber here
Strong in the faith till the last breath
That Christ on earth will yet appear
To bid their mouldering bodies rise
And change immortal for the skies"

CALVIN BATES
died March 29 1855
aged 77 years

ELIZABETH
his wife
died March 6 1842 aged 62 years

REBEKAH W. BATES
died Sept. 25 1857
aged 28 yrs 6 mos & 10 dys

Peaceful are thy slumber Rebekah
Thy sufferings now are O'er
Our God has called thee home
To dwell among the saints forevermore

SARAH A.
dau. of Joseph S. & Sarah Bates
died Oct. 29 1858
aged 34 yrs 11 mos

"We have loved her on earth
May we meet her in Heaven"

RUTH BATES
Died May 8 1866
Aged 78

CAPT. THOMAS M. BATES
died Feb. 22 1858
Aged 71 years

Sleep dear father thou hadst no fear
Of death for Christ to thee was nigh
He heard thy voice he heard thy prayer
And raised thee to his courts on high

GEORGE BATES
Died June 14 1859
aged 51 yrs 5 mo 11 days

Wife, children, friends, a short adieu we
soon shall meet again as deathless as the
angels are and free from mortal pain
Then do not pry beneath this Stone in
quest of one you love nor bury hope
within the grave but let it soar above.

SARAH
wife of Joseph S. Bates
died Nov. 4 1863
aged 75 yrs 5 mos

Peaceful be thy rest dear mother
All thy trials here are o'er
Weary days and nights of anguish
Never shall afflict thee more
"Freed from earth among the loved ones
Thou art gone in Heaven to dwell
And we bow in meek submission
For 'He doeth all things well' "

SYLVIA WING
wife of Capt. Thomas M. Bates
died Dec. 17 1864
aged 78 yrs. & 11 mo.

" Life hath many a weary burden
Many a crushing care and cross
They are but dust within the balance
When weighed against a mother's loss "

WALTER
Son of Paul & Freelove Bates
Born June 24 1810
Died Dec. 27 1869

LYDIA C. BATES
Died Oct. 16 1872
Aged 51 years

JOSEPH S. BATES
died June 19 1873
aged 80 yrs 4 mos

We will not mourn for him we love
he is from pain and sickness free;
but trust in yon bright home above
that Reunited we shall be.

SYLVANUS W. BATES
Died June 27th 1878
aged 59 yrs 6 mo's 4 dys

RUFUS BATES
died Sept. 11th 1878
aged 84 ys 5 mos 26 dys

HULDAH KEITH
wife of Rufus Bates
died Jan. 4th 1874
aged 72 yrs. 9 mo's.

(Square & Compass)
Father
(reverse)
MARTIN S. BATES
Died Sept. 14 1881
Aged 68 yrs 2 mos

SILAS W. BATES
died Dec. 12 1879
aged 29 yrs

RUSHA A.
wife of Hira W. Bates
1839—1882

THOMAS O. BATES
died Jan. 16 1883
aged 72 yrs

ANGIE S.
wife of Henry S. Bates,
died Mch. 10 1885
aged 53 yrs 4 mos.
"My wife Angie"

TEMPERANCE C.
wife of Paul Bates,
died July 8, 1885,
aged 78 yrs 4 mos 18 dys

ALBERT E. BATES
1858—1887

HIRA BATES
1796—1889

LUCY D. BATES
1796—1891

LUCY W.
wife of George Bates
died Aug. 10th 1889
aged 77 years 2 mos 23 days

JOSHUA BATES
born March 22, 1802
Died July 2d 1891

MARY S. PARMER
his wife
born July 5th 1806
Died Aug. 3d 1849

Dying is but going home

Sacred
To the Memory of
MRS. TRYPHENA BEAL
Wife of Mr. Zadock Beal
died Aug. 21 1821
in the 30th year of her age

Also
HOMER
Son of Mr. Zadock & Mrs.
Tryphena Beal
died Aug. 11 1821
Aged 5 weeks

Farewell all earthly friends we say
Be your connections what they may
When God shall call you must die
And hasten to Eternity
O may your souls be washed from sin
Eer your eternity begins
I hope when the Lord shall call you here
If you are young you need not fear

PRISILLA
dau. of Zadock & Tryphena
Beal
Died May 6 1824
6 yrs 7 mos 24 ds

O can this lovely flower be dead
That on our hearts such joy did shed
No it doth still in beauty Bloom
Beyond the confines of the tomb

J. WALDO H.
son of Alfred & Julia A Belcher
died July 15 1857
aged 7 yrs. 10 m. 26 ds

"Tho far from us who loved him
Still let him be with thee"

JOHN H. BENNER
Died Nov. 22d 1882
aged 71 yrs 3 mo's 6 dys

HANNAH S. his wife
died April 20th 1854
aged 36 yrs 7 mos 27 dys

There are no parting's in Heaven

MARY IDA
Wife of J. W. Bean
Died Jan. 10 1870
Æ 24 years

LUCY F. Dau. of
Horace M. & Eliza M. Billings
Died Dec. 7th 1860
aged 8 mo's

This blighted bud will bloom in Heaven

LILA R. dau. of
Annie L. & Lorenzo Bisbe
died Aug. 28 1879
Æ 16 yrs 10 mos

"Beloved Lila, tho' lost to earth
In memory thou art with us still"

ANNA A.
wife of Uriah Brett
died Feby 27 1857
aged 85 yrs 4 mos

HATTIE
(reverse)
Harriette S.
eldest daughter of
Lloyd & Sarah E. Briggs
died June 23 1879
aged 19 y'rs 4 mo's and 25 d's

ANN M. BRIGGS
dau. of Joseph & Jane Briggs
died Sept. 24 1858
aged 27 yrs 3 mos

"No weeping friends could keep her
No skillful hand could save
With aching hearts we clothed her
And laid her in the grave

"Farewell thou dearly loved one
Full many an eye shall weep
That thou in lifes bright morning
So early fell asleep"

J. GILMAN BRIGGS
1823—1893

JOSEPH BRIGGS
died Aug. 28 1861
aged 67 yrs
"With earth shall blend his precious dust
Till he ascend with all the just"

JANE P. BRIGGS
wife of Joseph Briggs
died Sept. 26 1882
Æ 84 yrs 6 mos
"He giveth his beloved sleep"

JOSEPH BROOKS
Tomb
1790

EDWARD G. BROOKS
Oct. 3d 1842
MARY A. his wife
Nov. 24 1842

ELIZABETH dau. of
Dea. John & Amy Brooks
died Dec. 3, 1846
aged 1 yr. 1 mo.

GEO. NELSON, son of
Dea. John & Amy Brooks
died May 12 1850
aged 8 mos 18 dys

SAMUELL BROOKS
died Aug. 26th 1858
aged 64 years

LEVI C. BROOKS.
*A member of Co. K.
38th Reg. Mass. Vol.*
**KILLED IN ACTION AT
CANE RIVER LA.**
April 23d 1864 aged 37 years
We asked for him Life, and God hath given it him, "even length of days for ever and ever"

JOSEPH LEWIS son of
Joseph Jr. & Emily T. Brooks
died Sept. 13 1865
aged 23 yrs 10 mos 14 days
"Death has entered our loved circle
And has taken from our band
One we loved and cherished fondly
To a bright and fairer land"

Brooks Children
CARRIE S.
born Aug. 15 1867
Died Feb. 26 1878
JAMES E.
Mch. 30 1871   April 4 1871

NANCY C.
wife of John S. Brooks
died Apl. 11 1868
aged 42 yrs. 4 mos.
"At Rest"

JANE BROOKS
Died Nov. 22, 1871,
aged 57 years, 2 mo. 18 ds.
One less to love on earth,
One more to meet in heaven

GEORGE GILBERT son of
Chas. C. & Sarah J. Brooks
died Aug. 11 1872
aged 5 mos

AMY BROOKS
wife of Dea. John Brooks
Died June 21 1876
Aged 73 yrs 2 mos

In thy presence is fullness of joy at Thy right hand there are pleasures forever more

LIZZIE and GEORGIE
Suffer little children to come unto Me

DEA. JOHN BROOKS
died Octo. 4 1878
aged 76 yrs 21 days

"Thanks be to God who giveth us the victory through our Lord Jesus Christ"

GILBERT BROOKS
Died June 27 1888
aged 67 years
SYBIL H. his wife

MEHITABLE
wife of Samuel Brooks
died July 21st 1889
aged **91 YRS 6 MOS**

Thou the Christians path hast trod
Dearest mother rest with God

Also their infant Dau's
ANNIE & LIZZIE

ELIZA F.
wife of John S. Brooks
Dec. 24 1836—Sept. 25 1890

Father I will that they also whome thou hast given me, be with me where I am

---

JAMES BROOKS
Born March 21st 1817
Died Jan. 22d 1894

MARY E. dau. of
Allen F. and Mary R. Bonney
died Mch. 12 1846
aged 16 mo's.

And he took the little Children in his arms and blessed them.

EVERETT son of
Allen F. & Mary R. Bonney
died Sept. 27th 1849
aged 2 mos. 20 dys.

Our darling boy we loved so well
Has gone to heaven with Christ to Dwell
He took him from this world of Pain
Where we all hope to meet again.

JOSIAH W. BONNEY
departed this life Apl. 8 1870
Æ 46 yrs 6 mos 21 days.

"We three shall meet again"
"I will be a father to the fatherless and the widows God"

JOSIAH BONNEY
died May 8 1872
aged 77 yrs 5 mos

Marcy W.
wife of Josiah Bonney
died May 23 1875
aged 78 yrs 2 mos

Allen F. Bonney
died July 5th 1885
aged 65 yrs 2 mos 11 dys

Ann W. Burgess
Mar. 15 1837
13 mos

Augustus W. Burgess
Dec. 4 1837
3 yrs 6 mos

T. Benton Burgess
Oct. 15 1839
14 mos

B. F. Burgess
Oct. 28 1888
78 yrs. 9 mos

Sarah W. Burgess
Feb. 10 1861
18 yrs 4 mos

Josiah Burgess
Feb. 1 1862
8 yrs 5 mos

Franklin Burgess
Nov. 15 1842
2 yrs

Elvira Burgess
Dec. 6 1844
6 mos

Melvina Burgess
Oct. 4 1848
4 mos

Bowers
Tomb

Burt
Charles D. Burt
1876—1892

John H. Cary
**DIED
IN NEW ORLEANS LA.
MAY 6 1863**
aged 43 yrs 5 mos
*A member of Co. G.
42nd Reg. Mass. Vol.*

Ann Adelia
died Dec. 19 1849
aged 6 yrs & 9 mos
John Francis
died Jan. 6 1850
aged 4 yrs & 9 mos
only children of
John H. & Fanny Cary

To me the glorious Saviour said
Suffer the children now to come
Tho in the dust their forms be laid
Forbid them not their heavenly home
Why will ye weep each form will rise
Triumphant o'er the silent tomb
Each with its soul in lasting ties
In pure immortal bliss to bloom

In Memory of
Mrs. Phebe wife of
Mr. Nath. F. Chamberlin
who died May 23 1836 aged 27
also their child
aged 6 mos, & 16 dys

NATHANIEL M.
son of Nathaniel F. &
Phebe Chamberlin
died Sept. 24 1840
aged 6 yrs 11 mos & 4 days

In Memory of
MRS. PRISCILLA wife of
Freedom Chamberlin
who died April 21st 1846
in her 84 years

NATHANIEL F. CHAMBERLIN
died Feb. 12 1854
aged 52 years & 6 days

Chamberlain Monument

PHILIP HERBERT
Sept. 20 1853
Mch. 8th 1865

ELIZA JAMES
Feb. 19th 1861
Oct. 8th 1861

PHILIP CHESTER
Aug. 2d 1867
Jan. 4 1893

God calls our loved ones
While angels bear them Home

JOSIAH CHAMBERLIN
died Nov. 4 1876
Æ 77 yrs 11 mos 17 ds
" I am the resurrection and the life "

EMMA S. dau.
Dea. F. & D. A. Chamberlin
born April 16 1881
died July 21 1882

SOPHIA wife of
Josiah Chamberlin
died Oct. 23 1881
Æ 79 yrs 5 mos 8 ds
" Because I live ye shall live also "

RALPH HARLAN son of
F. & D. A. Chamberlin
died Aug. 18 1885
aged 8 mos 11 ds

NORMAN CHAMBERLAIN
Died Jan. 30 1886
aged 67 years 9 mos.

WM. HENRY CHAMBERLAIN
1827—1889

FRANK W. CHAMBERLAIN
Born Dec. 28 1867
**DROWNED AT NO. SCITU-
ATE** May 20th 1890

Robert
April 6 1890 April 19 1891
Son of H. E. *and* A. E.
Chamberlain

SARAH E.
wife of Saml. S. Church
died Dec. 28 1850
Æ 42 yrs
"Farewell husband and children farewell
Follow Christ's example and with Him
dwell"

ALICE R. dau. of
Saml. S. & Sarah E. Church
died Mch. 10 1851
Æ 5 mos 4 ds

MARY H. CHURCH
died May 30 1857
aged 44 yrs
We have loved her on earth
May we meet her in heaven

WM. CHURCH JR.
CO. I. 58 MASS. VOL.
*Born in Hanover
died in Beverly New Jersey 1863*
aged 37 years
A Reunion in Heaven

LEWIS C. CHURCH
Died Dec. 9 1866
Aged 50 yrs
ANGELINE
His wife
Died Mar. 17 1860
Aged 41 yrs
AMELIA F. BARSTOW
Their Daughter
Died April 24 1862
Aged 21 yrs & 3 mos

EDDIE C. son of
S. H. & E. C. Church
died Mar. 11 1876
Æt 7 yrs 7 mos 20 days

LULU S. CHURCH
Until the day breaks
And the shadows Flee away
(Reverse)
Lulu S. Church
*Born in Hanover
died in Galveston Texas*
June 7 1882   Aged 20 years

DEA. SAML. S. CHURCH
died May 7, 1883,
Æ 81 yrs. 3 mos.
"Asleep in Jesus, Blessed sleep in
which none ever wake to weep."

BENJAMIN CHURCH,
died Dec. 22, 1889,
aged 45 yrs 10 mos.
"We miss thy kind and willing hand
Thy fond and loving care
Our home is darkness without thee
We miss thee everywhere"

CAROLINE STETSON
wife of Martin Church
died June 18, 1883.
Aged 77 yrs. 6 mos
"Blessed are the dead which die in
the Lord"

FREDERICK W. CHURCH
1859—1892

HENRY
(reverse)
Henry Elliot son of
Andrew & Jane C. Clark
Jan. 7 1885 May 14 1890
Will meet thee in Heaven

ROBERT S. CHURCH
CO. G. 43D REGT. M. V. M.
Jan. 18 1842   Nov. 21 1891
For him who sleeps our love is not quenched

ELIZABETH R. CHURCH
Died July 29 1892
Aged 84 yrs 5 mos
Safe in the arms of Jesus.

ZEBULON CLARK
1781—1857
CHRISTIANA
his wife
1791—1881

SARAH B.
wife of Andrew Clark
died Apr. 23 1863
aged 31 yrs & 3 mos
" Christ is my hope"
" He leadeth me beside the still waters"

GEORGE EDWARD son of
Andrew & Sarah B. Clark
died Apr. 28 1868
Æ 8 yrs 8 mos 19 ds
"Gone but not forgotten"

CHAS. CARROLL only son
of Chas. H. and Sarah *Clark*
a member of Co. I.
4th Reg. Mass. Vol.
**DIED AT NEW ORLEANS
JULY 17 1863**
Aged 17 yrs 9 mos

NELLIE E. dau. of
Henry & Ann E. Clark
died Dec. 4 1873
aged 16 yrs

HENRY CLARK
died Feb. 8 1876
aged 43 yrs
"Asleep in Jesus"

HENRY L. son of
Andrew & C. Maria Clark
died Aug. 15 1876
Æt 2 mos 8 ds
WALDO B. son of
Andrew & C. Maria Clark
died Oct. 13 1878
Æt 3 mos 3 dys

GEORGE EDWARD 2nd son of
Andrew & C. Maria Clark
died Nov. 2 1881
aged 11 yrs 10 mos 29 ds

HENRY ELLIOT son of
Andrew & Jane C. Clark
Jan. 7 1885—May 14 1890
"Will meet thee in Heaven "

C. MARIA
wife of Andrew Clark
died Nov. 10 1881
aged 40 yrs 6 mos 21 ds

Gone but not forgotten

E. BURTON son of
J. A. & E. F. Cole
died June 5 1888
Aged 2 mos

MRS. MARY E. COOPER
wife of Joseph A. Cooper
died Mch. 25 1888
aged 41 yrs 11 mos 9 ds

" The morning cometh "

" A precious one from us has gone
A voice we loved is stilled
A place is vacant in our home
Which never can be filled

GEORGE LLOYD CORBIN
died May 1 1883
Æt 9 yrs 1 mo

CAPT. JOSEPH CRADDOCK
died June A. D. 1812
aged 88 years

Sacred to the Memory of
MRS. MARY
wife of Ensign Crocker
Born May 24th 1809
Died May 24 1841

MARY E.
Dau. of Ensign Jr. & Mary
Crocker
died Oct. 6th 1845
aged 10 yrs 6 mos

Suffer little, children to come unto me

NATHANIEL CROCKER
Died June 20th 1847
aged 63 years

ENSIGN CROCKER
Died Jan. 7th 1853
aged 83 years

HANNAH
his wife
Died April 13th 1853
aged 79 years

Prepare to meet thy God.

ARTHUR
son of Ensign Jr. and
Sylvia Crocker
died Oct. 13 1857
aged 5 mos 2 dys

Of such is the kingdom of Heaven

ENSIGN CROCKER JR.
died Jan. 11th 1869
aged 62 years

Be ye also Ready

FRED. M. son of
Charles E. & Viola Crocker
Died Oct. 11th 1877
aged 8 yrs 5 mos 13 dys

Without a sigh a change of feature
or a shaded smile she gave her hand
to the stern mess'gr and as a glad
Child seeks its father went Home

ELLA M. dau. of
Charles E. & Viola Crocker
died Sept. 28th 1880
aged 24 ys 10 mos

God's finger Touched she slept

CARRIE E. dau. of
Charles E. & Viola Crocker
Died Nov. 29th 1880
aged 19 ys 18 dys

Father
JOHN CUDWORTH
Born Sept. 15 1831
Died Oct. 5 1890
Gone before

Mother
Mary H.
wife of John Cudworth
Born Dec. 17 1830
Died Oct. 10 1890
At Rest

SARAH JANE CUDWORTH
1835—1892

EXSPERENCE CURTIS
Daughter To Mr. Joseph Curtis
Dyed *June ye 25th* 1732 and
Aged 4 years

STEPHEN CURTIS
Son of Mr. Joseph Curtis
Dyed **JULY YE 14 INS 1739**
& Aged 10 Months

DEBORAH CURTIS
daughter to Mr. William Curtis
Dyed **AUG. YE 12TH 1739**
& aged 10 days

Here lyes the Body of
MR. WILLIAM CURTIS who died
JANY THE 20 1749
in the 44th year of his age

MRS. MARY CURTIS
ye vertuous *Consort* of
Mr. Joseph Curtis
Tis Dyed *April* **Ye 9 1750**
& Aged 46 years

Here Lyes The Body of
MR. JOSEPH CURTIS
Who Died December The 1 1753
In The 60 year of his age

In Memory of
MR. RICHARD CURTIS
Who died April 28th 1766
in the 64 year of his age

In Memory of
MISS ALATHEA CURTIS
she died April ye 16th 1801
in the 23rd year of her age

In Memory of
GERSHOM
son of Mr. Gershom Curtis
and Mrs. Elizabeth his wife
he died Dec. ye 15th 1779
aged 15 Days

In Memory of
MRS. TIBASHA
ye wife of Mr. Gershom Curtis
she died Jan. ye 25th 1780
in ye 25th year of her age

In Memory of
MRS. MARTHA CURTIS
the wife of Mr. William Curtis
who died Nov. ye 30th 1786
in the 73rd year of her age
*In faith she dy'd in dust she lies
But faith foresees that dust shall rise
When Jesus calls while hope assumes
And blests' her joy among the tombs*

In Memory of
MR. JOHN CURTIS
who died Sept. ye 27th 1799
in the 58th year of his age
"Oh cruel death who would not spare
A tender husband and a father dear
But's taken him to the world Above
To sing the praises of Eternal Love"

The grave of
SOPHIA
dau. of Seth & Percis Curtis
died 1807 Æ 4 years

In Memory of
MISS CHARLOTT CURTIS
the Dau. of Mr. John Curtis
& Mrs. Anne his wife
who died Aug. ye 23rd 1800
in the 33rd year of her age
" *Ye loving mortals Come and see
The wondrous change that's past on me
Like you I once was young and gay
But now am mouldering back to clay* "

In Memory of
MR. JOB CURTIS
who died April ye 6th 1804
in the 68th year of his age
" *Great God I own the sentence just
And nature must decay
I yield my body to the dust
To dwell with fellow clay* "

In Memory of
MR. SETH CURTIS
died June 4th 1812
in the 53 year of his age

A sinner born redeemed by blood
& rest till the great day of God
then will this slumbering dust arise
to blissful mansions in the skies

Vile sinner saved by grace divine
high in the world of glory shine
but walking in the downward road
they fall beneath the frownes of God

Sacred to the Memory of
MRS. PERCIS CURTIS
wife of Seth Curtis
died Oct. 2d 1825
aged 56 years

Mrs. Zinthia S.
wife of Ebenezer Curtis
Died Aug. 14th 1813
Aged 33 years
also their son
William B.
Died Aug. 14th 1813
Aged 1 year 7 mos

Sacred to the Memory of
Mrs. Abigail
wife of Reuben Curtis
Died Dec. 24th 1841
aged 74 years

Hail sweet repose now shall I rest
no more with sickness be distressed
from sin and sorrow find release
my soul shall dwell in endless Peace

In Memory of
John Curtis Jr. son of
Mr. John & Mrs. Sally Curtis
died Mch. 14 1817
aged 15 yrs 6 mos & 14 days

"Death like an overflowing stream
Sweeps us away: our life's a dream
An empty tale: a morning flower
Cut down and withered in an hour"

In Memory of
Martin Curtis
who died Aug. 29 1848
In his 39 yr.

*" Farewell my wife & children too
I can no longer stay with you
My portion in heaven I wish to share
Prepare for death and meet me there"*

The grave of
Benjamin Curtis Son of
Mr. John and Mrs. Sally Curtis
who died Aug. 28 1833
aged 26 years

*" The earth for a short period
may confine the body & even cause
the tenement of the active mind to
dissolve in dust : but the soul of the
just unfettered by the clods of the
valley flies to the bosom of its God"*

John Curtis
died Dec. 5 1851
aged 80 years

" A man of rare integrity, independent in his opinions, gentle and modest in his disposition, devoted and active in his **OPPOSITION TO NEGRO SLAVERY,** *unlike most men more enthusiastic in that opposition, and in the welcome of all new truth as he advanced in age; meeting his death at last most serenely with an unfaltering trust in God and the final triumph of justice"*

"Like one who wraps the drapery
of his couch about him and lies down
to pleasant dreams"

Luther Curtis
died Aug. 25 1843
aged 52 yrs.

LEVI CURTIS
died May 15 1853
aged 65 years
He is gone but many morrows
Yet may dawn ere we forget
Though his death awaken sorrows
In our hearts he liveth yet

ROBERT CURTIS
died Feby. 15 1858
aged 66 yrs 10 mos 14 dys
" E'ven so Father, for so it seemeth good in thy sight "

ROBERT SNOW son of
Robert S. & Rachel C. Curtis
died Sept. 16 1860
aged 1 yr 3 mos 8 dys
"Another little voice is hushed
And a little angel born"

RACHEL C.
wife of Robert S. Curtis
died June 13 1862
aged 41 yrs 7 mos
" Jesus can make a dying bed
Feel soft as downy pillows are "

RUTH CURTIS
died April 27 1863
aged 80 years

SALLY
wife of John Curtis
died Aug. 29 1865
aged 88 years

BENJAMIN CURTIS
Member of Co. G. 12 Mass. Vol.
KILLED IN BATTLE OF ANTIETAM MD. SEPT. 16TH 1863
Aged 22 years
Said'st thou that our sons were dying, Pouring out their blood in vain
God forbid they lay their lives down that our Country may be free   Not a drop of blood is wasted tis the price of Liberty

---

BATHSHUA wife of
James **PRATT** *& formerly wife of Luther Curtis*
died July 12 1868
aged 69 yrs

WILLIAM CURTIS
died Jan. 6th 1871
aged 67 years 4 mos

ROBERT S. CURTIS
died April 1 1873
aged 46 years
" Therefore be ye also ready for in such an hour as ye think not the Son of man cometh "

MERIEL
wife of Loring Curtis,
died May 11, 1873,
aged 72 yrs.

CASSANDRA
wife of Wm. Curtis
Died Nov. 23d 1875
aged 70 yrs 4 mos

Curtis Monument
Father & Mother
G. C.
1807—1875
N. B. C.
1804—1887
Husband and Wife
Almighty God tis right, tis just,
That earthly frames should turn to Dust
But Ah! forgive that wishful Tear
That would detain their Spirits here

KETURAH STUDLEY
wife of Robert Curtis
died Dec. 22 1880
aged 79 yrs 9 mos
"There remaineth a rest for the people of God"

LORING CURTIS
died Feb. 4 1881
aged 83 yrs 4 mos 1 day

In Memory of
DEBORAH
wife of Martin Curtis
died April 5 1881
aged 71 yrs 1 mo 4 ds

NATHANIEL CUSHING only son
of Dr. E. D. & D. S. Cushing
died Aug. 12 1864
aged 47 yrs

WARREN V. CUSHING
Died March 7th 1889
aged 73 ys 7 mos
At rest

JOHN CUSHING
Born June 14th 1800
Died Oct. 30 1871
his wife SARAH C.
born June 3d 1801
Died Mch. 1 1879
their dau. SARAH E.
wife of Godfroid Turcotte
Born Dec. 30 1835
Died Feb. 24 1882

MISS LYDIA B. CUTLER
Died Dec. 18 1858
Aged 63 yrs

MISS FRANCES CUTLER
Died June 28 1868
Aged 70 yrs

S. GARDNER CUTLER
Died Feb. 12 1869
Æt 33 yrs
We Shall Rise For Christ Has Risen

REV. SAMUEL CUTLER
Died July 17 1880
Aged 75 yrs
Waiting for the kingdom

ELIZABETH D. CUTLER
Died July 21 1888
Aged 79 yrs
Come Lord Jesus come

JOHN A. DAME
July 4 1835
Dec. 4 1891
MELISA
wife of John A. Dame
Apr. 4 1849
June 11 1889

FRANKLIN N.
Dec. 25 1869
Drowned
July 29 1880
AUGUSTA
Aug. 13 1874
Mar. 13 1875
CHAS. C.
Aug. 25 1888
Oct. 29 1888
Children of John & Melisa Dame

EDGAR L. son of
Bernard & Lydia A. Damon
died Sept. 22 1855
Æ 10 mo's & 2 da's

"Away away to thy home in the skies
Thou beautiful child with the love lit eyes
We have ever loved thee in doubtful fear
For brief have we felt would thy stay be here
Thou art all too fair for thy earthly home
And spirit voices are bidding thee come
Back to thy father in loveliness drest
Back to thy home in the land of the blest
We weep for ourselves but never for thee
For we know tis bliss where thy home will be
And we know full well that no blight will come
And naught to distress in that peaceful home

In Memory of
MRS. SARAH
wife of Mr. Zachariah Damon
died April 4 1847
aged 72 years

Hark, from on high my Saviour calls
I come my lord, my love,
Devotion breaks the Prison walls
And speeds my last Remove

HANNAH M. Dau. of
John & Martha S. Damon
Died June 23 1847
Aged 8 mos

Dear wife and daughter take thy rest
Where pain & parting never come
O may we find among the blest ,
With thee a bright eternal home

MARTHA S.
wife of John Damon
Died June 6 1849
aged 38 years

In Memory of
Zachariah Damon
died July 1858
aged 82 years 7 mo's
EELLS DAMON his father
drowned near Bonn Island Me.
Aug. 26th 1805 aged 43 years
also his wife HULDAH
died March 12 1830 aged 72 years

LIZZIE EVA dau. of
Bernard & Lydia A. Damon
died Sept. 4 1861
Æ 1 yr 4 mos

"They have gone to Heaven before us
But they turn and wave their hand
Pointing to the glories o'er us
In that happy spirit land"

LILIAN FRANCES dau. of
Geo. F. & Sarah T. Damon
died Aug. 5 1864
aged 1 yr 3 mos 19 ds
"She faltered by the wayside
And angels took her home"

JOSEPH DAMON son of
Chas. & Sarah B. Thomas
*Member 2nd Heavy Artillery
Mass. Vol's. DIED IN PRISON
AT ANDERSONVILLE
SEPT. 1864*
Aged 33 yrs 6 months
*He died a Prisoner in Anderson's
living tomb
We see his gaunt and wasted form
When we lay down to sleep
And know he died with hungers Pain
When we'd enough to eat*

EMMA
wife of Chas. H. Damon
died Dec. 14th 1871
aged 23 years 9 mos 23 days
HENRY F. their son
died March 13th 1872
aged 4 mo's

WILBUR B.
son of Joseph & Mary Damon
died Nov. 4 1877
aged 5 yrs 4 mos
"I take this little lamb said He
And lay him on my breast
Protection he shall find in me
And be forever blest"

ANNIE
youngest dau. of
Alfred C. & Lucy S. Damon
Sept. 1862—Sept. 1885
" A light is from our household gone
A voice we loved is stilled
A place is vacant in our hearts
Which never can be filled"

HENRY A. DAVENPORT
1852—1891

To the Memory of
MRS. AMY B.
wife of William Dawe
and relic of Cap't. Edward
Barstow
died Aug. 29th 1855
aged 58 years

WILLIAM DAWE'S
Died Feb. 19th 1867
aged 77 years

ALICE F.
wife of Rufus E. Delano
died May 2 1885
Æ 23 yrs 3 mos

MINNIE F.
wife of Clinton M. Delano
Apr. 5 1861 Sept. 9 1893
Severed only till he comes

In Memory of
JEDEDIAH & AVIS *Dweele*
ye son and Daughr of
Lieut. Joshua *Dweele*
& Mrs. Avis his wife
He died Nov ye 21st 1786
in ye 18th year of his age
She died August ye 27th 1786
in ye 16th year of her age

Here lies the body of
Lieut. JOSHUA DWEELE
who died Mch. 15th 1787
in the 51st year of his age

ALMIRA
dau. of Mr. Joshua Dwelly
died Dec. 9 1807
aged 2 yrs 4 mos

JOSHUA son of
Joshua & Betsey Dwelley
1825—1825

In Memory of
MRS. AVICE
wife of Mr. Joshua Dwelly
died Mch. 19 1831
aged 90 yrs & 1 day

"Our God is love his promises are sure
Great is his power none can his wrath endure
Oh do not slight this loud and solemn call
And while you mourn for me make Christ yonr all"

In Memory of
MRS. RACHEL
wife of Mr. Joshua Dwelly
died Dec. 11 1831
in the 57th year of her age

1825
ROBERT E. DWELLEY
1827
MARY L. his wife
Children
EDWIN B. 1850
EUGENE 1854

JOSHUA DWELLY
died Dec. 13 1847
aged 81 yrs

"*Draw near my friends and take a thought
How soon the grave may be your lot
Make shure of Christ while speech remains
And death will be eternal gain*"

Dwelley Monument
No lettering

LEMUEL DWELLY
Tomb
No Inscription

GEORGE W. son of
Joshua & Betsey (or Kezia)
Dwelley
1841—1841

In Memory of
DR. MELZAR DWELLY
died Nov. 25 1829
aged 58 years
SALLY his wife
who died Jan. 27 1841
aged 66 years
their son JOSEPH DWELLY
died Nov. 23d 1838
aged 19 years
their Dau. HARRIET DWELLY
died Dec. 14th 1818
aged 17 years
and their Dau.
ABIGAIL W. DWELLY
died Oct. 18th 1812
aged 2 ys 2 mo

JOSHUA DWELLY
1798—1842
BETSEY His wife
1799—1825
KEZIA His wife
1807—1890
Gone Home

JOHN DWELLY
Died Nov. 8 1857
aged 55 yrs 3 mos
In the midst of life we are in death

NATHAN H. son of
Nathan and Huldah B. Dwelly
Died June 16th 1862
aged 30 years
Meet Me in Heaven

FREDRICK DWELLEY
died May 26 1866
aged 53 years

HOSEA DWELLY
Died June 27 1866
aged 29 yrs 6 mos

To the Memory of
ALMIRA A. DWELLY Daugh. of
Mr. John & Mrs. Mary Dwelly
Died May 3 1839
aged 6 years 3 months & 10 Days

Farewell dear parents we must part
Death aims at me a mortal dart
Sweet child your Savior bid you come
And heaven above shall be your home

JOSEPH DWELLY
Died Feb. 7 1868
Aged 54 yrs 10 mos

Hope for upon that happy shore
Sorrow and sighing will be O'er
And friends will meet to part no more

HULDAH B.
wife of Capt. Nathan Dwelly
died July 23d 1868
aged 66 yrs 5 mo's
To know her was to love her

JOSEPH S. DWELLY
Died Feb. 1 1874
aged 34 yrs 4 mos 16 Days

SALLY
wife of Joseph Dwelly
Died April 20 1879
Aged 66 yrs 6 mos
To part no more

Amy M. Dwelly
Died April 5 1880
Aged 79 years
There is Rest in Heaven

Capt. Nathan Dwelly
died Mch. 17 1882
aged 85 years
After the work is over the Master's word well done

In Memory of
Huldah B. Dau of
Capt. Nathan & Huldah B. Dwelly
who died March 6th 1833
aged 2 yrs 9 mo's
This lovely bud so young and fair
Fallen by early doom
Just came to show how sweet a flower
In Paradise will bloom

J. Wilton Dwelley
Nov. 17 1803
July 9 1883

Huldah B. dau. of
Nathan & Huldah B. Dwelly
Born July 2d 1834
Died Jan. 20 1888
Faithfull in all things

Mary
wife of John Dwelly
Died Aug. 19 1893
aged 89 yrs 5 mos
Not dead but Resting

Mrs. Lucia (*Harlow*) dau. of
Capt. Ellis & Sarah Harlow
late of *Harvard Mass.*
wife of Rev. Abel G. Duncan
Pastor of First Cong. Church
in Hanover
died Sabbath Eve. Oct. 12 1851
aged 54 years
*She was a descendent of the
Pilgrims*
She was lovely in life and in death
Adorned both by Nature and Grace;
"Precious Jesus," was on her last Breath
When gently she passed to the Place
Prepared by the Lord for the Blest
And entered her glorious Rest
Erected by the ladies of the
Congregation

Sacred to the Memory of
REV. ABEL G. DUNCAN
Born June 25th 1802
Died April 23d 1874
Simply to thy cross I cling

Theodore Dyer
Born Sept. 19 1836
Died Aug. 29 1891

Infant son of
Robert & Mary T. Eells
died Jan. 3 1843
& Infant dau. died June 3 1844

HENRY DYER
1801—1889
his wife RUTH (REED)
1802—1839
their children
HERVEY R.
1827—1847
RACHEL R.
1829—1845
R. CORNELIA
1832—1851
his wife LYDIA R. (HOWES)
1815—1891
their children
WARREN A.
1845—1847
WILLIAM
1846—1847

ROBERT JR.
son of Robt & Mary T. Eells
died Aug. 17 1846
Æ 6 mos

MARY
dau. of Robt & Mary T. Eells
died Sept. 14 1847
Æ 5 mos

ELLEN A.
dau. Robt & Mary T. Eells
died Sept. 12 1847
Æ 7 yrs 5 mos

DEA. GEORGE W. EELLS
died May 23 1857
aged 37

MARY E.
dau. of Robt & Mary T. Eells
died Oct. 8 1852
Æ 3 yrs 4 mos

MARTHA FOBES
dau. of John P. & Anna Eells
born Nov. 10 1854
died June 6 1856

GEORGE H. EELLS
died Oct. 6 1857
aged 3 yrs
"God's time is the best"

CHARLES H. EELLS
died June 8 1861
Æt 19 yrs

ROBERT EELLS
died Feb. 5 1872
aged 57 yrs 10 mos

JOHN P. EELLS
born Aug. 12 1822
died Nov. 25 1883

In Memory of
MRS. RUTH ELLIS
ye wife of Mr. David Ellis
She died January ye 10th A. D.
1772
In ye 22d year of her age

In Memory of
NATHANIEL ELLIS
Died Feb. 5 1817
aged 60 years
also
MARY his wife
died Jan. 21st 1848
aged 76 years

Rest sleeping dust in silence rest
In the cold Grave that Jesus blest
In faith and hope we lay thee there
Safe in our heavenly Father's care

FRANCES B. ELLIS
died Nov. 2 1843
aged 47 years

"Into thy hands my Saviour God
I did my soul resign
In firm dependence on thy truth
That made salvation mine"

LUCY J.
wife of Nathaniel B. Ellis
Died June 7th 1859
aged 25 years 7 mo's 3 days

CALVIN C. ELLIS
*A member of Co. C.
38th Reg. Mass. Vol.*
**DIED AT NEW ORLEANS,
LA. JUNE 23 1863**
aged 24 yrs 6 mos

" He marched from his home at his dear country's call
His guiding star, Duty, his hearts light sweet love
Now marches all over and battles all fought
He waits for his loved ones in Christ's home above "

SOLOMON EWELL
died April 28 1858
aged 27 yrs 7 mos 4 days

We shall meet again
To part no more
And with celestial welcome greet
On an immortal shore

LUCY LITTLE
wife of Francis B. Ellis
died Oct. 18 1866
aged 59 yrs 7 mos

"Be ye therefore ready, for in a day or an hour when ye think not the Son of man cometh"

CALVIN C.
twin child of F. B. & S. J. Ellis
died Feb. 7 1876
aged 4 yrs 5 mos 9 ds

EVELYN B.
twin child of F. B. & S. J. Ellis
died Jan. 21 1876
aged 4 yrs 4 mos 21 ds

ANNIE F.
dau. of F. B. & S. J. Ellis
died Feb. 19 1876
aged 14 yrs 8 mos 27 ds

MARY ELLIS
died Aug. 13th 1880
aged 68 yrs 6 mos 29 dys

JOSEPH ELLIS
Died Dec. 5th 1880
aged 73 years 6 mos 17 dys

In Memory of
MR. RICHARD ESTES
he died March ye 11th 1797
in the 52nd year of his age
Also
ELIJAH son of
Mr. Richard Estes &
Mrs. Marcy his wife
he died Oct. ye 28th 1790
in the 8 year of his age

To the Memory of
ROBERT ESTES J.
who died Sept. 11 1843
aged 28 years 2 mos & 7 days
Son of Mr. Robert & Mrs.
Expe Estes

Farewell my true and loving wife
My children and my friends
I hope in heaven to meet you all
When all things have an end
Weep not for me but dry your tears
Nor heed the bitter sigh
My body rests beneath this stone
My soul with God on high

ROBERT ESTES
Died May 8 1867
Aged 78 y'rs
EXPERIENCE
His wife
Died April 2 1857
Aged 67 y'rs

SARAH J.
wife of Rufus T. Estes
died Dec. 28th 1850
aged 23 years 6 months
We have loved her on earth
May we meet her in Heaven

GEORGE H. ESTES
died May 12 1859
aged 27 yrs 2 mos

The grave of
BEULAH W. ESTES Daugh. of
Mr. Robert & Exp. Estes
died May 27 1835
Aged 11 years 7 mos & 24 Days

*My young companions come & see
Those earthly clods that cover me
My body once alive like thine
Though in a coffin now confined
And you like me must sleep in death
When God is pleased to take your
breath*

In Memory of
ALONZO W.
son of John W. & Polly Estes
died Dec. 24 1851
aged 7 yrs 4 mos & 13 days

A few short years thy sweet blue eyes
Did beam with brightness on our way
But God has called thee to that sky
Where angels love do grace thy stay

JOHN W. ESTES
Died Aug. 11 1872
Æt 55 yr 7 mo 26 days

Thy task is accomplished
Thy victory won
Thy work on this earth
Is finished and done
Thy spirit is strengthened
Thy frame is at rest
There is health there is peace
In the land of the blest

JOHN ESTES
Died Sept. 27 1878
Æ 86 yrs 5 mos

ELIZABETH B.
wife of John Estes
died May 10 1875
Æ 83 yrs 10 mos 18 ds

Beloved parents tho lost to earth
In memory tho art with us still

ANN MARIA
wife of Robert Estes
Born Nov. 1 1816
Died June 11 1886

Father & Mother Reunited

HENRY C. ESTES
died May 16 1891
aged 69 years

F. OTIS EVERSON
born Jan. 1 1840
died June 19 1867

"*Though I walk through the valley of the shadow of death I will fear no evil for thou art with me*"

E. ROWENA EVERSON
born Nov. 20 1839
died May 9 1889

REUBEN T. FOSTER
Died Sept. 20th 1848
aged 35 years

CHARLIE (*Fish*)
Marble Lamb

AGNES L.
wife of Alexander Fraser
Died Octo. 6 1863
aged 23 yrs

"Adieu dear husband here below
My Saviour calls and I must go
But on that peaceful shore we'll meet
And cast our crown at Jesus feet"

GEORGIANA
dau. of Alex. & Agnes L. Fraser
died Oct. 13 1863
Aged 7 mos

JOHN O. FRENCH
Died Sept. 28 1887
Aged 66 years

MARTHA B.
wife of John O. French
Died April 27 1859
Aged 40 years

NANCY W.
wife of John O. French
Died Feb. 11 1877
Aged 52 years

MARTHA P. Daughter of
John O. French M. D.
Died Apr. 7 1886
Aged 24 years

ANDREW GARDNER
died Jan. 10 1878
aged 71 yrs 8 mo's 28 ds

EVERETT WEBSTER
son of Andrew & Louisa Gardner
died Nov. 28 1837
aged 2 yrs & 22 days

"As the sweet flower which decks the morn
But withers in the rising days
Thus lovely was my Everett's dawn
Thus swiftly fled his life away"

MARIAH F. dau. of
Andrew & Louisa Gardner
died Aug. 6 1839
aged 6 yrs 5 mos 20 ds

"Departed soul whose poor remains
This hallowed lowly grave contains
Whose passing storm of life is o'er
Whose pains & sorrows are no more
Blessed be thou sister with the blest above
Where all is joy and purity & love

JULIA JACKSON dau. of
Andrew & Louisa Gardner
died May 7 1840
aged 1 yr 9 mos 24 ds

"Bud of the spring thou promised (flower)
To pay tenfold thy parent's care
We hoped to see thee bloom
That hope has vanished as a dream
The child so late our darling theme
Yon slumber in the tomb"

LOUISA M. dau. of
Andrew & Louisa Gardner
died Nov. 25 1846
aged 2 yrs 7 mos

"Sleep on sweet sister sleep, so early gone
To us a child is lost, to heaven a cherub born"

LOUISA B. GARDNER
wife of Andrew Gardner
died July 4 1861
aged 57 yrs 6 mos

"Mother thou art gone to rest
Thy toils and cares are o'er
And sorrow pain and suffering now
Shall ne'er distress thee more"

"Mother thou art gone to rest
And this shall be our prayer
That when we reach our journey's end
Thy glory we may share"

EMMA M.
wife of John D. Gardner
Died Dec. 1 1868
Aged 19 y'rs 9 mos

By the hand of God thou wert taken from me
Yet remember you shall always be

ADDIE L. dau. of
A. & A. A. Gardner
died Apr. 5 1871
aged 2 mos 13 ds

CELIA
wife of George W. Goodrich
Died Feb. 5 1865
Aged 56 yrs & 5 Days

PEREZ S. GOODRICH
CO. I. 58 REGT. MASS. VOL'S.
Died of disease contracted while in service July 28 1866
Aged 23 yrs

GEORGE H.
son of Geo. & Agnes M. Green
born Sept. 9 1860
died Nov. 14 1888

GEORGE GREEN
died Aug. 12 1880
aged 54 yrs 7 mos

AGNES M.
wife of George Green
died Aug. 18 1880
aged 50 yrs 6 mos

CAPT. WILLIAM E. HANDY
Lost at sea 1848
aged 44 years

ISABELLA wife of
Capt. William E. Handy
died Jan. 19 1856
aged 43 years

ANNIE dau. of
W. E. & Isabella Handy
died Mar. 1 1883
aged 49 years
Fear not, for I am with thee. Is. 43-5.

TOWN OF HANOVER
Tomb
Erected
By the town of Hanover
A. D. 1845

MELZER E. son of
Elisha R. & Laura A. Hanson
died Dec. 13 1859
aged 5 mos 6 ds

NELLIE R. dau. of
Elisha R. & Laura A. Hanson
died Jany. 23 1865
aged 10 mos 13 ds

EVERETT W. son of
Elisha R. & Laura A. Hanson
died Mar. 16 1865
aged 4 yrs
" Beloved children tho' lost to earth
In memory thou art with me still "

MEHITABLE (BROOKS)
wife of Robert A. Hanson
died June 25 1892
aged 68 years
Was a kind mother, a true wife
she was by many virtues blest
and piety among the best
At Rest

EVERETT L. son of
Seth W. & Cynthia J. Harden
died Oct. 27 1851
Æ 2 yrs 4 m's & 19 days
No ill can reach him now he rests
above
Safe in the bosom of celestial love

IRVING C. son of
S. W. & C. J. Harden
Died Aug. 12 1862
Aged 3 mos 18 das
Of such is the kingdom of Heaven

SARAH ANN dau. of
Cha's & Dorcasma Harlow
Born Oct. 19 1837
Died Oct. 8 1838
Beautiful babe thy Crumbling dust
to passing Mortals Speaks, Prepare
for endless scenes & Judgment Just
make Christ your Hope and heaven
your care

JAMES J. HARRIS
died Nov. 27 1886
aged 67 years
"To die is landing on some silent shore
Where billows never break nor tempests
roar"

BENJAMIN W.
son of Ezekiel T. & Jane Hatch
died Dec. 19 1853
Æ 16 yrs 4 mos 19 ds

REBECCA D.
dau. of Ezekiel T. & Jane Hatch
died Dec. 31 1853
Æ 11 yrs 10 mos 19 ds

JOHN HATCH
died July 14 1873
Æ 64 yrs 5 mos

ALICE HATCH
died Mar. 18 1878
Æ 37 yrs

SANFORD HATCH
died April 24 1882
Æ 34 yrs

ZILPHA A. HATCH
Died May 13 1882
Æ 33 yrs

ELIZABETH
wife of John Hatch
died May 24th 1891
aged 80 years
Asleep in Jesus

To the Memory of
MRS. ANN M. HENDERSON
Died June 8 1812
aged 33 years
The world can never give
the bliss for which we sigh
tis not the whole of life to live
nor all of death to die

To the Memory
MISS ANN M. HENDERSON
died June 8 1842
aged 33 years
"The world can never give
The bliss for which we sigh
Tis not the whole of life to live
Nor all of death to die"

WM. FREDERIC
son of Wm. & Sarah Henderson
died Sept. 16th 1845
aged 6 mo's 11 ds
And he hath gone so young and fair
Called hence by early doom
Just come to show how fair a flower
In Paradise will bloom

WILLIAM HENDERSON
Died in Cal. Dec. 27 1850
Æ 54 yrs
MARY
wife of William Henderson
died Jan. 6 1884
Æ 82 yrs 7 mos
At Rest
Father & Mother

EMERY W.
son of Wm. & Sarah Henderson
died Aug. 10th 1863
aged 3 ys 12 dys
Like a summer flower he faded
Now so full of life so soon to die
But he has gone to brighter scenes above
To live with angels in the skies

JOSEPH M. HENDERSON
Died June 14 1869
Aged 29 yrs

IDA F. dau. of
Wm. L. & Sarah Henderson
died June 26 1879
aged 20 yrs 7 mos
She was loved by all

LLOYD G. HENDERSON
died Dec. 5 1868
Aged 31 y'rs 10 mos
Also
Infant Dau. of
L. G. & Mary A. Henderson
died Nov. 17 1866

In Memory of
MRS. JANE
wife of Mr. David Hersey
who died April 12 1847
In her 55 year

In Memory of
MISS JANE HERSEY
who died March 1 1847
in her 27 year

In Memory of
DAVID HERSEY
Died Dec. 29 1861
aged 77 yrs

ROBERT HERSEY
Died April 23 1878
Aged 54 yrs

LUCY S.
wife of Robert Hersey
1824—1875

MARY W. child of
Mr. Heman & Mary B. *Holmes*
Died Apl. 6 1828
aged 19 mos

ALBERT HOLBROOKE
Died May 5 1862
aged 55 years
Also his wife
MARCIA HOLBROOKE
Died June 4 1835
aged 31 years
Also his two sons
ALBERT W.
Died May 17th 1848
aged 16 years
JOSHUA B.
Died Aug. 27 1845
aged 10 years
Erected by his son
Josiah Holbrook

ELIZA
wife of Albert Holbrook
Died Jan. 21st 1888
aged 86 yrs 3 mo's

ABBIE D. HOLLIS
died Oct. 20 1882
aged 25 yrs 6 mos 20 days
"Nearer my God to thee"

HANNAH B.
wife of Silas Hollis,
left the form March 9th 1894
aged 81 y 25 d
Not dead Translated to a higher
State
To which the angel Death swings
wide
The gate, we too, must pass,
And therefor us will wait

In Memory of
MRS. HANNAH
wife of Mr. Samuel House
she died Sept. 22 1822
in her 84 year

In Memory of
MR. SAMUEL HOUSE
who died July 14 1828
in his 88 year

To the Memory of
MRS. RUTH
wife of Mr. Samuel House
died Oct. 17 1840
Aged 57 years

WILLIAM E.
son of Wm. & Asenath C. House
died Feby 11 1857
aged 1 yr 9 ms & 20 ds
Also an infant daughter
"Parents their infant children mourn
When from their arms are taken
By faith & hope there is borne
That in heaven they will awaken"

ASENATH C.
wife of Wm. House
died Feby 23 1863
aged 27 yrs 5 mos 10 ds
" Here pause and shed affections tear
A youthfull wife lies burried here
Beneath this mouldering sod
The partner of her early choice
No more on earth shall hear her voice
She's gone to meet her God"

SAMUEL HOUSE
died May 6 1860
Æ 81 yrs 6 mos

ASENATH AUGUSTA
dau. of Wm. & Asenath C. House
died April 8 1863
aged 1 yr 7 mos 3 ds
"Sleep on sweet babe and take thy rest
God called thee home he thought it best"

JAMES W. HOUSE
died Dec. 17 1885
Æ 57 yrs

Mary Washburn Howe's
Born July 15th 1816
Died feb. 28th 1891

FREDERICK H. HOWES
Born Aug. 29th 1879
Drowned
July 2d 1894

ALVIN W. HOWLAND
died Sept. 26 1864
Æ 56
"Affectionate remembrance prompts this last tribute of respect of a widow'd wife in commemoration of the virtues of a beloved husband & rever'd father"

LYDIA S.
wife of Orien Iris
died Sept. 21st 1858
aged 31 years

In Memory of
DR. PETER HUBBART
he died October the 20 *1793*
in the 43th year of his age
*Thousands of journeys night and day
Ive traveld weary on the way
To heal the sick but now I am gone
A journey never to return*

AMELIA J.
wife of Sidney Humphrey
Born May 16th 1836
Died Feb. 11th 1855
aged 18 yrs 9 Mos
The deathless record is made upon my physical form, but the spirit is unfolded in beauty and in Love.

MARY E.
wife of James Iris
died May 2d 1866
aged 36 years

LUCY ANN
dau. of Christopher B. & Katherine J. Jones
died Oct. 6th 1840
aged 6 months
Sleep on sweet babe thy months were few
And suffering was thy lot Below
Jesus called thou has't obeyed
And left a world of Peace and woe

NELLIE MARIA dau. of
Silas B. & Maria E. Jones
born June 10 1861
died June 12 1863

DAVID P.
son of Christopher &
Katherine J. Jones
died Jan. 22d 1845
aged 18 years 11 days

I'll take this little lamb to me
And lean them on my breast
Protection they shall have in me
In me they shall have rest

REBECCA E.
wife of Silas B. Jones,
Died May 13, 1853,
aged 22 years 4 mons.

Then lingering pains her bosom tore
Resigned she kissed chastening rod.
Each mortal pang she meekly bore,
And smiled in death to meet her God

MINNIE HOWARD, dau. of
Silas B. & Maria E. Jones,
born Oct. 11, 1855,
died Oct. 3, 1863.

WILLIAM F. son of
Wm. H. & Susan Johnson
died July 27 1860
aged 4 yrs 9 mos

GEORGE W. son of
Wm. H. & Susan Johnson
died Aug. 17 1863
aged 10 mos

WILLIAM H. JOHNSON
died Aug. 18 1879
aged 43 yrs 10 mos

SUSAN
wife of Wm. H. Johnson
died Mar. 26 1864
aged 24 yrs 5 mos

JAMES L. JOHNSON
died Mar. 8 1882
aged 30 yrs 2 mos 22 days

" Tho' lost to sight to memory dear "

MRS. RUTH JOSSELYN
Ye Vertuous Consort of
Capt. Josselyn who Dyed
JANUARY THE 15TH 1742
aged 47 year's

Erected in Memory of
MR. JOHN JOSSELYN
and
MRS. SAGE JOSSELYN
his wife
She died Nov. ye 6th *1775*
in the 33d year of her age
he died July ye 30th 1770
in ye 36 year of his age

This small stone points out the
spot where the immortal part of
MRS. OLIVE JOSSELYN
wife of
Mr. Stockbridge Josselyn
left its Clay tenement to moulder
into dust till it shall again by
its Master Builder *be repaired*
and fitted up for
Immortallity
Died Sept. 10th 1803
aged 55 years

Here Lies the body of
JOSEPH JOSSELYN ESQ.
who departed this life
April the 30th *1787*
in the 88th year of his age

OREN C.
Died April 6 1819
aged 2 years

JANE R.
Died Jan. 2 1830
aged 7 mos

Children of Oren & Mary C. Josselyn

Why do we mourn departing friends
Or shake at deaths alarms
Tis but the voice that Jesus sends
To call them to his arms

In Memory of
MRS. LUCY E. JOSSELYN
wife of Mr. Ozen Josselyn
Died Nov. 27 1842
aged 41 years
Also
EDWIN B.
son of Ozen & Lucy E. Josselyn
died April 6 1833
aged 3 ms & 8 days

In Memory of
SARAH *Twin* dauth. of
Ozen & Lucy E. Josselyn
died Sept. 29 1843
aged 11 mos & 20 days

In Memory of
HANNAH F. JOSSELYN
wife of Eli C. Josselyn and dau.
of Timothy & Hannah (Robbins)
Died July 15th 1846
aged 21 yrs 11 mos 16 dys

How few the days & short the Hours
of our expected bliss;
Mourn not for me my partner dear
for I am gone to rest.

ANNA AMELIA
dau. of Ira & Sarah A. Josselyn
who passed to Spirit Life
Sept. 10 1849
aged 4 yrs 2 mos

FRANCIS HERBERT
son of Ira & Sarah A. Josselyn
who passed to Spirit Life
Sept. 7 1852
aged 1 yr 1 mo

ELEANOR T.
wife of Eli C. Josselyn
died April 27th 1853
aged 27 years 6 mo's

I know that my Redeemer lives

MARY C. JOSSELYN
wife of Oren Josselyn
died Aug. 2 1854
aged 60 years 7 months

In Memory of
ELIZA wife of
Stephen Josselyn & dau. of
Jabez & Chloe M. Studley
died Feb. 24 1854
aged 50 ys 7 ms 14 ds

"Jesus can make a dying bed
Feel soft as downy pillows are
While on his breast I lean my head
And breath my life out sweetly
there"

ALMERIN JOSSELYN
Born July 16 1775
Died Mch. 30 1855

In Memory of
MR. OZEN JOSSELYN
who died in Kansas Oct. 3 1855
aged 57 years

CHLOE WHITING
wife of Alverin Josselyn
Born Mch. 20th 1780
Died Nov. 14 1857

ELEAZER JOSSELYN
Died May 9 1868
aged 80 yrs 6 mos

HANNAH
wife of Eleazer Josselyn
died Oct. 14 1857
aged 72 yrs 8 mos

Beloved parents tho lost to earth
In memory thou art with me still

Erected in Memory of
RACHEL F.
wife of Charles Josselyn
who left this earth sphere
Nov. 13 1859
aged 27 yrs 5 mos

In Memory of
STEPHEN JOSSELYN
died Oct. 27 1871
aged 59 years 10 ms

"Friend after friend departs
Who hath not lost a friend
There is no union here of hearts
That finds not here an end"

JOANNA
wife of Chas. Josselyn and former
wife of Thorndike (Felton)
died Jan. 12th 1874
aged 84 yrs 3 mos

Remember time swift away
And life with you will soon be ore
Prepair yourselves then while you may
To follow me to that blest Shore

In Memory of
HOPE wife of
Stephen Josselyn and dau. of
Friend & Hope T. Cushing
died Sept. 16 1883
aged 60 yrs 7 m's & 16 ds

"The mother who waited for us is here
Wearing a smile so sweet
Now waits on the hill of Paradise
For her childrens coming feet"

Oren Josselyn
Died June 23 1880
Æ 86 yrs 11 mos

Sarah Loring
dau. of Ira & Sarah A. Josselyn
who *passed to Spirit Life*
Mch. 28 1884
aged 41 yrs 4 mos

Ralph son of
Stephen & Hope C. Josselyn
died Mar. 30 1885
aged 24 yrs 6 mos 22 ds

G. Everett Josselyn
died May 26 1888
aged 31 years 9 mos 16 days
"Gone but not forgotten"

Robert Josselyn
Died Aug. 29 1889
Aged 74 yrs 9 mos 29 ds
With life and name unstained the good man dies

Dryden Judd
died July 14 1850
aged 76 years

Celia
wife of Dryden Judd
died July 14 1860
aged 77 years
"Angels that trace the airy road
Shall bear us homeward to our God"

KEONI KALUA
son of Kalua K. and Hana W.
Born on Hawaii H. I.
died in Boston June 6 1887
aged 17 years
" Maluhia "

Elmer L. only son of
Samuel & Joanna S. Keene
died Feb. 24 1871
aged 15 yrs 11 mos 3 ds
"Like a flower cut down at the rising of sun
At the morning of life his labour was done"

Isaac son of
Peleg J. & Ruth P. Keene
died Jan. 19 1873
aged 23 yrs 3 mos 10 ds
" Meet me in heaven "

Peleg J. Keene
died May 15 1883
aged 73 yrs 11 mos
"Asleep in Jesus, blessed sleep"

In Memory of
Mrs. Priscilla
wife of Mr. Charles Leach
who died Nov. 6 1836
in the 28 year of her age
Also her Infant Child
Sister thou hast gone and left us
Why should we thy loss deplore
Thou hast gone to be with Jesus
There to live and die no more

KEONI KALUA.

LESTER S. son of
George H. & Lizzie M. Larkum
died Sept. 2 1883
Æ 2 mos 3 ds

AARON LEAVITT
died June 6 1875
aged 84 years

EUNICE T. LEAVITT
died Apl. 3rd 1884
aged 85 years

Erected
to the Memory of
MR. MARTIN LINDSEY
died July 21 1843
aged 32 years

My loving friends dry up your tears
I must be here till Christ appears
Now I am gone my grave you see
Prepare yourself to follow me

OLIVE H.
wife of Martin Lindsey
Died Aug. 2 1863
Æt 71 yrs 10 mos 3 days

MARTIN A. LINDSEY
Died July 9 1871
Æt 38 yrs 3 mo 5 days

LEWIS LITCHFIELD,
died March 8, 1890,
aged 78 yrs 5 mos 13 days

LUCY L.
wife of Lewis Litchfield,
died Mch. 4, 1864,
aged 46 yrs 2 mos 4 days
&
Infant dau. LAURA E.

MICHEL
wife of George Lovewell
died Oct. 26 1863
aged 58 yrs 11 mos

" *Call and see as you pas by*
That there are many graves here
shorter than you or I
O that you may all realize that
you are not too young to die
O prepare for death and follow
me "

GEORGE B. LOVEWELL
died Apl. 2 1888
aged 81 yrs

CALVIN LOVIS,
died Sept. 17, 1863,
aged 44 yrs

" *The one we loved has passed from earth*
We know that he's at rest
We trust that we one day may meet
In the Kingdom of the blest "

MARY
wife of Nelson Lowell
June 18th 1827
March 8th 1891

JAMES A. LYON
Co. D. 38th Regt. Mass. Vols.
WOUNDED AT BISLAND
the 14 & died the 18 April 1863
Æt 30 years
WILLARD AUSTIN LYON
Died May 24 1863
Æ 2 years
Husband and Child

1812 ABIGAIL LYON 1893

In Memory of
MRS. BETTEY MACOMBER
wife of Mr. Thomas Macomber
who died July 22d 1807
aged 43 years
*Death is a debt to Nature due
which I have paid & so Must you*

EDWARD IRVING son of
George I. & Mary B. McLauthlin
died Aug. 6 1863
aged 1 yr 4 mos

MORRIS C. son of
G. I. & M. B. McLauthlin
died Dec. 3 1876
Æ 12 yrs 3 mos

MARY B. E. CHURCH
wife of Geo. I. McLauthlin
died Aug. 27 1883
Æ 44 yrs 9 mos
"Through the Grave to Glory"

SNOW MAGOUN
1812—1853
RUTH E. MAGOUN
1817—1862

LACIE M. MAGOUN
died July 25 1860
aged 3 mos 19 ds

Little AUSTIN Infant son of
Horatio B. & Catharine B.
Magoun
died Sept. 12, 1863;
aged 1 yr 1 day.
Our little Austin precious baby boy—
Whose presence filled our home with
so much joy,—We yield thee now to
deck the angel bowers,—Jesus only
lent thee still we call thee ours.

JANE C. dau. of
Abner & Mary H. Magoun
died Aug. 22 1855
Æ 15 yrs 8 mos
" Weep not dear father & mother
Why mourn sweet sister & brothers
For in that happy spirit land
My voice has joined the angel band "

ALONZO I. son of
A. B. & C. W. Magoun
died Aug. 25 1866
aged 4 yrs
"These blighted buds all bloom in
Heaven"

Mary Homer wife of
William F. Stetson & dau. of
Abner & Mary H. Magoun
died Apl. 16 1867
Æ 33 yrs

Abner Magoun
Died Nov. 19 1868
Æ 68 yrs 9 mos
A kind husband and father,—
A friend to good order,—
We miss him on earth,—
May we meet him in Heaven.

Frank W. son of
H. B. & C. B. Magoun
died March 17 1881
aged 21 yrs 1 mo
"We have lent another treasure
To deck the Angels Home
We cannot give our darling
We must call him still our own"

In Memory of
Mrs. Martha Man
ye wife of Mr. Benjamin Man.
she died Jan'y ye 25 *1769*
in ye 68 year of her age

In Memory of
Mr. Benjamin Man
he died Mch. ye 2nd *1770*
aged 72–3 years and 3 days

Mrs. Abigail Mann
died *1785*

In Memory of
Ezra ye son of
Mr. Benjamin Man and
Mrs. Abigail his wife
he died at Weymouth
Nov. ye 26th *1775*
in ye 20th year of his age

Mrs. Anna Mann
wife of Levi Mann
died Mch. 14th *1789*
aged 33 years

Molly Mann 2nd
Departed this life Sept. 23 *1792*
aged 7 years & 8 days

In Memory of
Mr. Caleb Mann
died Feb. 23 1810
In the 64th year of his age

Sacred to the Memory of
Mr. Benjamin Mann
died Mch. 27 1816
in the 89th year of his age

In Memory of
Almira
dau. of Capt. Benja. and
Mrs. Lydia Mann
died Nov. 1 1817
aged 1 year
So fades the lovely blooming flower
Frail smiling solace of an hour
So soon our transient comforts fly
Any pleasure only blooms to die

Erected to the Memory of
MR. LEVI MANN
died Jan. 12 1818
aged 60 years

In Memory of
MR. BENJ. MANN
Died Dec. 12 1820
In the 68 year of his age

CHARLES MANN
Died Sept. 12 1825
Æ 59 yrs
ABIGAL his wife
died Apr. 27 1845
Æ 74 yrs

Sacred
to the Memory of
CAPT. JOSHUA MANN
Who departed his life
December 20th 1827
aged 68 years

In Memory of
MISS SARAH MANN
dau. of Levi & Patience Mann
died Dec. 21st 1832
aged 33 years

Oh wipe away that gathering tear
No cause for grief is witnessed here
There is naught but dust Beneath this sod
The soul we trust is with its God

In Memory of
MRS. HANNAH MANN
wife of Benjamin Mann 2d
died May 21 1827
aged 75 years

Beloved in life lamented at her death
calm and resigned she spent her last breath
freed from life's cares and every earthly l'ain
our loss we trust is her eternal gain

In Memory of
MRS. LYDIA
wife of Benjamin Mann Esq.
who died Sept. 11 1834
aged 43 years

The grave of
PEREZ MANN son of
Mr. David & Mrs. Betsey Mann
died Aug. 20 1835
Aged 1 year & 6 Months

Sacred To the Memory of
MISS HENRIETTA
Daughr. of Benja. Mann Esq.
who departed this life
April 30 A. D. 1838
Aged 16 years
Infant of B. & LYDIA MANN
aged 10 months

ABIGAIL
wife of Chas. Mann
died April 27 1845
Æ 74 yrs

Sacred to the Memory of
PATIENCE I. MANN
Relic of Levi Mann
who died Mch. 8 1846
aged 85 years
She loved the Savior, lived to him
Enjoyed the hope he gave
And though her limbs are streched
in death
Behold in Christ she lives

Sacred to the Memory of
WIDOW MOLLY MANN
Relict of Capt. Joshua Mann
died July 2 1849
Aged 93
Blessed

In Memory of
MARGARET MANN
wife of Levi Mann
died Nov. 4 1849
aged 63 yrs 10 mos

NEWTON MANN
Died August 7 1850
Aged 25 years

In Memory of
LEVI MANN
who died April 11 1853
Aged 71 yrs 4 mos
Blest are the pure in heart

LUCY A. MANN
died Jan. 24 1855
aged 26 yrs

GEORGE T.
son of C. G. & A. S. Mann
died Octo. 18 1858
aged 1 yr 1 mo
Infant son of
C. G. & A. S. Mann
died Mch. 18 1871
agèd 6 mos 19 dys

BENJAMIN MANN ESQ.
died Dec. 11 1861
Aged 74 years
Tis sweet to visit now his grave
And dwell on scenes long since
gone by
To treasure thoughts of one so pure
And learn to feel that all must die

HORACE MANN
Co. E. *13th Mass. InF.*

ALBERT G. son of
Benjamin & Lydia C. Mann
Died June 28 1865
Aged 22 years
Fearless of hell and ghastly death
I'd break through every foe
The wings of love and arms of faith
Would bear me conqueror through

BETSEY
wife of Caleb Mann
Died Apr. 26 1867
Aged 91 yrs 8 mos 20 days

HENRY MANN
died Mch. 6th 1887
aged 58 yrs 5 mos 3 dys

BETSEY
wife of David Mann
Died Jan. 29 1873
Aged 73 yrs 6 mos 28 dys
Tho lost to sight to memory dear

ANNER J. dau. of
Caleb G. & Amanda S. Mann
died Aug. 26 1873
aged 11 yrs 1 mo 4 ds

In Memory of
WILLIAM MORRIS
son of Wm. & Margaret Morse
died Jan. 30th 1839
aged 2 yrs 4 mo's 18 dys

In Memory of
MR. SHUBAEL MUNRO
he died June 14th 1795
in the 75th year of his age
Ive bid adieu to all on earth
And dwell Among the dead
And left my friends & children dear
To mourn their loving friend

TEMPERANCE C.
wife of Hiram Munroe
died Mch 6 1885
aged 72 yrs 9 mos
" Draw near my friends dry up your tears
Here I must lie till Christ appears"

SARAH M. dau. of
Truman E. & Leanora L. Niles
died Sept. 30 1855
aged 1 yr 2 mos 26 ds

WALTER JOSSELYN
son of Francis M. & Arabella W.
Munroe
born Jan. 27 1869
died Feb. 10 1887
"Gone where the flesh can no longer control
The freedom and faith of the God given soul"

HANNAH F. dau. of
Truman E. & Leanora L. Niles
died Oct. 6 1855
aged 4 yrs 11 mos 16 ds
" We loved thee on earth
May we meet thee in heaven "

OTIS B. OAKMAN
died June 8 1864
aged 29 yrs 10 mos 20 dys
"God calls our loved ones
But we loose not wholly
What he hath given
They live on earth
In thought and deed, as
Truly as in his heaven"

GEO. B. OLDHAM
1839—1879
LUCY P. (STOCKBRIDGE)
wife of Geo. B. Oldham
1853—1872

FRANCIS C. Son of
Alfred D. & Julia M. Paine
Died Sept. 7th 1864
aged 3 yrs 2 mos 7 dys

Sacred
To the Memory of
MARGARET PACKARD
wife of Isaac Packard &
Daughter of Levi (Mann)
who died May 18 1842
Aged 28 years

In Memory of
MARY E. dau. of
Martin & Rachel Palmer
who died March 5 1846
aged 16 years

*Death with his dart has pierced my
heart, when I was in my prime
When this you see dont weep for me
Tis God's appointed time*

SYLVANUS PERCIVALL
Born June 20 1796
Died June 7 1879
HENRY C. son of
Sylvanus & Selah Percival
Died at Baltimore June 18 1852
aged 23 years
SELAH
wife of Sylvanus Percival
died March 28 1860
aged 72 years

ANN
Wife of Ozias Perkins
died Sept. 25 1831
aged 28 years

May God grant endless peace to each
departed shade
And to their ashes in the earths' cold
bosom laid

OZIAS PERKINS
died June 17 1874
aged 69 years
MARY G. His wife
died Feb. 13 1873
aged 67 years

Change Change eternal Change
All human life shall burn on through
Death to meet forms more lovely
On the immortal shores of time

P. P. PETERSON
Co. F. 43d Mass. Inft.

JOHN STETSON & ISRAEL PERRY
Tomb
1806

THATCHER PERRY
son Elijah & Chloe
Died Mar. 1st 1811
Aged 4 years

CHLOE Dau. of
Isaiah & Susan Stetson
Died Dec. 27th 1812
Aged 26 years

Little Georgie
GEORGE
son of George & Eva Pardy
died May 12th 1885
aged 2 years

ELIJAH PERRY
son of Seth & Hannah
Died Oct. 9 1814
Aged 31 years

Sacred to Memory
MR. ADAM PERRY
Died Aug. 23 1830
In the 79th year of his age

Twas hard with you my friends to part
It wrung with grief each tender heart
Me in this world no more to see
Prepare my friends to follow me

CATHERINE PERRY
Dec. 15 1817
Jan. 30 1832
FRANKLIN PERRY
May 17 1821
July 3 1893
HENRY N. PERRY
April 17 1828
April 12 1872
LEVI H. PERRY
1793—1871
GIDEON PERRY
Mar. 23 1787
Sept. 8 1859
KATIE His Wife
May 16 1794
Jan. 3 1832

ROSILLA C.
dau. of E. & R. Perry
died Mch. 4 1839
Æ 2 yrs 7 mos

Sacred
To the Memory of
MRS. ELIZABETH
wife of Mr. Adam Perry
who died Feb. 11 1845
aged **90 YEARS**

She sleeps in Jesus & is blest
How sweet her slumbers are
From suffering & from sin released
And freed from every snare

SETH PERRY
son of Samuel & Eunice
Died Sept. 26 1846
Aged **92 YEARS**

BRADFORD
son of Levi & Anna Perry
Died Aug. 14 1848
Aged 3 months

Sleep on my child while o'er thy grave
A mother drops her tears
Sleep on dear cherub take thy rest
Till Jesus Christ appears

ADELINE
wife of G. B. Perry
died Aug. 18 1852
Æ 28 years

" Taken from earth in earthly life "

HANNAH PERRY
Dau. Henry & Ann (Josselyn)
Died Oct. 13 1854
Aged **99¾ YEARS**

CEMETERY RECORDS. 269

CLARENCE H. son of
Josiah F. & Sarah C. Perry
died Aug. 8 1855
aged 1 yr 17 dys

MARY B. PERRY
Dau. Edward Y. and Mary B.
Born and died Sept. 12 1855

NABBY PERRY
born Aug. 22d 1796
Died May 9 1856

WILLIE S. son of
E. Thacher & Louise M. Perry
died Nov. 9 1856
Æ 9 mos 2 dys

MARIA AGUSTA
wife of Cephas Perry Jr.
died Sept. 9th 1858
aged 24 *years* 8 mo's 2 days
also
CLARA GENEVA dau. of
Cephas & Maria A. Perry
died Oct. 17 1858
Aged 1 year 1 mo 17 days

GEORGE A. son of
E. Thacher & Louise M. Perry
died Sept. 22 1858
Æ 7 weeks 21 ds
"*a twin*"

SARAH L. dau. of
E. Thacher & Louise M. Perry
died Apr. 6 1859
Æ 8 mos 4 days
"*a twin*"

SARAH L. dau.
E. Thacher & Louise M. Perry
died July 27 1862
Æ 2 yrs 2 mos 15 dys

GEORGE B. PERRY
died Oct. 31 1863
Æ 39 yrs 9 mos
"Soon called to join those gone before"

NANCY
wife of G. B. Perry
died Sept. 23 1866
Æ 42 yrs
"At rest in peace"

ROSILLA
wife of Ethan Perry
died Octo. 23 1867
aged 65 yrs 1 mo
"Remember me as you pass by,
For as you are now so once was I,
As I am now so you must be,
Prepare for death and follow me."

FREDDIE S. son of
E. Thacher & Louise M. Perry
died Feb. 16 1868
Æ 5 yrs 1 mo 6 dys

EDWARD Y. PERRY
son Elijah and Chloe
MARY B. PERRY
Dau. David and Deborah Oldham

CHLOE S. PERRY
Dau. Isaiah S. & Julia A.
Died June 26 1873
Aged 40 years

MARY PERRY
Dau. Ichabod & Polly Thomas
Died Feb. 16 1877
Aged 82 years

In Memory of
ETHAN PERRY
died July 10 1880
Æ 78 yrs 2 mos
" At rest with loved ones "

DIANA A.
wife of Samuel Perry
died Mch 2 1881
aged 81 yrs 5 mos

ISAIAH S. PERRY
Son Elijah & Chloe
Died June 8th 1883
Aged 73 years

JOSHUA PERRY
son of Seth & Hannah
Died Sept. 2 1883
Aged 87 years

ALFRED PERRY
Died May 30 1888
Aged 43 yrs 9 ms 28 ds
There is rest in Heaven

SARAH C.
wife of Josiah F. Perry
born Mar. 29 1819
died Aug. 23 1888
" We will meet again "

JAMES H. PERRY
born Mar. 5 1844
died Dec. 19 1889
Co. G. 18 Mass. Regt.
" At Rest "

JOSIAH F. PERRY
born Sept. 17 1809
died Mar. 5 1890
"Gone home"

JULIA A. PERRY Dau. of
David & Deborah (Oldham)
Died Feb. 18 1891
Aged 85 years

EDGAR W.
son of E. W. & G. G. *Phillips*
died May 25 1881
aged 9 weeks
" When angels bore our treasure hence
We laid the casket here "

EDMUND PHILLIPS
a member of *Co. K.*
38 Regt. M. V. M.
died Aug. 2nd 1883
Æt 75 yrs 4 mos

RENA W.
dau. of E. W. & G. G. *Phillips*
died Octo. 26 1884
Æt 1 yr 5 days
"Sheltered and safe from sorrow"

JOANNA PHILLIPS
Died Jan. 1st 1888
Age 65 yrs 4 Mos 4 Ds
Rest dear mother thy earthly toil is o'er

INA S.
dau. of E. W. & G. G. *Phillips*
died July 2 1888
aged 1 yr 10 mos 6 days
"Gone but not forgotten"

CALVIN TILDEN PHILLIPS
son of Ezra & Catharin Tilden
Phillips
Born March 3d 1836
Died Jan. 15th 1892
I wait to meet the,
be of cheer, for all is well

GEORGE WALDRON PHILLIPS
1864—1889

LOTTIE
Died June 16th 1869
aged 3 yr 10 mo 16 dys
God gave, he took, he will restore
he doeth all things well

SUSIE
She has left a memory Fragrant with
wise Counsels, generous deeds, and
loveing devotion
She is not dead God keeps her safe
through his eternal years
1842—1882

SUSIE J.
wife of Joseph W. Phinney
Born Jan. 18th 1842
Died Dec. 8 1882

LYDIA J.
wife of John Pool
died April 11th 1852
aged 37 years
And must we say to thee farewell
Companion Son and Daughter too
Those whome on earth thou loved so well
Must they all bid a long adieu

ALONZO N.
son of John & Lydia Pool
died March 14th 1853
aged 1 yr 3 mos 28 dys
Sleep lovely babe and take thy rest
God called the home he thought it
Best

NANCY H.
wife of John Poole
died Dec. 9th 1871
aged 46 yrs 10 mos 12 dys

DEBORAH G.
wife of Joseph Pool
died Sept. 8 1859
aged 44 yrs 2 mos
Beloved companion though lost from earth in memory with me still

JOSEPH POOL
Died Dec. 21 1863
aged 47 yrs 4 mos
I shall be satisfied when I awake with thy likeness

WILLIE M.
son of L. & M. E. Poole
died Sept. 25 1875
Æ 6 yrs 4 mos 11 ds

EMMA B. dau. of
Benj. B. & Lusanna M. Poole
died Nov. 7 1877
aged 13 yrs 4 mos 9 days
"Gone but not forgotten"

ANDREW J. POOLE
1831—1880
ELLEN A. POOLE
his wife
1834—1891

LYDIA C. dau. of
Benj. C. & Rebecca E. Pratt
died Feb. 9 1823
aged 10 days

In Memory of
NATHANIEL PRATT
Who Died Feb. 24 1844
aged 41 years

In Memory of
MRS. REBECCA E.
wife of Benj. C. Pratt & dau.
of Robert & Lucy Sylvester
died Dec. 1 1847
aged 48 years

LYDIA C. PRATT
youngest dau. of Benj. C.
& Rebecca E. Pratt
born Dec. 28 1834
died July 6 1856
aged 21 yrs 6 mos 8 ds
"She is not dead but sleepeth"

LUCY B. PRATT dau. of
Benj. C. & Rebecca E. Pratt
died Jan. 11 1868
aged 43 yrs 11 mos 11 ds
"Asleep in Jesus"

BENJAMIN C. PRATT
Died June 16 1875
Aged 85 yrs 7 mos 7 dys

EMELINE H. (TRIBOU)
wife of Seth Pratt
died Jan. 30 1882
Æ 57 yrs 8 mos 28 ds

STONE BEARING THE OLDEST INSCRIPTION RECORDED IN THE CEMETERY.

MR. THOMAS RAMSDELL, DIED 1727.
MRS. SARAH RAMSDELL, DIED 1773.

In Memory of
MRS. ABIGAIL (STUDLEY)
wife of Mr. John Puffer
who Died Dec. 22d 1850
aged 46 years 3 mo's

BETSEY
wife of Thomas Quindley
died Jan. 1838
Æ 63 years

We mark the spot where kindred sleep
Where earthly ties are o'er
Yet why should we in anguish weep
They are not lost but gone before

MRS. MARY RAMSDELL
wife of Joseph Ramsdell
died *June ye 1st 1754*
and in ye 46 year of her age

In Memory of
MR. THOMAS RAMSDELL
he died March ye 13th *1757*
in ye 21st year of his age

In Memory of
MRS. SARAH RAMSDELL
wife of Mr. Thomas Ramsdell
she died August *ye 4th 1773*
in ye 91ST *year* of her age

In Memory of
MR. JOSEPH RAMSDELL
he died Aug ye 24th *1788*
in the 81st year of his age

In Memory of
ye Children of Ens'n Joseph
Ramsdell and Elizabeth his wife
PRISEA
died July ye 28th *1774*
in ye 2d year of her age
PRISEA
died Oct. ye 18th *1777*
aged 3d months

Mrs. Mary Ramsdell
In Memory of
MRS. ELIZABETH
ye wife of Joseph Ramsdell
died June ye 19th *1786*
in the 45 year of her age

In Memory of
MRS. MARCY RAMSDELL
wife of Mr. Joseph Ramsdell
she died Jan. ye 1st 1800
in the 82d year of her age

In Memory of
MISS HANNAH RAMSDELL
who died Aug. 11th 1807
in the 52d year of her age

In Memory of
MRS. ELIZABETH RAMSDELL
wife of Ens'n Joseph Ramsdell
died Oct. 20th 1811
aged 58 years

In Memory of
ENS'N JOSEPH RAMSDELL
died Aug. 6 1817
aged 74 years

MARY E. dau. of
Jacob L. & Elizabeth Ramsdell
died Jan. 10th 1864
aged 2 yrs 4 mos
Of such is the Kingdom of Heaven

S. LYMAN RAMSDELL
died Apl. 4th 1871
Æ 25 yrs 11 mos 27 days

"Thou art dear to me still"

"Dear spot of earth! Here with thee may we rest
As one by one we sleep on earth's cold breast
With thy pure spirit mid the happy throng
With golden harps together join the song
The ransomed ever sing on Canaan's shore
There may we meet again to part no more"

In Memory of
MR. ELIJAH RANDALL JR.
Died Novr. 15 1810
Aged 21 years

In Memory of
MISS HANNAH RANDALL
Died Augt. 15 1809
Aged 18 years

Stop reader as you pass by as you are living so was I But suddenly God called me here To sleep till Christ my Judge appear

---

HERBERT E. REED
Dec. 19 1845
May 12 1883

BETHIA A.
daughter of Isaac T. & Nancy N. Reed
died July 10 1851
Æ 2 yrs & 24 dys

Our babe has gone to Jesus arms
And left its parents dear
Could we but realize its joys
We could not wish her here

LUCY J. REED
Died June 6 1881
Aged 63 yrs 21 dys

FRANK ABBOTT REED
1854—1889
EVERETT HOWARD REED
1850—1852

REV. SILAS RIPLEY
May 7 1868

God's finger touched he slept
Morning and Night
Even as thou wast, I see thee still,
There's not a charm of soul or brow
Of all we knew and loved in thee
But lives in glorious Beauty now
Baptized in Immortality

Mrs. Mary F. W. Ripley
died in Boston Mch. 18 1881
Aged 72 yrs 4 mo's
Thou art not in Heaven
Still still our own
Blessed are the Mercifull

In greatfull Remembrance of
Mrs. M. F. R. Ripley
wife of Rev. Silas Ripley
who died in Boston Mch. 19 1881
aged 72 yrs 4 mos
She was a successfull teacher a true wife and a generous benefactor, her heart was deeply touched by the unmerited sufferings of the humbler creatures and she did what she could for their protection the infinite love of God was to her a fact and an inspiration
Together may we rise
and sing our morning hymn
One household stlll
A Household Bond to faith how dear
Not Lost, Gone before
S. R.
True in Word, tried in Deed
My Sudden frost was sudden gain
and gave all Ripeness to the grain
it might have gained from after heat

RIPLEY LOT

Nathaniel Robbins
died June 17 *1775*
aged 60 years
Also his wife
Hannah
Died Jan. 7 1807
aged 86 years

Capt. Thomas Robbins
Was *drowned* At Cohasset
April 14 *1790*
aged 38 years

Sacred to the Memory of
Dea. Timothy Robbins
died May 18 1807
in the 65th year of his age

In Memory of
Mrs. Mary Robbins
Wife of Dea. Timothy Robbins
died Feb. 8 1826
in the 75 year of her age.
There all the millions of the saints
Shall in one song unite
And each the bliss of all shall view
With infinite delight

Sacred to the Memory of
Mr. John Robbins
Who died Sept. 8 1838
in his 53 year
Blooming youth had passed away
Manhoods riper years had come
Longer here I thought to stay
But alas the grave my home

In Memory of
Eleanor T. Robbins
dau. of Timothy & Hannah
Robbins
died Jan. 29th 1843
aged 29 years
Farewell loved one from care set free
No more shall pain thy Bosom swell
Nor friendship throw her arm around thee,
For thou art gone from home to dwell

In Memory of
TIMOTHY ROBBINS son of
Timothy & Hannah Robbins
died Aug. 14 1850
aged 35 yrs 7 mos 9 dys

Farewell Father Farewell Mother
God will heal your deepest Pain
Farewell too, dear weeping sister
Soon in Heaven we'll meet again

In Memory of
SIBIL T. ROBBINS dau. of
Timothy & Hannah Robbins
died Jan. 23d 1854
aged 37 year 4 mo

*Calm be the spot where her form now
reposeth
May the friends who so loved Re-
visit the grave
And feel though the cold sod her ashes
enclothes
She lives in the presence of him who
can save*

In Memory of
TIMOTHY ROBBINS
who died Feb. 22 1856
aged 74 yrs 6 mos

His words were truth his actions good
His friends will drop the parting tear
In justice firm he always stood
His death was calm without a fear

SARAH Dau. of
Timothy & Mary Robbins
Died Feb. 26 1857
aged 73 years.

Departed this life
BETHIAH ROBBINS
Daughter of Deacn. Timothy
Robbins
Aged 27 years wanting 8 days

She was a dutiful child & loving sister
From the great Lord of life & death
As we receive our vital breath
And at thy sovereign call resign
That vital breath that gift divine

In Memory of
HANNAH ROBBINS
wife of Timothy Robbins
Died Jan. 5 1860
aged 78 yers

That countenance which death hath
veiled thou shall in brighter worlds behold

Erected
In Memory of
MRS. HANNAH ROGERS
wife of Mr. Caleb Rogers
died May 12 1807
In the 66th year of her age

Erected
In Memory of
MR. CALEB ROGERS
died March 26 1833
in the 80th year of his age

MARY RUMNEY
died Mar. 25 1886
Aged 83 years

LABAN T. ROSE
died Apr. 21 1851
Æ 24 yrs 8 mos

To my wife and children and all my friends so dear
When you stand around my grave shed not one bitter tear
Although you know my body lies beneath the silent sod
But my spirit is still living and seeking others good

HENRY W. ROSE
son of Laban & Emily Rose
died April 12 1854
aged 25 yrs 5 mos & 23 days

Farewell Father Farewell Mother
God will heal your deepest pain
Farewell too dear sisters & brothers
Soon in heaven we will meet again

Our Father and Mother
LABAN ROSE
Died Nov. 8 1860
Æ 65 yrs & 6 mos
EMILY YOUNG
his wife
died July 30 1860
Æ 64 yrs & 5 mos

We shall meet again

ARTHUR W.
son of H. F. & L. P. Rose
died Feb. 3 1877
Aged 6 mos 20 days

WILLIAM P. RUSSELL
Died June 24th 1879
aged 64 yrs 8 mos 9 dys

Myrtie
MARY J. M.
wife of Calvin W. Russell
1859—1886

A little while we part

JOHN SIME
Died May 16 1871
aged 48 years
also his wife
MARTHA B.
died Mar. 31 1853
aged 25 years

ELIZABETH A.
wife of Clarence E. Simonds
dau. of Geo. & Agnes M. Green
July 9 1852—Mch. 21st 1893

Sleep till that Morning,
Peacefully sleep

ROBERT SALMOND JR.
died at Louisville Kentucky
April 19 1822
Æt 33

PETER R. SALMOND
died at Baltimore May 18 1828
Æt 26

Erected in Memory of
ROBERT SALMOND
a native of Scotland
who died May 5 1829
Æt 80

In Memory of
WILLIAM SALMOND
son of Robt & Mary Salmond
died Mch. 11 1842
aged 49 years

In Memory of
JOHN SALMOND
son of Robert and Mary Salmond
died Apl. 3 1845
aged 54 years

ROBERT
son of Samuel & Eliza Salmond
Died Oct. 18th 1845
Aged 18 years

In Memory of
MARY
widow of Robert Salmond
who died Sept. 5 1847
aged 79 years

Erected in Memory of
MISS MARY SALMOND
Daut. of Mr. Robert & Mrs. Mary Salmond
died July 15 1848
aged 23 years

"*Few years she passed and then resigned her breath*
In life beloved lamented much in death
Hence reader learn how few the hours we have
Improve them well and live beyond the grave"

SAMUEL
son of Samuel & Eliza Salmond
died Aug. 14 1850
aged 11 weeks

SAMUEL SALMOND
Born Aug. 2d 1788
Died May 28 1859

ELIZA SALMOND
Born Mar. 20th 1801
Died Jan. 5th 1891

JOHN SMITH
born Dec. 10 1797
Died Sept. 5 1813
THOMAS M. SMITH
born Aug. 15 1799
died Jan. 7th 1803
SARAH B. SMITH
born Nov. 25 1802
died Nov. 28 1802
Children of Albert & Ann L. Smith

In Memory of
ALBERT SMITH Esq.
who died May 28 1823
aged 60 years
&
ANNA L. SMITH his wife
who Died May 7th 1835
Aged 70 years

Oh that men would Praise the
Lord for his goodness, and
For his wonderful works
To the children of men.

ANDREW TILDEN SMITH
Died at Manilla East Indias
April 29 1831
Aged 20 yrs

Thy will be done

———

ANNA L. SMITH
Died Dec. 12 1846
aged 58 years

———

In Memory of
RUTH SOPER
the wife of Mr. Joseph Soper
she died March the 9th *1777*
in the 77th year of her age

———

In Memory of
MR. JOSEPH SOPER
he died May the 1st *1790*
in the 88th year of his age

———

Children
ROBERT SPEAR
1851
HELEN
1869
ROBERT WARREN
1868—1871

In Memory of
CAPT. JOSEPH SOPER
ob. Mch. 30 1804
in the 67th year of his age

———

In Memory of
MR. DAVID STANDISH
who died June 4th 1795
in the 70th year of his age
Death is a debt to Nature due
Which I have paid and so must you

———

In Memory of
MRS. HANNAH
wife of Mr. David Standish
She died Aug. 23d 1803
in her 75th year
My God I cry with every breath
For sum kind Power to save
To break the yoke of sin & lead
And then redeem the slave

———

In Memory of
ZILPHA
the Daughter of Mr. Samuel
Stetson & Mrs. Zilpha his wife,
she died Nov. ye 29th 1800
aged 11th months

———

In Memory of
MRS. ZILPHA
wife of Mr. Samuel Stetson Jr.
who died Jan. 5 1807
aged 33 yrs
She sleeps in Jesus and is blest
How sweet her slumbers are
From suffering and from sin released
And freed from every snare

Sacred
To the Memory of
Mrs. Temprance
Wife of Mr. Nath. Stetson
died Nov. 6 1808
Æ 34 years
Stop passenger as you pass by
On my grave you cast an eye
Our sun like mine go down at noon
Our soul be called for very soon

In Memory of
Mrs. Lydia
wife of Mr. Turner Stetson
who died Jan. 22 1819
aged 50 years

In Memory of
Mr. Aristides
son of Mr. Turner & Mrs. Lydia
Stetson
who died Oct. 16 1839
aged 36 yrs

Harriet Ann
dau. of John & Ann Stetson
died Apl. 13 1846
aged 2 mos

Nathaniel Stetson
Died July 19 1846
aged 76 years
Also his wife
Joanna Pratt
Died Aug. 23 1841
aged 62 years
Though lost to sight
To memory dear

Nathaniel M.
son of Seth & Desire O. Stetson
Died May 10 1845
Aged 2 yrs 2 mos & 10 ds
Here little Martin lies
Beneath this silent clod
His little body moulders here
His spirit rests with God

In Memory of
Zilphia Ann daughter of
Albert Stetson & Weltha his wife
who died May 7 1843
aged 11 yrs 3 mos & 16 days
The Lord is Righteous in all his
ways and Holy in all his works

In Memory of
Mr. Turner Stetson
who died Feby 25 1844
aged 76 yrs

In Memory of
Elisha C. Stetson
born May 23 1796
Died Jan. 21 1845
aged 48 years 7 months & 28 days
Consumption comes God's will be done
Let every murmur cease
To Jesus fly prepare to die
And find eternal peace

Mrs. Nabby
wife of Ephraim Stetson
died Mch. 22d 1851
Aged 60 years

ALBERT STETSON
born Feb. 14 1843
died March 27 1845
aged 2 years 1 month & 13 days
SARAH MARIA STETSON
born Nov. 15 1839
died April 24 1845
aged 5 years 5 months & 9 days
Children of Elisha C. &
Betsey Stetson

Our path on earth was quickly trod
And now our spirits rest with God
Dry up your tears make Christ your
care
Death is what fate all must share

MICHAL
wife of Thomas Stetson
died May 17 1851
aged 71 years
" I know that my Redeemer lives "

TURNER
son of Turner & *Juletta* S. Stetson
born June 3 1855
died June 5 1855

HENRY MARTIN
son of John & Ann Stetson
died Aug. 7 1855
aged 11 yrs 3 mos 15 ds

JOHN EDWARD
son of John & Ann Stetson
died Sept. 5 1855
aged 3 yrs 7 mos 27 ds

ABBY F.
Daut. of Bery & Eliza Stetson
Died May 3 1858
Aged 14 yrs 9 mos

THEODORE STETSON
son of Harrison & Olive L.
Stetson
1850—1858

SAMUEL STETSON
died Aug. 16 1859
aged 87 yrs 3 mos & 9 dys

Peace to the mournful spot
Where hid my ashes lies
I ask no monumental praise
Over this dust to rise

Of you I claim no tear
Weep for yourselves my friends
The sigh of penitence secures
Rapture that never ends

ROBERT C. son of
Turner & Juletta S. Stetson
born Jan. 17 1860
died Apr. 5 1860

CORDELIA E.
wife of Andrew O. Stetson
Died Aug. 22 1860
Aged 26 yrs 8 mos

Weep not for me for my spirit has
fled To mansions in the sky
The one you have loved is not sleeping and but gone to her father on high

JAMES E.
son of Bery & Eliza Stetson
Died Dec. 12 1862
Aged 22 years
*A member of Co. G. 18th Regt.
Mass. Vols.*

EMMIE DELIA
died Sept. 9 1865
aged 4 yrs 2 mos 5 dys
ELIZA ANDREWS
died Mar. 22 1864
aged 6 mos
WILLIE ANDREWS
died Jan. 19 1865
Aged 2 weeks
*Children of Andrew O. &
Eliza M. Stetson*

MARY E.
Dau. of S. & D. O. Stetson
Died Nov. 30 1864
Æ 18 yrs 3 mos 20 Ds
Safe in the arms of Jesus

RACHEL E.
Dau. of S. & D. O. Stetson
Died July 3 1880
Æ 28 yrs 2 mos 20 Ds
We shall meet by and by

JASON E. son of
Wm. F. & Mary H. Stetson
died Dec. 30 1864
Æ 4 yrs 9 mos

SETH STETSON
died Jan. 30 1865
Æ 63 yrs 3 mos 12 Ds
He is not dead but sleeping

WILLIE M.
son of Wm. F. & Mary A. Stetson
died Jany 4 1865
Æ 3 yr 9 mo
"God loaned us this treasure
To be recalled at his pleasure"

SARAH E. dau. of
Turner & Juletta S. Stetson
born Aug. 23 1861
died Jan. 9 1865

BENJAMIN STETSON
born Sept. 28 1790
died June 6 1866
"We have loved him on earth may
we meet him in Heaven"

ELIZA M.
wife of Andrew O. Stetson
died Sept. 12 1869
Æ 29 yrs 10 mos 29 days

EMILY
wife of Jeremiah Stetson
died June 28 1870 aged 33 yrs

SAMUEL L. son of
Jeremiah & Emily L. Stetson
died July 25 1870
aged 1 yr 4 mos

SUMNER STETSON
1806—1873
ELIZA W. his wife
1801—1851

ZILPHA STETSON
died Jan. 31 1873
aged 64 yrs 1 mo
"Gone home"

ALBERT STETSON
Born Aug. 8 1802
Died Mar. 28 1874
also his wife
WELTHA
Born Feb. 10 1797
Died Dec. 10 1883

ABIGAIL S.
wife of Samuel Stetson
died Sept. 13 1874
Aged 83 yrs
At Rest

LUCY
wife of Benjamin Stetson
born June 26 1799
died Oct. 3 1875
" Weep not for the weary
There's rest for them in heaven "

JER' STETSON
died Mch. 9 1876
Æ 49 yrs 10 mos
"Absent but not forgotten"

SAMUEL STETSON
June 28 1799
Nov. 3 1876

MARY H. dau. of
Turner & Juletta S. Stetson
born Sept. 8 1865
died Oct. 29 1877

SAMUEL STETSON
June 28 1799
Nov. 3 1876
LYDIA T. STETSON
Nov. 26 1803
Feb. 19 1880
CATHERINE AMANDA STETSON
Oct. 20 1827
Dec. 5 1889
Husband
JOHN *Studley*
Died Oct. 29 1892
Aged 66 years 4 ms
Father
JOSHUA S. *Rose*
Mar. 17 1824
May 17 1893

LYDIA T. STETSON
Nov. 26 1803
Feb. 19 1880

ALICE R. STETSON
died Apl. 8 1880
Æ 73 yrs 3 mos

ELIZA
wife of Benj. Stetson
died Feb. 21 1881
Æ 67 yrs 8 mos
Not lost but gone before

———

BETSEY
wife of Elisha C. Stetson
Died Sept. 25 1881
Aged 85 years
Come unto me and I will give you rest

———

RUTH STETSON
died Apl. 30 1882
Æ 84 yrs 8 mos

———

In Loving Memory of
JOHN H. STETSON
who *entered into the Life everlasting*
Nov. 9 A. D. 1882
Æ 25 yrs 10 mos 8 ds
"I thank my God upon every remembrance of you"

———

DESIRE O.
wife of Seth Stetson
Died July 8 1890
Æ 75 yrs 9 mos 26 ds
In loving remembrance

———

Stetson
Not my will but Thine be done
REUBEN STETSON
Oct. 31 1810—Feb. 26 1892

CATHERINE AMANDA STETSON
Oct. 20 1827
Dec. 5 1889

———

JANE R. OLDHAM
Wife of I. Gilman Stetson
1825—1892

———

HARRISON STETSON
Born Jan. 26 1814
Died June 4 1892
Though lost to sight to Memory Dear

———

MARY EMMA dau. of
Rolinem & W. H. Stewart
died Mch. 26 1864
aged 2 yrs 6 mos

———

This Monument is Erected
In Memory of
MR. STEPHEN STOCKBRIDGE
Youngest son of
Wm. & Ruth Stockbridge
Born April 3d 1799
Died May 14th 1818
Aged 19 years 1 mo 11 dys
Death like an overflowing stream
Sweeps us away our life's a dream
An empty tale a waning flower
Cut down and withered in an hour

———

FRANCIS I. son of
Wm. & Mary A. Stockbridge
died Aug. 17th 1847
aged 2 years 10 mo's 9 ds

STONE ERECTED TO MR. JOHN STOCKBRIDGE, WHO DIED "A. DOMINI 1768."

FREDRIC W. son of
Wm. & Mary A. Stockbridge
died Jan. 17 1853
aged 10 years 5 mo's 9 days

In Memory of
BETSEY HOMER Dau. of
Lebbeus & Lydia Stockbridge
died *Nov. 16th 1833*
aged 12 years
Prepare to meet thy God

Sacred
to the Memory of
MRS. RUTH
wife of David Stockbridge Esq.
who died April 11 1833
In her 72 year
Hark from on high my Saviour calls
I come my Lord my love
Devotion breaks the prison walls
And speeds my last remove

In Memory of
WM. STOCKBRIDGE
died feb. 20th 1841
aged 88 yrs
Also
MRS. RUTH STOCKBRIDGE
wife of Wm. Stockbridge
died Dec. 9 1839
aged 85 years

WILLIAM BAILY son of
Wm. & Mary A. Stockbridge
died May 8 1866
aged 11 year 1 mo 20 dys

Sacred
to the Memory of
DAVID STOCKBRIDGE ESQ.
who died Feb. 26th 1843
Aged 88 years
Blessed are the dead who die in the Lord

LEBBEUS STOCKBRIDGE
died June 30 1855
aged 67 year 7 mo's
Also his Wife
LYDIA
died Jan. 16th 1869
aged 78 yr 1 mo'

JOSEPH C. STOCKBRIDGE
1799—1860
ANN W. his wife
1813—1837
PAMELIA his wife
1803—1884
AMELIA F. GARDNER
1844—1889
Children of J. C. & P.
Stockbridge
PAMELIA F.
1839—1849
Infant Son
1845

LEBBEUS STOCKBRIDGE
Co. K. 2nd Regt. M. V. M.
died June 30 1884
aged 59 yrs 4 ms 16 ds
"Gone but not forgotten"

WILLIAM STOCKBRIDGE
died April 10th 1890
aged 78 yrs 5 mo's

———

ELIZABETH F.
wife of Frank Stockbridge
July 30 1850
Dec. 19 1891
At Rest

———

Sacred to the Memory of
ABBY SARAH H. STODDARD
who died May 4 1844
aged 18 years

Come my dear mates as you pass by
This monument where I do lie
Think of my early sudden doom
And let me teach you from the tomb
Though healths warm current swelb
Your veins acute disease with racking
Pains may take away your vital Breath
Be wise while here Prepare for Death

———

DUNCAN T. STODDARD
Died Jan. 6 1868
Aged 44 yrs 10 mos

———

ANNA K. STODDARD
Dec. 2d 1792
March 16th 1877

———

MELVIN STODDARD
died Sept. 3 1882
aged 73 yrs
"Gathering home one by one"

ABIGAIL J.
wife of Melvin Stoddard
died Mch. 17 1884
aged 64 yrs
"Nearer my God to thee"

———

HARRY
son of J. A. & J. M. Stoddard
died March 7 1887
aged 14 yrs 10 mos 6 days
"Ever in remembrance"

———

In Memory of
BENONI STUDLEY
died Nov. 14 *1746*
aged 75 years
ABIGAIL his wife
Dau. of John Stetson
Died Feb. 1st *1759*
aged 84 years

———

In Memory of
JOSHUA STUDLY
son of Benoni Studley
died May 15th *1759*
aged 52 years
LYDIA his wife
and Dau. of Joshua Pratt
died July 9th *1759*
aged 40 years

———

ROBERT C.
son of Jabez & Chloe M. Studley
died Jan. 19 A. D. 1817
aged 14 months

STONE ERECTED TO DEA. JOSEPH AND MRS. ANNA STOCKBRIDGE,
1783—1783.

The Lord spake and it was Dun
In Memory of
MR. JOSEPH STUDLEY
Who died by Lightning
June 16th 1766
25 years & 3 mos old

In Memory of
GIDEON STUDLEY
son of Joshua Studly
died Aug. 14th 1816
aged 75 years
ROSAMOND his wife
Dau' of Caleb Church
died Jan. 3 1832
aged 91 years

In Memory of
JOSHUA STUDLY
son of Gideon Studley
died feb. 27 1818
aged 63 years

In Memory of
LYDIA STUDLEY
dau. of Joshua Studley
died Sept. 27th 1828
aged 78 years

SARAH
Wife of Gideon Studley
Died July 9 1838
Aged 56 yrs
Dau. of John & Grace Butler
of Oakland Mass

MARY M. STUDLEY
died Mar. 5 1840
Æ 5 mos

Erected In Memory of
MRS. SARAH ANN
wife of Mr. Hiram Studley
who died Mch. 19 1844
aged 31 yrs

MARY ROBERSON
dau. of Hiram & Sarah Studley
died Aug. 16 1844
aged 5 mos 3 ds
" The dear delights we here enjoy
And fondly call our own
Are but short favours borrowed now
To be repaid anon "

In Memory of
SARAH STUDLY
dau. of Gideon Studley
died June 26 1847
aged 81 years

HIRAM AUGUSTUS
son of Hiram & Esther Studley
died Sept. 22 1849
aged 15 mos 11 ds
Adieu our dear Augustus
We give you up to God
With flowers we'll deck thy early grave
And bow beneath the rod
The blow to us has been severe
For we are left alone
God only lent you to us here
Now he has called you home

GIDEON STUDLEY
died Jan. 9 1850
Æ 73 y'rs
Son of Gideon & Rosamond
Studley

Sacred to the Memory of
HANNAH
wife of David Studly
who died May 19th 1850
aged 58 years

HIRAM AUGUSTUS
son of Hiram & Esther Studley
died Sept. 8 1854
aged 6 mos 12 ds

"Sleep on my babe thou loved and blest
I would not break thy peaceful rest"

HIRAM STUDLEY
Died July 28 1855
aged 43 yrs & 3 mos

Blooming youth had passed away—
Manhood riper years had surely come—
Longer here I thought to stay—But
alas the graves my home—

CHLOE M.
wife of Jabez Studley
died Octo. 18 A. D. 1861
aged 83 years

REBECCA STUDLEY
died Aug. 26th 1862
aged 92 years

Blessed are the dead who die in the Lord

ESTHER
Wife of Hiram Studley
Died June 15 1867
aged 51 yrs 7 mos

Hushed is our loving mother's voice
That soothed our childhood's fears
Whose tender accents cheered our hearts
When grown to riper years.

Oft as we tread this sacred spot
Our upheaved hearts will weep;
But sweet the thought that angel bands
Their virgils softly keep.

JOHN STUDLEY
died June 28 1867
Æt 61 yrs 11 mos 8 ds

JABEZ STUDLEY
died May 31 1868
aged 91 years 9 mos

SARAH E.
dau. of Hiram & Esther Studley
died July 9 1869
Æ 17 yrs 3 mo 25 ds

"Sister in that solemn trust
We commend thee dust to dust
In that faith we wait till risen
Thou shall meet us all in Heaven"

ABBIE A.
wife of George Gurney &
dau. of Hiram & Esther Studley
died Sept. 23 1870
Æ 20 yrs 1 mo 3 ds

"Happy consoling thought, that we
shall meet in Heaven"

DAVID STUDLEY
Died Oct. 30th 1873
aged *90* years 7 mo's
Death only moulded into nobler
Beauty the Statue of his life

BENJ. F. STUDLEY
born Feb. 21 1823
died Octo. 15 1874
"Gone, but not forgotten"

CARL WILLNER
Son of Edwin H. & Matilda T.
Studley
Died May 23 1875
Aged 5 years 2 mos

ROBERT H. STUDLEY
died May 1 1883
aged 64 yrs 4 mos 22 ds

PHILANDER STUDLEY
died Apl. 10 1885
Æ 70 yrs 5 ms 5 ds

RAY B.
son of F. A. & E. M. Studley
died Apl. 29 1890
aged 1 year 2 days

JUDITH
wife of Geo. Studley
Died Dec. 4 1893
aged 84 years 2 mos

LUCINDA & MARION
Daughters of
Joseph H. & Lucinda Studly
JOSEPH H. STUDLY
Died Dec. 24th 1885
Aged 69 years

LEVI STURTEVANT
Born Dec. 28th 1797
Died Mch. 7 1858
aged 60 years
My works for sin cannot atone
Christ must save and Christ alone
Marietta—Edward

REBECCA A.
wife of Rufus M. Sturtevant
died Nov. 22 1858
aged 27 yrs 10 mos
It was anguish dear husband from thee
to depart
From the child of my bosom the pride
of my heart
Though in darkness and silence this
body must rest
My spirit is with you to guide and to
bless

FRANKLIN F.
son of Rufus M. & Rebecca A.
Sturtevant
died Octo. 20 1864
aged 5 yrs 11 mos 17 ds
" Death came and nipped the budding
flower
Ere it had reached its bloom
And in an unexpected hour
Called a bright cherub home "

ISAAC K. STURTEVANT
1831—1871
children
ELIZA W.
1858—1862
ALICE B.
1865—1892

ABIGAIL D.
wife of Zenas G. Sturtevant
died June 3 1890
aged 64 yrs 4 mos 7 days
" Call not back the dear departed
Anchored safe where storms are o'er
On the border land we left her
Soon to meet and part no more

To the Memory of
MR. ELIJA SYLVESTER
died Dec. 28th 1828
Aged 61 yrs
Beloved his life lamented at his death
Calm and resigned he spent his last Breath
Free'd from lifes cares and every Earthly Pain
Our loss we trust is his Eternal gain

Sacred to the Memory of
MRS. MARY SYLVESTER
wife of Mr. Elijah Sylvester and
Dau' of Deac' Timothy Robbins
Died June 27 1829
Aged 56 years
Sleeping beneath the Earths Cold Sod
The bodys of our Parents lie
Their spirits Gone up to their God
To reign with Christ above the Sky

ZENAS G. STURTEVANT
died March 15 1885
aged 72 yrs 9 mos 16 days
" He rests from his labor his work being done "

In Memory of
LUCY PORTER Dau' of
Mr. Elijah and Lucy Sylvester
Died Oct. 14th 1833
Aged 2 years 7 mo's
Dear little babe thy months were few
And suffering was thy lot Below
But Jesus called thou hast obeyed
And left a world of pain and woe

M. ROBERT SYLVESTER
1825
His wife
EMILY S. (SPEAR)
1828—1851
His wife
ELIZABETH T. (WATERMAN)
1833—1856

Sylvester
Tomb
MICHAEL & ROBERT SYLVESTER
1852

To the Memory of
MR. ELIJAH SYLVESTER
Died June 6th 1852
aged 58 years
My husband dear oh can it be
And has thy spirit fled
And left us here to mourn for thee
For thou art with the dead

CEMETERY RECORDS.

Non Sibi Sed Patria
LOAMMI B.
son of Robert & Sarah Sylvester
*Clerk of Co. I 2d Regt. Mass. Vol.
Wounded at the Battle of Cedar
Mountain* Aug. 9 1862
Died in Hospital at Alexandria Va. Sept. 6th 1862
aged 31 years

MARY SALMOND
wife of E. Q. Sylvester
Born Dec. 26 1832
Died July 31 1864
"She sleeps in Jesus"

MARY SYLVESTER
Born July 24 1864
Died Sept. 8 1865

Infant son of
E. Q. & E. S. Sylvester
Born Sept. 21 1867
Died Feb. 12 1868

CHRISTIANA W. SYLVESTER
wife of Elija W. Sylvester
died Sept. 22d 1873
aged 49 years
ELIJA W.
died May 14 1864
aged 9 mo's
WALLACE B.
died Oct. 6th 1866
aged 1 year 5 mo's
*Children of E. W. & C. M.
Sylvester*

LUCY SYLVESTER
wife of Elijah Sylvester
Born April 13th 1800
Died April 19th 1885
Blessed are the dead which die in the Lord

LUCY W.
wife of Joseph B. Sylvester
died Sept. 16th 1891
aged 66 yrs 9 mos 26 Dys

Sylvester
ROBERT
1814 ——
M. ALMIRA
1832—1893

MATILDA
wife of William P. Taylor
died June 28th 1893
aged *91* years

AMY DWELLEY dau. of
Chas. E. & Mary D. Thayer
died Oct. 7 1863
aged 7 yrs 7 mos 11 ds

EDGAR IRVIN son of
Chas. E. & Mary D. Thayer
died Nov. 3 1863
aged 3 yrs 6 mo

S. HOWARD THAYER
died Apl. 2 1879
aged 25 yrs 7 mos

JAMES E. child of
Edward F. & Emma L. Thayer
died Sept. 25 1880
aged 2 yrs 23 ds

AMELIA J.
wife of Wendell P. Thayer
born April 29 1847
died May 28 1884
"The Lord is my Shepherd
I shall not want"

CHARLES THOMAS
Died Nov. 6 1847
aged 55 yrs 4 mos 21 ds
We loved thee on earth we hope to
meet thee in Heaven

CHAS. THOMAS JR.
son of Chas. & Mary S. Thomas
died Oct. 3th 1848
aged 11 months
Dear little one thy Pains are ended
Thou hast found a better home
Thy songs are now with angels blended
Where no death or sorrows come

SARAH B. THOMAS
March 16th 1801
Sept. 21st 1893
At Rest

LYMAN THOMPSON
died Mar. 2 1890
aged 72 yrs 10 mos

LEVI T. son of
Chas. & Sarah B. Thomas
Drowned July 27th 1850
aged 18 yrs 1 mo 25 dys
*Without a moments warning
His soul was snatched away
Dear reader stop as you pass by
And think of such a day*

BATHSHUA
wife of Lyman Thompson
died feb. 20 1892
aged 69 ys 4 mos

Here Lyes ye Body of
SARAH TILDEN
Daughter of Mr. Job &
Mrs. Elizabeth Tilden
who died April ye 8th *1751*
aged 4 yrs & 7 months & 26 days

Hear lies buried
MRS. ELIZABETH TILDEN
Wife of Lieut. Job Tilden
She died March ye 2d *1799*
in the 84 year of her age
Mourn not my friends wipe off your tears
Here I must lie till Christ appears

In Memory of
JOB TILDEN
Who died Sept. 30 1830
Aged 72 yrs
Also his wife
LYDIA
died Aug. 23 1848
Aged 87 yrs

CEMETERY RECORDS. 293

SALLY TILDEN
Died July 8 1880
Æ 89 yrs 11 mos 6 ds

In Memory of
BENJAMIN TOLMAN
died Sept. 17th 1852
aged 84 years

POLLY TOLMAN
Born 1808
Died 1884

WILLIAM TORREY
Died Oct. 19 1828
aged 77
MRS. MARY TORREY
Died Jan. 28 1826
aged 75
MRS. MARY LITTLE
Died June 9 1834
Aged 47
HAVILAND TORREY
Died Aug. 26 1865
Aged 74
SALOME (BARSTOW)
Wife of Haviland Torrey
Died May 3 1878
aged 76
GEORGE H. TORREY
Died Jan. 7 1832
aged 3
WILLIAM H. TORREY
Died Aug. 31 1837
aged 4
MARY S. TORREY
Died Sept. 1 1837
aged 2

GEORGE B. TOLMAN
Born 1820
Died 1887

WM. DEXTER TORREY
Feb. 25th *1835*—June 2d 1891
BENJ. D. TORREY
Nov. 16 1796—July 17th 1843
LOUISA his wife
Sept. 1st 1797—Feb. 26 1871
CLAYTON S. TORREY
July 17th 1857—Aug. 25th 1858
Father   Mother   W. D. T.   Baby
Torrey Monument

ANDREW W. TOTMAN
1839—1892
" Thy labors Ended,
thy rest is won."

Here Lies ye Body of
MRS. PARTES TOWER
ye wife of Mr. David Tower
She Died *June the 24th 1787*
In ye 86 year of her age

JANE
Wife of John S. Tower
died Aug. 25 1849
Æ 36 yrs

Infant son of
H. S. & H. A. Tower
Aged 4 mos

Mary P. Tower
died Jan. 22 1877
Æ 23 yrs 3 mos 28 ds

"Not for the dead in Christ we weep
Their sorrows now are o'er
The sea is calm the tempest past
On that eternal shore"

Charles C. Tower
died April 19 1882
Æ 19 years

"Just as I am without one plea
But that thy blood was shed for me
And that thou bid'st me come to thee
Oh Lamb of God I come I come"

In Memory of
Capt. John Tribou
who died Oct. 15 1848
in his 61st year

"Farewell my wife and children too
I can no longer stay with you
My portion in heaven I wish to share
Prepare for death and meet me there"

Walter S.
son of Mr. William F. &
Mrs. Janette Tribou
died April 6 1850
aged 1 yr 8 mos 5 d'ys

"Rest thou darling child
All thy pains are o'er
Thy spirit undefiled
Is blest forever more"

Levi W. Tribou
died Nov. 20 1877
aged 61 yrs

Ann Augusta
daughter of I. T. & M. B.
Tribou
died Mar. 17 1864
aged 19 yrs & 5 mo
(*reverse*)

We saw our household light grow dim
The while our eyes grow blind with tears
God came to take anew to him
The jewel lent in bygone years
For as God gives so he takes
Nor asks us whom nor when or where
And tis a loving hand that breaks
And desolates our hearts as now

Lucinda D.
wife of Levi W. Tribou
died Feb. 23 1882
aged 62 yrs 6 ms 16 ds

Melissa B.
wife of John T. Tribou
Died June 24 1892
Aged 76 yrs 2 mos 26 days

She's passed beyond all earthly woes
She smiles in a sunnier sphere

Mr. Joseph Tubbs
died Apl. 1 1854
aged 77 yrs 11 mos 18 ds

Lucy
widow of Joseph Tubbs
died Mch. 22 1866
Æt 89 yrs 1 mo & 11 ds

EUNICE W. TUBBS
died Feby. 22 1879
aged 81 yrs

JOSEPH TUBBS
died July 3 1885
aged 76 yrs 1 mo 24 ds

MARY B. TUBBS
died Jan. 23 1888
aged 87 yrs 3 mos 1 day

In Memory of
MRS. MARY
the wife of Mr. Isaac Turner
who died May 3d *1796*
In the 41st year of her age

Draw near my friends and take a thought
How soon the grave may be your lot
Make sure of Christ while there remain
Death shall be Eternal Gain

In Memory of
SILVIA
the Daughter of Mr. Isaac
Turner & Mrs. Mary his wife
She died Jan. ye 27th 1801
Aged 13 yrs

In Memory of
MRS. DEBORAH TURNER
Wife of Capt. Marlbry Turner
Died May 28 1824
In the 63 year of her age

THOMAS TURNER
1782—1829
DEBORAH STOCKBRIDGE
his wife
1790—1882
THOMAS JR.
1812—1813
RUTH STOCKBRIDGE
1813 ———
THOMAS 2d
1815 ———
CHARLES PHILLIPS
1823—1847
THOMAS TURNER
1815 ———
SUSAN MARIA THAYER
his wife
1818 ———
THOMAS JR.
1841—1841
SUSAN JANE
1842—1882
THOMAS 2d
1844—1849
ADALEIDE WARREN
1848 ———
CHARLES PHILLIP
1852 ———
MARY GREENE
1856 ———

In Memory of
MR. NATHAN TURNER
he Died at *Abington* Dec. 27th 1829
aged 15 years 6 mo's

Raise thoughtless sinner, raise thine eye
Behold Gods balance lifted high
Where should his justice be displayed
And there thy hope and life is weiyed

Sacred to the Memory of
MR. SETH TURNER
died at Hanson May 15 1823
Also
PRISCILLA *Beal*
died Nov. 20th 1818
aged 16 months
Also
PRISCILLA *Beal*
died Nov. 9 1820
aged 8 mos 6 days
Daughters of Mr. Seth Turner
and Mrs. Priscilla his wife
Draw near my friend and think how soon
The great I. AM. may seal your doom
Awake, arise, with speed Prepare
To meet at Gods impartial bar

MARY E.
daughter of George and Avis
Turner
died Oct. 31 1832
aged 7 mos & 24 ds
Before this lovely bud had bloomed
From parent stock it was riven
For Jesus took it for his own
To fully bloom in heaven

GEORGE GILBERT
Son of Mr. Saml. S. &
Mrs. Mary Ann Turner
died Oct. 6 1838
Aged 1 year
Thy little one is sleeping
Among the quiet dead
And thou art sadly weeping
Above his lowly bed

AVIS
Wife of George W. Turner
Died Jan. 2 1857
Aged 53 yrs 10 mos 4 ds
Let worms devour my wasting flesh
And crumble all my bones to dust
My God shall raise my frame anew
At the revival of the just

ELMA A. son of
Elma J. & Virginia A. Turner
died June 14th 1865
aged 1 year 2 mo's 17 days
O, mother weep not for thy babe
Why mourn you over my little grave
O Father Mother cease those broken sighs
Thy babe is Happy in the Skyes

JULIA A.
wife of James Turner
Died Dec. 20th 1870
Aged 34 years 10 mos
Faithfull and True

RUTH TURNER
died July 18th 1877
aged 84 yrs 4 mos
Death is swallowed up in Victory

MARY ANN
wife of Samuel S. Turner
Died Oct. 27 1877
Æ 66 years
Mother thou art gone to rest
And this shall be our prayer
That when we reach onr journey's end
Thy glory we may share

CEMETERY RECORDS. 297

ELDON W. son of
Ezekiel T. & Sarah S. Turner
died Aug. 13 1881
aged 12 yrs 2 ms 1 day
" Heaven retaineth now our treasure
Earth the lonely casket keeps
And the sunbeams love to linger
Where our darling loved one sleeps"

SAMUEL S. TURNER
Died Nov. 19 1887
Aged 77 years
We will meet again

JAMES VINAL
1835—1894
M. A. VINAL
1838—1894

FLORA JANE
dau. of Walter W. & Sarah Jane
Wardrobe
died Jan. 31 1860
aged 11 mo's
" Sweet Flora's eyes are closed in death forever
So fair a flower for earth was never made
Tis gone to blossom in a milder clime
Where flowers of love and beauty cannot fade "

ASA WARREN
1766—1807
JAMIMA KELLOGG
his wife
1766—1853
WARREN

IRA WARREN M. D.
1806—1864
RUTH STOCKBRIDGE (TURNER)
his wife
1813 ———
An eminent man of science
A wise and upright counsellor
A courteous and generous associate
A loyal and devoted friend
His memory is Cherished by all who knew him

LUCY A.
wife of Eben C. Waterman and
dau. of Nathl. & Abby R.
(Barstow)
Died Jan. 20 1873
Aged 33 years

In Memory of
MRS. SARAH L. WHITE
the wife of Mr. Cornelius White
who departed this life
August the 26th 1799
aged 25 years 2 days
All though my body lies in the cold tomb
The earths to scanty for my soul vast doom
His wings for heaven and took a hasty flight
To crowns of blessing in the heavens of light

Erected
In Memory of
MR. WILLIAM WHITING
he died February the 12 1780
In the 59 year of his age

In Memory of
MR. LEWIS WHITE
who was accidentally shot
April 3d 1813
Aged 31 years

How can my trembling hand support my pen
While sorrow mourns the loveliest best of men
The tear shall flow can genuine sorrow sleep
Know certainly in streams our eyes shall weep
Hes gone forever gone Lewis has taken flight
To yonder world of joy of peace & light
Gone to behold his Saviour and his God
Oh may we tread the peaceful paths he trod

ELIZABETH MAGOUN

In Memory of
LUIT' THOMAS WHITING
he died Sept. 23d *1793*
in the 75 year of his age

Thou turned man O Lord to d .
Of which he first was made
And when thou speak'est the word *Return*
Tis instantly Obeyed

In Memory of
MISS LUCY WHITING
Dau. of Leiu't Thomas Whiting
and Mrs. Lydia (or Mary)
his wife
she died Nov. 18th *1789*
in the 42 year of her age

Who can secure his Vital Breath
against the bold demands of Death

In Memory of
MRS. DEBBE
the wife of Mr. Asa Whiting
she died Jany. ye 8th *1787*
aged 24 yrs & 3 *mounths*

In Memory of
ASA
son of Mr. Asa Whiting &
Mrs. *betty* his wife
he died May 16 1793
in the 3d year of his age

In Memory of
MR. HOMER WHITING
he died October the 11th *1793*
In the 28 year of his age

In Memory of
MISS AVIS WHITING
she died October 14th *1793*
In the 36 year of her age

In Memory of
MRS. ANNE WHITING
Wife Mr. Homer Whiting
she died July the 24th *1789*
In the 27 year of her Age

In Memory of
CALEB
son of Mr. Caleb Whiting &
Mrs. Susa Gill his wife
he died September the 29 *1792*
in the 4th year of his age

SEE OPPOSITE PAGE.

In Memory of
ANNE
daughter of Mr. Homer Whiting
& Mrs. Anne his wife
she died October the 4th *1793*
In the 16th year of her age

In Memory of
SAGE MAN WHITING
daughter of Mr. Caleb Whiting
and Mrs. Susa Gill his wife
she died Oct. 11 *1793*
in the 9 month of her age
From death a rest no age is free
Young children too may die

In Memory of
MARTIN
son of Mr. Thos. Whiting
and Mrs. Rachel his wife
he died October the 18th *1793*
in the ——2nd year of his age
" Death like an overflowing stream
Sweep's us away our lifes a dream
An evening tale a morning flower
Cast down and wither'd in an hour "

JUSTUS WHITING
Tomb

MRS. LYDIA WHITING
1801
" Kind Reader pause and drop a tear
Think of the dust which slumbers here
And when you read the fate of me
Think of the glass which runs for thee "

In Memory of
MR. THOMAS WHITING JR.
died Sept. 2 1805
In the 29th year of his age
" That once lov'd form now cold and dead
Each mournful thought employs
And nature weeps her comforts dead
And wither'd all her joys
Hope looks beyond the bounds of time
When that we now deplore
Shall rise in full immortal prime
And bloom to fade no more "

Sacred
To the Memory of
MR. WILLIAM WHITING
of Hanover
died Mar. 29 1825
Aged 63 yrs
Peace all ye sorrows of the heart
And every tear be dry
The Christian ne'er can be forlorn
Who views his Saviour nigh
Let not your sorrows rise he says
Nor be your souls afraid
Trust in your God's almighty name
And trust your Saviours aid

Erected
In Memory of
MRS. MARY WHITING
widow of Mr. William Whiting
died June 11 1826
Aged 95 *years*
Yes we must follow soon we'll glad Obey
When a few suns have Rolled their cares away
Tired with vain life we'll close the willing Eye
Tis the great birthright of man ind to die

In Memory of
Mr. Abel Whiting
died Jan. 24 1822
In the 70th year of his age

In Memory of
Mr. Lewis T. Whiting
died Sept. 25 1826
aged 23 yrs

"Sweet youth alike to friends and strangers dear
O'er thy green turf will drop the tender tear
In vain thy soul was bright, thy bosom kind
In vain the tears of those thou *leavst* behind
Cold is thy form and dark thy lone abode
Yet thou but tread'st the vale thou Saviour trod
With Him fond hope again beholds thee rise
From transient earth to the superior skies"

In Memory of
Mrs. Sarah C. Whiting
wife of Mr. Oran Whiting
died Feb. 20 1827
In the 23d year of her age
Also *Their Daugh.*
Sarah Ann
died Sept. 28 1826
Æ 1 year

Mourn not for me my work is done
The combat is oe'r the prize is won
And now my mansion is above
Where all is life and peace and love
I left the world without a tear
Save for the friends I loved so dear
To sooth their sorrows Lord descend
And be their everlasting friend

In Memory of
Mrs. Betsey Whiting
wife of Mr. William Whiting
Died Mar. 17 1829
Aged 58 years

Come my dear children come behold
This stone of life the final goal
Approach it in your mothers tomb
The place where you must shortly come
I warn you all for death prepare
And make your souls your greatest care
Death soon will come & you must go
If not prepared to endless woe

Pyam Wilson son of
Pyam C. & Sarah D. Whiting
died Feb. 11th 1833
aged 7 mo's

Welcome dear babe to Jesus Breast
For ever there in joy to Rest
Welcome to Jesus courts above
To sing the great Redeeming Love

The grave of
Simeon son of
Mr. William & Mrs. Cynthia Whiting
died March 4 1839
Aged 7 months

Ere sin could blight or sorrow fade
death came with friendly care
The Opening bud to heaven convyd
And bade it blossom there

Soianus W. son of
Gilman C. & Diantha Whiting
Died July 2 1839
aged 2 yrs & 9 ms

To the Memory of
MISS SARAH MERITT
daugh. of Mr. Homer &
Mrs. Hannah Whiting
died April 11 1835
Aged 21 years

LUCY
daughter of Caleb Whiting
died June 15 1840
Æ 49

ABEL H.
son of Oran & Mary Whiting
Died Oct. 9 1842
aged 1 year & 2 mos

SUSAN G.
wife of Caleb Whiting
Died Nov. 25 1842
Æ 77

In Memory of
PYAM C. WHITING
died Aug. 12 1845
aged 34 years 1 mo 14 dys
Cease ye mourners cease to languish
Oer the Grave of those you love
Pain and death and might and anguish
Enter not the world above

MARY
wife of Caleb Whiting
died Sept. 1 1850
Æ 45 y'rs

MARY dau. of
Sylvanus & Lucy Whiting
died Dec. 9 1846
aged 1 mo 10 ds
"Sleep sleep thou dear departed Mary
Parents tears will wet thy sod
Early flowers will deck thy grave
While angels bear thee home to God

CALEB WHITING
Died May 20 1848
aged 86 years

In Memory of
PRISCILLA
wife of Abel Whiting
who died Jan. 15 1851
aged *91 years*
Father I give my spirit up
And trust it in thy hands
My dying flesh shall rest in hope
And rise at thy command

TRYPHENA
Wife of Homer Whiting
Died Nov. 7 1851
Æ 89 yrs 6 mos & 10 Days
*Mother forgive forgive thy children
dear
Why mourn thy exit from a world
like this
Forgive the wish that would have
kept thee here
And staid thy progress to the land
of bliss*

In Memory of
HOMER WHITING
who died Feb. 5 1854
aged 68 years & 6 mos

HANNAH M.
Daughter of Gilman C. &
Diantha Whiting
Died Sept. 27 1852
age 17

M. ELETTA dau. of
Lewis & Mary B. Whiting
died July 8 1856
aged 11 mos 1 day
"We loved thee fondly & thy smile
All innocence repaid our love
But oh thy soul too free from guile
For earth God called above"

MARY
wife of Oran Whiting
Died March 1 1857
aged 51 years & 3 mos

SYLVANUS WHITING
died Feby 11 1859
aged 51 years
"Beloved companion though lost from earth
In memory thou art with me still"

ALBERT son of
Oran & Mary Whiting
died Oct. 12 1859
aged 13 yrs 6 mos 18 dys

ABEL H. son of
Oran & Mary Whiting
died July 19 1863
aged 20 years & 5 days

IDA daughter of
Lucius A. & Lydia M. Whiting
died Aug. 9 1863
aged 4 yrs 8 mos
Ida farewell we give thee up
Our Father calls thee home
That Saviour folds you in his arms
Who said to children come

ORAN WHITING
Died Oct. 23 1866
aged 65 years

CALEB WHITING
Died Feb. 1 1867
Aged 67 years

CYNTHIA
wife of William Whiting
died Sept. 9 1868
aged 60 yrs 6 mos
Lo where the silent marble weeps
A friend a wife a mother sleeps
A heart within whose sacred cell
The peaceful virtues love to dwell

LILY BELLE
only child of
Anson & Cynthia Whiting
Died July 8 1870
Æ 11 mos
How hard is parting
How slow the submission
When our birdling has flown
From the tender home nest
And yet there is cheer in the hope
that is whispered Our baby has gone
to the clime of the blest

CEMETERY RECORDS. 303

DESIRE
wife of Jared Whiting
Died Aug. 3 1872
Aged 60 yrs 3 mos 28 ds

JOHN B. WHITING
Mch. 24 1848
Aug. 8 1875
" We have no home but heaven"

ELLA E. dau. of
Walter W. & Sarah J. Wardrobe
died Feb. 2 1874
aged 25 yrs 22 ds
"Safe in the tearless land"

JARED WHITING
Died Sept. 6 1876
Aged 72 years 4 mos 21 ds

ANNA
Wife of Caleb Whiting &
Daughter of Gideon & Sarah
Studley
Died March 20 1874
Aged 63 yrs 7 mos 22 d's

VESTA L.
wife of Benjamin F. Wood
died April 8 1878
aged 26 yrs 6 mos

Mother
SALLY CURTIS WHITING
died Sept. 10th 1874
75 years

HENRY W. WHITING
Co. G. 18th Mass. Vol.
Co. H. 32nd Reg. Inf.
Born July 28th 1843
Died Oct. 14 1879

Father
EZRA WHITING
died Oct. 3 1831
31 years

In Memory of
MARY Dau. of
William & Cynthia Whiting
Born April 12 1847
Died July 17 1881

EVA M. Dau. of
Lucius A. & Lydia M. Whiting
Died Sept. 20 1874
aged 3 mos 27 d's

JOSEPH WASHINGTON
born in North Carolina a **SLAVE**
died in Massachusetts **FREE**
1857—1881
"The reward of the faithful is certain"

LYDIA M.
wife of Lucius A. Whiting
Died May 26 1874
Aged 38 y'rs
She hath done what she could

WILLIAM WHITING
Died June 30 1886
Aged 75 yrs 4 mos

MARY W. (ESTES)
wife of John B. Whiting
Feby 7th 1849
Jany 9 1882
"Oh for the touch of a vanished hand,
and the sound of a voice that is still"

SARAH D.
wife of Pyam C. Whiting
died July 5th 1882
aged 70 years 3 mo's 6 dys

ROSETTAH
Wife of William A. Whiting
Died May 9 1887
Æ 37 yrs 7 mos 10 ds

SALLIE B.
wife of Lucius C. Whiting
Died June 2d 1887
Aged 55 yrs 8 mos

DIANTHA STODDARD
Wife of Gilman C. Whiting
Nov. 1 1804
Sept. 6 1894
Gone from home but
Not from Our Hearts

H. WM. WHITING JR.
Born Nov. 24 1873
Died Sept. 12 1894
Gone when his life was Brightest
From us who loved him so dear
Our burdens were always Brighter
When his cheerfull Presence was Here

DIANTHA S. WHITING
Sept. 27 1830
Oct. 12 1890
At Rest

GILMAN C. WHITING
Feb. 16 1800
"   2 1892

In Memory of
MR. ISAAC WILDER
died March 30 1818
Et 41 yrs
Peace to the mournfull spot
Where hid my ashes lies
I ask no monumental praise
Over this dust to rise
Of you I claim no tear
Weep for yourselves my friends
The sigh of penitence secures
Rapture that never ends

In Memory of
Caleb
son of Isaac & Ruth Wilder
died May 22d 1818
aged 17 mo's
Here lies an infant. No his dregs lie here
his better part the earth could not
confine
weep not ye friends his dust shall
reappear
we trust well known and in a form
divine

In Memory of
MR. JOHN WILDER
died Dec. 18 1828
aged 41 years
Departed saint thy conflict o'er
blissfull thy spirit flies
in peace we trust thy ashes rests
destined in joy to rise

In Memory of
MISS HANNAH B. WILDER
died Nov. 11 1829
aged 22 years

Nor pain nor grief nor anxious fear
invade the tomb No mortal woes
can reach the lonely sleeper here
while angels watch the soft repose
so Jesus slept — God's dying son
passed thro' the grave, and blessed
the bed
Rest here dear saint till from her throne
the morning break and pierce the
shade

MRS. RUTH WILDER
died Jan. 11 1867
aged 88 yrs 3 mos

Rest weary one
lie down to slumber in the peaceful tomb
light from above hath broken through its
gloom
here in the place where once the Savior lay
where he shall make the on a future day
like a tired child upon its mother's breast
Rest spirit Rest

LUCINDA E. WILDER
Died Aug. 2 1871
Æt 30 yrs

Oh sacred hope, O blissful hope
Which Jesus's grace has given
The hope when days and years are past
We all shall meet in heaven

JOSEPH C. WILDER
June 13 1815
July 19 1872
PRISCILLA his wife
May 18th 1813
Oct. 26 1880

JOSEPH E. WILDER
Q. M. Scrgt. 31st Mass. Vol.
**KILLED IN ACTION AT SA-
BINE CROSS ROADS LA.**
April 8 1864
Aged 25 yrs
Student at Amherst College
Enlisted in his Countrys
Service Nov. 1861
Reenlisted Feb. 1864

LUCINDA
Wife of Isaac M. Wilder
Died April 25 1876
Aged 71 yrs 11 ds

Calm on the bosom of thy God
Fair spirit rest thee now
Even while with us thy footsteps trod
His seal was on thy brow
Dust to its narrow hours beneath
Soar to its place on high
They that have seen thy looks in death
No more may fear to die

ISAAC WILDER
Died Sept. 1 1878
Aged 43 yrs 9 mos 17 ds

Gone to the land of peace
Gone where the tempest hath no longer
sway
And the shadows pass from the soul
away
And sounds of weeping cease

MATTIE C. WILDER
Oct.—1877
Oct.—1883

We miss you at home

Isaac M. Wilder
Died July 1 1879
Aged 74 yrs
There remaineth therefore a rest
to the people of God. Heb. IV. 9
And there shall be no more death
neither sorrow nor crying neither shall
there be any more pain for the former
things are passed away Rev. XXI. 4

Nettie L.
wife of John C. Wilder
died July 4 1885
aged 21 yrs 6 mos
" Rest in Hope "

Forrest L.
son of N. L. & J. C. Wilder
Died Nov. 27 1885
Aged 5 mos 5 d's
Our Darling

John Calvin
Sarah Elizabeth
Sarah H.
wife of John C. Wilder
Died April 1888
Aged 78 yrs
John C. Wilder
Died Mar. 15 1855
Aged 44 yrs 8 mos
Sarah Elizabeth
Died Sept. 28 1836
Æt 5 mos
John Calvin
Died Mar. 17 1840
Æt 2 yrs 7 mos
We shall go to them but they shall
not return to us

John C. Wilder
Died Oct. 24 1891
Aged 29 yrs 8 Mos
Reunited

In Memory of
Mrs. Mary S.
wife of Mr. Horatio C. Williams
died June 5th 1842
in the 29 year of her age
also their Dau'
died June 1st 1842
The voice of this alarming scene
May every heart obey
Nor be the Heavenly warning vain
Which call to watch and Pray
Great God thy saving grace impart
With cleansing healing power
This only can prepare the heart
For death's surprising hour

In Memory of
Mary Williams
daugh. of Caleb Whiting Jr.
& Mary his wife
died Sept. 25 1843
aged 14 years & 6 months
Dear as thou wert and justly dear
We cant suppress the falling tear
But when a few more days are oer
We hope to meet to part no more

Eliza D.
dau. of Daniel & Ruth D. Willis
Died April 12 1842
aged 7 mos 10 ds
Sleep, Sleep thou dear Departed Child
Parents tears will wet thy sod
Early flowers will deck thy grave
While angels bear thee Home to God

FERRIN WILLIS
Co. F. 1st. Mass. H. A.

DANIEL F.
son of Daniel & Ruth D. Willis
Died Nov. 28 1851
aged 8 years
Thy father will miss thee
His pride and his joy
Thy mother will mourn
For her dear dead Boy
Thy Brother thy only one
Lone will he be
While thy sweet infant sister
Will murmur of thee

Father & Mother
reverse
DANIEL WILLIS
Born Oct. 8 1820
Died June 12 1890
RUTH D. WILLIS
Born Apr. 7 1824
Died June 26 1894

ELIJAH WING
died Sept. 30 1840
aged 66 years
Great God
Let man that is formed of dust praise thee for in thy almighty power and infinite goodness rest the immortality Happiness and onward Progress of all mankind in eternal march of ages
God Eternal
Let all things be made to praise thee let the marble from Quarry praise thee for at thy command every atom of its dust would become living man

(M.)
CHARLES WINSLOW
Died Aug. 8 1891
Aged 88 yrs 2 mos 22 days

HENRY WRIGHT
Died Jan. 14 1887
Aged 55 years

RUTH D.
wife of Warren Wright
died Aug. 28th 1861
Aged 48 years
Jesus lover of my soul
let me to thy bosom fly

MARTHA E.
wife of Warren T. Wright
Died Oct. 22d 1893
My Beulah Land

WARREN WRIGHT
died May 11th 1894
aged 84 years 9 months
Blessed are the dead which die in the Lord

MARY B.
wife of Lewis Whiting &
dau. of Abner & Mary Wood
died Mch. 4 1857
aged 21 yrs 7 mos
"Happy soul thy days are ended
All thy mourning days below
Go by angel guards attended
To the arms of Jesus go"

MARY
wife of Abner Wood
died Jan. 12 1859
aged 57 yrs 7 mos 6 ds
" Her flesh shall slumber in the ground
Till the last trumpets joyful sound
Then burst the chains with sweet surprise
And in her Saviour's image rise"

CHARLES ROBERT
son of Abner & Mary Wood
died Jan. 10 1863
aged 14 yrs 7 mos 29 ds
" While young to God he gave his heart
Above his treasures lay
May we like Charlie choose the part
Death cannot take away "

Here Lies the Body of
CAPT. JOHN YOUNG
Who Died June the 9th 1781
in ye 51st year of His Age

ABNER WOOD
died Apl. 8 1882
aged 79 yrs 6 mos 10 ds
He has gone to his rest with his loved ones
His trials and troubles are done
His glorified spirit is happy
He has fought the good fight and he's won

Erected
In Memory of
MR. JOHN YOUNG
who died Sept. 11 1828
in the 65th year of his age
Also
MRS. RUTH his wife
who died June 4 1835
in the 67th year of her age
They that die in Jesus & are blessed
How sweet their slumbers are
From suffering & from pain released
And freed from every snare

INDEX.

[FOR NAMES OF PLACES SEE END OF THIS INDEX.]

	PAGE
A	
Abbe,	40
Abbott,	274
Adams,	97, 101, 162, 214
Aiken,	42, 44
Alden,	20, 48, 93, 115, 148, 167, 177
Allen,	29, 32, 34, 48, 49, 50, 51, 118, 214, 215, 231, 232
Ambrose,	155
Andrews,	282
Anson,	154, 302
Appleton,	11, 62
Arnold,	1, 22, 24
Atherton,	77, 95, 144, 145, 146, 148, 150, 152, 198, 201, 203
Austin,	100, 262
B	
Babcock,	39
Bachelor, Batcheldor,	120, 132, 182, 206, 207
	22, 35, 59, 60, 63, 70, 71, 76, 79, 89, 90, 91, 93, 95, 96, 97, 98, 99, 100, 101, 102, 103, 100, 107, 108, 109, 110, 111, 112, 113, 114, 116, 117, 118,
Bailey,	119, 120, 121, 122, 126, 128,
Baily,	131, 137, 138, 139, 140, 141,
Bayley,	143, 144, 145, 146, 147, 148,
Bayly,	149, 154, 155, 159, 160, 168, 181, 182, 183, 185, 186, 187, 188, 189, 190, 191, 192, 194, 195, 196, 198, 199, 200, 201, 202, 206, 207, 209, 215, 216, 217, 218, 235
Baker,	74, 93, 96, 104, 106, 120, 122, 154, 161, 169
Baldwin,	3, 7, 8, 9, 61, 62, 74, 78, 79, 99, 100, 136, 137, 138, 140, 142, 144, 146, 149, 151, 189, 193, 195, 196, 197, 218
Barden,	90, 134, 159, 163, 183
Barker,	64, 82, 84, 90, 97, 98, 101, 102, 106, 108, 112, 132, 136, 151, 155, 156, 158, 159, 160, 180, 182, 184, 186, 188, 200, 201, 212, 218
Barnes, Barns,	43, 61, 62, 90, 96, 148
Baron,	186
Barrel,	108, 209
Barry,	3, 12, 14, 51

	PAGE
Barstow,	3, 6, 15, 17, 23, 25, 27, 28, 46, 49, 58, 59, 63, 65, 66, 67, 68, 69, 70, 71, 74, 77, 78, 80, 81, 82, 84, 87, 88, 89, 90, 92, 93, 95, 99, 100, 101, 102, 103, 104, 105, 106, 108, 100, 110, 111, 112, 113, 114, 115, 117, 118, 119, 120, 121, 122, 123, 124, 125, 126, 127, 128, 129, 130, 131, 133, 134, 135, 136, 137, 138, 139, 142, 146, 147, 149, 152, 153, 154, 155, 156, 157, 158, 159, 160, 162, 165, 166, 170, 174, 179, 180, 181, 182, 184, 187, 188, 189, 193, 196, 201, 203, 204, 207, 208, 209, 210, 211, 212, 213, 218, 219, 220, 221, 222, 234, 293, 297
Bartlett,	164
Bass,	4, 5, 6, 7, 11, 15, 25, 27, 35, 39, 47, 55, 57, 59, 65, 66, 67, 70, 74, 75, 76, 79, 80, 81. 83, 91, 100, 101, 102, 103, 107, 109, 114, 115, 118, 119, 123, 141, 142, 144, 146, 148, 150, 151, 156, 157, 158, 159, 160, 161, 162, 163, 168, 170, 171, 173, 175, 176, 177, 179, 180, 187, 191, 198, 203, 205, 210, 211, 212, 222, 223, 224
Basset,	124
Bates,	58, 63, 65, 71, 73, 74, 75, 76, 77, 80, 82, 83, 84, 87, 88, 89, 92, 93, 94, 95, 96, 98, 100, 101, 103, 104, 105, 106, 107, 108, 109, 110, 111, 112, 113, 114, 118, 120, 122, 123, 125, 126, 128, 129, 130, 132, 133, 134, 137, 138, 140, 141, 142, 143, 144, 147, 148, 149, 151, 152, 153, 154, 156, 157, 159, 161, 162, 163, 172, 174, 181, 182, 184, 186, 188, 190, 191, 192, 193, 194, 195, 196, 197, 198, 199, 200, 201, 202, 203, 204, 205, 206, 207, 208, 210, 211, 213, 224, 225, 226, 227, 228
Real,	106, 228, 229, 296
Beales, Beals,	63, 100, 155, 156
Bean,	229
Belcher,	80, 140, 156, 164, 202, 229
Benner,	229
Bennett, Bennit,	92
Benton,	232
Berry, Bery,	93, 139, 141, 281, 282

	PAGE
Besse,	164
Bicknall, Bicknell,	16, 96
Bilhah,	88, 91, 187
Billings,	229
Bird,	17
Blabee,	2, 187, 229
Bishop,	95, 106
Blanchard,	115, 160
Bonney, Bonny,	99, 197, 231, 232
Booe,	193
Booth,	201
Borden,	87
Bosby,	187
Bourn, Bourne,	1, 71, 110, 112, 121, 122, 167, 182
Bowditch,	55
Bowen,	157
Bowers,	232
Bowker,	78, 95, 96, 147, 148, 150, 162, 194
Bowman,	85, 106, 174
Bozzard,	191
Bradbury,	76, 78, 82, 94, 99, 114, 123, 141, 143, 145, 146, 148, 149, 151, 158, 163, 179, 194, 210
Bradford,	29, 211, 268
Brainerd	39, 103
Bray,	73, 89, 93, 115, 123, 126, 129, 130, 132, 133, 135, 167, 186
Brett,	229
Brewster,	63, 98, 152
Briggs,	63, 82, 98, 99, 148, 150, 152, 153, 156, 190, 193, 196, 197, 198, 201, 202, 204, 205, 207, 208, 209, 229, 230
Brigham,	26, 161, 162
Brimhall,	95
Brisco,	89
Bristol,	199, 201
Briton,	128, 184
Brooks,	17, 63, 65, 66, 67, 68, 69, 75, 80, 100, 101, 102, 103, 105, 128, 130, 132, 144, 146, 148, 150, 152, 163, 187, 198, 200, 208, 209, 230, 231, 252
Brown,	122
Bryant,	75, 76, 87, 88, 89, 91, 94, 131, 141, 143, 145, 147, 149, 180, 190, 191, 192
Buck,	2, 3, 5, 55, 57, 70, 89, 108, 109, 117, 119, 120, 136

INDEX.

	PAGE
Buker,	88, 89, 90, 108, 109, 111, 133, 179, 180, 185
Bullard,	39
Bunker,	94
Bunting,	119
Burden, Burdin,	87, 99, 108, 139
Burgess,	164, 232
Burrell,	206
Burt,	232
Burton,	24, 276
Butler,	105, 165. 287
Byfield,	6, 59

C

	PAGE
Cain, Cane,	89, 180, 181, 184
Capron,	105
Carey, Cary,	85, 89, 165, 232
Carrell, Caryl, Carroll,	142, 146, 193, 235
Carver,	29, 95, 163, 211
Caswell,	89, 96 101, 150 194
Chaddock,	14, 15, 64, 69. 81, 104, 159, 160, 169, 205, 207. 236
	31, 35, 42, 45, 46, 47, 63, 65, 66. 67. 68, 79, 80, 83 85. 98, 100,
Chamberlain, Chamberlin,	106, 153, 155, 156, 157, 158, 161, 162, 163, 165, 173. 176, 177, 178, 196, 203, 211, 232, 233
Chandler,	114, 123
Chapin,	15, 16. 20. 21
Chapman,	35, 66, 76, 94, 112, 114, 141, 206
Chauncey,	152
Checkley,	57
Chester,	233
Chubbuck,	95
Church,	14, 27. 39. 40, 41, 42, 43, 44, 45, 46, 47, 49, 65, 86, 75, 76, 80, 82, 83, 84, 85, 93, 94. 97, 101, 128, 141, 142. 146, 154, 156, 157, 158, 159, 160, 161, 162, 163, 164, 171, 172, 175. 187, 193, 200, 207, 211, 234, 235, 262, 287
Clapp,	3, 65, 68, 75, 81, 144, 150 39, 63, 77, 80, 83. 85, 89, 93, 94, 95, 96, 99, 101, 102, 103,
Clark,	104, 105, 113, 114, 127, 128,
Clarke,	129, 132, 136, 144, 156, 159, 161, 164, 168. 174, 186, 190, 196, 202, 206, 207, 208, 209, 235, 236.
Clay,	111, 121, 106, 205
Clayton,	293
Coats,	165
Cobb,	131, 132, 185, 186, 211
Cochran,	105
Colburn,	69
Cole,	96, 236
Collamore,	72, 88, 94, 127, 131
Collier,	95
Colman,	28
Conner,	89, 90
Conneway, Conoway,	89, 93
Cook,	1, 23, 24, 25. 27, 31, 34, 35, 36, 37, 39, 40, 41, 42, 43, 44, 45, 46, 61,

	PAGE
Cooms,	82, 106, 161, 162, 165, 170, 171, 172, 175, 177, 178, 212, 213
Cooms,	101
Cooper,	208, 236
Copeland,	83. 84, 99, 139, 156, 158, 162, 163, 174, 206
Corbin,	85, 166 236
Cornish,	107, 108, 110, 112. 114 118, 121, 122, 124. 128, 180, 181, 183, 184, 186, 187
Corthell,	77, 90, 95 144. 150, 194
Cotherel,	198, 201, 202, 207
Cozeno,	100
Crane,	15. 34
Crocker,	214, 236, 237
Crooker,	94, 104, 182, 183
Crosby,	112, 113, 122, 123, 124
Cudworth,	31, 48, 93, 96, 237
	3, 4. 8, 60, 63, 65, 66, 67, 68, 71, 72. 73, 74, 75, 76, 77, 78, 79, 80, 81, 88, 89, 90, 91, 92. 93, 94, 95, 96. 97 98, 99. 100, 101, 102, 103, 104, 105, 106, 108, 109, 110, 111, 112, 113, 114, 115, 117, 118, 119, 120, 121, 122, 123. 124. 125, 126, 127, 128, 129, 130, 131,
Curtis,	132, 133, 134, 135, 136, 137,
Curtiss,	138, 139, 140, 141, 142, 148, 144, 145, 146, 147, 148, 149. 150, 151. 152, 153, 154, 155. 156, 157. 158, 162. 168, 180, 181, 182, 183, 184. 185, 186, 187, 188, 189, 190, 192, 193, 194, 195, 196, 197 198, 199, 200, 201, 202, 203, 204, 205. 206, 207, 208, 209, 237, 238, 239, 240, 241, 203
Cushing.	2. 3, 4, 5, 6, 7, 28 55, 57, 58, 59 82, 90, 95, 98, 99. 100, 101, 102, 108, 109, 111. 112. 114. 118, 119, 121, 122, 126, 134, 153, 155, 157, 160, 168, 179, 181, 183, 194, 197, 200, 241, 259
Cutler,	34, 44, 220, 241

D

	PAGE
Dame.	242
Damon,	31, 72, 85, 88, 96, 97, 102, 103, 104, 105, 106, 127, 130, 158, 165, 174, 207, 208, 242, 243
Darling,	106
Davenport,	100, 243
Davis,	149
Dawe,	82, 90, 103, 160, 169, 205,
Dawes,	243
Day,	159
Dean,	33, 178
Delano,	77, 143, 144, 147, 148, 156, 188, 192, 193, 243
Dexter,	293
Dillingham,	87. 88, 97, 106, 108, 109, 110, 111, 112, 114, 128, 179, 180, 201
Dilly,	181
Dodge,	61
Doggett,	183
Donald, Donnell,	204, 205, 206
Donham,	90
Doten,	206
Dowse,	140

	PAGE
Dowty,	140, 141
Dryden,	104, 260
Dunbar,	79, 94, 105
Duncan,	25, 26, 27, 29, 30, 31, 32, 33, 38, 41, 46, 83, 84, 85, 163, 174, 178, 210, 211, 246, 286
Dunning,	162
	3, 14, 49, 65, 74, 80, 81, 82, 83. 84, 93, 99, 102, 104, 133, 140, 141, 142, 144, 146, 148,
Dwelley, Dwelly,	155, 156, 157, 158, 159, 160, 162, 169, 179, 180, 181, 195, 197, 205, 208, 210, 212, 244, 245, 246, 291
Dwight,	2
Dyer,	31, 35, 36, 85, 166, 246, 247

E

	PAGE
Eames,	90
Eastman,	80, 168
Eddy,	77, 95, 143, 144, 146, 151, 155
Edwards,	44, 104, 208
Eells,	5, 35, 56, 57, 63, 75, 76, 79, 80, 81, 82. 83, 84, 85, 92, 94, 97, 99, 100, 101, 102, 103, 104, 105, 106, 109, 111, 112, 113, 114, 115, 116, 117, 118, 119, 121, 122, 123, 129, 130, 136, 137, 139, 140, 141, 142, 143, 145, 147, 148, 149, 151, 154, 155, 156, 158, 159, 160, 161, 162, 163, 164, 165, 174, 181, 189, 197, 202, 205, 206, 207, 209, 211, 220, 222, 242, 246, 247
Ekings,	92
Eldon,	165, 297
Elliott,	165, 235
Ellis,	99, 102, 103, 106, 163, 166, 186, 187, 191, 200, 204, 206, 208, 246, 247, 248
Ellms,	104
Elmer, Elmore.	108, 181
Emerson,	21
Emery,	164, 254
Estes,	46, 83, 102, 103, 105, 108, 107, 108, 109, 111, 113, 162, 165, 178, 179, 180, 182, 183, 184, 185, 197, 199, 201. 204, 206, 207, 208. 209, 249, 250, 304
Eustice,	97
Everson,	250
Everett,	231, 251, 252, 260, 274
Ewell,	75, 149, 168, 248

F

	PAGE
Fairfield,	125
Farrar,	146, 153, 156
Farron,	104
Farrow,	82
Felton,	259
Ferrin,	307
Ferris,	89
Ferry,	161
Fessenden,	58
Fillmore,	159
Fish,	103, 250
Fiske,	35. 39
Fitzgerald,	73, 74, 94, 109, 111, 127, 184, 186, 188
Fletcher,	22
Fobes,	247
Fogg,	161

INDEX. 311

Folger, ... 150, 215
Folsom, ... 218
Ford, 29, 73, 89, 94, 108, 109, 110, 112, 156, 174, 181, 183, 200, 201
Forrest, ... 91, 306
Foster, 82, 95, 135, 158, 161, 185, 207, 220, 250
Fox, ... 187
Frank, ... 87, 186
Franklin, . 164, 242, 268, 289
Fraser, ... 250
Freeman, 34, 35, 36, 37, 38, 46, 48, 85, 102, 165, 174, 175, 176
French, ... 250
Frost, ... 164
Fuller, ... 44

G

Gannitt, ... 205
Gardiner, { 74, 77, 78, 93, 97, 100, 102, 105, 136, 138, 139,
Gardner, { 141, 148, 149, 152, 160, 192, 199, 209, 222, 241, 250
Garner, ... 104
Garnett, . 141, 142, 144, 188, 206
Garratt, . 31, 85, 165, 174, 211
Gay, ... 57, 61
George I., ... 2
Gibbs, ... 92
Gilbert, 78, 97, 105, 147, 148, 150, 152, 200, 231, 296
Gilkie, } 191, 201
Gilky, }
Gill, 91, 99, 105, 126, 128, 129, 133, 140, 298
Gilman, . 229, 294, 300, 302, 304
Glass, ... 165
Gold, ... 91
Goodrich, ... 251
Gould, ... 91, 97
Graham, ... 97
Gray, } 106, 206
Grey, }
Green, } 16, 207, 252, 277, 295
Greene, }
Gregory XIII., . . . 52, 53
Griffin, ... 22
Groce, 75, 81, 89, 98, 99, 100, 102,
Grose, { 103, 106, 114, 156, 158, 192,
Gross, } 197, 201, 204, 205, 209
Guilford, 87, 88, 89, 113, 123, 125, 181
Gurney, ... 152, 288

H

Hale, ... 162
Hall, . . . 90, 129, 130
Halleck, ... 165
Handy, ... 252
Hanmar, } . 70, 117, 186, 206
Hanmer, }
Hanover, Duke of, . . 2
Hanson, ... 252
Harden, } . 91, 92, 94, 252, 253
Hardin, }
Harding, }
Harlan, ... 233
Harlow, 28, 163, 191, 192, 210, 211, 246, 253
Harris, . 22, 88, 106, 110, 253

Harrison, . . . 281, 285
Harvey, ... 164
Hatch, 5, 41, 45, 55, 57 63, 65, 70, 71, 74, 75, 76, 77, 81, 85, 87, 88, 93, 94, 95, 97, 99, 100, 102, 103, 106, 108, 109, 110, 111, 112, 113, 118, 119, 120, 133, 135, 136, 137, 138, 139, 141, 142, 143, 144, 145, 146, 148, 150, 153, 154, 155, 156, 158, 159, 160, 166, 167, 174, 180, 183, 184, 187, 189, 190, 192, 195, 201, 202, 205, 206, 209, 211, 212, 253
Hathaway, ... 102
Hatherly, . . . 134, 185
Haviland, . . . 221, 293
Hayes, . . 35, 36, 41, 44
Hayford, }
Hefford, } . 35, 179, 190, 206
Hifford, }
Healy, } . . . 103, 159
Hely, }
Heuchman, . . . 135, 188
Henderson, . . . 253, 254
Henry, ... 166
Hearsey, } 78, 85, 147, 148, 150, 156
or { 165, 166, 254
Hersey, }
Hervey, ... 247
Hessord, ... 90
Hill, 52, 77, 87, 92, 93, 98, 100, 113, 118, 123, 126, 128, 131, 133, 143, 190
Hitchcock, . 61, 62, 82, 97, 210
Hobart, 11, 57, 79, 103, 153, 199, 256
Hobbs, ... 99
Holbrook, } . . . 255
Holbrooke, }
Hollis, ... 255
Holmes, 84, 100, 128, 144, 145, 164, 169, 174, 187, 192, 254
Homer, 87, 141, 153, 155, 160, 164, 196, 199, 223, 263, 285, 298, 299, 301
Hopkins, ... 4
2, 3, 7, 46, 71, 73, 74, 76, 77, 84, 86, 88, 89, 91, 92, 94, 95, 97, 101, 107, 108, 109, 110, 111, 112, 113, 114, 115, 117, 118, 119, 121, 122, 123, 124, 125, 126, 127, 130, 132,
House, { 133, 134, 135, 136, 137, 138,
Howes, } 139, 140, 141, 142, 144, 145, 146, 147, 149, 151, 177, 182, 183, 184, 186, 188, 189, 190, 191, 192, 193, 194, 197, 201, 204, 213, 247, 255, 256
Howard, . 106, 257, 274, 291
Howland, 42, 84, 92, 93, 140, 174, 183, 256
Hubbard, } . . . 91, 256
Hubbart, }
Humphrey, ... 256
Hussey, ... 50

I

Iris, ... 256
Irvin, ... 291
Irving, . . . 253, 262

J

Jackson, . . . 92, 251

Jacob, { 65, 76, 81, 103, 139, 140, 142,
Jacobs, { 143, 147, 155, 156, 157, 190, 191, 122, 193, 202, 204, 205, 206, 208
James, ... 233
Jenkins, 60, 72, 74, 100, 102, 128, 129, 130, 136, 137, 162, 186
Jenks, , . . . 168
Jewett, ... 168
Johnson, . . 156, 205, 257
Jonas, . . . 91, 118, 184
Jones, . 88, 100, 109, 256, 257
2, 4, 5, 8, 9, 11, 23, 55, 57, 63, 65, 71, 73, 75, 76, 79, 80, 81, 83, 85, 90, 96, 97, 98, 99, 101, 102, 103, 105, 106, 109, 110, 111, 114,
Josselynn, { 115, 119, 120, 121, 123,
Joslyu, } 126, 131, 132, 134, 135,
Joslyn, } 136, 137, 139, 140, 141, 143, 145, 146, 147, 149,
Joslynn, 152, 153, 154, 155, 157, 158, 159, 163, 165, 166, 179, 180, 181, 185, 187, 189, 191, 193, 194, 195, 197, 200, 202, 204, 208, 211, 227, 257, 258, 259, 260, 266, 268
Joyce, ... 75
Judd, 42, 83, 104, 165, 212, 260
Judson, . . . 154, 225
Justice, ... 70, 117

K

Kane, . . 88, 180, 181, 184
Keen, } 88, 89, 101, 193, 260
Keene, }
Keith, ... 227
Kellogg, ... 297
Kennedy, ... 180
Kent, ... 100
Keoni Kalua, . . . 260
King, . . . 33, 38, 174
Kingman, . . 200, 201, 203
Kinsman, ... 150

L

Ladd, ... 74, 88
Lambert, 70, 72, 74, 77, 88, 95, 108, 110, 111, 112, 113, 114, 117, 118, 119, 120, 121, 123, 124, 125, 126, 128, 131, 144, 146, 147, 167, 181, 183, 185, 186, 187, 189, 191
Lane, ... 84, 161
Lapham, . . . 84, 165, 174
Larkum, ... 261
Latham, ... 93
Lawson, ... 187
Leach, ... 260
Leavit, } . . 101, 165, 261
Levett, }
Leed, ... 88
Lenthall, { 68, 99, 104, 130, 139, 140,
Lenthel, { 158, 202
Lenthell, }
Lester, ... 261
Lewis, 5, 28, 56, 57, 118, 123, 155, 230
Lincoln, . 87, 101, 109, 119, 153
Lindsey, ... 90, 261

INDEX.

	PAGE
Lisle,	158
Litchfield,	3, 10, 11, 178, 261
Little,	82, 97, 98, 210, 248, 293
Lloyd,	220, 236, 254
Long,	206
Longley,	104
Loring,	161, 240, 241, 260
Love,	87, 108, 109, 112, 181
Lovell,	
Lovewell, }	162, 163, 164, 212, 261
Lovis,	261
Low,	131, 155, 180
Lowell,	261
Lyman,	153, 274, 292
Lyon,	262

M

Maccarty,	88
Mackerdey,	70
Macomber, }	
Macumber, }	35, 89, 101, 200, 262
Macy,	50
Magoon, }	
Magoun, }	201, 262, 263, 298
Makepiece,	207
Man, Mann,	6, 58, 60, 62, 63, 70, 74, 78, 81, 89, 90, 91, 93, 95, 96, 99, 100, 102, 103, 105, 106, 107, 108, 109, 110, 111, 117, 118, 119, 120, 121, 125, 131, 132, 134, 135, 136, 139, 140, 141, 142, 144, 147, 148, 149, 150, 152, 153, 155, 156, 157, 158, 169, 180, 181, 183, 190, 191, 193, 196, 197, 198, 203, 204, 208, 200, 263, 264, 265, 266, 267, 299
Manson,	80, 97, 156
Marshal, }	
Marshall, }	153, 178
Martin, }	
Martyn, }	22, 106, 161, 281
Martindale,	22
McLauthlin,	262
Meed,	161
Mellen,	11, 12, 27, 62, 64, 66, 78, 79, 98, 99, 100, 151, 160, 168, 203, 211
Melvin,	286
Meriam, }	
Miriam, }	83, 161, 169
Merritt,	76, 87, 100, 105, 107, 109, 111, 138, 141, 150, 194, 301
Miller,	103, 157, 158
Mitchell,	161
Monro, Monroe, Munro, Munroe,	74, 75, 80, 81, 82, 89, 97, 99, 104, 124, 130, 132, 134, 135, 137, 140, 157, 162, 163, 164, 173, 174, 190, 196, 197, 200, 202, 206, 207, 208, 210, 266
Morgan,	96, 152
Morgridge	36
Morrice,	97
Morrill,	97
Morris,	266
Morse,	150, 266
Morton,	101
Mott,	96

N

	PAGE
Nash,	82, 99, 105, 161, 196, 209
Neal, }	63, 83, 91, 92, 94, 95, 100, 103, 128, 129, 147, 155, 156, 161,
Neil, }	184, 198, 199, 200, 210
Nelson,	230, 261
Newel, }	
Newell, }	161
Newton,	265
Nicholson, }	
Nicolson, }	95, 136, 188, 190
Nickerson,	94
Niles,	3, 50, 70, 88, 108, 109, 110, 118, 119, 182, 192, 195, 214, 250, 266
Norman,	233
North,	92, 181
Northy,	181
Norton,	64, 92
Nye,	14, 83, 169

O

Oakman,	266
Oldham,	96, 97, 105, 266, 270, 284
Orr,	77, 95, 145
Otis,	3, 50, 70, 88, 108, 109, 110, 118, 119, 182, 192, 195, 214, 250, 266
Ozias,	102, 267

P

Packard,	103, 163, 267
Paine,	266
Paley,	29, 33, 84
Palmar, Palmer,	13, 50, 76, 78, 87, 88, 93, 95, 96, 97, 102, 105, 110, 114, 118, 120, 122, 124, 129, 131, 133, 135, 137, 148, 179, 181, 183, 184, 185, 187, 189, 191, 193, 196, 201, 208, 209, 228, 267
Pardy,	267
Parker,	88, 99
Parkman,	94
Parmer,	228
Parris,	180
Parsons,	20
Payson,	33, 164
Peaks,	98, 145
Percival,	267
Perkins,	26, 28, 32, 267
Perry,	4, 27, 63, 77, 81, 83, 84, 91, 97, 98, 102, 103, 104, 105, 106, 107, 109, 111, 112, 113, 114, 118, 119, 121, 122, 123, 125, 144, 145, 147, 149, 151, 152, 153, 154, 155, 161, 162, 165, 168, 169, 170, 171, 179, 183, 200, 202, 205, 208, 209, 267, 268, 269, 270, 272
Peter,	74, 87, 88, 93, 95, 108, 110
Peters,	113, 180, 185, 191, 207
Peterson,	75, 93, 94, 105, 150, 194, 196, 209, 267
Philips, }	
Phillips, }	100, 106, 270, 271, 295
Phinney,	271
Pierce,	191
Pinchin,	92
Pool, }	
Poole, }	96, 103, 106, 205, 271, 272
Porter,	290
Powers,	28

	PAGE
Prat, Pratt,	65, 67, 68, 74, 75, 82, 87, 88, 89, 90, 93, 94, 98, 100, 101, 102, 103, 105, 114, 123, 125, 127, 128, 129, 132, 133, 135, 133, 141, 142, 143, 144, 146, 148, 151, 154, 155, 167, 179, 182, 184, 185, 188, 191, 196, 197, 207, 211, 240, 272, 280, 286
Prentice,	62
Prince,	105
Prior,	89, 91, 92, 93
Prouty,	72, 82, 90, 92, 111, 121, 128, 130, 131, 133
Puffer,	273

Q

Quincy,	161
Quindley,	273

R

Ramsdale, Ramsdel, Ramsdell,	6, 58, 61, 70, 71, 72, 73, 75, 77, 79, 87, 89, 90, 92, 93, 94, 95, 96, 97, 98, 99, 100, 102, 103, 104, 105, 106, 107, 108, 109, 110, 111, 112, 114, 115, 118, 119, 120, 121, 122, 123, 124, 125, 126, 137, 135, 136, 140, 145, 146, 148, 149, 151, 152, 156, 169, 180, 181, 182, 185, 187, 190, 192, 194, 195, 196, 200, 202, 204, 205, 206, 209, 273, 274
Randal, Randall,	72, 76, 78, 80, 91, 93, 97, 125, 127, 132, 134, 138, 139, 140, 141, 145, 147, 148, 150, 155, 183, 190, 192, 199, 206, 208, 274
Ransom,	164
Ray,	289
Read,	84, 96, 103, 106, 139, 151, 165,
Reed, }	247, 274
Riccards, }	83, 152, 154, 181
Richmond,	64, 142, 146, 192, 201
Ripley,	77, 90, 94, 127, 274, 275
Robbins, Robins,	11, 65, 75, 82, 89, 96, 97, 101, 102, 103, 104, 114, 123, 125, 124, 129, 130, 134, 135, 138, 145, 146, 147, 148, 151, 152, 154, 162, 185, 188, 192, 194, 197, 203, 205, 209, 258, 273, 276, 290
Roberson,	287
Robinson,	91, 287
Rockwood,	31, 35, 39, 41
Rogers,	65, 66, 68, 79, 82, 84, 88, 89, 90, 93, 94, 95, 98, 101, 110, 112, 113, 115, 123, 124, 125, 126, 128, 130, 131, 132, 133, 141, 152, 153, 161, 183, 184, 185, 187, 188, 189, 201, 204, 205, 206, 213, 276
Rose,	6, 11, 58, 59, 65, 71, 76, 78, 80, 81, 85, 90, 92, 93, 94, 101, 102, 108, 109, 111, 112, 114, 119, 120, 121, 122, 123, 125, 138, 140, 141, 142, 143, 144, 145, 147, 149, 157, 158,

INDEX. 313

	PAGE
	150, 160, 181, 189, 191, 194, 197, 204, 205, 206, 208, 209, 211, 277, 283
Rowland,	50
Ruggles,	58, 92, 149
Rumney,	276
Russel,	158, 159, 160, 161, 162, 163,
Russell,	164, 277

S

Salmon,	63, 99, 153, 154, 155, 156,
Salmond,	158, 209, 277, 278, 291
Sampson,	
Samson,	84, 88, 102, 104, 174
Sandford,	
Sanford,	21, 22, 25, 161, 253
Sedgwick,	22
Sessions,	48
Shaw,	97, 160
Sheldon,	71, 88, 110, 114, 121, 124
Sigourney,	214
Sime,	277
Simonds,	277
Simons,	133
Simmons, Symmonds,	51, 100, 101, 106, 127, 129, 131, 132, 133, 134, 136, 139, 141, 152, 153, 155, 156, 158, 175, 188, 198, 201, 205
Skiff,	5, 55
Smith,	12, 13, 20, 21, 22, 23, 24, 25, 42, 61, 65, 67, 68, 70, 79, 80, 83, 88, 99, 101, 103, 104, 106, 107, 108, 148, 154, 155, 156, 157, 158, 161, 162, 169, 204, 207, 212, 278, 279
Snow,	132, 147, 152, 153, 154, 155, 157, 200, 204, 240, 262
Soper,	10, 11, 80, 91, 94, 105, 193, 197, 204, 279
Soule,	3, 135
Southworth,	44, 46, 48, 99, 100, 213
Spear, Spcer,	72, 90, 126, 127, 279, 290
Spofford,	27
Sprague,	118
Spring,	17
Standish,	200, 204, 279
Staples,	5, 55, 73, 75, 77, 96, 113, 117, 118, 120, 129, 131, 133, 135, 136, 138, 144, 145, 147, 148, 150, 179, 180, 182, 185, 190, 191
Steel,	59
Sterling,	98, 198, 204
Sternhold,	4
Sternhold & Hopkins,	4, 6
Stetson,	2, 11, 12, 31, 39, 40, 43, 85, 66, 67, 69, 71, 72, 73, 74, 75, 76, 77, 80, 82, 83, 84, 85, 87, 89, 90, 91, 93, 94, 96, 98, 99, 100, 101, 102, 103, 104, 105, 106, 107, 108, 109, 110, 111, 112, 113, 114, 115, 116, 117, 118, 119, 120, 121, 122, 123, 124, 125, 126, 127, 128, 129, 130, 131, 132, 133, 134, 137, 138, 139, 140, 141, 142, 143, 144, 145, 146, 147, 148, 149, 150, 151, 152, 154, 157, 158, 160, 161, 162, 163, 164, 165, 160, 167, 168, 173, 181, 182, 184, 185, 186, 187, 188, 189, 190, 191, 192, 193, 194, 195, 197, 199, 200, 201, 202, 203, 204, 205, 206, 207, 208, 209, 210, 211, 212, 224, 234,

	PAGE
	263, 267, 279, 280, 281, 282, 283, 284, 286
Stevens,	43, 93, 110, 120, 163, 167, 189
Stewart,	284
Still,	94
Stockbridge,	5, 6, 9, 47, 55, 57, 58, 62, 72, 75, 78, 84, 88, 90, 93, 96, 97, 98, 100, 102, 103, 106, 111, 112, 113, 114, 115, 116, 119, 121, 122, 123, 124, 132, 133, 137, 143, 145, 146, 147, 148, 149, 150, 151, 152, 153, 154, 155, 157, 160, 161, 165, 174, 180, 181, 184, 185, 188, 192, 196, 200, 203, 204, 208, 209, 210, 214, 257, 266, 284, 285, 286, 295, 297
Stoddard,	42, 72, 83, 103, 104, 165, 181, 182, 191, 286
Stodder,	104
Stone,	160
Storer,	61, 127
Strong,	64
Studley, Studly,	10, 63, 65, 72, 74, 75, 77, 79, 80, 83, 88, 91, 92, 93, 94, 95, 96, 98, 100, 102, 103, 105, 106, 107, 109, 110, 111, 112, 113, 114, 117, 118, 119, 121, 122, 123, 124, 126, 127, 128, 130, 131, 133, 135, 137, 138, 141, 143, 146, 148, 149, 150, 152, 159, 160, 181, 182, 183, 184, 185, 188, 189, 190, 191, 192, 193, 194, 195, 197, 199, 201, 207, 208, 212, 241, 259, 273, 283, 286, 287, 288, 289, 303
Sturtevant,	289, 290
Sumner,	160, 283
Swift,	61
Sylvester,	2, 4, 7, 50, 63, 65, 67, 68, 71, 73, 76, 78, 80, 81, 83, 84, 86, 88, 89, 90, 91, 92, 93, 94, 95, 96, 97, 98, 99, 100, 101, 103, 104, 109, 111, 112, 113, 114, 115, 118, 120, 121, 122, 123, 124, 125, 126, 127, 128, 130, 131, 132, 133, 134, 135, 136, 137, 138, 139, 140, 141, 142, 144, 145, 146, 149, 152, 153, 154, 155, 156, 157, 161, 164, 165, 166, 174, 178, 180, 181, 183, 184, 186, 187, 188, 189, 190, 191, 193, 195, 197, 198, 200, 201, 202, 203, 204, 205, 206, 210, 215, 272, 290, 291
Symmods,	100

T

Tailor, Taylor,	1, 5, 55, 85, 89, 91, 92, 109, 110, 165, 181, 187, 291
Tamplin,	115
Tappan,	174
Tate & Brady,	6
Teague,	139, 140, 142, 144, 148, 150, 193, 194
Temple,	17
Thacher, Thatcher,	26, 101, 267, 269
Thayer,	38, 41, 43, 47, 83, 176, 291, 292, 295
Thomas,	26, 72, 81, 85, 96, 104, 106, 130, 162, 163, 243, 270, 292
Thompson,	160, 162, 292

	PAGE
Thorndike,	259
Thurston,	26
Tiffany,	181, 191
Tilden,	63, 72, 77, 91, 95, 104, 105, 106, 125, 127, 128, 130, 132, 135, 147, 152, 153, 154, 155, 156, 185, 186, 188, 202, 205, 206, 271, 279, 292, 293
Tileston,	1
Tilson,	97
Tobey, Toby,	57, 59, 71, 72, 87, 89
Titus,	124
Tollman, Tolman,	8, 31, 65, 81, 82, 83, 84, 85, 96, 102, 131, 156, 161, 163, 165, 168, 174, 210, 293
Torrey,	3, 6, 15, 58, 59, 65, 70, 71, 72, 75, 76, 77, 78, 81, 82, 88, 89, 90, 94, 95, 96, 97, 98, 106, 107, 110, 113, 114, 118, 122, 123, 124, 126, 127, 128, 129, 130, 131, 132, 133, 135, 136, 137, 138, 139, 140, 146, 147, 149, 150, 151, 153, 156, 164, 169, 180, 181, 183, 185, 186, 188, 190, 191, 192, 193, 194, 199, 201, 204, 205, 207, 209, 293
Totman,	106, 160, 293
Toto,	94, 130
Tower,	51, 91, 103, 105, 115, 160, 161, 195, 208, 293, 294
Towne,	22
Townsend,	148
Tribou,	165, 272, 294
Truman,	208
Tubbs,	102, 294, 295
Turcotte,	241
Turner,	2, 5, 7, 55, 58, 60, 65, 74, 75, 76, 77, 79, 80, 82, 85, 87, 89, 93, 94, 95, 96, 97, 99, 100, 101, 102, 106, 107, 108, 110, 111, 112, 113, 114, 115, 117, 118, 121, 122, 123, 124, 125, 126, 127, 128, 129, 130, 132, 135, 138, 139, 140, 141, 142, 145, 146, 149, 152, 153, 154, 155, 157, 158, 159, 160, 161, 162, 165, 166, 168, 174, 180, 182, 183, 185, 187, 189, 190, 192, 193, 194, 195, 198, 200, 201, 202, 203, 205, 208, 210, 211, 280, 281, 282, 283, 295, 296, 297

U

Utter,	90, 180

V

Viaughan,	105
Vinal,	106, 107, 118, 141, 179, 180, 181, 186, 187, 297

W

Wade,	106
Wadsworth,	182
Walt, Wate,	190, 208
Waldo,	106, 229
Waldron,	271
Wales,	61, 77, 95, 101, 144, 145, 146, 148, 150, 152, 198, 201, 203
Walker,	31, 35, 36, 43, 45, 105, 164

INDEX.

Wallace, ... 291
Ward, ... 28, 31, 148
Wardell, ... 92
Wardrobe, . . . 297, 303
Warren, 119. 161, 218, 241, 247, 279, 296, 297, 307
Washburn, . . 101, 145, 256
Washington, . . . 303
Waterman, 84, 97, 100, 136, 142, 143, 174, 175, 178, 190, 290, 297
Waters, ... 92
Wayford, ... 142
Webb, ... 99
Webster, . . . 89, 128, 251
Wendell, ... 302
Wheaton, . . . 50, 141, 214
Whitcomb, . . . 100
White, 31, 43, 63, 74, 77, 79, 89, 97, 103, 105, 111, 133, 134, 146, 151, 152, 154, 162, 180, 192, 194, 195, 197, 199, 204, 207, 297
Whitefield, ... 6
Whiten, { 74, 77, 78, 88, 91, 92, 97,
Whitten, { 103, 109, 120, 121, 129,
{ 131, 133, 134, 135, 136,
{ 137, 138, 139, 140, 141,
{ 143, 145, 146, 148, 149,
{ 150, 151, 186, 190, 191,
Whiting, 63, 65, 66, 67, 68, 79, 82, 83, 98, 99, 102, 151, 152, 153, 154, 155,

156, 157, 158, 159, 195, 196, 197, 198, 199, 202, 203, 204, 207, 209, 210, 211, 218, 259, 297, 298, 299, 300, 301, 302, 303, 304, 306, 307
Whitman, 13, 106, 155, 156, 158, 203
Whitmarsh, ... 31
Whitting, . 67, 68, 81, 105, 106, 209
Wight, . . 31, 32, 164, 175
Wilder, 48, 81, 82, 83, 103, 162, 163, 171, 174, 209, 210, 211, 304, 305, 306
Wilke, ... 88
Wilks, 57, 70, 73, 88, 107, 109, 110, 111, 113, 115, 118, 119, 120, 121, 123, 124, 127, 129, 135, 167, 180, 183, 184
Willard, ... 262
Williams, 160, 161, 162, 163, 165, 208, 306
Willis, . . 48, 85, 306, 307
Willet,
Willett, } . 77, 95, 101, 144, 145
Willitt,
Williston, ... 33
Willner, ... 280
Wilson, ... 300
Wilton, ... 246
Windsor, . . . 91, 118, 184
Wing, 63, 74, 88, 96, 99, 101, 105, 106, 107, 109, 110, 111, 120, 134, 155,

157, 158, 159, 182, 186, 187, 188, 189, 193, 194, 195, 206, 207, 208, 227, 307
Winslow, 35, 63, 65, 80, 89, 91, 102, 123, 124, 126, 131, 155, 208, 210, 307
{ 4. 74. 75, 76, 77, 79, 88,
{ 89. 90. 93, 94, 96, 97, 100,
Witherel, { 101, 113, 118, 138, 139,
Witherell, { 140, 141, 142, 143, 145,
{ 146, 147, 148, 160, 168,
{ 179, 180, 181, 184, 185,
{ 187, 189, 192, 199, 209
Witherly, ... 179
Withington, ... 102
Wood, 18, 89, 163, 164, 165, 303, 307, 308
Woodbury, . . . 24
Woods, ... 95
Woodward, 49, 61, 77, 143, 144, 187, 189, 192
Woodworth, 63, 89, 100, 103, 129, 143, 153, 154
Wright, 76, 83, 127, 136, 161, 162, 164, 183, 187, 192, 207, 307
Young, 63. 76, 79, 93, 98, 100, 101, 104, 109, 110, 112, 120, 121, 122, 139, 140, 141, 142, 143, 144, 146, 155, 156, 157, 158, 168, 182, 191, 194, 277, 308

INDEX OF TOWNS.

A

Abington, 1, 2, 11, 15, 17, 21, 26, 28, 35, 42, 61, 62, 64, 79, 85, 92, 94, 95, 96, 97, 100, 101, 103, 105, 106, 122, 167, 169, 178, 211, 295
Abington Centre, . . 31, 40
Acton, ... 61
Assonet, . . . 32, 46, 178
Andover, ... 15, 49
Attleborough, . . . 15, 105

B

Bangor, ... 26, 38
Barnstable, . . . 11, 62, 101
Barre, ... 105
Barrington, . . . 15, 16, 18
Bath, ... 54, 166
Belchertown, . . . 21
Belfast, ... 168
Bonn Island, . . . 242
Boston, 3, 22, 24, 25, 32, 33, 39, 45, 50, 51, 54, 55, 57, 82, 95, 168, 275
Boylston, . . . 22, 23, 25
Braintree, . . . 4, 21, 26, 28
Bridgewater, 32, 88, 90, 91, 93, 97, 100, 104, 106, 106, 118
Brooks, ... 26, 81

C

Cambridge, . . . 11, 33, 62
Camden, . . . 102, 106
Cape Breton, . . . 120
Carver, ... 40, 45
Centre Abington, . . 175
Centre Hanover, . . 214
Chester, ... 26
Chesterfield, . . . 96, 168
Chiltonville, . . . 43, 44, 45
Cincinnati, . . . 169
Cohasset, . . 21, 32, 100, 275
Coleraine, . . . 49, 50
Concord, ... 100

D

Dartmouth, . . . 89
Dedham, . . . 2, 20, 52
Devonshire, . . . 7
Dorchester, . . . 102
Dunbarton, . . . 22
Durham, ... 104
Duxbury, . . 75, 89, 99, 105, 177

E

East Abington, . . 31, 43
East Haddam, . . . 15
Eastham, ... 38
Easthampton, . . . 33
East Haverhill, . . . 28
East Jaffrey, . . . 49
Edgartown, ... 169
Elmwood, ... 64

F

Falmouth, . . . 59, 219
Francistown, . . . 168
Frankfort, ... 35
Freeport, . . . 168, 199
Freetown, . . 33, 46, 178

G

Gardner, ... 51
Granville, ... 15
Greenland, ... 100

H

Halifax, 15, 23, 39, 43, 64, 97, 103
Hall's Hill, . . . 43
Hanson, 21, 31, 35, 41, 44, 46, 48, 211, 213, 296
Harpswell, ... 167
Haverhill, . . . 22, 24
Hebron, ... 22
Hillsboro', ... 15
Hingham, 31, 35, 57, 61, 88, 90, 91, 92, 96, 99, 102, 103, 105, 120
Hopkinton, . . 12, 22, 25
Hubbardston, . . 49, 50, 51
Hull, ... 95
Hunter, ... 15

J

Jackson, ... 26

K

Kingston, 23, 45, 49, 100, 101, 124
Kittery, ... 11

L

Lancaster, . . 60, 62, 78

Limerick, ... 168
Lunenburg, . . . 100

M

Mansfield, ... 15
Marlboro', ... 13
Marshfield, 35, 48, 61, 81, 84, 86, 89, 90, 96, 100, 101, 102, 104, 106, 177, 183, 192, 222
Mashpee, ... 6, 58
Massillon, ... 22
Medway, . . . 15, 22
Mendon, ... 15
Middleborough, . . 64, 105
Milford, ... 178

N

Nantucket, . . . 50, 94
Newark, ... 22
Newburyport, . . . 22
New Bedford, . . . 169
New Salem, . . . 168
North Abington, . . 31
North Adams, . . 33, 38, 174
North Bridgewater, . 17, 211
North Marshfield, . 39, 174
North Scituate, . . 48, 233
North Wrentham, . . 26
North Yarmouth, . . 60, 169
Norton, . . . 49, 50

O

Oakham, ... 14
Oakland, ... 237
Orrington, ... 38

P

Pelham, . . . 49, 50
Pembroke, 4, 5, 56, 57, 61, 62, 81, 87, 88, 89, 91, 92, 93, 94, 95, 96, 97, 98, 99, 100, 101, 102, 103, 105, 106, 124, 128, 167, 170, 181, 187, 192
Perkins, ... 28
Pittsfield, ... 168
Plymouth, . 7, 15, 23, 44, 90, 91, 98
Plympton, . . 41, 43, 94
Pompey, ... 22
Poultney, . . . 22, 23
Prospect, ... 37
Providence . . . 16

INDEX.

Q	PAGE
Quincy,	4

R	
Randolph,	26, 64
Reading,	12, 13, 62
Rehoboth,	15
Rochester,	14, 58, 64, 93, 95
Rockland,	43
Rowley,	15
Roxbury,	4

S	
Salem,	99
Sandwich,	6, 58, 167, 182
Sandy Point,	38
Scituate,	1, 2, 3, 5, 10, 21, 27, 28, 31, 48, 56, 57, 58, 61, 62, 75, 81, 82, 84, 85, 87, 88, 89, 90, 91, 92, 93, 94, 95, 96, 97, 99, 101, 102, 104, 106, 119, 121, 128, 129, 130, 164, 168, 174, 175, 178
Scotland,	32
Searsport,	26
Sharon,	55
Sherborn,	94
South Abington,	44
South Marshfield,	38, 48
South Plymouth,	39, 42, 45
South Weymouth,	27, 28, 41, 44
Spencer,	97, 167
Stafford,	93, 167
Sterling,	11, 12
Stockton,	38, 44, 85
Strong,	38
Sudbury,	7, 12, 61
Sylvester,	168

T	
Taunton,	3, 33, 49, 101, 178
Temple,	55
Thetford,	24
Tinmouth,	22
Tiverton,	88
Tolland,	59
Townsend,	104
Turner,	100, 101

U	PAGE
Uxbridge,	15

W	
Washington,	22
Watertown,	14, 61
Waverly,	178
Westfield,	88
Westminster,	22
West Prospect,	26
West Roxbury,	50
Westerly,	85, 164
Weston,	61, 100, 106, 169
Weybridge,	22
Weymouth,	21, 26, 28, 64, 81, 82, 104, 106, 263
Wheaton,	50
Williston,	33
Woburn,	7, 84
Wrentham,	15

Y	
York,	11, 48

ERRATA.

Page 3. For "Bush" read "Buck."
" 12 and 13. The page heading should be "Rev. John Mellen" not "Rev. Calvin Chaddock.'
" 37. For " Joseph " Cook read "Isaac " Cook.
" 14. The page heading should be "Rev. Calvin Chaddock" not " Rev. Seth Chapin."
" 48. Read " I. M. Wilder." instead of " J. M. Wilder."
" 95. " Gamaliel " instead of " Gamabiel."
" 97. " of " not " or," in 23rd line.
" 174. " North Adams " not " North Aams."
" 236. " Chaddock" instead of " Craddock."
" 240. " Sept. 16th, 1862 " instead of " Sept. 16th, 1863."

www.ingramcontent.com/pod-product-compliance
Lightning Source LLC
Chambersburg PA
CBHW031432230426
43668CB00007B/503